LAW LIBRARY OF CONGRESS

COMPARATIVE ANALYSIS

REGULATION OF FOREIGN AID IN SELECTED COUNTRIES

Executive Summary

Foreign development assistance has played a significant role in the history of both the United States and Europe. International cooperation in this area surged following World War II and has resulted in the adoption of the Millennium Development Goals (MDGs) that set economic, environmental, and welfare objectives for the promotion of world development.

A 1970 UN General Assembly Resolution included 0.7% of countries' GNI as a target for official development assistance (ODA). Among the countries surveyed, European and Nordic countries tended to proportionally donate more than other regions surveyed.

Australia, India, Israel, Japan, Kuwait, South Korea, New Zealand, the Russian Federation, and South Africa were found to have directed large proportions of their ODA activities toward neighboring countries or those in their geographic region. Former colonizing powers, such as France, apparently favor assistance to their former colonies; countries that still have overseas territories, such as the UK, give priority assistance to these areas.

Countries surveyed usually directed their ODA based on particular substantive areas of focus, such as elimination of poverty, health, education, food security, good governance, etc. Finland, Norway, and Sweden, were found to have given special attention to gender equality; similarly, Israel demonstrates contribution to rural-area training programs specifically for women. The promotion of the rights of the child was another area that influenced the aid policies of the EU, Finland, and Israel. Other criteria for prioritization applied in Australia, Finland, Sweden, the UK, and the EU were found to include levels of poverty as well as the aid's potential effectiveness.

In addition to other policy considerations for selection of recipients Australia, Finland, and Japan considered potential peace building and national security; Brazil and Israel the development of diplomatic relations, and France the facilitation and management of migratory flows.

Australia, Brazil, France, Germany, Japan, Norway, and the UK implement ODA policies through agencies that are dedicated to ODA distribution. Finland, New Zealand, and Israel have special departments within their Ministries of Foreign Affairs (MFAs) that implement ODA. In South Korea, *some aspects of ODA planning and implementation are shared between the MFA and the Ministry of Strategy and Finance. Kuwait and Saudi Arabia conduct their international development assistance mainly through public institutions governed by boards of directors. ODA implementation was found to be fragmented in the Russian Federation, South Africa, and India, with some institutional changes expected in these countries in the future.*

ODA implementation was found to be still lacking with regard to the untying of aid in countries such as Germany and the Russian Federation. Restrictions on aid qualifying for dual use and prohibitions on exports in violation of military embargoes were imposed in countries like Finland, France, Israel, and the United Kingdom. All countries surveyed appear to employ at least one oversight mechanism to ensure proper implementation of their ODA policies.

Whereas Australia, Germany, France, New Zealand and Sweden designate ODA as an independent budget allocation, in the UK, Finland, Israel, the Russian Federation, and India, ODA derives from general allocations to ODA dispensing agencies. Kuwait and Saudi Arabia generally channel their ODA through special funds that are governed by boards of directors. Japan and South Korea combine ODA with other financial resources. In general, annual EU budgets are based on a multiannual financial framework (MFF) that is agreed upon by the European Parliament, Council, and Commission in an inter-institutional agreement.

The United Kingdom was by far the largest donor of private donations for foreign aid purposes, followed by Sweden, Finland, Germany, and France. Additional types of foreign development assistance provided by the countries surveyed include emergency aid, scholarships to foreign students, guest worker programs, facilitation of remittances, and debt relief. Further aid-related activities include a focus on trade-enabling policies by Australia, and the creation of incentives for companies to invest in research, development, and production capacity for new vaccines in the United Kingdom.

I. Introduction

This collection of reports provides an overview of the way the European Union and eighteen selected countries from different continents around the world have handled their contributions to foreign development aid. Countries selected include members as well as nonmembers of the Organization for Economic Co-operation and Development (OECD) including countries with established and emerging economies. The collection is composed of individual country and European Union studies prepared by the research staff of the Global Legal Research Center of the Law Library of Congress during 2011 and early 2012. Each report provides information that was available at the time of its completion. Appendix A includes GIS maps that depict various aspects of the survey;[1] Appendix B, a compilation of official

---

[1] GIS maps utilize the geographic information system (GIS) for capturing, managing, analyzing, and displaying relevant geographically referenced information. *See What Is GIS?,* GEOGRAPHIC INFORMATION SYSTEMS,

development assistance (ODA) data in table format, reflects percentage change in ODA between 2003 and 2010. Although the United States was not surveyed, some US data is reflected in the maps for comparison purposes only.

The reports provide historical and background information on international cooperation agreements regarding ODA and statistical data regarding both ODA and private contribution figures. The reports further highlight priorities utilized by donor countries in selecting recipients and in determining the types of development assistance they provide.

The reports include information on foreign agencies that are responsible for ODA planning and implementation, and discuss foreign countries' appropriations processes for allocation of their ODA budgets. The reports list restrictions imposed under foreign countries' laws on the provision of ODA as well as on private contributions.

In addition to ODA and private donations, the reports discuss the contributions of foreign countries to development assistance by additional means, for example by providing scholarships to foreign students, instituting guest worker programs, facilitating remittances, and providing emergency aid.

Foreign countries' experience may be relevant to the current discussion regarding foreign aid development appropriations in the United States.[2] The recent global economic downturn seems to have reignited a debate in the United States and other countries over the role, extent, and impact of foreign aid on foreign policy.[3] Facing budgetary cuts in domestic programs, as

---

http://www.gis.com/content/what-gis (last visited Mar. 1, 2012). The maps in Appendix A were produced by Colin Hess, Law Library of Congress intern, under the supervision of Professor Brian Rizzo of the University of Mary Washington, Fredericksburg, Virginia, based on information derived from the attached individual reports as well as from data posted on Feb. 6, 2012, on the OECD website, http://stats.oecd.org.

[2] *See, e.g., The Agency for International Development and the Millennium Challenge Corporation: Fiscal Year 2012 Budget Requests and Future Directions in Foreign Assistance: Hearing Before the H. Comm. on Foreign Affairs,* 112th Cong. (2011), http://www.foreignaffairs.house.gov/112/65301.pdf. Foreign aid has been described by the current US administration "as 'smart power' . . . , one that emphasizes diplomacy and development as a complement to American military power." Steven Lee Myers, *Foreign Aid Set to Take a Hit in U.S. Budget Crisis,* N.Y. TIMES (Oct. 3, 2011), http://www.nytimes.com/ 2011/10/04/us/politics/foreign-aid-set-to-take-hit-in-united-states-budget-crisis.html?pagewanted=all; *see also* David Gartner, *Congress and Foreign Aid,* BROOKINGS INSTITUTION (Jan. 20, 2012), http://www.brookings. edu/opinions/2011/1005_congress_foreign_aid_gartner.aspx. Polls have shown, however, that the majority of Americans support foreign economic aid cuts to the federal budget. *See* Harris Interactive, *Cutting Government Spending May Be Popular But Majorities of the Public Oppose Cuts in Many Big Ticket Items in the Budget,* HARRIS INTERACTIVE (Mar. 1, 2012), http://www.harrisinteractive. com/NewsRoom/HarrisPolls/tabid/447/ctl/ReadCustom%20Default/mid/1508/ArticleId/972/Default.aspx.

[3] *See, e.g.,* Clare Feikert-Ahalt, *The UK: Foreign Aid and Political Pressures,* IN CUSTODIA LEGIS (Jan. 19, 2012), http://blogs.loc.gov/law/2012/01/the-uk-foreign-aid-and-political-pressures/. For Canada, *see Budget to Cut Spending Nearly $6B Over 3 Years,* CTVNEWS (Mar. 29 2012), http://www.ctv.ca/CTVNews/]TopStories/20120329/federal-budget-flaherty-ottawa-20120329 /; for Australia *see* Ben Packham & James Massola, *Julie Bishop Wins in Row Over Budget Cuts, Preventing Proposed Axe for Africa Aid,* THE AUSTRALIAN (Feb. 08, 2011), http://www.theaustralian.com.au/national-affairs/treasury/julia-bishop-wins-in-row-over-budget-cuts-preventing-proposed-axe-for-africa-aid/story-fn8gf1nz-1226002007187, *and* Phil Mercer, *Australian Business Group Wants Government to Cut Foreign Aid,* VOICE OF AMERICA (Feb. 14, 2011), http://www.voanews. com/english/news/asia/Australian-Business-Group-Says-Government-to-Cut-Foreign-Aid--116148489.html.

well as other austerity measures to revamp the economy, some have called for a reevaluation of donor countries' undertakings to provide international assistance and in particular for a reevaluation of the aid's effectiveness.

This study provides some comparative perspectives relevant to the discussion of foreign development aid.

II. International Cooperation in Providing Foreign Aid

A. Historical Background

Foreign aid is not a new concept in world affairs. In US history the significance of French assistance during the American Revolution is well known;[4] its impact on the donor, however, was said to have "plunged France into a precarious financial situation and accelerated the crisis of the monarchy."[5]

International development cooperation has surged in the last century, particularly after the American Marshall Plan to help Europe following World War II.[6] On January 13, 1960, the Development Assistance Group (DAG) was created as a forum for consultations among donors on assistance to developing countries. The DAG at that time included Belgium, Canada, France, Germany, Italy, Portugal, the United Kingdom, the United States, and the Commission of the European Economic Community, with Japan and the Netherlands joining shortly thereafter.[7] With the entry into operation of the Organization for Economic Co-operation and Development the DAG merged with the Development Assistance Committee (DAC). The OECD's Development Co-operation Directorate (DCD) works with the DAC on formulating international development commitments.[8]

B. The Millennium Development Goals

In 2000, the UN General Assembly adopted the Millennium Development Goals (MDGs), which consist of eight specific objectives, including

- eradication of extreme poverty and hunger;
- achievement of universal primary education;

---

[4] *Milestones: 1776–1783, French Alliance, French Assistance, and European Diplomacy during the American Revolution, 1778–1782*, UNITED STATES DEPARTMENT OF STATE OFFICE OF THE HISTORIAN, http://history.state.gov/milestones/1776-1783/FrenchAlliance (last visited Jan. 24, 2012).

[5] *The American Revolution (1775–1783)*, SITE FOR LANGUAGE MANAGEMENT IN CANADA, http://www.salic-slmc.ca/ (last visited Jan. 24, 2012).

[6] *Containment and the Marshall Plan, Postwar Challenges*, US HISTORY: PRE-COLUMBIAN TO THE NEW MILLENNIUM, http://www.ushistory.org/us/52c.asp (last visited Mar. 19, 2012).

[7] OECD, DAC IN DATES, THE HISTORY OF OECD'S DEVELOPMENT ASSISTANCE COMMITTEE 8 (2006 ed.) http://www.oecd.org/dataoecd/3/38/1896808.pdf.

[8] OECD, THE DAC: 50 YEARS, 50 HIGHLIGHTS at 6, http://www.oecd.org/dataoecd/22/26/47072129.pdf?contentId=47072130 (last visited Mar. 26, 2012).

- promotion of gender equality and empowerment of women;

- reduction of child mortality;

- improvement of maternal health;

- combating HIV/AIDS, malaria, and other diseases;

- ensuring environmental sustainability; and

- building a global partnership for development.[9]

These goals were accepted by major donor countries as guiding principles for their assistance activities.

C. The Four High-Level Forums on Aid Effectiveness

Four High-Level Forums on Aid Effectiveness (HLFs) sponsored by the DAC Working Party on Aid Effectiveness (WPAE) have been convened since 2000 to assess and meet the ambitious targets set by the MDGs; in Rome (2003), Paris (2005), Accra (2008), and Busan (2011).[10] The following is a brief summary of the principles adopted at these forums.[11]

1. HLF1 (Rome, 2003)

The Rome forum resulted in the adoption of the following priority actions, embodied in the Rome Declaration:[12]

- that development assistance be delivered based on the priorities and timing of the countries receiving it
- that donor efforts concentrate on delegating co-operation and increasing the flexibility of staff on country programmes and projects
- and that good practice be encouraged and monitored, backed by analytic work to help strengthen the leadership that recipient countries can take in determining their development path.[13]

---

[9] *Official List of MDG Indicators, Millennium Development Goals Indicators*, UNITED NATIONS, http://mdgs.un.org/unsd/mdg/Host.aspx?Content=Indicators%2fOfficialList.htm (last visited Jan. 24, 2012).

[10] *Id.*

[11] For additional information *see* Marian Leonardo Lawson, Cong. Research Serv., R 41185, FOREIGN AID: INTERNATIONAL DONOR COORDINATION OF DEVELOPMENT ASSISTANCE 4–6 (Apr. 5, 2010).

[12] Rome Declaration on Harmonisation (Feb. 2003), http://www.oecd.org/dataoecd/54/50/31451637.pdf.

[13] *The High Level Fora on Aid Effectiveness: A History*, OECD, DEVELOPMENT CO-OPERATION DIRECTORATE (DCD-DAC), http://www.oecd.org/document/63/0,3746,en_2649_3236398_46310975_1_1_1_1,00.html (last visited Jan. 25, 2012).

2. HLF2 (Paris, 2005)[14]

The Paris Declaration, a product of HLF2, outlined the following five fundamental principles for making aid more effective:

1. **Ownership**: Developing countries set their own strategies for poverty reduction, improve their institutions and tackle corruption.

2. **Alignment**: Donor countries align behind these objectives and use local systems.

3. **Harmonisation**: Donor countries coordinate, simplify procedures and share information to avoid duplication.

4. **Results**: Developing countries and donors shift focus to development results and results get measured.

5. **Mutual accountability**: Donors and partners are accountable for development results.[15]

3. HLF3 (Accra, 2008)

This forum convened in order to strengthen and deepen implementation of the Paris Declaration. The Accra Agenda for Action (AAA) centered on capacity development and proposed improvement in ownership, partnerships, and the delivery of results.[16] The key points agreed as part of the AAA are:

- **Predictability** – donors will provide 3–5 year forward information on their planned aid to partner countries.

- **Country systems** – partner country systems will be used to deliver aid as the first option, rather than donor systems.

- **Conditionality** – donors will switch from reliance on prescriptive conditions about how and when aid money is spent to conditions based on the developing country's own development objectives.

- **Untying** – donors will relax restrictions that prevent developing countries from buying the goods and services they need from whomever and wherever they can get the best quality at the lowest price.[17]

---

[14] *The Paris Declaration on Aid Effectiveness and the Accra Agenda for Action*, OECD, http://www.oecd.org/dataoecd/11/41/34428351.pdf (last visited Jan. 25, 2012).

[15] DCD-DAC, *supra* note 14.

[16] *Id.*

[17] *The Accra High Level Forum (HLF3) and the Accra Agenda for Action*, OECD, http://www.oecd.org/document/28/0,3746,en_2649_3236398_43553372_1_1_1_1,00.html (last visited Jan. 25, 2012).

4. HLF4 (Busan, 2011)[18]

The Busan Partnership for Effective Development Co-operation reinforced the principles that were adopted in the three earlier forums and specifically reemphasized the following:

- Ownership of development priorities by developing countries
- Focus on results
- Inclusive development partnerships
- Transparency and accountability to each other[19]

III. Official Development Assistance and the 0.7% Gross National Income Goal

A. Definition of ODA

The DAC adopted the concept of Official Development Assistance (ODA) in 1969 to standardize the measurement of the resource flows from DAC government donors to developing countries. According to the DAC, ODA is composed of

[t]hose flows to countries and territories on the DAC List of ODA Recipients and to multilateral development institutions which are:

    i. provided by official agencies, including state and local governments, or by their executive agencies; and

    ii. each transaction of which:

        a) is administered with the promotion of the economic development and welfare of developing countries as its main objective; and

        b) is concessional in character and conveys a grant element of at least 25 per cent (calculated at a rate of discount of 10 per cent).[20]

The OECD website has further clarified that ODA reporting should not include military aid or antiterrorism activities. The cost of using donors' armed forces to deliver humanitarian aid and some closely defined developmentally relevant activities within peacekeeping operations are, however, included. Additionally, nuclear energy is reportable as ODA, provided it is for civilian purposes. Support for cultural programs for the purpose of building "the cultural capacities of recipient countries" is similarly reportable, unless the programs are "one-off tours by donor country artists or sportsmen, and activities to promote the donors' image."[21]

---

[18] *Fourth High Level Forum on Aid Effectiveness*, OECD, http://www.aideffectiveness.org/busanhlf4/images/stories/hlf4/OUTCOME_DOCUMENT_-_FINAL_EN.pdf (last visited Jan. 25, 2012).

[19] *Id.* at 3.

[20] *Official Development Assistance – Definition and Coverage*, OECD, http://www.oecd.org/document/4/0,3746,en_2649_34447_46181892_1_1_1_1,00.html#Definition (last visited Feb. 3, 2012).

[21] *Id. See also Is It ODA?*, OECD (Nov. 2008), http://www.oecd.org/dataoecd/21/21/34086975.pdf.

B. The 0.7% Goal

The world's governments have repeatedly committed to donate 0.7% of donor countries' gross national income (GNI) to Official Development Assistance. The 0.7% target was first pledged thirty-five years ago in a 1970 UN General Assembly Resolution, and has been affirmed in many international agreements over the years. To date, most donor countries have not met the 0.7% target.[22]

IV. Foreign Development Assistance by Selected Countries

The attached reports address various policies and regulatory frameworks that are applied by selected foreign countries and by the European Union in providing foreign development aid. Individual foreign countries surveyed include members as well as nonmembers of the OECD as highlighted in Map 1 (Appendix A). In some cases, specifically those of newly emerging donor countries, surveyed jurisdictions were both donors as well as recipients of ODA.

A. ODA Contribution Amounts[23]

The following reports and Maps 2–4 (Appendix A) indicate ODA expenditure in 2003 and 2010 by the European Union and the countries surveyed. A table depicting actual figures is set forth in Appendix B.

Map 2 illustrates that in 2003, with the exception of the European Union (at US$41,427.53 million, hereafter M), the highest donor was Japan, with a US$12,970.87M contribution. Without the strong outlier (EU), US$3,958M was the average amount given by the countries surveyed in 2003. By comparison, the United States gave US$18,257.49M in 2003, about 4.6 times more than the average amount given by the surveyed countries.

Map 3 reflects that in 2010, with the exception of the European Union (at US$73,733.23M), the highest amount was again given by Japan, at US$18,861.66M. That year, without the strong outlier (EU), the average amount given by the surveyed countries was US$5,622.91M. By comparison, the United States gave US$31,159.3M, over 5.5 times more than the average.

A comparison between ODA monetary contributions in 2003 and in 2010 in the countries surveyed (illustrated in Map 4[24]) shows that all the countries contributed more in 2010 than in 2003, and the largest change was in Australia, with a 314% increase. The United States, in comparison, increased its ODA contribution by 171%.

---

[22] *The 0.7% Target: An In-Depth Look*, UN MILLENNIUM PROJECT (2006), http://www.unmillennium project.org/press/07.htm.

[23] Figures quoted in this section reflect data derived from the OECD website, http://stats.oecd.org (Feb. 6, 2012), as well as the attached country and EU reports (individually dated).

[24] Due to the absence of ODA GNI percentages for 2003, the percentage change between 2003 and 2010 is not provided.

Map 5 (Appendix A) shows the makeup of ODA contributions relative to each country's GNI in 2010. The lowest percentage was Brazil, with just 0.03% of GNI related to ODA contributions. The highest percentage was Norway, which devoted 1.1% of its GNI towards ODA contributions. The average percentage given by the countries surveyed was 0.39%. Overall, the Continental European and Nordic countries tended to donate more proportionally than other regions. Data regarding the makeup of ODA contributions as a percentage of the countries' GNI in 2003 has not been identified.

Considering the recent global economic downturn, mainly in Europe and in the US, patterns of ODA contributions and ODA GNI percentages, as demonstrated in Maps 4 and 5, may change, with traditional "rich" donors potentially limiting their spending and emerging market countries increasing their aid involvement.

B. Private Donations

In addition to ODA rates, private contribution figures were surveyed. Some have argued that private donations can be considered as an indirect form of states' assistance because tax exemptions or credits associated with such donations include an element of a state concession.[25]

According to the attached country reports, the United Kingdom was by far the largest donor of such aid, with an estimated US$17,000M given for 2009–2010, followed by Sweden, Finland, Germany, and France. The lowest amount, US$18M, came from Norway. This contrasts with governmental aid from Norway, which is the highest of any surveyed country.

C. Geographic Focus

A survey of the geographic focus of foreign aid activity, represented in Maps 6–9 (Appendix A), partially reflects donor countries' geopolitical interests. The Russian Federation, for example, has directed its foreign aid assistance to neighboring countries, mostly members of the former Soviet Union. Assistance to other regions, focusing on specific sectors of industry and the public sector, was mainly formulated under the influence of the Russian Federation's presidency of the G8 in 2006.

A geographical focus is also reflected in the policies of Kuwait, which for the fiscal year 2009/2010 contributed 53.94% of its total aid to the Arab countries, and the rest to countries in Africa, Southeast Asia, the Pacific region, Europe, Latin America, and the Caribbean. Israel, a country that has entered into regional peace agreements with some of its neighbors, refocused its aid from Africa and Asia, which were the focus during the 1970s and 1980s, to Egypt, Jordan, and the Palestinian Authority in the mid to late 1990s. South Africa, a country that has undergone significant transformation since the end of apartheid eighteen years ago, has also engaged in foreign development assistance with a focus on other African countries.

---

[25] Charles O. Flickner Jr., Former Staff Director, House Appropriations Committee, Subcommittee on Foreign Operations, Statement at Woodrow Wilson Center Seminar: Is Foreign Aid Worth the Cost? (Jan. 23, 2012).

A preference in favor of assisting neighboring countries was also found in Australia and in New Zealand, countries that primarily provide aid to East Asia and the Pacific region. Such preference is also found in India, where the focus is on neighboring countries such as Bhutan, Afghanistan, Nepal, and Burma. In the last decade, however, India has reportedly attempted to broaden its influence through aid to Africa. Like other Asian countries, Japan and South Korea have historically aided countries in the region.

In addition to a geographical focus on neighboring countries, this study also found that former colonizing powers, such as France, tend to favor assistance to their former colonies; countries that still have overseas territories, such as the UK, give priority assistance to these areas.

D. Substantive Focus Areas

Areas of contribution vary among the countries surveyed. Whereas some countries tend to focus on health, education, food security, good governance, and economic growth, others tend to focus on professional training and technical assistance, development of energy sources, and agriculture in recipient states.

The major objective of the foreign aid policy of the EU is the reduction and the eventual elimination of poverty. In pursuing its foreign aid policy, the EU aims to promote human rights, gender equality, democracy, the rule of law, access to justice and civil society, the rights of the child and indigenous people, protection of the environment, and the fight against HIV/AIDS. A similar focus is shared by individual countries such as Japan, Norway, Sweden, and Finland.

According to the attached country reports, Finland, Norway, and Sweden give special attention to gender equality; Israel provides rural-area training programs specifically for women.

The reports on the EU and Finland as one of the EU Member States specifically highlight promoting the rights of the child in foreign aid recipient countries; the report on Israel additionally lists youth programs and early childhood education as areas of prioritization of such aid.

E. Selection of Recipients

The survey indicates donors' prioritization of recipients based on general principles of poverty status as well as the aid's potential effectiveness. Such prioritization is applied in Australia, Finland, Sweden, the UK, and the EU as a community.

Finland and Germany also consider recipients' political situations and respect for human rights as determining factors in the prioritization of aid. France funds emerging market countries such as Brazil and China. Brazil, a recipient as well as a donor, selects aid recipients based on whether they share similar social and economic problems as those of Brazil itself.

F. Policy Considerations

Countries surveyed view foreign aid as contributing to both regional and to global economic and security interests. The Australian government, for example, has agreed to the following core purpose statement relating to Australia's aid program:

> The fundamental purpose of Australian aid is to help people overcome poverty. This also serves Australia's national interests by promoting stability and prosperity both in our region and beyond. We focus our effort in areas where Australia can make a difference and where our resources can most effectively and efficiently be deployed.[26]

Finland's policy of foreign aid is said to include the provision of "support for peace-building processes."[27] South Africa's current assistance programs similarly emphasize cooperation with African countries through promotion of conflict resolution. South Africa's assistance disbursement patterns further show that its aid policy favors peacekeeping assistance in addition to education.[28]

A concern for regional stability is specifically expressed by Japan's current Official Development Assistance Charter, which provides that "[t]he objectives of Japan's ODA are to contribute to the peace and development of the international community, thereby helping to ensure Japan's own security and prosperity."[29]

According to the Russian Federation's International Development Assistance (IDA Concept), its economic and political interests will be met by "strengthening Russia's international position and credibility; stabilizing [the] socioeconomic and political situation in the partner countries; establishing a belt of good neighborliness; prevent[ing] the occurrence of potential focal points of tension and conflict, primarily in the regions neighboring Russia; [and] creating a favorable external environment for Russia's own development."[30]

The focus on developing diplomatic relations plays an important role in the policies of Brazil and Israel. Although Brazil is generally said to provide aid to foreign countries independent of any conditions or political goals in exchange for grants, the Brazilian Agency for Cooperation defines technical assistance "as a contribution to the strengthening of Brazilian relations with developing countries."[31]

---

[26] *See* country report, AUSTRALIA, *infra*, at 48–49.

[27] *Finland's Development Policy Programme*, MINISTRY OF FOREIGN AFFAIRS OF FINLAND (Feb. 22, 2008), http://www.formin.fi/public/default.aspx?nodeid=15319&contentlan=2&culture=en-US; *see also* country report, FINLAND, *infra*, at 98, note 29.

[28] *See* country report, SOUTH AFRICA, *infra*, at 230.

[29] *See* country report, JAPAN, *infra*, at 161.

[30] *See* country report, RUSSIAN FEDERATION, *infra*, at 212–13.

[31] *See* country report, BRAZIL, *infra*, at 69.

Israel's selection of recipients is similarly viewed as furthering diplomatic goals, including the use of development cooperation to forge bonds of peaceful cooperation with Israel's neighbors based on its peace agreements.

Although representing a small part of its total ODA, France has instituted a special program that gives ODA preferential treatment to countries that have signed agreements with France for the concerted management of migratory flows, in an effort to facilitate the management of migratory flows and encourage immigrants to voluntarily return to their countries of origin.[32]

V. Legal Framework

A. Implementing Agencies

Some countries surveyed, as well as the European Union, have special agencies that provide advice on and implement aid policies and programs. These agencies usually enjoy discretion in spending ODA appropriations, subject to guiding policies and legal restrictions. Although dedicated to planning, coordinating, developing, and delivering aid programs, ODA agencies are often not the only ones handling foreign development assistance in their countries; some aspects of ODA may be handled by other agencies.

Examples of countries that have dedicated agencies for foreign development assistance include Australia, Brazil, France, Germany, Japan, Norway, and the UK. In addition, special departments for ODA exist within the Ministries of Foreign Affairs (MFAs) of New Zealand, Finland, and Israel. These departments work on policy development, planning, financing, and other activities relevant to foreign aid. Both Finland and Israel utilize the services of public companies to implement various ODA tasks. In South Korea some aspects of ODA planning and implementation are shared between the MFA and the Ministry of Strategy and Finance. In addition, about thirty institutions, including national government agencies and municipal governments, participate in the execution of ODA programs.

Instead of government agencies or ministries' departments, Kuwait and Saudi Arabia conduct their international development assistance through public institutions governed by boards of directors.

At the time the reports on the Russian Federation, South Africa, and India were completed (in November 2011 and September 2011, respectively), these countries did not have a specialized government agency for development assistance. Their delivery of ODA was therefore fragmented among many organizations and lacked centralized implementation. In the Russian Federation, however, plans to establish such an agency were announced by the Finance Ministry on August 26, 2011. The agency is expected to be subordinate to the Ministry of Finance and to coordinate its activities with the Ministry of Foreign Affairs.

---

[32] *See* country report, FRANCE, *infra*, at 114.

B. Restrictions

In 2001 the DAC recommended the untying of ODA to the least developed countries. The goal of untying ODA was also recognized by the Paris Declaration on Aid Effectiveness as a commitment designed to get "better value for money."[33] In 2008 at HLF3 in Accra the OECD Development Assistance Committee (DAC) further agreed to extend the original 2001 recommendation to cover additional countries.[34] The concept of untying aid was again reaffirmed at HLF4 (Busan, 2011).[35]

A review of the policies of the countries surveyed, however, indicates that in 2008, 41% of German technical assistance was provided in the form of tied aid; in the Russian Federation that percentage for 2008 was estimated at approximately 25%. Data indicates that France has already untied up to 91% of its total aid; Australia and the United Kingdom claim to have untied 100% of their ODA.

A review of additional current restrictions imposed on development assistance by the countries surveyed indicates the continued existence of limitations related to dual use and to prohibitions on exports in violation of military embargoes (e.g., Finland); or to export to hostile states (e.g., France, Israel, and the UK).

France links ODA to a requirement from the recipient state to promote democratic values, the rule of law, and human rights and principles as guaranteed by the UN Charter and by international law. Norway specifically conditions aid by requiring "gender-equal" implementation.

C. Oversight

Countries surveyed maintain a variety of systems of ODA oversight. These include an internal annual performance report, such as in Australia; an audit by a national auditor or state comptroller, as is the case in Finland, Israel, New Zealand, and South Africa; a governmental audit, as in Japan and the Russian Federation; an audit by the ODA agency itself, as is the case in South Korea; or a combination of national, parliamentary, ministerial, and judicial audits, as is the case in France, Germany, Sweden, and the United Kingdom.

VI. Regulation of Private Contributions

To encourage private donations, Australia authorizes donors to receive tax deductions under specified conditions relating to the identity and operation of the NGO concerned. Australia also grants income and other tax concessions and exemptions to NGOs that are involved in foreign aid. Israel, Japan, New Zealand, Norway, the Russian Federation, and South

---

[33] OECD, The Paris Declaration on Aid Effectiveness (2005) and the Accra Agenda for Action (2008) at 19, http://www.oecd.org/dataoecd/11/41/34428351.pdf. The untying of aid is listed as the eighth indicator of progress under the objective of "Alignment." *Id.*

[34] *Id.*, The Accra Agenda for Action § 18.

[35] *Fourth High Level Forum on Aid Effectiveness, supra* note 19, para. 18e.

Africa similarly provide for tax deductions or credits to qualified charitable organizations. The UK provides a tax refund for registered domestic charities under certain circumstances.

Donations to the Red Cross Society of China (RCSC) for the purpose of international humanitarian aid may trigger a full deduction for the purpose of corporate or personal income tax, provided that the RCSC meets the qualifications for accepting donations.

The French General Tax Code provides for a number of tax incentives for private contributions. These include tax credits for individual donations to officially approved public-interest and charitable organizations for recipients located in the EU, Norway, or Iceland; and for donations to organizations that provide food, lodging, and health care. French law further exempts donations from estate tax, and reduces corporate tax for donations to nonprofit organizations.

German law exempts nonprofit corporations, associations, and foundations from corporate income tax liability and allows individuals and corporations to deduct a certain percentage of their annual income for qualifying "nonprofit purposes," including for development aid. Alternatively, such bodies may elect to be limited in their qualifying nonprofit spending. Individual taxpayers also enjoy certain tax deductions over a one- to ten-year period if they donate funds toward the establishment of a charitable foundation. As preconditions for tax benefits Germany requires proof that the aid enhances its image and that donor organizations do not engage in subversive or extremist conduct. These two requirements are controversial and their constitutionality has been challenged by the Tax Authority.[36]

It is important to remember that countries' export rules also apply to development aid, just as those rules apply to other types of goods and services. Development aid is therefore subject to dual use restrictions in some countries—for example Sweden and Finland.

VII. Foreign Aid Appropriations Process

An ODA budget allocation is usually included in the surveyed countries' annual budget bills, which are typically proposed by their governments for parliamentary approval based on the advice and submissions by executive agencies and ministries. Several variations exist, however, as summarized below.

A. ODA as an Independent Budget Allocation(s)

In some countries, such as in Australia, ODA is an independent item in the annual Budget and is separate from that of the Department of Foreign Affairs and Trade. The Australian agency for development, AusAID, prepares its own advice and documentation in support of its request for annual appropriation.

New Zealand similarly has a separate appropriation for ODA in its appropriation bill and any supplementary estimates bills. Following a review of ministerial and executive agencies'

---

[36] *See* country report, GERMANY, *infra*, at 131–33.

proposals, the New Zealand Cabinet makes final budget decisions according to the government's budget strategy and submits its bill for parliamentary approval. New Zealand ODA budget allocations include funding for multilateral and bilateral aid. In addition to the specified ODA budget, other agencies may receive ODA-related funding as part of their own appropriations, particularly the New Zealand Police and New Zealand Defence Force.

Swedish budget allocations for ODA are also specified in the annual budget law, based on a governmental request. After approval, ODA is distributed by the government to implementing agencies that are notified by "letter of appropriation" of their relevant allocation of both bilateral and multilateral aid, as well as administrative costs.

Instead of a single designation of ODA, the French government presents its draft Finance Law in the form of major public policies, called "missions," to be examined and approved by Parliament. In 2011, French ODA comprised twenty-three programs that were distributed among ministries. Additional French ODA expenditures can be found under other missions and programs whose resources are only partly earmarked for development assistance.

While specifically allocated in its annual budget laws, ODA allocations in Germany frequently employ commitment plans extending three to five years, which may include reservations allowing the Federal Cabinet to block funds if other contributor countries do not live up to their obligations. The consent of parliamentary committees may sometimes be required to unblock such funds.[37]

B. ODA Funded by Agencies from Their Appropriated Budgets

Unlike countries where ODA is either listed as an independent item or as an item in a yearly appropriations bill, in several countries surveyed ODA funding is derived from the general appropriations to agencies that dispense ODA.

In the UK, for example, the ODA budget is not specified in the annual budget but rather constitutes a part of the budget allocation for the Department for International Development. In Finland, ODA likewise constitutes a component of the budget allocated to the Ministry of Foreign Affairs.

Israel's foreign aid budget is allocated to a number of government agencies, including the Bank of Israel, the Foreign Ministry (MASHAV), the Ministry of Finance, the Ministry of Industry and Trade, and the Ministry of Labor, among others. The budget is set according to a government plan and is discretionary.

Similarly, the Russian Federation's ODA is composed of budget allocations to various official bodies and ministries based on approval of the government's appropriation bill. ODA appropriations involve the submission of yearly proposals by different federal agencies to the Ministry of Finance based on ODA volumes agreed upon with the Ministry of Foreign Affairs,

---

[37] *Id.* at 133.

together with each agency's justification for the inclusion of its proposals in the long-term financial plans and the federal budget.

In India, funding for foreign assistance programs is proposed in an appropriation bill submitted by the Ministry of Finance (MoF) based on multiple ministries' proposals. Funding requires parliamentary approval. The MoF's expenditure proposal for 2010-2011 included separate allocations to multinational organizations, and for multilateral and bilateral cooperation agreements.

Additional countries where ODA allocation amounts are not clearly identified include the emerging market countries of Brazil and China. In Brazil there are more than 100 institutions of the Brazilian federal government, ministries, and related entities that are directly involved in international cooperation.

Similarly, in China each department authorized to handle respective foreign aid matters under the State Council draws up its own budget for foreign aid projects separately every year and submits it to the Ministry of Finance for examination, and then to the State Council and the National People's Congress for approval and implementation. Each department controls and manages its own funds for foreign aid projects in its budget.

C. ODA Through Public Institutions Governed by Board of Directors

Kuwait and Saudi Arabia have other arrangements for allocating ODA. Kuwait channels its ODA through the Kuwait Fund for Arab Economic Development, a public institution, based on its charter. Similarly, Saudi Arabia distributes ODA according to decisions by the Board of Directors of the Saudi Fund for Development. In addition, both countries contribute to regional and international development institutions.[38]

D. ODA Combined with Other Financial Sources

In South Korea the ODA budget supports the activities of the Ministry of Foreign Affairs and Trade (MOFAT), which controls grants and technical cooperation, as well as of the Ministry of Strategy and Finance (MOSF), which is responsible for loans to developing countries. The South Korean budget for development assistance consists of several sources: the government's general and special budget account for loans and funds from other financial sources, such as contributions from governmental funds, deposits from the National Bond Management Fund, and profit earned from the operation of the Economic Development Cooperation Fund of Korea's Export-Import Bank. South Korea's allocation of ODA from government funds is included in the government appropriation bill based on proposals made by ministries and agencies to the Ministry of Planning and Budget. The appropriation bill has to be approved by both the State Council and National Assembly.

Japan's development assistance budget incorporates four financing sources: the General Account, the Special Account, issuance of government bonds, and fiscal loans and investments.

---

[38] *See* country report, SAUDI ARABIA, *infra*, at 220–21.

The General Account portion of funding is approved by the Diet (Japan's Parliament) based on requests submitted by different ministries. In 2010 the General Account consisted of 35% of the gross ODA budget.[39]

E. EU ODA

In general, annual EU budgets are based on a multiannual financial framework (MFF) that is agreed upon by the European Parliament, Council, and Commission in an inter-institutional agreement. The MFF establishes the annual limits on appropriations in the EU budget for the various EU policy areas and sets an annual ceiling on payments and commitments. In June 2011, the European Commission proposed a budget for the period 2014–2020.[40] The total amount dedicated to foreign aid in the proposal was €70 million (about US$92.06 million).[41]

VIII. Other Types of 'Aid'

In addition to ODA allocations, countries have contributed to foreign aid in a variety of ways. Most countries surveyed, as well as the European Union, contributed emergency aid beyond their ODA appropriations.

Most countries surveyed have also extended scholarships to foreign students. In addition, Australia and New Zealand have operated guest worker programs. These countries as well as Finland, the Russian Federation, Sweden, and South Korea facilitated remittances. China and the European Union authorized debt relief.

Trade-enabling policies can also be viewed as additional means of foreign aid. For instance, the Swedish project *Kosmopolit* allocates special funds to stimulate and increase foreign trade with immigrants' native countries.[42]

While not allocating funds specifically for such a purpose, Australia recognizes that a rules-based multilateral trading system and freer trade and investment are of great benefit to developing countries. Trade-enabling policies therefore form part of the Australian overall approach to foreign policy and international development.

Among health-related types of aid, the United Kingdom provided financing to the Advance Market Commitment (AMC), which aims to create a market for vaccines in developing

---

[39] *See* country report, JAPAN, *infra*, at 167.

[40] News Release, European Commission Financial Programming and Budget, The Commission Proposes the Next Multiannual Financial Framework, 2014–2020 (June 29, 2011), http://ec.europa.eu/budget/news/ article_en.cfm?id=201106292310.

[41] *See Annex of Proposal for a Council Regulation Laying Down the Multiannual Financial Framework 2014–2020*, COM (2011) 398 final (June 29, 2011), http://ec.europa.eu/budget/library/biblio/documents/fin_fwk 1420/proposal_council_regulation_COM-398_en.pdf; *see also* country report, EUROPEAN UNION, *infra*, at 40–42.

[42] *See* country report, SWEDEN, *infra*, at 257.

countries by creating incentives for pharmaceutical companies "to invest in research, development and production capacity for new vaccines that serve the poor."[43]

IX. Concluding Remarks

The list of donors to foreign development aid has expanded in recent years beyond the traditional donor countries to include new emerging markets. Some countries appear to be both recipients as well as donors of aid. Such countries' contributions naturally fall into different geographic and substantive categories than those of donor-only countries.

The accompanying individual reports illustrate the experience gained by eighteen countries and by the European Union in formulating ODA policies and legislation and in streamlining their ODA activities during the past several decades. These reports are intended to provide a comparative perspective for consideration of the issue.

Prepared by Ruth Levush, Coordinator
Senior Foreign Law Specialist
March 2012

---

[43] *See* country report, UNITED KINGDOM, *infra*, at 278.

LAW LIBRARY OF CONGRESS

EUROPEAN UNION

REGULATION OF FOREIGN AID

Executive Summary

The European Union's (EU) foreign aid policy to third countries is guided by the principles on which the EU was founded: democracy and respect for human rights, fundamental freedoms, and the rule of law. A key objective of the EU's policy on foreign aid, as mandated by the Lisbon Treaty of 2009, is the reduction and eventual elimination of poverty. Foreign aid is a field that is shared by the EU and its twenty-seven Member States. All are required to coordinate their actions, and complement and reinforce each other, to deliver better and more efficient foreign aid.

In addition to reduction of poverty, other priorities of the EU's development policies under the "European Consensus on Development" include promoting sustainable development and protecting the environment, establishing and consolidating democracy and the rule of law, achieving the Millennium Development Goals (MDGs), and improving aid effectiveness in the least developed and lowest-income countries, including fragile states, which have priority in receiving larger amounts of foreign aid.

Foreign aid is distributed on the basis of multiannual programs and strategies prepared by the European External Action Service (EEAS) created by the Lisbon Treaty and EuropeAid, which is a newly created Directorate-General (DG) of the European Commission responsible for implementing the EU's development policies. In 2010, the Organisation for Economic Co-operation and Development (OECD) estimated that EU institutions provided US$12,985.87 million in foreign aid. The EU has made an ambitious commitment to increase its foreign aid gradually to a level of 0.7% of gross national income (GNI) by 2015. However, the EU and its members missed their intermediate collective target of 0.56% by 2010. The Commission has urged the largest members with solid economies to do more than their share in order to reach the EU's collective target.

The EU implements its foreign aid policy based on geographic and thematic instruments. The geographic programs extend to five regions: Latin America, Asia, Central Asia, the Middle East, and southern Africa (specifically South Africa). Foreign aid to sub-Saharan Africa, except South Africa; the African, Caribbean, and Pacific (ACP) countries; and the overseas countries and territories (OCTs) is provided on the basis of the European Development Fund

(EDF, established under the Cotonou Agreement). Some thematic instruments deal with a variety of issues, including migration, asylum, and investing in people.

The EU has, to a large extent, espoused a policy of delivering untied aid for the last twenty-five years with the objective of increasing transparency and accountability. Currently, ownership, participation of the beneficiary countries in the management of aid, and accountability of local authorities constitute the cornerstones of the EU's development policy.

Under EU law, foreign aid to third countries may be reduced or discontinued, wholly or partially, if such countries fail to respect international law, human rights, and the rule of law.

The European Parliament possesses the right to scrutinize any development assistance financed by the general budget. The budget support programs are subject to review by the European Court of Auditors. In its 2010 report, the Court of Auditors criticized the Commission's lack of criteria for determining the level of budget support to be allocated.

I. Introduction

The EU, in conducting its development policy, is guided by the fundamental principles on which it was founded: liberty, democracy, and respect for human rights and the rule of law. The EU's mandate in foreign aid, including the granting of humanitarian assistance, is based on the 2009 Lisbon Treaty and secondary legislation.[1] Eradication of poverty worldwide is at the heart of the foreign aid policy pursued by the EU. The EU also continues to endorse the European Consensus on Development (ECD) adopted in 2005[2] and to pursue the Millennium Development Goals (MDGs).[3] The ECD established the foundation for a common EU vision on

---

[1] Article 21 of the Treaty on European Union states that in its international relations the Union shall be guided by the universality and indivisibility of human rights and fundamental freedoms, respect for human dignity, the principles of equality and solidarity, and respect for the principles of the UN Charter and international law. Consolidated Version of the Treaty on European Union, Feb. 7, 1992, 2010 OFFICIAL JOURNAL OF THE EUROPEAN UNION [O.J.] (C 83) 13, http://eur-lex.europa.eu/LexUriServ/LexUriServ.do?uri=OJ:C:2010:083:0013:00 46:EN:PDF.

[2] The Consensus reaffirmed the EU commitments made in the 2005 Paris Declaration on Aid Effectiveness. Joint Statement by the Council and the Representatives of the Governments of Member States Meeting within the Council, the European Parliament and the Commission on European Union Development Policy: 'The European Consensus,' 2006 O.J. (C 46) 1, http://eur-lex.europa.eu/LexUriServ/LexUriServ.do?uri=OJ:C:2006:046 :0001:0019:EN:PDF.

[3] For additional information see Commission Staff Working Paper: Annual Report 2011 on the European Union's Development and External Assistance Policies and Their Implementation in 2010, at 5, SEC (2011) 880 final (July 6, 2011), http://eur-lex.europa.eu/LexUriServ/LexUriServ.do?uri=SEC:2011:0880:FIN:EN:PDF; and accompanying document, Report from the Commission to the Council and the European Parliament Annual Report 2011 on the European Union's Development and External Assistance Policies and Their Implementation in 2010, COM (2011) 414 final (July 6, 2011), http://eur-lex.europa.eu/LexUriServ/LexUriServ.do?uri=COM:2011: 0414:FIN:EN:PDF.

development designed to deliver increased and more effective aid, and also led to the adoption of the EU Code of Conduct on Complementarity and Division of Labour in Development Policy in 2007.[4] The EU Code of Conduct is designed to harmonize donor practices and increase cooperation and collaboration in joint cofinancing programs with other donors.[5]

Foreign aid is an area in which the EU and the twenty-seven Member States enjoy a shared and parallel competence. Individual Members began their foreign aid programs at the end of World War II based on historical, economic, and social relations with a particular country or region. The EU's independent policy on foreign aid does not prevent the EU Members from exercising their own competencies. Division of competence between the EU and its Members is regulated by article 208 of the Treaty of the Functioning of the European Union (TFEU), which calls for complementation and reinforcement of Union and Members' development policy.[6] In the same vein, the EU Code of Conduct clarifies that community policy is intended to be complementary to the policies pursued by the EU Member States.[7]

Within their respective fields of competence, the EU and its Members States aim to promote a multilateral approach to delivering foreign aid and promoting cooperation with other multilateral and regional organizations and bodies. In some areas, the Commission plays a more dynamic and enhanced role as a donor than any EU Member State. In the so-called fragile countries,[8] which became the focus of EU aid in 2007, the Commission is often the only donor present because the EU Members have withdrawn their support.[9]

Currently, at the EU level, a number of foreign aid–related issues have raised concerns and are subject to debates and public consultations. The quantity and quality of aid reaching its destination, and aid effectiveness and ownership of development strategies, are often discussed.[10] The Commission is strongly committed to ensuring increased ownership of development strategies by recipient countries, along with involvement of all segments of society. Two main

---

[4] European Union Code of Conduct on Complementarity and Division of Labour in Development Policy [EU Code of Conduct], *approved by* the Council of the EU on May 15, 2007, http://register.consilium.europa.eu/pdf/en/07/st09/ st09558.en07.pdf.

[5] *Id.*; *see also* Holger Murle, Towards a Division of Labour in European Development Cooperation: Operational Options (German Development Institute Discussion Paper, June 2007), *available at* http://www.oecd.org/dataoecd/60/23/46859449.pdf.

[6] *See* discussion in text, *infra*, at 12.

[7] European Consensus, *supra* note 2, at 1; EU Code of Conduct, *supra* note 4.

[8] Fragile countries are often referred to as "aid orphans" because they attract few international donors and low aid levels. EU Code of Conduct, *supra* note 4. For additional information on EU's policy on fragile states, *see* Maurizio Carbone, Aid and Security in the Development Policy of the European Union 15 (paper prepared for a workshop on "Transforming Political Structures: Security, Institutions, and Regional Integration Mechanisms," Florence, Italy, Apr. 2009), *available at* http://erd.eui.eu/media/carbone.pdf.

[9] Joint Statement by the Council and the Representatives of the Governments of the Member States Meeting Within the Council, the European Parliament and the Commission, European Consensus, *supra* note 2, at 16.

[10] *See, e.g.*, OECD, European Community – Development Assistance Committee (DAC) Peer Review 12–25 (2007), http://www.oecd.org/dataoecd/57/6/38965119.pdf.

issues are open for public consultation: (1) the future of EU development policy, which is addressed by the Commission's *Green Paper: EU Development Policy in Support of Inclusive Growth and Sustainable Development*;[11] and (2) the use of budget support as a means to deliver EU aid. This issue is examined in the Commission's *Green Paper: The Future of EU Budget Support to Third Countries.*[12]

Internationally, the EU is actively engaged in a constructive dialogue with competent international partners on foreign aid and especially with the UN and the OECD. The European Commission, as a Member of the OECD and the Development Assistance Committee (OECD/DAC), has endeavored to ensure greater impact of foreign aid, improve aid effectiveness, and reach the targets of the Paris Declaration of 2005 and the Accra Agenda for Action of 2008.[13]

A. Official Development Assistance Figures

OECD statistics indicate that in 2010 EU institutions provided US$12,679.15 million in net disbursements of official development assistance (ODA).[14] The EU's 2011 Report on Development and External Assistance states that in 2010 the EU (Member States plus EU institutions) granted the largest amount of foreign aid (€53.8 billion, about US$68.15 billion) and that the Commission alone is one of the biggest donors of foreign aid worldwide, providing €11 billion.[15] In 2005, the EU committed itself to an even more ambitious goal by providing, by 2015, 0.75% of its collective gross national income (GNI) in ODA, for a total of US$122 billion annually.[16] For the period 2007–2013, the European Commission has allocated around €52

---

[11] Green Paper: EU Development Policy in Support of Inclusive Growth and Sustainable Development: Increasing the Impact of EU Development Policy, COM (2010) 629 final (Nov. 10, 2010), http://eur-lex.europa.eu/LexUriServ/LexUriServ.do?uri=COM:2010:0629:FIN:EN:PDF.

[12] *Green Paper: The Future of EU Budget Support to Third Countries*, COM (2010) 586 (Oct. 19, 2010), http://eur-lex.europa.eu/LexUriServ/LexUriServ.do?uri=COM:2010:0586:FIN:EN:PDF.

[13] The Paris Declaration on Aid Effectiveness and the Accra Agenda for Action of 2008, OECD, http://www.oecd.org/dataoecd/30/63/43911948.pdf. The Paris Declaration of 2005 is an international agreement, signed by one hundred countries that pledged to improve aid effectiveness. The signatories made the following important commitments: (1) ownership: developing countries establish their own plans for poverty reduction; (2) alignment: donor countries support national strategies for recipient countries; (3) harmonization: donor countries coordinate their actions and share information; (4) results: accomplishing targets is emphasized; and (5) mutual accountability: donors and recipient countries are accountable for development aid results.

[14] *ODA by Donor*, OECD.STATEXTRACTS, http://stats.oecd.org/Index.aspx?DatasetCode=ODA_DONOR (last visited Feb. 1, 2012).

[15] European Commission, *2011 Annual Report on the European Union's Development and External Assistance Policies and Their Implementation in 2010*, at 5, http://ec.europa.eu/europeaid/files/publications/europeaid_annual_report_2011_en.pdf. *See also The European Union: Leading Provider of Development and Humanitarian Aid*, EU INSIGHT (Sept. 2006), http://www.eurunion.org/News/eunewsletters/EUInsight/2006/EUInsightDev2006.pdf.

[16] Communication from the Commission to the European Parliament, the Council, the Economic and Social Committee, and the Committee of the Regions, Enhancing EU Accountability on Financing for Development Towards the EU Official Development Assistance Peer Review, at 2 & 5, COM (2011) 218 final (Apr. 19, 2011), http://eur-lex.europa.eu/LexUriServ/LexUriServ.do?uri=COM:2011:0218:FIN:EN:PDF.

billion (US$67.62 billion) for its development program, or approximately €9 billion annually (US$11.70 billion).[17]

In 2006, the EU and its Members reached their intermediate target of 0.39% of ODA/GNI, but in 2010 failed to meet their collective goal of 0.56%[18] due to the current economic crisis, which has affected several EU Members. In 2009, the EU and its Member States disbursed €20.5 billion in foreign aid to Africa. EU's collective 2005 commitment to give at least 50% of the combined aid to sub-Saharan Africa was not achieved.[19] With respect to foreign aid to the least developed countries, in 2008, the EU and its Members promised to spend at least 0.15% of combined GNI on ODA by 2010. Preliminary data indicates that this goal was also missed; in 2010 the combined EU ODA to the least developed countries amounted to 0.13% of GNI.[20]

Nine EU Members met or exceeded the 2010 individual minimum targets and the majority reached their national ODA targets. The remaining EU Members missed their individual 2010 minimum targets and, hence, the EU missed its collective target of 0.56%.[21] The Commission attributed the EU's failure to meet the 2010 target partly to the economic crisis currently unfolding among some EU Members but also to a number of Members not adhering to their commitments to achieve the collective EU goal.[22] In the Commission's opinion, such failure undermines the principle of fair internal EU burden sharing and has an adverse impact on aid delivery. On the other hand, the EU expects Members with large economies, such as France, Germany, Italy, and the United Kingdom (UK) to augment the average aid levels to achieve the targets set. These Members account for 70% of the gap to be filled between 2010 and 2015; therefore, the EU can meet its collective target of 0.7% ODA/GNI by 2015 only if the large-economy countries contribute more than their share.[23]

In its 2011 EU Accountability Report on Financing for Development, the European Commission categorized the twenty-seven EU Members into four groups based on their contributions and outlook on achieving their individual goals by 2015:

---

[17] *See Frequently Asked Questions on EU Aid*, DEVELOPMENTPORTAL.EU, http://www.development portal.eu/wcm/faq-on-eu-aid.html (last visited Feb. 2, 2012). For a summary table of the fifteen EU/DAC Members' commitments and performance, *see DAC Members' Commitments and Performance: Summary Table of OECD Secretariat Projections*, OECD (Feb. 15, 2010), http://www.oecd.org/dataoecd/20/19/44607047.pdf.

[18] Communication from the Commission, *supra* note 16, at 5.

[19] *Id.* at 6.

[20] *Id.*

[21] Commission Staff Working Document, EU Accountability Report 2011 on Financing for Development, Review of Progress of the EU and its Members States, Accompanying Document to the Communication from the Commission to the European Parliament, the Council, the Economic and Social Committee and the Committee of the Regions Enhancing EU Accountability on Financing and Development Towards the EU Official Development Assistance Peer Review vol. I at 25, SEC (2011) 500 final (Apr. 19, 2011), http://eur-lex.europa.eu/LexUriServ/ LexUriServ.do?uri=SEC:2011:0500:FIN:EN:PDF.

[22] *Id.*

[23] *Id.* at 34.

1. Denmark, Luxembourg, the Netherlands, and Sweden already achieved their 0.7% target. The multiannual budgets of Denmark, the Netherlands, and Luxembourg indicate that their aid will remain the same in nominal terms until 2015.

2. Belgium, Cyprus, Finland, France, Ireland, and the UK have reached their 2010 targets or missed by a small margin. The Commission expects that these Members could achieve their individual targets (ranging from 0.7% to 0.33%) on time.

3. Austria, the Czech Republic, Estonia, Germany, Lithuania, Malta, Poland, Slovenia, and Spain missed the 2010 targets.

4. Bulgaria, Greece, Hungary, Italy, Latvia, Portugal, Romania, and the Slovak Republic have fallen behind their commitments, and the Commission expects that these countries will not meet their individual targets by 2015.[24]

The Commission urged EU Members to make the following commitments:

• Increase ODA to 0.7% of the combined GNI by 2015

• Reach individual ODA targets as soon as possible by drafting national action plans

• Take additional national measures, if necessary, to achieve the target by 2015, including the option to enact legislation to make the ODA target legally binding

• Share information with each other on their actions

• Publicize their actions to gain public support for foreign aid[25]

B. Overview of Foreign Aid Activity

The general principles that guide the EU's policy on foreign aid are to give priority to the least-developed countries and lowest-income countries with the long-term objective of achieving the MDGs. In pursuing its foreign aid policy, the EU aims to promote human rights, gender equality, democracy, the rule of law, access to justice and civil society, the rights of the child and indigenous people, protection of the environment, and the fight against HIV/AIDS.[26]

Based on country or regional strategy papers[27] and annual action programs, which are jointly prepared by the European External Action Service (EEAS) and the newly established

---

[24] *Id.* at 35.

[25] *Id.* at 35–36.

[26] Regulation (EC) No. 1905/2006 of the European Parliament and of the Council of December 18, 2006, Establishing a Financing Instrument for Development Cooperation art. 3, 2006 O.J. (L 378) 41, recitals 2–7, http://eur-lex.europa.eu/LexUriServ/LexUriServ.do?uri=OJ:L:2006:378:0041:0071:EN:PDF.

[27] These are general strategy papers for the period 2007–2013, either Country Strategy Papers (CSPs) or Regional Strategy Papers (RSPs), for example for the African, Caribbean and Pacific (ACP) countries and other

Directorate-General of the Commission, EuropeAid, the EU provides foreign aid through two main methods: (1) by funding various projects through grants or related projects; and (2) by providing budget support. The first method supports specific initiatives with a fixed budget and a specific time period, and the second involves mainly the transfer of funds directly to the national treasury of the recipient country based on a number of agreed-upon performance indicators.

In the transfer of budget support funds, three points are important: (1) the EU transfers funds to the recipient country's central bank, (2) the central bank credits the national treasury with the transferred amount in national currency, and (3) the transfer to the central bank is made only if agreed-upon conditions for payment are met. The European Commission prefers the budget support method. Budget support is provided if the recipient country manages public spending in a transparent, reliable, and effective manner and has established microeconomic policies reviewed or endorsed by main donors and/or international financial institutions.[28]

Budget support may also involve the provision of funds for a specific sector, such as education or health.[29] However, a salient element of budget support is conditionality; that is, the fulfillment of three eligibility criteria by the recipient country and additional conditions agreed upon in advance to ensure that results are met. The requirements include the existence of: (1) a national or sectoral development or reform policy, (2) a stability-oriented microeconomic framework, and (3) a strong and credible program to improve public financial management.[30] The funds are transferred only if the above criteria and all agreed-upon conditions are met.[31] Upon transfer, the recipient country's authorities and especially its auditing authorities assume responsibility for overseeing, controlling, and auditing the funds granted.

1. Thematic Programs

Foreign aid is implemented through geographic and thematic programs. Thematic programs have a wider scope of application than geographic programs because they cover a specific area of development policy not limited by geography. The EU strives to tailor external aid to specific themes, and often the thematic instruments supplement the geographic instruments.[32] Thematic strategy papers outline the EU's plan for the theme concerned; its

---

non-EU countries. *How the Commission Provides Budget Support*, EUROPEAN COMMISSION: DEVELOPMENT AND COOPERATION – EUROPEAID, http://ec.europa.eu/europeaid/how/delivering-aid/budget-support/index_en.htm (last updated Oct. 13, 2011).

[28] EUROPEAID, GUIDELINES ON THE PROGRAMMING, DESIGN & MANAGEMENT OF GENERAL BUDGET SUPPORT 10, http://ec.europa.eu/europeaid/what/economic-support/documents/guidelines_budget_support_en.pdf (last visited Mar. 2, 2011).

[29] European Commission, EuropeAid Co-operation Office, Partnership for Change: The EU's Development Cooperation with African, Caribbean and Pacific Countries 14 (2010), http://ec.europa.eu/development/icenter/repository/europeaid_brochure_partnership_for_change_en.pdf.

[30] *Id. See also* EUROPEAN COMMISSION, *supra* note 27.

[31] EUROPEAN COMMISSION, *supra* note 27.

[32] *Id.*

priorities as determined by the Commission; the specific objectives, anticipated results, and performance indicators; and consistency with the objectives and principles established in Annex IV of Regulation No. 1905/2006.[33] There are five thematic programs:

(1) Investment in people

(2) Environmental protection and sustainable management of natural resources, including climate change and energy

(3) Non-state actors and local authorities in development

(4) Food security

(5) Migration and asylum[34]

2. Geographic Programs

Geographic strategy papers must apply the principles of aid effectiveness, which include national ownership, partnership, coordination, harmonization, and alignment of EU support with the recipient's national development strategies, reform policies, and procedures. Strategy papers must also aim to improve cooperation and mutual accountability between partner governments and donors, and promote local expertise and local employment. Geographic and thematic strategy papers are reviewed either at mid-term or ad hoc, if necessary.[35]

The geographic programs extend to five regions: Latin America, Asia, Central Asia, the Middle East, and southern Africa (specifically South Africa). The African, Caribbean, and Pacific (ACP) states are covered by the European Development Fund (EDF). The EU's overarching objective for delivering foreign aid to these countries is the eradication of poverty and the achievement of the MDGs. In particular, it supports the following actions: primary education and health of the local population; promotion of social cohesion and employment, democracy, human rights, and institutional reforms; sustainable development through environmental protection and better management of natural resources; and assistance in post-crisis situations.[36]

For the period 2007–2013, the EU has adopted three geographic instruments to implement external assistance: the EDF, the European Neighborhood and Partnership Instrument (ENPI), and the Development Cooperation Instrument (DCI).[37]

---

[33] Regulation (EC) No. 1905/2006, *supra* note 26, art. 20 & Annex IV.

[34] *Id.* arts. 12–15.

[35] *Id.* art. 19.

[36] A Budget for Europe 2020: The Current System of Funding, the Challenges Ahead, the Results of Stakeholders Consultation and Different Options on the Main Horizontal and Sectoral Issues, at 193, SEC (2011) 868 final (June 29, 2011), http://ec.europa.eu/budget/library/biblio/documents/fin_fwk1420/SEC-868_en.pdf.

[37] *How We Finance*, EUROPEAN COMMISSION, DEVELOPMENT AND COOPERATION – EUROPEAID, http://ec.europa.eu/europeaid/how/finance/index_en.htm (last updated Dec. 6, 2011).

a. European Development Fund

Foreign aid to sub-Saharan Africa (except South Africa), the ACP countries, and the overseas countries and territories (OCTs) is provided on the basis of the EDF. The legal basis for providing assistance is the Cotonou Agreement, which has been revised regularly, most recently in 2010.[38] Cooperation with other countries financed by the EU budget is based on Regulation No. 1905/2006. The EDF is not part of the EU budget.[39]

The EDF, whose duration is usually five years, provides support for the ACP countries in the areas of economic, social, and human development and regional cooperation and integration.[40] It is composed of several instruments: (a) grants managed by the Commission; (b) risk capital and loans to the private sector managed by the European Investment Bank; and (c) the "FLEX" mechanism designed to remedy the adverse effects of instability of export earnings.[41]

The 10th EDF (2008–2013) is concluded on the basis of the ACP–European Community partnership agreements and the amended Overseas Association Decision. The 10th EDF has a budget of €22,682 million (US$29,969 million): of this amount, €21,966 million is allocated to the ACP countries, €286 million to the OCTs, and €430 million to the Commission for expenditures related to implementation of the EDF.[42] The EDF is not funded by the general budget, but it is funded by the Member States. Each Member must contribute a specific amount.

b. European Neighborhood and Partnership Instrument

The ENPI is designed to support the EU's European Neighborhood Policy, which, based on good neighborliness goals, focuses on providing development assistance to the countries and territories listed in the Annex of Regulation No. 1638/2006 on Establishing a European Neighborhood and Partnership Instrument.[43] The beneficiary countries and territories include Algeria, Armenia, Azerbaijan, Belarus, Egypt, Georgia, Israel, Jordan, Lebanon, Libya, Moldova, Morocco, the Palestinian Authority of the West Bank and Gaza Strip, the Russian

---

[38] Partnership Agreement Between African, Caribbean and Pacific Group of States and the European Community and Its Members, signed in Cotonou on June 13, 2000. The Cotonou Agreement is the most comprehensive partnership agreement between the above countries and the EU. It was revised in 2005 and 2010. *See* Second Revision of the Cotonou Agreement – Agreed Consolidated Text, EU–ACP, Mar. 11, 2010, http://ec.europa.eu/development/icenter/repository/second_revision_cotonou_agreement_20100311.pdf.

[39] Commission Staff Working Paper, Annual Report 2011, *supra* note 3.

[40] Council Regulation (EC) No. 617/2007 of May 14, 2007, on the Implementation of the 10th European Development Fund Under the ACP-EC Partnership Agreement, 2007 O.J. (L 152) 1, http://eur-lex.europa.eu/LexUriServ/LexUriServ.do?uri=OJ:L:2007:152:0001:0013:EN:PDF.

[41] *European Development Fund (EDF)*, EUROPEAN COMMISSION, DEVELOPMENT AND COOPERATION – EUROPEAID, http://ec.europa.eu/europeaid/how/finance/edf_en.htm (last updated July 8, 2011).

[42] *Id.*

[43] Regulation (EC) No. 1638/2006 of the European Parliament and the Council of October 2006 Laying Down General Provisions Establishing a European Neighborhood and Partnership Instrument, 2006 O.J. (L 310) 1, http://ec.europa.eu/world/enp/pdf/oj_l310_en.pdf.

Federation, Syria, Tunisia, and Ukraine.[44] The overall aim of EU assistance is to promote enhanced cooperation and progressive economic integration between the EU and partner countries and to facilitate the implementation of partnership, cooperation, and association agreements. The ENPI supports measures in the areas of promoting legislative and regulatory approximation of partner countries with EU legislation; effective implementation of policies included in association and cooperation agreements; promoting the rule of law and good governance, poverty reduction, social development, health, education and training, and protection of human rights and freedoms, including women and children's rights; ensuring secure border management; development of civil society; and promoting participation in EU research and innovation activities.[45] Measures financed based on Regulation No. 1638/2006 are eligible for cofinancing by Member States, their local authorities and public agencies, international and regional organizations, companies, firms, and private organizations.[46]

The amount allocated for the period 2007–2013 is €11.181 billion. A minimum of 95% of this amount will be allocated for a country or multi-country programs, and 5% will be allocated for cross-border cooperation programs.[47]

c. Development Cooperation Instrument

The DCI includes three components: (a) geographic programs; (b) thematic programs; and (c) programs for accompanying measures for the eighteen ACP Sugar Protocol countries with the objective of assisting them in adjusting in the aftermath of the reform of the EU sugar regime. The geographic programs support cooperation with forty-seven developing countries in Latin America, Asia and Central Asia, the Gulf region (Iran, Iraq, and Yemen), and southern Africa (South Africa). The areas of support include poverty eradication and progress on the MDGs; essential needs of the population, especially in education and health; employment; governance, democracy, and human rights; sustainable protection of the environment and natural resources; assistance in post-crisis situations and fragile states; and others.[48] The thematic component benefits all developing countries, including those covered by the ENPI and the EDF. It supports measures in the areas of investing in people, non-state actors and local authorities in development, food security, migration and asylum, and environmental protection and sustainable management of natural resources.[49]

3. Special Measures

In case of unforeseen circumstances and in exceptional cases due to natural disasters, civil unrest, or crisis, the Commission has the authority to adopt special measures not provided

---

[44] *Id.*, Annex, "Partner Countries Referred to Article 1 [of Regulation No. 1638/2006]."

[45] *Id.* art. 2.

[46] *Id.* art. 17.

[47] *Id.* art. 29.

[48] *Development Cooperation Instrument (DCI)*, EUROPEAN COMMISSION, DEVELOPMENT CO-OPERATION INSTRUMENT – EUROPEAID, http://ec.europa.eu/europeaid/how/finance/dci_en.htm.

[49] *Id.*

for in strategy papers or action programs.[50] Special measures may be used to fund initiatives to facilitate the transition from emergency aid to long-term development operations and to enable people to deal better with crises.

The Commission adopted special measures following the recent events in North Africa and the Middle East—the so-called "Arab Spring." As Catherine Ashton, the EU High Representative, stated recently, a key priority of the Commission's policy in those regions is to support not only "deep and sustainable democracy but also economic recovery."[51] Following the adoption of a joint Communication by the Commission and the EU High Commissioner, "A New Response to a Changing Neighborhood,"[52] the Commission adopted four new decisions that endorse democracy and provide support for growth, job creation, microfinance, and higher education:

(1) The SPRING program (Support for Partnership, Reform, and Inclusive Growth), a major initiative in the amount of €350 million (US$472.5 million). It is designed to assist emerging democracies in institution building and economic growth and is customized to each country's specific needs.

(2) Special measures to alleviate poverty in Tunisia, to increase employment and generate job growth, and to improve living conditions. Its total value is €20 million (US$27 million).

(3) The Erasmus Mundus Program, to increase academic and student mobility through various study abroad programs and exchanges of knowledge and skills. Its total value is €66 million (US$89 million).

(4) The Neighborhood Civil Society Facility, to enable civil society, promote reform, and increase public accountability. Its total value is €22 million (US$29.7 million).[53]

---

[50] Regulation (EC) No. 1905/2006, *supra* note 26, art. 23.

[51] *EU Launches Four Ambitious New Support Programs in Response to the Arab Spring*, EUROPEAN UNION @ UNITED NATIONS (EU/UN email alert, Sept. 30, 2011), http://www.eu-un.europa.eu/home/index_en.htm.

[52] Joint Communication to the European Parliament, the Council, the Economic and Social Committee, and the Committee of the Regions, A New Response to a Changing Neighborhood, COM (2011) 2 (May 25, 2011), http://ec.europa.eu/world/enp/pdf/com_11_303_en.pdf.

[53] *Id.*

II. Legal Framework

A. Regulation of ODA

1. Overview

Title III of the Treaty on the Functioning of the EU (TFEU), as amended by the Lisbon Treaty, provides the legal framework for the EU's development policy. In particular, article 208 of the TFEU on Cooperation with Third Countries and Humanitarian Aid establishes the principles on which foreign aid policy must be conducted and the objectives to be achieved. It also delineates the competence of the EU and its Members and obliges them to fulfill their commitments and take into account the objectives endorsed within the UN framework and other international organizations. Specifically, article 208 stipulates that the EU must exercise its development policy within the framework of the principles and objectives of its external actions; that "the Union's development cooperation policy shall have as its primary objective the reduction and, in the long term, the eradication of poverty"; and that the Union's development policy and that of its Members "complement and reinforce each other."[54]

Acquisition of legal personality by the EU by virtue of the Lisbon Treaty means that the EU now has the authority to conclude agreements with third countries and international organizations.[55] Article 209 gives the mandate to the EU to enter into agreements, with third countries or international organizations, to achieve its objectives in the area of development policy. The EU's authority does not impair the capacity of the EU Members to enter into agreements with third countries.[56] Article 209 also authorizes the European Bank to implement EU policies on foreign aid. Legislation on foreign aid is adopted on the basis of the ordinary legislative procedure, which involves a proposal by the Commission, adoption by the Parliament and the Council, and review by the European Court of Justice.[57] The Commission may take any initiative to promote coordination between the EU and its Members.[58]

Article 210 of the Treaty on the Functioning of the EU specifies the forms of collaboration between the EU and its Members, while article 212 deals with cooperation between the EU and its members in relations with international organizations. To improve complementarity and ensure efficiency of their activities on foreign aid, the EU and its Members must cooperate by

- coordinating their policies on development cooperation;
- consulting with each other on various aid programs;

---

[54] Consolidated Version of the Treaty on the Functioning of the European Union (TFEU) art. 208, 2010 O.J. (C 83) 47, 141, http://eur-lex.europa.eu/LexUriServ/LexUriServ.do?uri=OJ:C:2010:083:0047:0200:EN:PDF.

[55] *Id.* art. 209.

[56] *Id.*

[57] *Id.*

[58] *Id.* art. 209, para. 2.

- undertaking joint actions, as necessary;

- contributing to the implementation of the EU's programs;[59] and

- cooperating with third countries and international organizations.[60]

The following additional initiatives also introduced by the Lisbon Treaty are anticipated to have a positive impact on delivering foreign aid to third countries:

- The establishment of the position of High Representative for Foreign Affairs and Security Policy, who is also the Vice-President of the European Commission, chairs the Foreign Affairs Council, and is in charge of implementation of the EU's external policy.

- The creation of the European External Action Service, which serves the High Representative for Foreign Affairs, the President of the Council, and the Commission.

- New opportunities for enhanced cooperation among EU Members and the possibility of joint programs.[61]

a. Regulation No. 1905/2006 on Establishing a Financial Instrument for Development Cooperation

The objective of eradicating poverty is also expressly stated in article 2 of Regulation No. 1905/2006, on Establishing a Financing Instrument for Development Cooperation,[62] which stipulates that "the primary and overarching objective of cooperation . . . shall be the eradication of poverty in partner countries and regions."[63] To this end, the Regulation provides for the financing of

- measures designed to support cooperation with developing countries, territories, and regions included in the OECD/DAC list of aid recipients, which was updated in 2009 by virtue of Regulation No. 960/2009; and

- thematic programs countries, territories, and regions eligible for foreign aid, under a geographic program provided for in this regulation, or for a geographic cooperation under the EDF.[64]

---

[59] *Id.* art. 210, para. 1.

[60] *Id.* art. 212.

[61] For institutional changes that affect foreign aid, *see Commission Staff Working Paper, Annual Report 2011, supra* note 3, at 6.

[62] 2006 O.J. (L 178) 41, *as amended by* Commission Regulation (EC) No. 960/2009 of October 14, 2009, Amending Regulation (EC) No. 1905/2006, http://eur-lex.europa.eu/LexUriServ/LexUriServ.do?uri=OJ:L:2009:270:0008:0011:EN:PDF.

[63] Regulation (EC) No. 1905/2006, *supra* note 26, *as amended by* Regulation No. 960/2009, Annex I, O.J. (L 270) 8, http://eur-lex.europa.eu/LexUriServ/LexUriServ.do?uri=OJ:L:2009:270:0008:0011:EN:PDF.

[64] *Id.* art. 1.

The amount allocated for the implementation of this Regulation during the period of 2007–2013 is €16,897 million (about US$22,671 million). Under this Regulation, the geographic programs encompass five regions: Latin America (eighteen countries), Asia (nineteen countries), Central Asia (five countries), the Middle East (four countries), and southern Africa (one country, South Africa).[65] EU aid delivered to these regions is designed to support actions in a number of critical areas of cooperation, including

- eradication of poverty and achievement of the MDGs;

- focusing on essential needs of the local population, especially primary education and health;

- promotion of democratic governance and human rights;

- promotion of sustainable development by protecting the environment and natural resources; and

- assistance in post-crisis situations and fragile states.[66]

Under Regulation No. 1905/2006, the thematic programs deal with a specific area of activity directed to a group of recipient countries, irrespective of geographic criteria. Five thematic programs are established: (1) investing in people, (2) environmental protection and sustainable development of natural resources, (3) non-state actors and local authorities, (4) food security, and (5) cooperation in the field of asylum and migration.[67]

In addition, Regulation 1905/2006 establishes a program that accompanies measures in favor of the eighteen ACP Sugar Protocol countries and that assists them through the adjustment period due to the reform of the EU sugar regime.[68] As article 25, paragraph 2{ of the Regulation specifies, EU foreign aid cannot be used for paying taxes or duties in beneficiary countries.[69]

Financing is done either under an agreement or grant or procurement contract, or under an employment contract. It may take the following forms:

- Projects and programs

- Budget support

- Sectoral support

- Sectoral and general import programs in exceptional cases

- Interest-rate subsidies, especially for loans for environmental projects

- Debt relief under internationally agreed-upon debt relief programs

---

[65] *Id.*

[66] Regulation (EC) No. 1905/2006, *supra* note 26, art. 5.

[67] *Id.* arts. 12–16.

[68] *Id.*, Annex III.

[69] *Id.* art. 25.

- Grants to finance certain projects

- Funding for twinning programs between public institutions and local authorities

- Contributions to international funds managed by international or regional organizations[70]

> b. *Regulation No. 1889/2006 on Establishing a Financing Instrument for the Promotion of Democracy and Human Rights Worldwide*

Regulation No. 1889/2006,[71] which establishes a financing instrument to provide assistance for the period of 2007–2013, aims to contribute to the achievement of the development policy objectives contained in the European Consensus on Development and to establish and consolidate democracy and the rule of law. The amount allocated for the implementation of this Regulation amounts to €1,104 billion (about US$1,458 billion).

Pursuant to the objectives of the instrument cited above, EuropeAid drafted a European Instrument for Democracy and Human Rights (EIDH) Strategy Paper 2011–2013.[72] The Strategy Paper has the following objectives: (a) to enhance respect for human rights in countries where such rights are most at risk; (b) to improve the role of civil society in promoting human rights; (c) to support EU actions on human rights issues, such as the death penalty, torture, children in armed conflict, violence against women, and others; and (d) to support democracy through a fair and transparent electoral process.

In April 2010, in implementation of the MDGs, the Commission adopted a Communication, "A Twelve-Point EU Action Plan in Support of the Millennium Development Goals.[73] The Action Plan focuses on delivering foreign aid to countries in great need, such as those experiencing internal conflict—the so-called fragile countries—where the Commission is often the only donor. The Commission proposed that EU Members adopt a number of measures to increase the amount of aid and make it more effective. Some of the key recommendations include

- establishing realistic annual action plans to reach goals and publishing such plans before September 2010;

- increasing aid effectiveness by coordinating national aid programs at the EU level;

---

[70] *Id.* art. 29.

[71] Regulation EC No. 1889/2006 of the European Parliament and of the Council of December 20, 2006, on Establishing a Financing Instrument for the Promotion of Democracy and Human Rights Worldwide, 2006 O.J. (L 386) 1, http://eur-lex.europa.eu/LexUriServ/LexUriServ.do?uri=OJ:L:2006:386:0001:0011:EN:PDF.

[72] *European Commission – External Relations, European Instrument for Democracy and Human Rights (EIDHR) Strategy Paper 2011–2013* (Apr. 21, 2010), http://ec.europa.eu/europeaid/what/human-rights/documents/eidhr_strategy_paper_2011_2013_com_decision_21_april_2011_text_published_on_internet_en.pdf.

[73] Communication from the Commission to the European Parliament, the Council, the European Economic and Social Committee and the Committee of the Regions: A Twelve-Point EU Action Plan in Support of the Millennium Development Goals, at 6, COM (2010) 159 final (Apr. 21, 2010), http://eur-lex.europa.eu/LexUriServ/LexUriServ.do?uri=COM:2010:0159:FIN:EN:PDF.

- promoting "ownership" of MDGs in developing countries;

- supporting initiatives on innovative financing with high revenue potential and ensuring that such financing assists the poorest; and

- focusing more on the least developed countries and fragile states.[74]

2. Implementing Agencies

On January 1, 2011, a new Directorate-General (DG) for Development, EuropeAid, was created through a merger of the former DG for Development and EuropeAid DGs.[75] Its organizational structure was finalized on June 1, 2011. The rationale for having a single agency is that such a one-stop shop will facilitate access to information on foreign aid within and outside the EU.[76]

At the EU level, EuropeAid is tasked with implementation of external assistance instruments in a transparent, accurate, and accountable manner. It is also subject to the Court of Auditors' review. The European Parliament exercises a right to scrutiny, but only when it comes to funds from the EU budget. With regard to how the Commission makes use of the EDF, the Commission must forward a copy of a country or region strategy paper to the Joint Parliamentary Assembly EU/ACP for review.[77]

Internationally, the EEAS represents the EU through its delegations in 136 countries. The EEAS was established based on the Lisbon Treaty and performs a crucial role in the implementation of aid delivery.[78] The EU delegations play a key role in promoting the aid effectiveness agenda, ensuring a division of labor and burden sharing among donors, and ensuring more government ownership of the aid process.[79] For example, the EU Delegation established in Washington, DC, acts as a liaison between the Directorate of the European Commission and US government agencies such as the Department of State and the US Agency for International Development (USAID), international organizations including the World Bank and the International Monetary Fund (IMF), nongovernmental organizations (NGOs), and various "think tanks" based in the DC area.[80]

---

[74] *Id.*

[75] *Who We Are*, EUROPEAN COMMISSION, DEVELOPMENT AND COOPERATION – EUROPEAID, http://ec.europa.eu/europeaid/who/index_en.htm (last updated June 23, 2011).

[76] *Id.*

[77] *Programming*, EUROPEAN COMMISSION, DEVELOPMENT AND COOPERATION – EUROPEAID, http://ec.europa.eu/europeaid/how/finance/ programming_en.htm (last updated Mar. 4, 2011).

[78] *What We Do*, EUROPEAN UNION EXTERNAL ACTION, http://eeas.europa.eu/what_we_do/index_en.htm (last visited Oct. 2011).

[79] Commission Staff Working Paper, Annual Report 2011, *supra* note 3, at 30.

[80] *How We Ensure Aid Effectiveness*, EUROPEAN COMMISSION, DEVELOPMENT AND COOPERATION – EUROPEAID, http://ec.europa.eu/europeaid/how/ensure-aid-effectiveness/index_en.htm (last updated Nov. 18, 2011).

The delegations prepare the External Assistance Monitoring Reports (EAMRs), which compare the outcome and results of assistance with the benchmarks of the Paris Declarations, and assist the DG in assessing its performance against the four benchmarks of the Paris Declaration of 2005.

To qualify for aid delivery, an NGO must

- be an autonomous nonprofit organization with its head office in a Member state;

- provide audited financial statements for the two previous years;

- indicate sufficient administrative activity;

- follow a voluntary code of conduct that adheres to the principles of impartiality, independence, and neutrality in distributing humanitarian assistance; and

- confirm the moral integrity of the management board and the overall organization.[81]

3. Restrictions

Untying aid has been the focus of discussions at the international level, in particular by the Development Assistance Committee of the OECD/DAC. In March 2001, the DAC adopted a Recommendation on Untying Official Development Assistance to the Least Developed Countries.[82] At the EU level, for more than twenty-five years, the former European Community has largely espoused a policy of untied aid as an effective tool to increase transparency and accountability in the management of aid.[83] Its policy has even gone further than the recommendation of the OECD/DAC. Currently, more than two-thirds of aid delivered via geographical or thematic instruments is untied.[84] All EU Members have agreed to extend further the scope of this recommendation and have urged the untying of food aid and food aid transport.

Financial Regulation No. 1905/2006 embodies the policy of untied aid pursued by the EU. In allocating funds, the Commission considers a number of objective and transparent criteria based on the needs and performance of each recipient country or region. The needs criteria include population, income per capita, income distribution, and level of poverty and social development. The performance criteria include political, economic, and social progress;

---

[81] Regulation No. 1257/1996 Concerning Humanitarian Aid art. 6, 1996 O.J. (L 163) 1, http://eur-lex.europa.eu/LexUriServ/LexUriServ.do?uri=OJ:L:1996:163:0001:0006:EN:PDF.

[82] Development Assistance Committee of the OECD/DAC, Recommendation on Untying Official Development Assistance to the Least Developed Countries, OECD/DAC 2001 Report vol. 3, no. 1, at 46 (2002).

[83] The first Convention of Lomé I, signed in 1973 between the then-European Community and the ACP, was based on partnership, which presupposes ownership.

[84] Communication from the Commission to the Council and the European Parliament, Financing for Development and Aid Effectiveness – The Challenges of Scaling Up EU Aid 2006–2010, COM (2006) 85 final (Mar. 2, 2006), http://eur-lex.europa.eu/Result.do?T1=V5&T2=2006&T3=85&RechType=RECH_naturel &Submit=Search.

progress in good governance; effective use of aid; and especially how the recipient country uses its own resources.[85]

Assistance may be suspended by the Council of the EU based on a proposal by the Commission. Suspension may occur if a beneficiary country continues to fail to adhere to the principles while refusing consultations with the Commission or when such consultations do not reach a satisfactory outcome for both parties.[86]

4. Discretionary Aid

The Emergency Aid Reserve is designed to assist third countries that experience a crisis that was unforeseen when the budget was prepared. The EU also has at its disposal the Flexibility Instrument, which provides funding in a given financial year for identified expenses that could not be covered by one or more headings without going beyond their expenditure ceilings.[87] The maximum amount allocated to the Flexibility Instrument is €200 million annually.

5. Oversight

Financing provided in any legal form, whether as a financing or grant agreement or as a procurement or employment contract, must include clauses that (a) entitle the Commission and the Court of Auditors to perform audits, including review of documents or on-the-spot audits, inspections, and checks of any contractor that received funds from the Commission; and (b) ensure that the EU's financial interests are protected, especially in cases of fraud, irregularities, or any other illegal activity.[88]

The funds are managed by the European Investment Bank. An observer from the bank participates in meetings convened by the Commission and the committee, which assists the Commission in monitoring and reviewing the impact of foreign aid policy.

a. European Commission

The Commission, assisted by a committee, must monitor its programs at regular intervals and evaluate the implementation of thematic and geographic instruments. To accomplish an objective evaluation of its foreign policy aid, and to ensure that objectives are met, the Commission must engage all relevant stakeholders, including private donors, local authorities, and NGOs. The Commission does not evaluate its own programs but assigns review tasks to independent external authorities. Evaluations are considered by the Commission in drafting recommendations for more effective implementation of its foreign aid policy.[89] Subsequently,

---

[85] Regulation (EC) No. 1905/2006, *supra* note 26, art. 18, para. 2.

[86] *Id.* art. 37.

[87] *Flexibility Instruments*, EUROPEAN COMMISSION, FINANCIAL PROGRAMMING AND BUDGET, http://ec.europa.eu/budget/explained/budg_system/flex/flex_en.cfm#flex (updated Jan. 19, 2012).

[88] Regulation (EC) No. 1905/2006, *supra* note 26, art. 30.

[89] *Id.* art. 33.

the Commission forwards its evaluation reports to the European Parliament and the committee. EU Members may request evaluation reports.[90]

The Commission prepares annual reports on the implementation, major accomplishments, shortcomings, and impact of foreign assistance. Such reports are submitted to the European Parliament, the Council of the EU, the Economic and Social Committee, and the Committee of the Regions. The annual reports contain a wealth of information on the measures financed; the outcome of the evaluations; implementation of budget commitments; and payments by country, region, and sector. The Commission, through the use of measurable indicators, assesses its role in providing assistance and any progress made toward achieving the MDGs.[91]

b. European Parliament

In October 2010, the European Parliament urged more use of article 290 of the Treaty on the Functioning of the EU as amended by the Lisbon Treaty,[92] which provides for the possibility of using delegated acts. Pursuant to article 290, a legislative act may delegate the Commission to adopt nonlegislative acts of general application. Such delegated acts could be used to regulate the financing of instruments on foreign assistance. Because article 290 grants the Parliament the right to revoke a delegated act and the right to veto it, the Parliament could exercise its authority to make amendments.

As Gay Mitchell, the Parliament's rapporteur on the Development Cooperation Instrument, explained, "[w]hat we are asking is to be treated on equal footing with the Council when exercising the democratic scrutiny rights."[93]

c. European Court of Auditors

The European Court of Auditors (ECA) has carried out audits to evaluate whether the European Commission has fulfilled its role in managing its general budget support (GBS) programs effectively in ACP, Latin American, and Asian countries.[94] One such audit covered the period from 2001 to 2009. The Court's auditors made on-site visits in Benin, Laos, Paraguay, and Uganda. Two additional countries, Nicaragua and Vietnam, were included in the audit through questionnaires. The Commission also convened with World Bank and International Monetary Fund officials.

---

[90] *Id.* arts. 33, 35.

[91] *Id.* art. 34.

[92] Consolidated Version of the Treaty on the Functioning of the EU (TFEU) art. 290, 2010 O.J. (C 83) 47, 173, http://eur-lex.europa.eu/LexUriServ/LexUriServ.do?uri=OJ:C:2010:083:0047:0200:EN:PDF.

[93] Press Release, European Parliament, Guaranteeing MEP's Over Development and Human Rights Funding (Feb. 3, 2011), http://www.europarl.europa.eu/en/pressroom/content/20110203IPR13105/html/Guaranteeing-MEPs'-right-of-scrutiny-over-development-and-human-rights-funding.

[94] *European Court of Auditors, The Commission's Management of General Budget Support in ACP, Latin American and Asian Countries* (Special Report No. 11, 2010), http://eca.europa.eu/portal/pls/portal/docs/1/7090728.PDF.

The Commission has used budget support during the last decade as the preferred method of aid delivery to reduce poverty. The total package of GBS programs consists of three components: (1) transfer of funds linked to the objectives of the particular program and agreed upon between the Commission and the recipient countries; (2) capacity-building measures through technical assistance; and (3) communication with the recipient country on the design, implementation, and outcome.[95] The difference between budget support and sector budget support is that the latter aims to support a particular sector rather than a national policy. One of the benefits of foreign aid delivered through GBS programs, rather than the traditional approach through projects, is that more aid can be forwarded to the recipient country and also more control of aid and improvements in the management of the public financing system of the recipient country and strengthening of accountability are possible. This may also improve dialogue between the donor and recipient countries, and certainly improves the efficiency of donor aid delivery and reduces costs.[96]

The ECA found that in general during the last decade, the Commission has made progress toward its goal of delivering better and more effective aid through its GBS; however, the ECA did identify some flaws in the methodology and management of GBS programs. In particular, the ECA found that the Commission's approach is problematic in specific areas due to

- lack of sound risk management framework to evaluate and reduce the risks of its programs, especially when a large amount of money is given through public budgets in developing countries;

- lack of clear grounds and rationale that prompt the Commission to decide on the amount of funds to be allocated in each country;

- lack of clear criteria to assess whether true and satisfactory progress has been made;

- ineffective use of policy dialogue with beneficiary countries (the Commission must define clearly a dialogue strategy that outlines its objectives, contents, and goals to be achieved, and needs to ensure that Delegations of the European Union are equipped with expert staff to ensure effective dialogue); and

- insufficient information on the actual impact of aid delivery through budget support (the Commission needs to develop an evaluation methodology that provides concrete information on whether and under what circumstances budget support can contribute effectively to reducing poverty, and needs to improve on the reporting of the effectiveness of budget support programs).[97]

In particular, the ECA held that the objectives of the GBS do not take into account the specific circumstances and the changing priorities of each recipient country. The Commission has not paid full attention to the need to increase the capacity of oversight bodies, including audit

---

[95] *Id.* at 9.

[96] *Id.* at 12.

[97] Press Release, European Court of Auditors, Special Report: The Effectiveness of the Commission's Management of General Budget Support in ACP, Latin American and Asian Countries (Feb. 16, 2011), http://eca.europa.eu/portal/pls/portal/docs/1/7106723.PDF.

institutions, parliaments, and organizations tasked to oversee how funds are allocated and spent by governments in recipient countries. The Court also referred to another problem associated with GBS: its programs are not used to support other objectives related to health and education.

d. European Anti-Fraud Office

The European Anti-Fraud Office (*Office Européen de Lutte Anti-Fraude*, or OLAF) is part of the Commission but also enjoys some administrative and budgetary autonomy. Its mission is to protect the financial interests of the EU by combating fraud, corruption, and other illegal activities against the EU and misconduct by EU institutions.[98] OLAF has the authority to conduct independent external investigations on illegal activities perpetrated by natural or legal persons.[99] Its website cites a number of cases involving external aid and misuse of funds.

6. Policy Considerations

During the past twenty-five years, the EU has evolved into a dynamic and powerful economic player with regional and strategic security interests. Its external policies worldwide and in particular its development policy on third countries are guided by the same principles that initially laid the foundation and cornerstone for the establishment of the Union: the principles of freedom, democracy, respect for human rights and fundamental freedoms, and the rule of law.[100] These principles have been reaffirmed by the Lisbon Treaty.

Further EU instruments adopted to advance and promote development policy are based on the same principles and reflect similar policy considerations. For instance, the European Consensus on Development outlines the policy priorities of the EU, which focus on four main objectives:

(1) Reducing or eradicating poverty

(2) Promoting sustainable development

(3) Improving aid effectiveness

(4) Meeting the objectives of the MDGs[101]

The European Commission's 2011 Communication on a Budget for Europe describes a number of financial instruments to support the implementation of the following external policies:

---

[98] *Our Mission*, EUROPEAN ANTI-FRAUD OFFICE, http://ec.europa.eu/dgs/olaf/mission/index_en.html (last visited Feb. 1, 2012).

[99] *Id.*

[100] *See* Consolidated Version of the Treaty on European Union art. 21, Feb. 7, 1992, 2010 O.J. (C 83) 13, 28, http://eur-lex.europa.eu/LexUriServ/ LexUriServ.do?uri=OJ:C:2010:083:0013:0046:EN:PDF; Consolidated Version of the Treaty on the Functioning of the European Union (TFEU) art. 205, 2010 O.J. (C 83) 47, 139, http://eur-lex.europa.eu/LexUriServ/LexUriServ.do?uri=OJ:C:2010:083:0047:0200:EN:PDF.

[101] European Consensus, *supra* note 2.

- Promoting and defending EU values abroad, especially human rights, democracy, and the rule of law

- Addressing major global challenges, including climate change, biodiversity loss, and the protection of global public resources

- Improving the impact of EU development cooperation towards eradication of poverty by allocating aid resources according to needs, capacities, and commitments

- Supporting the long-term prosperity and stability of the EU's neighborhood by assisting candidate countries to join the EU, and by reinforcing and expanding its neighborhood policy

- Improving crisis prevention and resolution[102]

B. Regulation of Private Contributions

Regulation 1905/2006's section on co-financing of measures from other donors deals with contributions provided by private donors. The list of private donors includes Member States and their regional and local authorities; other donor countries; international and regional organizations; companies, firms, businesses, and other private entities; and other non-state actors.[103]

A distinction is made between parallel and joint cofinancing. In the event of parallel cofinancing, the particular program or project is divided into separate components that can be easily identified and that are each financed by a different partner. In the event of joint cofinancing, the total cost of a project or a program is divided among the donors who provide the financing. The total funds and resources available are gathered together so that it is not possible to discern the source of financing. The Commission may also receive and manage the funds in the event of joint cofinancing.[104]

III. Foreign Aid Appropriations Process

In general, annual EU budgets are based on a multiannual financial framework (MFF)[105] that is agreed upon by the European Parliament, Council, and Commission in an interinstitutional agreement.[106] The MFF establishes the annual limits on appropriations in the EU budget for the

---

[102] Communication from the Commission to the European Parliament, the Council, the European Economic and Social Committee and the Committee of the Regions, A Budget for Europe 2020 – Part II: Policy Fiches, at 42–43, COM (2011) 500 final (June 29, 2011), http://europa.eu/press_room/pdf/a_budget_for_europe_2020_-_part_ii_policy_fiches_en.pdf.

[103] Regulation (EC) No. 1905/2006, *supra* note 26, art. 27, para. 1.

[104] *Id.* art. 27, para. 2.

[105] *Financial Framework 2007–2013*, EUROPEAN COMMISSION FINANCIAL PROGRAMMING AND BUDGET, http://ec.europa.eu/budget/figures/fin_fwk0713/fwk0713_en.cfm#cf07_13.

[106] Interinstitutional Agreement (IIA) of May 17, 2006, Including the Multiannual Financial Framework 2007–2013, 2006 O.J. (C 139) 1, http://eur-lex.europa.eu/LexUriServ/LexUriServ.do?uri=OJ:C:2006:139:0003:0003:EN:PDF.

various EU policy areas (headings) and sets an annual ceiling on payments and commitments.[107] The category "appropriation for payments" relates to the actual money to be financed from EU Members within specific years, whereas the category "appropriations for commitments" indicates the amounts authorized for programs or projects that can be entered into in a specific year and concern a specific beneficiary. The ceiling for payment commitments is expressed as a percentage of GNI and takes into account economic activity.[108]

In June 2011, the European Commission proposed the budget for the period 2014–2020.[109] The total amount dedicated to foreign aid was €70 million (about US$92.06 million).[110]

The Commission, in its Communication on a Budget for Europe 2020, proposed enhanced oversight of external aid delivery through the delegated acts of article 290 of the Treaty and by placing the European Parliament and the Council of the EU on an equal footing as the two co-legislators. Moreover, the EDF, which has been outside the review of the Court of Auditors, will also be subject to review.[111] The overarching objective of the budget for 2020 remains the eradication of poverty. The EU remains committed to delivering aid where it is most needed, improving aid coordination, and ensuring adequate financing for development. The Commission introduced a number of initiatives related to external aid for 2020. It proposed a reinforced European Instrument for Democracy and Human Rights to improve the EU's ability to deal with human rights crises and provide more support for electoral processes and observation missions.[112] It also proposed a new Partnership Instrument to provide support, as needed, to developing and nondeveloping nations with an emphasis on strategic partners and emerging economies.[113] It further proposed the creation of a pan-African instrument to support implementation of the Joint Africa-Europe Strategy. Another proposal was a single pre-accession instrument to ensure that candidate countries fully adopt the *acquis communautaire* (EU body of law) prior to accession. The current Development Cooperation Instrument (DCI) will be reinforced and the EDF will remain outside of the budget for the next MFF.[114] The

---

[107] Frequently Asked Questions(FAQs): Budget and Financial Perspectives: MEMO/04/30, EUROPA (Feb. 10, 2004), http://europa.eu/rapid/pressReleasesAction.do?reference=MEMO/04/30&format=HTML&aged=1&language=EN&guiLanguage=fr.

[108] *Id.*

[109] News Release, European Commission Financial Programming and Budget, The Commission Proposes the Next Multiannual Financial Framework, 2014–2020 (June 29, 2011), http://ec.europa.eu/budget/news/article_en.cfm?id=201106292310.

[110] *See Annex of Proposal for a Council Regulation Laying Down the Multiannual Financial Framework 2014–2020*, COM (2011) 398 final (June 29, 2011), http://ec.europa.eu/budget/library/biblio/documents/fin_fwk 1420/proposal_council_regulation_COM-398_en.pdf.

[111] Communication from the Commission to the European Parliament, the Council, the European Economic and Social Committee and the Committee of the Regions, A Budget for Europe 2020 – Part II: Policy Fiches, COM (2011) 500 final (June 29, 2011), http://europa.eu/press_room/pdf/a_budget_for_europe_2020_-_part_ii_policy_ fiches_en.pdf.

[112] *Id.* at 44.

[113] *Id.*

[114] *Id.*

European Neighborhood Policy instrument will be enhanced to improve cooperation with neighbor countries, with an emphasis on "more for more."[115]

IV. Other Types of 'Aid'

A. Humanitarian Aid

The EU also plays a preeminent role in delivering emergency and humanitarian aid and aims to respond immediately to man-made or natural disasters and conflict situations. The EU is among the largest contributors of such aid worldwide.[116] Humanitarian aid is designed to assist third countries outside the EU, based on need relating to the catastrophic effects of man-made or natural disasters.

Since the entry into force of the Lisbon Treaty of 2009, humanitarian aid has acquired the status of a legally binding policy of the EU. Pursuant to article 214 of the Treaty on the Functioning of the EU, the EU operations in the field of humanitarian aid "shall be intended to provide ad hoc assistance and relief and protection for people of third countries who are victims of natural or man-made disasters, in order to meet the humanitarian needs resulting from these different situations."[117] Humanitarian aid is not the exclusive domain of the EU; rather, both the EU and the Member States share competence and act in synergy with each other. The European Commission may take any initiative to promote coordination among the measures taken by the EU and those of the Member States. In delivering humanitarian aid, the EU must comply with international law and the principles of humanity, impartiality, neutrality, and independence.[118]

Humanitarian aid, which encompasses food, water, sanitation, shelter, health services, protection of victims of conflict, and disaster preparedness, is administered through the European Commission's DG for Humanitarian Aid (ECHO). In 2010, the EU spent about €1,115 million (US$1,450 million) through ECHO by providing humanitarian aid to 151 million people in eighty non-EU countries.[119] It was established in 1992 and operates through the conclusion of two types of Framework Partnership Agreements (FPAs): with international organizations, and with NGOs. In addition, ECHO has concluded a Financial and Administrative Framework Agreement between the EU and the UN that regulates humanitarian aid financed by ECHO and dispersed by UN humanitarian services.[120] ECHO does not operate directly in the countries affected but provides funds to two hundred partners, NGOs, UN agencies, and the International

---

[115] *Id.*

[116] *See Annual Report on Humanitarian Aid Policy and Its Implementation in 2009*, SEC (2010) 398, COM2010/138 final (Apr. 9, 2010), http://eur-lex.europa.eu/LexUriServ/LexUriServ.do?uri=COM:2010:0138:FIN:EN:PDF.

[117] Consolidated Version of the Treaty on the Functioning of the European Union (TFEU) art. 124, 2010 O.J. (C 83) 47, 99, http://eur-lex.europa.eu/LexUriServ/LexUriServ.do?uri=OJ:C:2010:083:0047:0200:EN:PDF.

[118] *Id.* art. 214, para. 2.

[119] European Commission, Humanitarian Aid & Civil Protection, Annual Report 2010 at 5, http://ec.europa.eu/echo/files/media/publications/annual_report/annual_report_2010.pdf.

[120] Summary, Framework Partnership Agreement with Humanitarian Organizations (2008–2012), in force Jan. 1, 2008–Dec. 31, 2012, EUROPA, http://europa.eu/legislation_summaries/humanitarian_aid/r10007_en.htm.

Committee of the Red Cross, which further distribute the funds as needed. In 2009, 47% of humanitarian assistance was granted to NGOs, UN agencies received 39%, and other international organizations about 14%.[121]

B. Trade-Related Assistance

The EU Aid for Trade Strategy was adopted by the Council of the EU in 2007 with the objective of increasing quantitative Aid for Trade (AFT) in order to reach the European Commission's and the Member States' collective spending on trade-related assistance of €2 billion annually.[122] The EU and its Members accounted for about 37% of AFT from the world's major multilateral and bilateral donors in 2008–2009 and collectively are deemed to be the largest provider of AFT worldwide. Individually, the EU trails after Japan, which is the largest donor of AFT. The EU represents 11.4% of the world's total.[123]

C. Reducing the Debt Burden of Developing Countries

The EU continues to provide support to developing countries to cope with economic crises. In particular, the EU supports the following two initiatives: the Heavily Indebted Poor Countries Initiative, and the Multilateral Debt Relief Initiative.[124]

D. Remittances

Migrant remittances from the EU to developing countries amount to the same as the total amount of EU foreign aid. In 2008, the EU pledged to lower the cost and facilitate remittance transfers in recognition of the effect of such remittances on the living conditions of family members in developing countries. As a result, expenses in sending remittances fell in some EU Members but were increased in others.[125]

---

[121] *Id.*

[122] Conclusions of the Council and of the Representatives of the Governments of the Member States Meeting Within the Council on EU Strategy on Aid for Trade: Enhancing EU Support for Trade-Related Needs in Developing Countries (Oct. 29, 2007), http://register.consilium.europa.eu/pdf/en/07/st14/st14470.en07.pdf. Council of the EU, EU Strategy on Aid for Trade: Enhancing EU Support for Trade-related Needs in Developing Countries (Oct. 11, 2007), *available at* http://register.consilium.europa.eu/pdf/en/07/st13/st13070.en07.pdf.

[123] Commission Staff Working Document, *EU Accountability Report 2011 on Financing for Development*, at 69, SEC (2011) 500 final, http://ec.europa.eu/europeaid/how/accountability/eu-annual-accountability-reports/documents/working-document-vol1_en.pdf.

[124] *Debt Relief*, EUROPEAN COMMISSION, DEVELOPMENT AND COOPERATION – EUROPEAID, http://ec.europa.eu/europeaid/what/development-policies/intervention-areas/debt/index_en.htm. *See also Heavily Indebted Poor Countries (HIPC) Initiative*, EUROPA, http://europa.eu/legislation_summaries/development/least_developed_countries/r12402_en.htm (last updated Dec. 14, 2005).

[125] Communication from the Commission to the European Parliament, the Council, the Economic and Social Committee and the Committee of the Regions, Enhancing EU Accountability on Financing for Development Towards the EU Official Development Assistance Peer Review at 8, COM (2011) 218 final (Apr. 19, 2011), http://eur-lex.europa.eu/LexUriServ/LexUriServ.do?uri=COM:2011:0218:FIN:EN:PDF.

Prepared by Theresa Papademetriou
Senior Foreign Law Specialist
October 2011

LAW LIBRARY OF CONGRESS

AUSTRALIA

REGULATION OF FOREIGN AID

Executive Summary

> *The Australian government recently released a report setting out the policy framework for its aid program in response to an independent review. The review was aimed at ensuring the program's effectiveness as its budget is increased to 0.5% of GNI over the next five years. Features of the program include a lead government agency (AusAID); a geographic focus on East Asia and the Pacific; a commitment to the Millennium Development Goals; an emphasis on partnerships with recipient countries, other government agencies, and non-governmental organizations; a focus on core objectives, results, and value for money in aid allocation and in procurement and evaluation processes, with nearly all aid being untied; a separate annual appropriation for the program; and internal and external oversight and reporting mechanisms. Australia also regulates the private donation system through an accreditation process and engages in different development assistance initiatives apart from direct aid to countries, such as providing scholarships and addressing issues in the remittance system.*

I. Introduction

A. Official Development Assistance Figures

The Australian government's total Official Development Assistance (ODA) budget for the 2011-12 fiscal year is AU$4.84 billion (about US$5.14 billion).[1] This is estimated to be equivalent to 0.35% of Australia's Gross National Income (GNI). This is an increase upon the previous year when the ODA expenditure was estimated to amount to 0.33% of GNI.[2]

There is bipartisan agreement in Australia to raise the ODA budget to 0.5% of GNI by 2015-16. To reach this target, the government has stated that it expects to increase the ODA budget to around 0.38% of GNI in 2012-13, 0.42% of GNI in 2013-14, and 0.46% of GNI in

---

[1] Australian Government, *Summary of Australia's Overseas Aid Programme 2011-12: Budget Highlights* (May 10, 2011), http://www.ausaid.gov.au/budget/budget11/pdf/budget-highlights-2011-12.pdf.

[2] *Id.* The most recent OECD donor statistics available show that Australia's total gross ODA disbursements in 2010 amounted to US$3.848 billion, which was estimated to be about 0.32% of GNI. In terms of net disbursements, this figure included US$3.466 billion for bilateral ODA and US$0.32 billion for multilateral ODA. OECD donor country statistics are *available at* http://stats.oecd.org/Index.aspx?DatasetCode= ODA_DONOR (last visited Sept. 1, 2011).

2014-15.[3]   Beyond this, Australia has a longstanding "aspirational goal" of increasing expenditure to 0.7% of GNI (the target first agreed to by donor countries in 1970 and used as a reference point by the OECD[4]).[5]

B. Private Contribution Figures

It is estimated that Australians contribute about AU$800 million (about US$856 million) per year to non-governmental organizations (NGOs) operating in the area of international aid.[6] According to the Australian Council for International Development, this represents approximately 73% of total funds raised by agencies. A further 14.5% of total funds managed by the sector consists of government funding received by NGOs through the government agency AusAID, while 12.6% is made up of grants from other Australian and multi-lateral donors.[7] There are more than one hundred overseas development NGOs operating in Australia, including affiliates of international organizations as well as wholly local organizations.[8]

C. Snapshot of Foreign Aid Activity

In 2011-12, Australia will provide bilateral aid to around 35 countries. An additional 78 countries will receive assistance through regional and global initiatives. The geographic focus of the program is currently East Asia (33%) and the Pacific (31%), with the top five recipients of Australian aid for the year expected to be Indonesia, Papua New Guinea, Solomon Islands, Afghanistan, and Vietnam.[9]

In total, approximately 73% of AusAID's administered funding (about AU$3 billion) will go toward country and regional programs. Funding for global and multilateral initiatives, including humanitarian assistance and contributions to United Nations (U.N.) agencies, the World Bank, the Asian Development Bank, and non-governmental organization and volunteer programs, is estimated to constitute 27% of AusAID's budget (about AU$1.1 billion).[10]

---

[3] Australian Government, *Australia's International Development Budget Statement 2011-12: Statement by Hon. Kevin Rudd MP* [Ministerial Budget Statement] 3 (May 10, 2011), *available at* http://cache.treasury.gov.au/budget/2011-12/content/download/ms_ausaid.pdf?v=1.

[4] *The 0.7% ODA/GNI Target – A History*, OECD DEVELOPMENT CO-OPERATION DIRECTORATE (DCD-DAC), http://www.oecd.org/document/19/0,3343,en_2649_34447_45539475_1_1_1_1,00.html (last visited July 27, 2011).

[5] Australian Government, *An Effective Aid Program for Australia: Making a Real Difference—Delivering Real Results* [Government Response] 1 (July 2011), *available at* http://www.ausaid.gov.au/publications/aidreview-response/effective-aid-program-for-australia.pdf.

[6] Australian Government, *Independent Review of Aid Effectiveness* [Independent Review] 3 (Apr. 2011), *available at* http://www.aidreview.gov.au/report/.

[7] *Facts and Figures*, AUSTRALIAN COUNCIL FOR INTERNATIONAL DEVELOPMENT, http://www.acfid.asn.au/resources/facts-and-figures (last visited Aug. 22, 2011).

[8] *What is an NGO?*, AIDWATCH, http://aidwatch.org.au/where-is-your-aid-money-going/non-government-organisations/what-is-an-ngo (last visited Aug. 22, 2011).

[9] Ministerial Budget Statement, *supra* note 3, at 6.

[10] *Id.*

Half of the total aid expenditure "is expected to go towards projects in the areas of education, health, and economic growth."[11]   Australia emphasizes that it is committed to the implementation of the Millennium Development Goals, which "underpin the Australian aid program."[12]

Due to the established goal of increasing the ODA budget to 0.5% of GNI by 2015-16, in late 2010 the government sought an independent review of the effectiveness of Australia's aid program, with the aim of ensuring that the increased funding is spent in the most effective manner. The independent panel reported back to the government in April 2011, and its report, along with the government's response, was released in early July 2011.[13] The response sets the strategic direction for the aid program for the next four years and includes activities aimed at improving transparency and oversight, as well as making the program "more focused on results and on real, measurable value for money."[14]

In terms of the specific actions arising from the Independent Review, the government has stated that it will:[15]

- Develop a four-year, "whole of ODA" budget strategy, which will be considered as part of the 2012 Budget process, and ensure regular reviews of the program;[16]

- Ensure value for money in designs, procurements, and grants, as well as greater selectivity and larger average program size;[17]

- Improve risk management and performance oversight, including through stronger fraud control and enhanced evaluation programs;[18]

- Develop a "Transparency Charter" with clearer and more accessible reporting of aid activities;[19]

- Ensure that budget reporting is linked to results and that decisive action is taken on non-performing programs;[20]

---

[11] Department of Foreign Affairs and Trade, *Portfolio Budget Statements 2011-12: Australian Agency for International Development (AusAID)* 106 (May 2011), *available at* http://www.dfat.gov.au/dept/budget/2011_2012_pbs/2001-12-PBS-Foreign-Affairs-and-Trade-ausaid.pdf.

[12] *The Millennium Development Goals: The Fight Against Global Poverty and Inequality,* AUSAID, http://www.ausaid.gov.au/keyaid/mdg.cfm (last visited Aug. 22, 2011). See also Government Response, *supra* note 5, at 7.

[13] *See generally* INDEPENDENT REVIEW OF AID EFFECTIVENESS, http://aidreview.gov.au/index.html (last visited Aug. 22, 2011).

[14] Government Response, *supra* note 5, at 1.

[15] See id. at 2.

[16] *Id.* at 19.

[17] *Id.* at 20.

[18] *Id.* at 21–23.

[19] *Id.* at 24.

- Enhance the involvement of the Australian community, including through increased volunteer and NGO support and partnerships with business and academia.[21]

Several other reviews relating to Australia's aid program have been conducted in recent years, including reviews of remuneration rates for contracted technical advisers, fraud control policies, grant guidelines, Annual Reviews of Development Effectiveness, as well as an OECD Development Assistance Committee peer review in 2008.[22] A review of the procurement system is expected to be completed in 2011.[23]

II. Legal Framework

A. Regulation of ODAs

1. Overview

Australia's aid program is established through executive decision-making processes (i.e., Ministers and the Cabinet) as well as being subject to parliamentary approval and oversight in the context of the appropriations process and the reporting requirements that apply to all government agencies and Ministers.[24]

As noted above, the policy framework and strategic direction for the aid program, including the criteria upon which decisions on the funding of various activities will be based, was recently set out in the government's response to the Independent Review of Aid Effectiveness. This states that decisions on aid allocation (i.e., to countries, regions, and sectors) will be based on sets of goals and objectives, as well as three broad "aid allocation criteria": poverty-related need, effectiveness (or "capacity to make a real and measurable difference"), and Australia's national interests.[25]

As a result of the Independent Review, the government agreed to the following core purpose statement relating to Australia's aid program:

> The fundamental purpose of Australian aid is to help people overcome poverty. This also serves Australia's national interests by promoting stability and prosperity both in our

---

[20] *Id.* at 23–24.

[21] *Id.* at 25–26.

[22] *See DAC Peer Review of Australia – Main Recommendations and Findings (2008)*, OECD website, http://www.oecd.org/document/56/0,3343,en_2649_34603_41877687_1_1_1_1,00.html (last visited Aug. 22, 2011).

[23] *See* Government Response, *supra* note 5, at 20.

[24] For information about the Australian government accountability frameworks, *see generally Foundations of Government: Accountability,* AUSTRALIAN PUBLIC SERVICE COMMISSION, http://www.apsc.gov.au/foundations/accountability.htm (last visited Aug. 22, 2011). For information about the structure and operations of Australia's public service, *see Foundations of Government: Introduction,* AUSTRALIAN PUBLIC SERVICE COMMISSION, http://www.apsc.gov.au/foundations/introduction.htm (last visited Aug. 22, 2011).

[25] Government Response, *supra* note 5, at 27.

region and beyond. We focus our effort in areas where Australia can make a difference and where our resources can most effectively and efficiently be deployed.[26]

From this fundamental purpose, the government has articulated five "core strategic goals" for the overall aid program that will be taken into account in decision-making and evaluation processes: [27]

- Saving lives;[28]

- Promoting opportunities for all;[29]

- Investing in food security, sustainable economic growth, and private sector development;[30]

- Supporting security, improving the quality of governance, and strengthening civil society;[31] and

- Preparing for and responding to disasters and humanitarian crises.[32]

Ten "individual development objectives" that give effect to these goals are also set out in the government's response to the Independent Review.[33] The response then lists five approaches that the government intends to use to deliver aid more efficiently and effectively. These are reflected in the specific actions set out above.

In addition to working within this policy framework, AusAID and entities with which it contracts must meet operating requirements that are set out in a number of statutes. They include the following areas of federal law: [34]

- Anti-discrimination legislation;[35]

- Legislation setting out employer obligations;[36]

---

[26] *Id.* at 1, 17.

[27] *Id.* at 2.

[28] *Id.* at 28–29.

[29] *Id.* at 30–32.

[30] *Id.* at 33–36.

[31] *Id.* at 36–38.

[32] *Id.* at 38–39.

[33] *Id.* at 2.

[34] *See* AusAID, *Lists of Laws and Guidelines for Contractors Undertaking Activities for AusAID* (June 2010), *available at* http://www.ausaid.gov.au/business/pdf/lists-of-laws-and-guidelines-for-contractors-2010.pdf.

[35] Including the Age Discrimination Act 2004 (Cth), Equal Opportunity for Women in the Workplace Act 1999 (Cth), Sex Discrimination Act 1984 (Cth), Disability Discrimination Act 1992 (Cth), Racial Discrimination Act (Cth), and the Human Rights and Equal Opportunity Commission Act 1986 (Cth). *See Respecting the Diversity of the Australian Community in Providing Services,* AUSTRALIAN PUBLIC SERVICE COMMISSION, http://www.apsc.gov.au/foundations/respectingdiversity.htm#legislativeframework (last visited Aug. 22, 2011).

- Legislation that applies to the conduct and oversight of the public sector;[37]
- Sector legislation;[38] and
- Criminal legislation.[39]

Government agencies, contractors, and NGOs must also comply with regulations made under the Charter of the United Nations Act 1945 to implement sanctions imposed by the U.N. Security Council against member countries, as well as individuals and entities. The guidance provided to AusAID contractors states that:

> Under the Regulations, it is a criminal offence to deal in a specified range of goods or services with particular countries, or to use or deal with the assets of a number of specified individuals or entities, or to make assets available to a number of specified individuals or entities. The offences created by the Regulations apply to conduct in Australia and to conduct by Australians anywhere in the world. The Regulations are supported by parallel regulations and ordinances made under other legislation, for example the Customs (Prohibited Imports) Regulations and Customs (Prohibited Exports) Regulations.[40]

For example, the most recent regulations made under the Charter of the United Nations Act relate to the sanctions against Libya,[41] while others from 2010 relate to sanctions against specified entities in Iran[42] and the sanctions against Eritrea.[43]

The approach to delivering the aid program is also guided by various procedural instructions,[44] including the Commonwealth Grant Guidelines, Commonwealth Procurement Guidelines,[45] Commonwealth Fraud Control Guidelines,[46] Australian Government Investigations

---

[36] For example, the Occupational Health and Safety Act 1991(Cth) and Fair Work Act 2009 (Cth).

[37] Including the Public Services Act 1999 (Cth), Auditor-General Act 1997 (Cth), Ombudsman Act 1976 (Cth), Freedom of Information Act 1982 (Cth), Privacy Act 1988 (Cth), and Archives Act 1983 (Cth). In addition, the Financial Management and Accountability Act 1997 (Cth) provides the framework for the proper management of public money and public property.

[38] For example, the Building and Construction Industry Improvement Act 2005 (Cth), Banking Act 1959 (Cth), and Corporations Act 2001 (Cth), as well as the Environment Protection and Biodiversity Conservation Act 1999 (Cth), which requires prior approval for actions that are likely to have a significant impact on the environment anywhere in the world if the action is undertaken by the Commonwealth.

[39] For example, the Criminal Code Act 1995 (Cth) and Crimes Act 1914 (Cth).

[40] *Lists of Laws and Guidelines for Contractors*, *supra* note 34, at 7.

[41] Charter of the United Nations (Sanctions – Libyan Arab Jamahiriya) Regulations 2011 (Cth), *available at* http://www.comlaw.gov.au/Details/F2011C00208.

[42] Charter of the United Nations (Sanctions – Iran) (Specified Entities) List 2010 (Cth), *available at* http://www.comlaw.gov.au/Details/F2010L02236.

[43] Charter of the United Nations (Sanctions – Eritrea) Regulations 2010 (Cth), *available at* http://www.com law.gov.au/Details/F2011C00256.

[44] See *Lists of Laws and Guidelines for Contractors*, *supra* note 34, at 7–8.

Standards,[47] Lobbying Code of Conduct,[48] and any relevant AusAID policy documents, such as "Family Planning and the Aid Program: Guiding Principles."[49]

2. Implementing Agencies

Of the 2011-12 ODA budget, AU$4.87 billion, or around 89%, will be administered by the Australian Agency for International Development, or "AusAID."[50] The remaining 11% of the budget will go toward programs run by a variety of government agencies, about a quarter of which is used for international programs operated by the Australian Federal Police.[51]

AusAID is an administratively autonomous agency under the Department of Foreign Affairs and Trade portfolio.[52] It was established as a government agency in 1974 to bring together roles previously performed by different departments since an aid program to Papua New Guinea began in 1946. In 1976, the agency was renamed and became part of the Department of Foreign Affairs portfolio. Then, in July 2010, AusAID was established as an executive agency within the Foreign Affairs and Trade portfolio. Its role involves advising the government on

---

[45] Under the Financial Management and Accountability Regulations (Cth) ss 7 and 7A, *available at* http://www.comlaw.gov.au/Details/F2011C00555, both the Commonwealth Procurement Guidelines and the Commonwealth Grant Guidelines must be applied by officials performing duties in relation to procurement or grants.

[46] Under the Financial Management and Accountability Regulations (Cth) s 16A, the Fraud Control Guidelines must be applied by officials performing duties in relation to the control and reporting of fraud.

[47] All Australian government agencies that must apply the Commonwealth Fraud Control Guidelines "must also comply with the minimum standards for investigations set out in the Australian Government Investigations Standards." *Investigation Standards*, AUSTRALIAN FEDERAL POLICE, http://www.afp.gov.au/policing/fraud/investigation-standards.aspx (last visited Aug. 22, 2011).

[48] In 2008, the Australian government introduced the Lobbying Code of Conduct and established a Register of Lobbyists "to ensure that contact between lobbyists and Commonwealth Government representatives is conducted in accordance with public expectations of transparency, integrity and honesty." *About the Register*, DEPARTMENT OF THE PRIME MINISTER AND CABINET, http://lobbyists.pmc.gov.au/index.cfm (last visited Aug. 22, 2011).

[49] This is stated as being "a comprehensive reference document for AusAID staff, partner organisations and contractors who are preparing, designing, implementing or monitoring any AusAID funded aid program or activity involving reproductive health and family planning." It clarifies the government's approach to supporting family planning activities in the aid program, which is "to support a comprehensive approach to family planning and reproductive health" and is in line with the 1994 Cairo International Conference on Population and Development (ICPD) Programme of Action. AusAID, *Family Planning and the Aid Program: Guiding Principles* (Aug. 2009), *available at* http://www.ausaid.gov.au/publications/pubout.cfm?ID=5045_1822_5780_5045_6070&Type.

[50] Ministerial Budget Statement, *supra* note 3, at 6.

[51] *Id.* at 114–18. The International Deployment Group of the Australian Federal Police (AFP) provides officers for the Australian government's "domestic and international stability and security operations" and seeks to contribute to "the development, maintenance or restoration of the rule of law in countries that seek Australia's support, as well as to United Nations and domestic initiatives." *International Deployment Group*, AUSTRALIAN FEDERAL POLICE, http://www.afp.gov.au/policing/international-deployment-group.aspx (last visited Aug. 22, 2011).

[52] *See Organisation Structure*, AUSAID, http://www.ausaid.gov.au/about/org.cfm (last visited Aug. 22, 2011).

development policy, management of the implementation of Australia's overseas development programs, and planning and coordination of Australia's response to humanitarian disasters.[53]

There is an emphasis on whole-of-government engagement in the management of the aid program. A Development Effectiveness Steering Committee, made up of senior representatives from central agencies, provides "a whole-of-government coordination mechanism" at the strategic level and oversees the effectiveness of the aid program. AusAID also states that it takes a collaborative approach to working with other agencies, including in developing strategic priorities and delivering the aid program.[54]

3. Restrictions

In discussing the strategic direction and policy framework of the aid program, Australia stresses that there are direct national security and national economic interests at stake within its immediate region. For example, in terms of economic benefits, the government states that "by lifting people out of poverty, we also grow the global economy and that is good for Australian business."[55] In addition, the Australian government emphasizes that it has "broader interests and values in enhancing the stability and fairness of a global rules-based order."[56] This principle of "good international citizenship" seeks to promote a recognition that the government's ODA policy "together with our foreign policy, security policy, and our international economic and environmental policies, all have an impact in supporting a stable and humane order that benefits all countries in the world."[57]

The linkages of the aid program to Australia's national interests do not include requirements that suppliers be Australian entities. In 2002, as part of an international initiative, AusAID began untying some aid components to Least Developed Countries, and by 2005 had untied the "vast majority" of its aid to these countries.[58] Australia then untied the remainder of its aid expenditure in 2006, except for the Australia Indonesia Partnership for Reconstruction and Development.[59] Instead, aid contracts are subject to a procurement process that involves preferred bidders being selected on the basis of value for money. This is in line with the

---

[53] AusAID, *Annual Report 2009-10: Agency Overview* (2010), *available at* http://www.ausaid.gov.au/anrep/rep10/agencyoverview.html.

[54] Id.

[55] Government Response, *supra* note 5, at 6.

[56] *Id.* at 7.

[57] Id.

[58] Australian Government, *Australian Aid: Promoting Growth and Stability (A White Paper on the Australian Government's Overseas Aid Program)* 22 (2006), *available at* http://www.ausaid.gov.au/publications/pdf/whitepaper.pdf.

[59] *Untied Aid Opportunities*, AUSAID, http://www.ausaid.gov.au/business/untied.cfm (last visited Aug. 22, 2011); *see also Eligibility Criteria for AusAID Contracts*, AUSAID, http://www.ausaid.gov.au/business/eligibility.cfm (last visited Aug. 22, 2011).

Commonwealth Procurement Guidelines, which also "prohibit discrimination based on foreign ownership, affiliation or location."[60]

AusAID states that its "procurement framework encourages competition and ensures that the agency uses its resources efficiently, effectively, and ethically, and makes decisions in a transparent and accountable manner."[61] A range of mandatory and recommended due diligence checks are made before AusAID enters into a contracting agreement with an entity. These seek to "identify and manage key reputational and programmatic risks associated with implementing partners, such as fraud, misrepresentation, financial mismanagement and corruption."[62] For example, AusAID's fraud control policy requires that any company or non-governmental organization on fraud blacklists are to be automatically excluded from bidding AusAID contracts.[63]

An internal audit section reviews the fraud control mechanisms of partners, such as non-governmental organizations, contractor firms, and academic institutions.[64] Partner government systems are also carefully assessed, and assistance is provided where needed; for example, to implement systems aimed at managing fraud and corruption.[65]

4. Policy Considerations

In terms of the mechanisms available for implementing the aid program, in addition to non-governmental organizations, other government agencies, and contracted companies, AusAID includes "regional governments" in its list of partners, stating that "Australia increasingly looks to opportunities to use partner country processes and systems to deliver the aid program."[66] It refers to the 2005 Paris Declaration on Aid Effectiveness, which calls for "closer partnerships between aid agencies and partner countries through the delivery of aid via the partner country's budget and the use of its procurement and financial management systems where possible."[67] In addition, Australia, along with New Zealand and other Pacific Islands Forum countries, signed the Cairns Compact on Strengthening Development Coordination in the Pacific in 2009.[68] This agreement includes principles relating to mutual responsibilities and the

---

[60] *Id.* The Commonwealth Procurement Guidelines (2008) are *available at* http://www.finance.gov.au/procurement/procurement-policy-and-guidance/CPG/index.html.

[61] AusAID, *Annual Report 2009-10: Management and Accountability – Purchasing and Assets* (2010), *available at* http://www.ausaid.gov.au/anrep/rep10/purchasing.html (last visited Aug. 22, 2011).

[62] Id.

[63] Government Response, *supra* note 5, at 22.

[64] Id.

[65] Id.

[66] *Regional Governments*, AusAID, http://www.ausaid.gov.au/partner/countries.cfm (last visited Aug. 22, 2011).

[67] Id.

[68] Pacific Islands Forum, *Cairns Compact on Strengthening Development Coordination in the Pacific* (2009), *available at* http://www.forumsec.org/resources/uploads/attachments/documents/Cairns%20Compact%202009.pdf.

involvement of the recipient countries in determining and achieving development priorities in Pacific Island countries.

The Australian government's response to the Independent Review stated that it would continue to use a range of possible partnerships for delivering aid on a direct country-to-country basis. This included national delivery through developing country government systems, which is stated as having the benefit of reducing the administrative burden on partner governments and enabling greater ownership, as well as leveraging national resources and facilitating "greater alignment with partner government priorities."[69] However, the response also states that, "to guard against the risk that aid funds will be poorly managed, we will only use partner government systems where we assess these as being robust. Where they are not, we will work to strengthen these before any Australian funds are provided."[70]

Direct partnerships with governments are seen by Australia as a better option in countries where it is the lead or major donor. In such countries, the government says that it will "pursue results across a range of sectors," including a partnership approach with the country's government.[71] However, in countries where Australia is a relatively small donor, or where aid is only a small proportion of the partner government resources, the focus "will be even more selective and our effort combined with that of other partners to achieve impact."[72]

Australia has now signed Pacific Partnerships for Development agreements with eleven Pacific Island countries, where it is a major (if not the primary) donor.[73] These agreements are aimed at improving the focus of Australia's aid on a defined number of mutually-agreed sectors. The fundamental principles underlying the agreements are mutual respect and mutual responsibility:

> **Mutual respect:** the Partnerships take country ownership seriously and respect partner country leadership of their own national development plans. Australia and partners will also acknowledge accountability to our respective Parliaments for the impact and effective use of development assistance.

> **Mutual responsibility:** the Partnerships will be explicitly based on mutual, long-term and measurable commitments for development results. Australia will commit to provide new and additional bilateral assistance over time in return for commitments by Pacific partners to improve governance, enhance private sector development, increase investment in economic infrastructure, achieve better outcomes in health and education and in other areas. Jointly, we will assess progress towards development outcomes and hold each other accountable for the commitments we make in the Partnerships. Australia will not

---

[69] Government Response, *supra* note 5, at 54.

[70] *Id.*

[71] *Id.* at 27.

[72] *Id.*

[73] *See Pacific Partnerships for Development*, AUSAID, http://www.ausaid.gov.au/country/partnership.cfm (last visited Aug. 22, 2011).

engage in conditionality—all commitments made by Pacific partners will be jointly identified and agreed and draw from partners' own national development plans.[74]

The agreement for which implementation has been most advanced is that with Papua New Guinea, which was signed in 2008.[75] AusAID states that it is supporting the country's own priorities by focusing on four key areas: health (including HIV), education, transport infrastructure, and law and justice.[76] In 2011-12, AusAID expects to spend AU$436.5 million on projects in Papua New Guinea, while other agencies will also contribute AU$45.8 million.[77]

5. Discretionary Aid

In addition to the funding allocated to specific ODA activities through the appropriations process, which is explained below, Australia provides funding on a discretionary basis to local projects in various countries through competitive grant programs.[78] This includes two programs through which NGOs that have been established in developing countries can apply for funding: the Direct Aid Program (DAP) and the Small Activities Scheme (SAS).

The DAP is a "flexible, small grants program funded by the Australian Government through AusAID and managed by the Department of Foreign Affairs and Trade."[79] It involves the disbursement of funds at the discretion of the Australian Head of Mission in different countries. Each post has a DAP strategic plan and a DAP Committee, which makes recommendations to the Head of Mission, who makes the final funding decision.[80] Each overseas post may have slightly different processes and criteria, but will focus on ensuring that projects "have developmental outcomes, and are consistent with the international relations and public diplomacy objectives of the Post."[81] Furthermore, the emphasis is on projects that have a direct benefit to those most in need in the local community.

In 2010-11, the total DAP budget was AU$8.25 million. The budgets of the individual posts range from AU$10,000 to AU$510,000.[82] The Independent Review recommended that the

---

[74] Id.

[75] The Partnership for Development Between the Government of Australia and the Government of Papua New Guinea (2008), *available at* http://www.ausaid.gov.au/publications/pdf/png-partnership08.pdf. *See also Papua New Guinea–Australia Partnership for Development*, AUSAID, http://www.ausaid.gov.au/country/partnership/png.cfm (last visited Aug. 22, 2011).

[76] *Papua New Guinea*, AUSAID, http://www.ausaid.gov.au/country/papua.cfm (last visited Aug. 22, 2011).

[77] Id.

[78] *See Annual Plan 2010-2011 for Competitive Grant Programs*, AUSAID, http://www.ausaid.gov.au/business/grants-annualplan.cfm (last visited Aug. 22, 2011).

[79] *Direct Aid Program (DAP)*, DEPARTMENT OF FOREIGN AFFAIRS AND TRADE, http://www.dfat.gov.au/direct_aid_program/index.html (last visited Aug. 22, 2011).

[80] *Direct Aid Program (DAP) General Guidelines*, DEPARTMENT OF FOREIGN AFFAIRS AND TRADE, http://www.dfat.gov.au/direct_aid_program/dap_guidelines.html (last visited Aug. 22, 2011).

[81] Id.

[82] *Direct Aid Program (DAP)*, *supra* note 79.

budget for the DAP should at least double, with the highest increases made in countries with no country program. The government agreed in principle with this recommendation, with the details to be determined through the 2012-13 budget process.[83]

The SAS is aimed at contributing to "the reduction of poverty and the achievement of sustainable development through small scale interventions."[84] It is normally administered by the resident AusAID officer in the Australian Embassy or High Commission within a country. For example, in China, the scheme is managed by AusAID in consultation with the Chinese Ministry of Commerce. It "provides grants for small-scale development cooperation activities in poorer, remote and minority group areas, especially in the national poverty counties."[85] The maximum funding available for each project is AU$100,000.[86]

In addition to these programs for developing country NGOs, there is a Human Rights Grants Scheme that provides funding to NGOs and human rights organizations based or operating in developing countries. The scheme is overseen by an expert panel that makes recommendations to the Minister for Foreign Affairs. Grants are awarded to projects that achieve one or more of the following objectives:

- prevent or end gross human rights violations
- promote positive change in policies or actions of government or relevant non-state actors in the area of human rights
- monitor, seek redress for and/or report on human rights violations, including supporting victims of human rights abuses
- educate and/or train human rights victims, workers or defenders
- promote observance and implementation of international human rights standards
- promote and strengthen national or regional human rights institutions or mechanisms.[87]

Grant programs operated by or on behalf of AusAID are subject to the standard Commonwealth Grant Guidelines.[88]

---

[83] Government Response, *supra* note 5, at 60.

[84] *Funding to Developing Country NGOs*, AUSAID, http://www.ausaid.gov.au/ngos/devel_ngos.cfm (last visited Aug. 22, 2011).

[85] *China: NGO Funding Schemes*, AUSAID, http://www.ausaid.gov.au/china/community.cfm (last visited Aug. 22, 2011).

[86] Id.

[87] *Human Rights Grants Scheme*, AUSAID, http://www.ausaid.gov.au/business/other_opps/human rights_scheme.cfm (last visited Aug. 22, 2011).

[88] *Grant Funding Arrangements*, AUSAID, http://www.ausaid.gov.au/business/grants-funding.cfm (last visited Aug. 22, 2011). The Commonwealth Grant Guidelines are *available at* http://www.finance.gov. au/publications/fmg-series/23-commonwealth-grant-guidelines.html (last visited Aug. 22, 2011).

6. Oversight

The aid program is subject to both internal and external oversight mechanisms that seek to ensure financial and program accountability and to identify possible improvements. This includes annual performance reports within the internal quality assurance system that assess the performance of a country or regional program in terms of its progress against the country or region's development goals, the contribution of Australian aid, and aid management.[89] In addition to these reports, there are quality reports on individual aid activities as well as independent evaluations of significant activities commissioned at least once every four years.[90] AusAID also commissions a number of "cross-program evaluations at the sectoral and country strategy level" each year.[91] The Performance Review and Audit Section of AusAID is responsible for conducting particular internal reviews as well as for developing and overseeing AusAID's fraud control framework.[92]

The Office of Development Effectiveness was established in 2006 as a separate unit within AusAID.[93] The Office reports directly to the Director General of AusAID and is separate from the other parts of the agency that are responsible for managing the aid program. It is guided by the Development Effectiveness Steering Committee, which is chaired by the Director General and comprises deputy secretaries from the Department of the Prime Minister and Cabinet, the Department of Foreign Affairs and Trade, the Treasury, and the Department of Finance and Deregulation.[94] This committee advises the government on major aid policy and budget priorities and concerns. The Office undertakes annual reviews of development effectiveness that are tabled in Parliament, as well as evaluations of particular matters. These reports are available on the Office's website.[95] The Office also checks the robustness of the internal quality reporting system.

In terms of external oversight, the Australian National Audit Office's annual work plan of performance audits includes audits of aspects of Australia's aid program.[96] AusAID must also

---

[89] Government Response, *supra* note 5, at 22.

[90] *Id.* at 23.

[91] Id.

[92] *See* AusAID, *Annual Report 2009-10: Management and Accountability – Internal Audit* (2010), *available at* http://www.ausaid.gov.au/anrep/rep10/03management.html (last visited Aug. 22, 2011).

[93] *About ODE*, AUSAID OFFICE OF DEVELOPMENT EFFECTIVENESS, http://www.ode.ausaid.gov.au/ (last visited Aug. 22, 2011).

[94] Id.

[95] *Annual Review of Development Effectiveness*, AUSAID OFFICE OF DEVELOPMENT EFFECTIVENESS, http://www.ode.ausaid.gov.au/publications/arde.html (last visited Aug. 22, 2011).

[96] Government Response, *supra* note 5, at 23. *See, e.g.*, Australian National Audit Office, *AusAID's Management of the Expanding Australian Aid Program* (Nov. 2009), *available at* http://www.anao.gov.au/ Publications/Audit-Reports/2009-2010/AusAIDs-Management-of-the-Expanding-Australian-Aid-Program.

develop an annual report that is tabled in Parliament in October each year, as required by the Financial Management and Accountability Act 1997.[97]

Australia's aid program is also subject to peer reviews by other donor countries as part of the OECD Development Assistance Committee (DAC) arrangements. The last peer review of Australia was conducted in 2008.[98]

B. Regulation of Private Contributions

NGOs involved in overseas aid activities may be granted income tax exempt status, as well as being eligible for other tax concessions and exemptions relating to Goods and Services Tax and Fringe Benefit Tax, under Australia's tax legislation as it applies to non-profit entities.[99] Not-for-profit (NFP) or charitable organizations must also comply with the registration and other regulatory requirements under either the Corporations Act 2001 (Cth) or state legislation applicable to incorporated associations.[100] As part of Budget 2011, the government announced that a new body, the Australian Charities and Not-for-profits Commission (ACNC), will be established and commence operations on July 1, 2012.[101] This agency will "initially be responsible for determining charitable, public benevolent institution, and other NFP status for all Commonwealth purposes; providing education and support to the sector; implementing a 'report-once use-often' general reporting framework for charities; and establishing a public information portal by 1 July 2013."[102]

Donations collected by organizations for their overseas aid activities can be claimed as tax deductions by donors if the organization "has been admitted to the Overseas Aid Gift Deduction Scheme (OAGDS) and been endorsed by the Australian Taxation Office (ATO) as a deductible gift recipient (DGR) for the fund that it operates."[103] This process involves the Minister for Foreign Affairs declaring that an organization is an "approved organization"

---

[97] *See Accountability: Annual Reporting,* AUSTRALIAN PUBLIC SERVICE COMMISSION, http://www.apsc.gov. au/foundations/accountability.htm#annualreporting (last visited Aug. 22, 2011). AusAID's Annual Reports for the past ten years are *available at* http://www.ausaid.gov.au/publications/pubout.cfm?ID=8691_5877_871_8496_ 1205&CFID=3328295&CFTOKEN=90652321 (last visited Sept. 1, 2011).

[98] *DAC Peer Review of Australia, supra* note 22.

[99] *See generally Income Tax Guide for Non-profit Organisations,* AUSTRALIAN TAXATION OFFICE (ATO), http://www.ato.gov.au/nonprofit/content.aspx?doc=/content/29074.htm (last visited Aug. 22, 2011).

[100] *See Registering Non-for-profit or Charitable Organisations,* AUSTRALIAN SECURITIES & INVESTMENTS COMMISSION (ASIC), http://asic.gov.au/asic/asic.nsf/byheadline/Registering+not-for-profit+or+charitable+ organisations?openDocument (last visited Aug. 22, 2011).

[101] Press Release, Hon. Tanya Plibersek MP & Hon. Bill Shorten MP, Making it Easier for Charities to Help Those Who Need It (May 10, 2011), http://assistant.treasurer.gov.au/DisplayDocs.aspx?doc=press releases/2011/077.htm&pageID=003&min=brs&Year=&DocType=0.

[102] Id.

[103] *Overseas Aid Funds: Introduction,* ATO, http://www.ato.gov.au/nonprofit/content.aspx?doc=/ content/30677.htm&pc=001/004/006/008/002&mnu=44782&mfp=001/004&st=&cy (last visited Aug. 22, 2011). For information on the treatment of deductible donations, *see Making Tax Deductible Donations*, ATO, http://www.ato.gov.au/nonprofit/content.aspx?doc=/content/8568.htm&pc=001/004/013/007/001&mnu=44802&mf p=001/007&st=&cy=1 (last visited Aug. 22, 2011).

following an approval process that is run by AusAID. The organization's overseas aid fund must also be a "public fund" established "solely for the relief of people in a country declared by the Minister for Foreign Affairs to be a developing country," and that the Treasurer has declared to be a "relief fund."[104] Various requirements must be met for an overseas aid fund to qualify as both a "public fund" and a "relief fund" for the purposes of the scheme, as well as for the organization to be endorsed by the ATO.[105]

Non-governmental aid organizations may also need to register under and comply with each Australian state's fundraising legislation.[106] Other legislation that must be complied with includes the Anti-Money Laundering and Counter-Terrorism Financing Act 2006 (Cth), Spam Act 2003 (Cth), and Privacy Act 1988 (Cth). Organizations must also comply with the regulations implementing U.N. sanctions, as noted above, and must not deal with listed terrorist organizations under the Criminal Code Act 1995 or the Charter of the United Nations (Terrorism and Dealing with Assets) Regulations 2002 (U.N. Charter Regulations).[107]

To receive any government funding, an NGO must be accredited by AusAID.[108] Organizations must submit a range of evidence and are assessed against accreditation criteria. They must also be signatories of the Australian Council for International Development Code of Conduct for Non-Government Organisations in order to receive accreditation.[109] This is a self-regulatory code that sets out standards of governance, management, financial control, and reporting. Organizations must submit an annual report to the Council that is used to assess compliance with the code. Various other voluntary codes of practice can also be signed by NGOs, and adherence to these can provide assurances to donors regarding the practices and integrity of the organizations.[110]

A new draft accreditation guidance manual was released for comment in June 2011.[111] In addition to the accreditation process, the risk management framework relating to the funding of

---

[104] *Overseas Aid Funds*, ATO, http://www.ato.gov.au/nonprofit/content.aspx?menuid=44782&doc=/content/30677.htm&page=2#P17_762 (last visited Aug. 22, 2011).

[105] *Overseas Aid Funds: DGR Endorsement*, ATO, http://www.ato.gov.au/nonprofit/content.aspx?menuid=44782&doc=/content/30677.htm&page=3&H3 (last visited Aug. 22, 2011).

[106] *See State and Territory Government Requirements – Fundraising*, ATO, http://www.ato.gov.au/nonprofit/content.aspx?menuid=0&doc=/content/56555.htm&page=1&H1 (last visited Aug. 22, 2011).

[107] *See Terrorist Organisations*, ATTORNEY-GENERAL'S DEPARTMENT, http://www.ag.gov.au/www/agd/agd.nsf/Page/Nationalsecurity_Terroristorganisations (last visited Aug. 22, 2011).

[108] *See List of Accredited NGOs*, AUSAID, http://www.ausaid.gov.au/ngos/accredited.cfm (last visited Aug. 22, 2011).

[109] *Code of Conduct*, AUSTRALIAN COUNCIL FOR INTERNATIONAL DEVELOPMENT, http://www.acfid.asn.au/code-of-conduct (last visited Aug. 22, 2011). *See also Code of Conduct FAQs*, AUSTRALIAN COUNCIL FOR INTERNATIONAL DEVELOPMENT, http://www.acfid.asn.au/code-of-conduct/faqs (last visited Aug. 22, 2011).

[110] *See, e.g., Codes of Conduct and Standards*, OXFAM AUSTRALIA, http://www.oxfam.org.au/about-us/how-we-work/legal-and-ethical-responsibilities (last visited Aug. 22, 2011).

[111] AusAID, *NGO Accreditation Guidance Manual (Draft)* (June 2011), *available at* http://www.ausaid.gov.au/ngos/pdfs/draft-accreditation-man-jun2011.pdf.

NGOs includes accreditation reviews that are undertaken every five years, as well as audits, spot-checks, and cluster evaluations that assess the capacity of NGOs receiving funding.[112]

III. Foreign Aid Appropriation Process

The ODA budget is determined as part of the annual appropriations process that is primarily governed by the Financial Management and Accountability Act 1997 and associated regulations,[113] as well as the Australian Constitution. Broadly, under the Constitution, "no money shall be drawn from the Treasury of the Commonwealth except under appropriation made by law."[114] The mechanisms for this include annual appropriations bills that contain appropriations of specified amounts for government operations. Additional appropriations bills can be introduced during the financial year "in order to meet requirements that have arisen since the last Budget."[115] Annual appropriations bills that form part of the Budget are accompanied by Portfolio Statements. These are "the most comprehensive and inform Members of Parliament and the public of the proposed allocation of resources to government outcomes."[116]

The ODA budget, including for both bilateral and multilateral activities and expenditure by all government agencies involved in the delivery of the aid program, is a separate item within the annual Budget – it is not combined with the appropriations and portfolio statements relating to the Department of Foreign Affairs and Trade. AusAID prepares its own advice and documentation required by the Financial Management and Accountability Act 1997 in accordance with its status as a "prescribed agency" under that legislation.[117]

IV. Other Types of 'Aid'

The following are examples of different types of development assistance provided by the Australian government that do not involve the provision of direct aid to countries for particular activities.

---

[112] *Accreditation Risk Management*, AUSAID, http://www.ausaid.gov.au/ngos/accred_risk.cfm (last visited Aug. 22, 2011).

[113] Financial Management and Accountability Act 1997 (Cth), *available at* http://www.comlaw.gov.au/Details/C2011C00328; Financial Management and Accountability Regulations 1997 (Cth), *available at* http://www.comlaw.gov.au/Details/F2011C00555.

[114] Commonwealth of Australia Constitution Act s 83, *available at* http://www.comlaw.gov.au/Details/C2004C00469.

[115] *The Commonwealth's Appropriation Framework – An Introduction,* DEPARTMENT OF FINANCE AND DEREGULATION, http://www.finance.gov.au/budget/budget-process/appropriation-bills.html (last visited Aug. 22, 2011).

[116] Id.

[117] *See* Financial Management and Accountability Regulations 1997 (Cth) sch 1. "Prescribed agencies" do not handle any money other than public money.

A. Debt Relief

Australia contributes to international debt relief initiatives, including the Heavily Indebted Poor Countries Initiative (HIPC), the Multilateral Debt Relief Initiative (MDRI), and World Bank arrears clearance activities.[118]　In addition, Australia has entered into bilateral debt relief arrangements and "has provided 100% debt forgiveness to those HIPC qualified countries that owe money directly to Australia."[119]

B. Scholarships

The Australian government has established an "Australian Awards" program "to promote knowledge, education links and enduring ties between Australia, our neighbours and the global community."[120]　One aspect of the program is Development Awards, which are administered by AusAID. Such awards have been part of the overseas aid program since the 1950s. The current Development Awards include:

- Australian Development Scholarships (ADS), which "provide opportunities for people from developing countries to undertake full time undergraduate or postgraduate study at participating Australian universities and Technical and Further Education (TAFE) institutions";[121]

- Australian Leadership Award Scholarships (ALA Scholarships), which target "high achieving applicants" from developing countries wishing to undertake postgraduate study in Australia;[122]

- Australian Regional Development Scholarships (ARDS), which provide opportunities to people from developing countries in the Pacific to study at selected education institutions outside Australia;[123]

- Australian Leadership Awards Fellowships (ALA Fellowships), which "provide short term opportunities for study, research and professional attachment programs in Australia, delivered by Australian organisations, to nominated fellows from eligible countries";[124]

---

[118] *See Budget 2011-12: Part 2 – Expense Measures*, AUSTRALIAN GOVERNMENT, http://www.budget.gov.au/2011-12/content/bp2/html/bp2_expense-11.htm (last visited Sept. 1, 2011).

[119] *The Values and Virtues of Debt Relief*, AUSAID, http://www.ausaid.gov.au/hottopics/topic.cfm?ID=7830_2129_2610_4042_8214 (last visited Sept. 1, 2011).

[120] *Australian Awards*, AUSAID, http://www.ausaid.gov.au/scholar/ (last visited Aug. 22, 2011).

[121] *Australian Development Scholarships*, AUSAID, http://www.ausaid.gov.au/scholar/studyin.cfm (last visited Aug. 22, 2011).

[122] *Australian Leadership Award Scholarships*, AUSAID, http://www.ausaid.gov.au/scholar/ala.cfm (last visited Aug. 22, 2011).

[123] *Australian Regional Development Scholarships*, AUSAID, http://www.ausaid.gov.au/scholar/studyout.cfm (last visited Aug. 22, 2011).

[124] *Australian Leadership Awards Fellowships*, AUSAID, http://www.ausaid.gov.au/scholar/alafellow.cfm (last visited Aug. 22, 2011).

- Prime Minister's Pacific-Australia Awards, which provide a combination of work placement and leadership training for recipients of development awards who "are leaders or potential leaders of their country";[125] and

- AusAID Short Course Awards, which "aim to reduce the impact on partner countries of long-term absences of key personnal [sic]."[126]

C. Guest Worker Pilot Program

The Department of Education, Employment and Workplace Relations administers the Pacific Seasonal Worker Pilot Scheme.[127] Under this program, workers from Kiribati, Papua New Guinea, Tonga, and Vanuatu who receive an employment offer from an approved employer may receive a special visa to work in Australia for four to six months. The program started in 2008-09 to "place workers in regional Australia where there is unmet demand for low skilled workers for employment in horticultural positions."[128] As of May 2011, 468 visas had been issued to Pacific seasonal workers under the program.[129]

D. Remittances

The Australian government is highly aware of the significance of remittances by workers in Australia to developing countries, particularly in the Pacific region.[130] AusAID therefore undertakes various activities related to ensuring that the remittance system is fair, effective, and secure.

A key initiative, funded by AusAID in partnership with the New Zealand Aid Programme and developed and managed in conjunction with a private development consultancy, is a remittance database that aims to improve transparency and competition in the remittance system, thereby reducing costs in the long term.[131] The resulting website, www.sendmoneypacific.org,

---

[125] *Prime Minister's Pacific-Australia Awards*, AUSAID, http://www.ausaid.gov.au/scholar/pmpa.cfm (last visited Aug. 22, 2011).

[126] *AusAID Short Course Awards*, AUSAID, http://www.ausaid.gov.au/scholar/sca.cfm (last visited Aug. 22, 2011).

[127] *Pacific Seasonal Worker Scheme*, DEPARTMENT OF IMMIGRATION AND CITIZENSHIP, http://www.immi.gov.au/skilled/pacific-seasonal-worker/ (last visited Aug. 22, 2011). *See also Pacific Seasonal Worker Pilot Scheme Home*, DEPARTMENT OF EDUCATION, EMPLOYMENT AND WORKPLACE RELATIONS, http://www.deewr.gov.au/Employment/Programs/PSWPS/Pages/default.aspx (last visited Aug. 22, 2011).

[128] *See* Press Release, Chris Bowen MP, Visa for Pacific Island Seasonal Worker Scheme (Sept. 23, 2008), http://www.minister.immi.gov.au/media/media-releases/2008/ce08090.htm.

[129] Department of Immigration and Citizenship, *Pacific Seasonal Worker Visa Grants as at May 2011* (May 2011), *available at* http://www.immi.gov.au/skilled/pacific-seasonal-worker/_pdf/factsheet-pswps.pdf.

[130] *See* Australian Government and New Zealand Government, Trends in Remittance Fees and Charges (Oct. 2010), *available at* http://www.ausaid.gov.au/publications/pdf/TrendsinRemittance.pdf.

[131] *See* Press Release, Amanda Rishworth MP, Remittance Website to Help Pacific Islanders (Mar. 27, 2009), http://www.ausaid.gov.au/media/release.cfm?BC=Media&ID=5409_6262_8387_3545_1745.

provides information to people in the two countries about remittance methods, operators, and fees.[132]

In addition, AusAID has a partnership with the Westpac Banking Corporation to provide financial literacy training to Pacific seasonal workers prior to their entry into Australia as part of the Pacific Seasonal Worker Pilot Scheme,[133] as well as to rural or vulnerable communities in some countries. This latter program, the Pacific Financial Inclusion Program,[134] receives funding from AusAID along with international development agencies.[135]

In terms of the efficiency and accessibility of payment systems, Australia and New Zealand have also partnered with the International Finance Corporation and the World Bank Group to develop the Pacific Payments, Remittances and Securities Settlement Initiative.[136] AusAID is also a member of the Pacific Financial Inclusions Donors Group, which seeks to coordinate efforts and develop strategies to further their vision to "optimize collaboration amongst donor partners in the Pacific with a view to expanding access to financial services to an additional two million Pacific Islanders by 2012 in an effective, efficient and sustainable manner."[137]

In October 2010, a joint Australian and New Zealand report on remittance costs to Pacific countries was presented to the Pacific Islands Forum Economic Ministers Meeting. Following a discussion of the report, the Ministers agreed "to explore and prioritise support for domestic initiatives in both sending and receiving countries to promote lower remittance costs."[138]

In seeking to ensure that the remittance system is protected from misuse for criminal or terrorism purposes, Australia regulates remittance service providers through the standard financial and regulatory system that applies to financial institutions such as banks, as well as placing restrictions on remittance dealers that operate outside that system. In the latter situation, the government agency AUSTRAC (Australian Transaction Reports and Analysis Centre) operates the Register of Providers of Designated Remittance Services, and monitors and enforces

---

[132] *See* Press Release, Hon. David Bradbury MP, Pacific Remittance Costs Come Down (July 26, 2011), http://ministers.treasury.gov.au/DisplayDocs.aspx?doc=pressreleases/2011/032.htm&pageID=003&min=djb&Year=&DocType.

[133] Trends in Remittance Fees and Charges, *supra* note 130, at 15. S*ee also Pacific Seasonal Employer Scheme: Obligations*, DEPARTMENT OF IMMIGRATION AND CITIZENSHIP, http://www.immi.gov.au/skilled/pacific-seasonal-worker/obligations.htm (last visited Aug. 22, 2011).

[134] PACIFIC FINANCIAL INCLUSION PROGRAMME, http://www.pfip.org/ (last visited Aug. 22, 2011).

[135] *See Donors,* PACIFIC FINANCIAL INCLUSION PROGRAMME, http://www.pfip.org/who-we-are/donors/ (last visited Aug. 22, 2011); *see also* Press Release, Bob McMullan MP, More Pacific Islanders to Benefit from Australian Support for Microfinance (Jan. 29, 2010), http://www.ausaid.gov.au/media/release.cfm?BC=Media&ID=7156_6955_7097_6889_9860.

[136] Trends in Remittance Fees and Charges, *supra* note 130, at 15.

[137] *Partners*, PACIFIC FINANCIAL INCLUSION PROGRAMME, http://www.pfip.org/who-we-are/partners/ (last visited Aug. 22, 2011).

[138] *Report Highlights Need for Remittance Reform*, AUSAID, http://www.ausaid.gov.au/hottopics/topic.cfm?ID=3970_7856_8433_988_4666 (last visited Aug. 22, 2011).

mandatory reporting processes.[139]   It is an offense for a person to provide a "registrable designated remittance service" if the person's name and other details are not entered on the register.[140]

E. Trade Enabling Policies

The Australian government has identified that "the adoption of more open and freer trade and investment by developed countries would allow developing countries greater access to markets, knowledge and technologies" and therefore that "an open and predictable rules-based multilateral trading system is crucial."[141]   It particularly highlights agricultural subsidies in developed countries as being a restrictive trade practice with harmful long-term effects, and advocates for their removal. It states that countries with these subsidies "exacerbate the current food security problem by insulating their producers from world price changes, shifting the adjustment burden to farmers in developing countries, and taking market share away from them."[142]

Prepared by Kelly Buchanan
Foreign Law Specialist
September 2011

---

[139] *See* Australian Transaction Reports and Analysis Centre, AUSTRAC Guidance Note: Register of Providers of Designated Remittance Services (July 2007), *available at* http://www.austrac.gov.au/files/ reg_pro_rem.pdf. *See also Reporting Policy,* AUSTRALIAN TRANSACTION REPORTS AND ANALYSIS CENTRE (AUSTRAC), http://www.austrac.gov.au/report_policy.html (last visited Aug. 22, 2011).

[140] Anti-Money Laundering and Counter-Terrorism Financing Act 2006 (Cth) s 74(2). *See Removal from Register of Providers of Designated Remittance Services*, AUSTRAC, http://www.austrac.gov.au/rrpds.html (last visited Aug. 22, 2011).

[141] Government Response, *supra* note 5, at 14.

[142] Id.

LAW LIBRARY OF CONGRESS

BRAZIL

REGULATION OF FOREIGN AID

Executive Summary

In 2010, the Brazilian government prepared the first survey designed to identify, recover, and systematize data and information concerning public investment for activities, projects, and programs of Brazilian cooperation (aid) for international development from 2005–2009. During this period, it was found that Brazil invested more than US$1.8 billion in international development cooperation.

According to the survey, more than one hundred institutions of the Brazilian federal government, including ministries and related entities, are directly involved in international cooperation. The Brazilian Agency for Cooperation is responsible for negotiating, coordinating, implementing, and monitoring Brazilian programs and projects of technical cooperation, performed based on agreements signed by Brazil with other countries and international organizations.

Brazil provides aid to foreign countries with no strings attached. No conditions or political goals are imposed in exchange for grants destined for international collaboration.

I. Introduction

A. Official Development Assistance Figures

In recent years, agencies and entities of the federal government increased the allocation of a portion of their resources for projects designed to promote the development of various countries.[1] However, the identification of this practice was neither quantified nor systematized within the federal public administration, which was a limiting factor in the use of this instrument for the execution of foreign policy objectives and recognition of the country's contribution to the socioeconomic development of others countries.[2]

---

[1] INSTITUTO DE PESQUISA ECONÔMICA APLICADA (IPEA) ET AL., COOPERAÇÃO BRASILEIRA PARA O DESENVOLVIMENTO INTERNACIONAL: 2005–2009 at 11 (Dec. 2010), http://www.ipea.gov.br/portal/images/stories/PDFs/Book_Cooperao_Brasileira.pdf.

[2] *Id.*

The decentralized nature of the actions implemented by institutions of the federal government posed a challenge to clearly defining the amount of investment in international cooperation.[3]   Aware of the importance of international cooperation for development, the Ministry of Foreign Affairs (*Ministério das Relações Exteriores – MRE*) proposed to the Presidency of the Republic the initial survey of Brazilian federal government funds invested for the purpose of contributing to the development of other countries.[4]

In January 2010, the Ministry of Foreign Affairs, through the Brazilian Cooperation Agency (*Agência Brasileira de Cooperação – ABC*), and the Institute of Applied Economic Research (*Instituto de Pesquisa Econômica Aplicada – IPEA*) partnered with the support of the Presidency of the Republic (*Casa Civil*) for the initial survey of these resources within the federal government, in order to identify, recover, and systematize the data and information of public investment for activities, projects, and programs of Brazilian cooperation for international development for the period 2005–2009 (hereinafter the survey).[5]

The classification of the quantified resources followed a set of predefined categories, created from an international review of methodologies, in order to allow a certain degree of comparability of the data collected with the data available internationally.[6]   Consequently, the resources were classified according to the nature of cooperation (bilateral or multilateral) and the type of cooperation (technical aid, scholarships for foreigners, humanitarian aid, aid to refugees in Brazil, peacemaking missions, and contributions from the Brazilian budget for international organizations).[7]

Throughout 2010, data were obtained from organs of the direct administration[8] and entities subordinated to the federal government.[9]   It was found that the total volume of investments for the 2005–2009 period was in the amount of approximately R$2.8 billion.[10]

In 2009, Brazil invested R$724 million[11] in international development cooperation, which was divided among humanitarian aid (12.02%), scholarships for foreigners (6.14%), technical cooperation (13.49%), and contributions to international organizations (68.35%).[12]

---

[3] *Id.*

[4] *Id.*

[5] *Id.*

[6] *Id.* at 13.

[7] *Id.*

[8] Direct administration is considered to be the body of public administrative services exercised directly by the government (federal, state, or municipal) through government organs, such as ministries and secretariats, that are integrated into the structure of the executive branch. 1 MARIA HELENA DINIZ, DICIONÁRIO JURÍDICO 123 (São Paulo, SP: Editora Saraiva, 2005).

[9] IPEA ET AL., *supra* note 1. A list with all the institutions that participated in the survey is available on page 14 of the study, Quadro 1 – Instituições que Participaram do Levantamento da Cooperação Brasileira para o Desenvolvimento Internacional.

[10] *Id.* at 12 (R$2,898,526,873.49, which is approximately US$1,868,932,151.32 at the current exchange rate of 1.5509).

B. Private Contribution Figures

The available data regarding Brazilian contributions deal with government-related transactions. No data was identified concerning private contributions to foreign aid.

C. Snapshot of Foreign Aid Activity

Two laws were recently enacted in regard to Brazil's current foreign aid activity. The first, on May 31, 2011 (*Lei No. 12.413, de 31 de Maio de 2011*),[13] authorized the executive branch of the federal government to make donations to the Global Alliance for Vaccines and Immunization (GAVI)[14] in the amount of US$20 million, distributed in equal and subsequent parts over a period of twenty years, in order to feed the financial platform, the International Finance Facility for Immunization (IFFIm),[15] which will finance vaccinations and immunizations in low-income countries.[16]   Law No. 12,413 also authorized the executive to make annual donations for an undetermined period of time to UNITAID,[17] in the proportion of US$2.00 per passenger boarding an aircraft within Brazil bound for abroad, except for passengers in transit through the country.[18]

The second law was enacted on June 20, 2011 (*Lei No. 12.429, de 20 de Junho de 2011*),[19] and authorized the federal government to make donations of certain products through the World Food Programme of the United Nations (WFP)[20] to Bolivia, El Salvador, Guatemala, Haiti, Nicaragua, Zimbabwe, Cuba, members of the Community of Portuguese Language Countries, the Palestinian Authority, Sudan, Ethiopia, the Central African Republic, the

---

[11] IPEA ET AL., *supra* note 1, at 20. R$724,420,126.16 is approximately US$467,096,605.94 (exchange rate: 1.5509). *Foreign Exchange Rates – H.10*, BOARD OF GOVERNORS OF THE FEDERAL RESERVE BANK (July 28, 2011), http://www.federalreserve.gov/releases/h10/current/. In 2009, the Brazilian investment corresponded to 0.02989% of Brazil's Gross National Income (GNI), which was US$1,562,411,914,397.00. *World dataBank*, THE WORLD BANK GROUP, http://databank.worldbank.org/ddp/home.do?Step=3&id=4 (last visited July 28, 2011).

[12] IPEA ET AL., *supra* note 1. A detailed table is available on page 20 (*Tabela 1*) of the study.

[13] Lei No. 12.413, de 31 de Maio de 2011, http://www.planalto.gov.br/ccivil_03/_Ato2011-2014/2011/Lei/L12413.htm.

[14] GAVI ALLIANCE, http://www.gavialliance.org/index.aspx (last visited Aug. 24, 2011).

[15] IIFIM, http://www.iffim.org/ (last visited Aug. 24, 2011).

[16] Lei No. 12.413, de 31 de Maio de 2011, art. 1, http://www.planalto.gov.br/ccivil_03/_Ato2011-2014/2011/Lei/L12413.htm.

[17] In 2006, Brazil, Chile, France, Norway, and the United Kingdom decided to create an international drug purchase facility financed with resources that would be both sustainable and predictable. The initiative was given the name UNITAID, and a tax on airline tickets was chosen as the most appropriate means of providing sustainable funding. *How UNITAID Came About*, UNITAID, http://www.unitaid.eu/en/about/-background-mainmenu-18/159.html (last visited Aug. 2, 2011).

[18] Lei No. 12.413 art. 2.

[19] Lei No. 12.429, de 20 de Junho de 2011, http://www.planalto.gov.br/ccivil_03/_Ato2011-2014/2011/Lei/L12429.htm.

[20] WORLD FOOD PROGRAMME, http://www.wfp.org/ (last visited Aug. 24, 2011).

Democratic Republic of Congo, Somalia, Niger, and the Democratic People's Republic of Korea (North Korea) for a period of up to twelve months after publication of the Law.[21] The products and their respective limits are identified in the Annex attached to the Law; listed products may be provided so long as the donation does not compromise service to people victimized by adverse events within Brazil's national territory.[22]

II. Legal Framework

A. Regulation of ODAs

1. Overview

During the Brazilian government's survey, the institutions that participated in the study[23] came up with a common definition for data collection[24] that differs from the definition of official development assistance (ODA) used by the Organisation for Economic Co-operation and Development (OECD).[25]

OECD defines ODA as

[g]rants or loans to countries and territories on the DAC List of ODA Recipients (developing countries) and to multilateral agencies which are: (a) undertaken by the official sector; (b) with promotion of economic development and welfare as the main objective; (c) at concessional financial terms (if a loan, having a grant element of at least 25 per cent). In addition to financial flows, technical co-operation is included in aid. Grants, loans and credits for military purposes are excluded. Transfer payments to private individuals (e.g. pensions, reparations or insurance payouts) are in general not counted.[26]

In Brazil, the definition created for cooperation for international development is the totality of resources invested by the Brazilian federal government (considered grants) in the government of other countries, nationals of other countries in Brazil, and international organizations for the purpose of contributing to international development, which is understood as the strengthening

---

[21] Lei No. 12.429 art. 1. The products listed in the Annex to Law No. 12,429 include rice (up to 500,000 tons), beans (up to 100,000 tons), corn (up to 100,000 tons), milk powder (up to 10,000 tons), and vegetable seeds (up to 1 ton).

[22] *Id.*, Annex.

[23] IPEA ET AL., *supra* note 1.

A list with all the institutions that participated in the survey is available on page 14 of the study, Quadro 1 – Instituições que Participaram do Levantamento da Cooperação Brasileira para o Desenvolvimento Internacional.

[24] *Id.*

[25] ORGANISATION FOR ECONOMIC CO-OPERATION AND DEVELOPMENT – OECD, http://www.oecd.org/pages/0,3417,en_36734052_36734103_1_1_1_1_1,00.html (last visited Aug. 24, 2011).

[26] *DAC Glossary of Key Terms and Concepts*, OECD, http://www.oecd.org/document/32/0,3343, en_2649_33721_42632800_1_1_1_1,00.html#ODA (last visited Aug. 24, 2011).

of the capacities of international organizations and groups or populations of other countries to improve their socioeconomic conditions.[27]

2. Implementing Agencies

According to the survey, which was designed to identify, recover and systematize data and information concerning public investment for activities, projects, and programs of Brazilian cooperation for international development,[28] more than one hundred institutions of the Brazilian federal government, including ministries and related entities, are directly involved in international cooperation.[29]

The Brazilian Agency for Cooperation is subordinated to the Ministry of Foreign Affairs.[30] The agency is responsible for negotiating, coordinating, implementing, and monitoring Brazilian programs and projects of technical cooperation, performed based on agreements signed by Brazil with other countries and international organizations.[31] To fulfill its mission, the agency follows the external policy of the Ministry of Foreign Affairs and the national development priorities as defined in plans and programs of the government.[32]

The Brazilian government believes that technical cooperation that it receives should contribute significantly to the socioeconomic development of the country and encourage national autonomy with regard to the subjects covered.[33]

The same concern applies to the technical cooperation provided by Brazil to other countries. The national mission of technical cooperation among developing countries is defined by the Brazilian Agency for Cooperation as a contribution to the strengthening of Brazilian relations with developing countries to expand their interchange, generation, dissemination, and use of technical expertise to give its human resources the necessary qualifications and strengthen its institutions.[34]

3. Restrictions

The international collaboration that Brazil grants to other countries does not impose any conditions or immediate political goals.[35] According to the survey, the federal government

---

[27] IPEA ET AL., *supra* note 1.

[28] *Id.* at 11.

[29] *Id.* at 16.

[30] *Introdução*, AGÊNCIA BRASILEIRA DE COOPERAÇÃO, http://www.abc.gov.br/abc/introducao.asp (last visited Aug. 24, 2011).

[31] *Id.*

[32] *Id.*

[33] *Histórico da Cooperação Técnica Brasileira*, AGÊNCIA BRASILEIRA DE COOPERAÇÃO, http://www.abc.gov.br/ct/historico.asp (last visited Aug. 24, 2011).

[34] *Id.*

[35] IPEA ET AL., *supra* note 1, at 7.

recognizes international cooperation to promote development in nations who share similar social and economic problems faced by Brazil as an instrument of foreign policy.[36] It also states that Brazilian cooperation for international development is driven by principles of equitable relations and social justice, forming an important instrument of foreign policy.[37]

4. Discretionary Aid

As noted, the survey states that Brazil implements international cooperation according to principles of equitable relations and social justice,[38] does not impose any conditions associated with its international cooperation, and apparently has no specific laws governing discretionary aid or required criteria and procedures for such aid. Brazil applies the knowledge obtained while resolving its own problems to support and help countries overcome their difficulties to achieve development[39] with no reservations or conditions.

5. Oversight

As Brazil does not impose any conditions or immediate political goals associated with its international cooperation, no oversight mechanism, safeguards against corruption, or technical and efficiency requirements could be identified. However, the Brazilian government believes that development cooperation is not limited to the interaction between donors and recipients; it is an exchange between similar people, which entails mutual benefits and responsibilities. According to the government, the model for cooperation is still under construction.[40]

The 2010 survey represents the first step towards building a policy of international cooperation that is integrated with Brazilian foreign policy goals, which is not subject to the priorities of each new administration but operates with a broader base of support that includes both the government and civil society. Brazilian cooperation for international development seeks to contribute to the renewal movement of the development agenda in the twenty-first century, marked by the search for development models that can combine economic growth with social inclusion, and sustainability with national prosperity and global stability.[41]

6. Policy Considerations

According to the survey, in an increasingly interdependent world, peace, prosperity, and human dignity do not depend only on actions at the national level and for Brazil, international development cooperation is a key element for the establishment of a more just and peaceful international order.[42]

---

[36] *Id.* at 11.

[37] *Id.* at 16.

[38] *Id.*

[39] *Id.* at 7.

[40] *Id.*

[41] *Id.*

[42] *Id.*

To this end, Brazil makes use of solutions created and developed internally on topics such as agriculture, education, and public safety to support countries with similar difficulties in overcoming their obstacles to development. Cooperation may be in the form of individual actions, such as donations of food and medicine to victims of natural disasters; technical cooperation projects; granting scholarships to foreign students; or contributions to international organizations. Regardless of the form, the principle of non-indifference inspires and drives Brazilian cooperation for international development.[43]

Balancing respect for sovereignty and the defense of self-determination, which are traditional characteristics of Brazilian diplomacy, Brazil has been developing its own way of cooperating with developing nations and, as previously mentioned, does not impose any conditions or immediate political goals on its international cooperation.[44]

Brazilian cooperation is specialized because it has the commitment of public agencies and entities, universities, and civil society organizations. It is also participatory, as it includes the partner countries from the negotiation phase, which adapt and contextualize actions to the local reality.[45]

B. Regulation of Private Contributions

Brazilian laws regarding private aid deals, essentially, with domestic related contributions. No limits on donors or recipients, or tax incentives to encourage private donations for foreign aid, have been identified.

III. Foreign Aid Appropriations Process

One of the main components of Brazilian foreign policy is the commitment to contribute to the promotion of global development, with an emphasis on Latin America, Africa, and Asia.[46] Brazil does not prioritize specific segments resulting from unilateral interests[47] and, as a result, the Brazilian agenda of international cooperation for development is advanced through interchange mechanisms, including bilateral, regional, or multilateral agreements.[48]

---

[43] *Id.*

[44] *Id.*

[45] *Id.*

[46] *Id.* at 10.

[47] *Id.*

[48] *Id.*

A. Bilateral Agreements

At the bilateral level, Brazil has partnered with more than seventy countries.[49] One example is the Ministry of Health, which has established several bilateral agreements with developing nations related to technical cooperation.[50] According to the Ministry, the cooperation between Brazil and other developing countries, called South-South Cooperation (*Cooperação Sul-Sul*) in the field of health is based on certain principles that guide the management of the Brazilian public health, which include among others health as a universal right and duty of the State, equal treatment, full medical service, universality of coverage of public health services, social participation and control, and the availability of cost-free services.[51]

The Ministry of Health has also determined that the principles governing cooperation in the field of health care include cooperation among peoples for the progress of humanity; respect for national sovereignty, economic independence, equal rights, and non-intervention in the domestic affairs of the nations; a horizontal approach to cooperation; respect for cultural diversity; and sustainability of actions.[52]

Aligned with these principles, Brazilian international technical cooperation for developing countries is guided by the successful experiences of certain cooperation projects that were previously developed and identified as a "model" for future cooperation projects.[53]

The International Advisory Board of the Ministry of Health (*Assessorial Internacional do Ministério da Saúde*) invests in the development of infrastructure projects and pilot initiatives such as the Malaria Project in Sao Tome and Principe, South-South Network (*Laços Sul-Sul*), a Project in Ghana dealing with sickle-cell disease, and Milk Bank Projects.[54]

The Malaria Project in Sao Tome and Principe is triangulated with the United States Agency for International Development (USAID) and is co-financed by the Brazilian Agency for Cooperation (*Agência Brasileira de Cooperação – ABC*). It aims to develop and strengthen the Epidemiological Surveillance System on Malaria (*Sistema de Vigilância Epidemiológica em Malária*) in order to improve the control of malaria cases and enhance knowledge for the implementation of an integrated and selective control of vectors with the goal of decreasing the

---

[49] *Id.* The website of the Ministry of Foreign Affairs lists the countries with which Brazil has bilateral and multilateral agreements. However, it was not possible to identify the seventy countries that the survey makes reference to and that are directly related to international aid. The list is available at http://www2.mre.gov.br/dai/quadros.htm (last visited Aug. 24, 2011).

[50] MINISTÉRIO DA SAÚDE, http://portal.saude.gov.br/portal/saude/odm_saude/area.cfm?id_area=1705 (last visited Aug. 4, 2011).

[51] *Cooperação Internacional em Saúde*, MINISTÉRIO DA SAÚDE, http://portal.saude.gov.br/portal/saude/odm_saude/visualizar_texto.cfm?idtxt=35204 (last visited Aug. 4, 2011).

[52] *Id.*

[53] *Acordos Bilaterais Técnicos em Vigor por País*, MINISTÉRIO DA SAÚDE, http://portal.saude.gov.br/portal/saude/odm_saude/visualizar_texto.cfm?idtxt=35205 (last visited Aug., 4, 2011).

[54] *Id.*

incidence of malaria in the population.[55]   In regard to resources for this project, ABC will contribute a total of about US$600,000 and the Ministry of Health about US$36,000.[56]

The South-South Network supports actions to prevent and control HIV/AIDS. Its main goal is to increase the number of health professionals trained in clinical management of antiretroviral drugs and implement or strengthen universal treatment in member countries of the Community of Portuguese Language Countries (*Comunidade dos Países de Língua Portuguesa - CPLP*) and in Latin America.[57]

Today, eight countries are part of the network: Brazil, Cape Verde, Guinea Bissau, Sao Tome and Principe, East Timor, Nicaragua, Paraguay and Bolivia. The initiative provides information exchange and joint development of strategies and action plans for coping with, treating, and providing care for HIV/AIDS, and for promoting solidarity among developing countries, through a model of horizontal cooperation.[58]   The Ministry of Health provides free antiretroviral treatments produced nationally and promotes training activities for health professionals, with an emphasis on the logistics of drugs and clinical management.[59]

Through the project Support to the Structuring of the National System for Complete Attention to People with Sickle Cell Disease in Ghana (*Apoio à Estruturação do Sistema Nacional de Atenção Integral à Pessoa com Doença Falciforme de Gana*), Brazil is committed to creating a center of excellence in the fight against sickle cell disease in Ghana, which will also serve as a center for training technicians from Ghana and other countries of the region regarding the identification and treatment of people living with sickle cell disease.[60]   No information regarding project resources is available.

The commitment of the Ministry of Health in the Milk Bank Project is to expand and strengthen the actions of cooperation between Brazil and developing countries in terms of human milk banks.[61]   Currently, twenty-one projects are being negotiated and executed in twenty-one different countries; these projects aim to establish and implement milk banks at hospitals and maternity facilities with the ultimate goal of reducing malnutrition and infant mortality.[62]   No information regarding project resources is available.

---

[55] *Id.*

[56] *Id.*

[57] *Id.*

[58] *Id.*

[59] *Id.*

[60] *Id.*

[61] *Id.*

[62] *Id.*

B. Regional Agreements

Regionally, Brazil is engaged in activities with the Union of South American Nations (*União das Nações Sul Americans – UNASUL*), the Southern Common Market (*Mercado Comum do Sul – Mercosul*), the Latin American and Caribbean Economic System (*Sistema Econômico Latino-Americano e do Caribe – SELA*), the Latin American Integration Association (*Associação Latino-Americana de Integração – ALADI*) and the Organization of American States (*Organização dos Estados Americanos – OAS*).[63]

C. Intergovernmental Mechanisms

In terms of intergovernmental mechanisms, Brazil is actively involved in forums such as the Community of Portuguese Language Countries (*Comunidade dos Países de Língua Portuguesa – CPLP*) and the Ibero-American General Secretariat (*Secretaria-Geral Ibero-Americana – SEGIB*).[64]

D. Multilateral Cooperation

With regard to multilateral cooperation, Brazil provides financial assistance to international organizations and supports the establishment of trilateral operations that involve the development of institutional, scientific, technological and human capacities.[65]

Prepared by Eduardo Soares
Senior Foreign Law Specialist
September 2011

---

[63] IPEA ET AL., *supra* note 1, at 10.

[64] *Id.*

[65] *Id.*

LAW LIBRARY OF CONGRESS

CHINA

REGULATION OF FOREIGN AID

Executive Summary

China does not have strict official development assistance (ODA) figures, although it has a long history of foreign aid (since the 1950s) that shares many common elements with the ODA standard. China implements a more flexible and broader foreign aid practice than is normally within the scope of ODA. Grants, interest-free loans, and concessional loans are the financial mechanisms for China's eight types of foreign aid, and these are allocated within the national budget and capital raised by the state-owned Export-Import Bank of China from the market.

China's foreign aid policy is based on the Eight Principles of Economic Aid and Technical Assistance to Other Countries and the framework of South-South Cooperation. The Chinese government has declared that its foreign aid is provided with no political attachment and with the purpose of seeking mutual cooperation and benefit. The largest proportion of Chinese aid flows to African countries.

The Ministry of Commerce is the lead authority in administering and supervising China's foreign aid activities in accordance with applicable laws and regulations. The Ministry of Finance is responsible for formulating the budget allocation relating to foreign aid programs upon receiving proposals from competent departments under the State Council. The Export-Import Bank administers and oversees concessional loans, which are provided at preferential interest rates.

Bilateral channels are still the cornerstone of China's foreign aid, although a rapid expansion to international platforms is currently underway. China's private donations at the civil level are limited and are often a portion of government projects.

I. Introduction

A. Official Development Assistance Figures

The Development Assistance Committee (DAC) of the Organisation for Economic Co-operation and Development (OECD) adopted the concept of Official Development Assistance (ODA) in 1969 to standardize the measurement of the resource flows from DAC member states to developing countries.[1] ODA is referred to as flows of concessional financing with a grant element of at least 25%, and are provided by official sectors with the primary objectives of promoting the aid recipients' economic development and public welfare.[2] China is a DAC-list ODA recipient and beneficiary; however, it has experienced soaring economic growth during the past two decades and has thus enabled itself, as an emerging development assistance contributor, to meet the development commitment it made under the United Nations Millennium Declaration (UNMD).[3]

Although China has undertaken extensive development assistance programs relating to other developing countries since 1950, the Chinese government has never reported official ODA statistics to the public; not only because it is a non-DAC state, but also due to the gap between the ODA standard and China's notion of development assistance.

On April 11, 2011, the State Council of China published its first White Paper on China's Foreign Aid (White Paper), which merged official development assistance into the undefined term "foreign aid".[4] The report declared China's aggregate financial flow to foreign aid by the end of 2009 for the nearly sixty years prior as amounting to a total of RMB256.29 billion (approximately US$37.68 billion), including RMB106.2 (approximately US$16.89 billion) in grants, RMB76.54 billion (approximately US$12.17 billion) in interest-free loans, and RMB73.55 billion (approximately US$16.89 billion) in concessional loans.[5] These figures should not be taken as equivalents to aggregate ODA statistics for the reasons that follow.

First, concessional loans are primarily raised by the Export-Import Bank of China (EIBC) from the market; the central government only subsidizes the interest gap arising from the difference between the concessional interest rate (usually between 2% to 3%) and the national benchmark interest rate.[6] Thus, whether China is able to meet the ODA ratio standard of "at least 25% grants" is in question, as illustrated by the commentary below:

> "For example, if [EIBC] gave out $100 million in a concessional loan with an interest rate of 2 percent, and the central bank lending rate was 6 percent, the annual subsidy

---

[1] *Official Development Assistance – Definition and Coverage*, OECD, http://www.oecd.org/ document/4/0,3746,en_2649_34447_46181892_1_1_1_1,00.html#Definition (last visited Jan. 30, 2012).

[2] *DAC Glossary of Key Terms and Concepts*, OECD, http://www.oecd.org/document/32/0,3343,en_2649 _33721_42632800_1_1_1_1,00.html#ODA.

[3] U.N. GAOR, 55th Sess., 8th plen. mtg., U.N. Doc. A/55/L.2 (Sept. 8, 2000). The signatories are committed to "grant more generous development assistance, especially to countries that are genuinely making an effort to apply their resources to poverty reduction." *Id.* pt. III, art. 15, http://www.un.org/millennium/declaration/ ares552e.htm.

[4] Zhongguo de Duiwai Yuanzhu Baipi Shu (《中国的对外援助》白皮书) [China's Foreign Aid (White Paper)] (promulgated by the State Council), CHINA DAILY (Apr. 21, 2011), at 4, http://www.eu-china.net/web/cms/ upload/pdf/nachrichten/2011-04-21Chinas-ForeignAid-WhitePaper.pdf.

[5] *Id.* at 4.

[6] Id.

would be 4 percent, or only $4 million. So a $100 million concessional aid loan given in 2009 'costs' the foreign aid budget only $4 million that year."[7]

Second, China permits aid for the purpose of military assistance in recipient states and aid that includes commercial purposes to benefit entities in the Chinese private sector. These forms of aid are generally not reportable as ODA.[8]

Third, the Chinese government has run counter to the ODA purpose of generating primary benefits for the aid recipients by directing China's foreign aid in a manner that supports reciprocity and mutual benefit. A number of researchers have asserted that China's foreign aid is more like a diplomatic and strategic tool to increase political influence and boost domestic economic development.[9]

Until the Chinese government explains these inconsistencies with the definition of ODA and interprets its methodology for measuring resource flows, the quantification of foreign aid provided by the Chinese government does not qualify as a report of ODA, although it shares some characteristics in common with ODA.

Although the White Paper does not include annual aid data, the central government in fact releases expenditures for foreign aid in the annual budget and final account reports. For example, the Ministry of Finance (MOF) reported a total of RMB14.411 billion (approximately US$2.99 billion, equating to 0.39% of 2010 Gross National Income (GNI)) of Chinese foreign aid expenditure in 2010; however, this is not reportable as an ODA figure due to the lack of transparency concerning its components, as noted above.[10]

---

[7] SVEN GRIMM ET AL., TRANSPARENCY OF CHINESE AID: AN ANALYSIS OF THE PUBLISHED INFORMATION ON CHINESE EXTERNAL FINANCIAL FLOWS 16 (Aug. 2011) (quoting DEBORAH BRAUTIGAM, THE DRAGON'S GIFT – THE REAL STORY OF CHINA IN AFRICA 167 (Oxford Univ. Press., 2009)), *available at* http://www.ccs.org.za/wp-content/uploads/2011/09/Transparency-of-Chinese-Aid_final.pdf.

[8] Duiwai Yuanzhu Zhichu Yusuan Zijin Guanli Banfa (对外援助支出预算资金管理办法) [Measures for Administration of Budgetary Disbursement for Foreign Aid] (promulgated by the Ministry of Finance on June 24, 1998; effective on the same day), arts. 7.1, *available at* http://www.people.com.cn/item/flfgk/gwyfg/1998/21 5210199808.html; Zhongguo Jinchukou Yinhang Duiwai Youhui Daikuan Zanxing Banfa (Jinchu Yin Youdai Fa [2000] No. 26) (中国进出口银行对外优惠贷款暂行办法(进出银优贷发(2000)第26号)) [Interim Measures of the Export-Import Bank on Concessional Loans to Foreign Countries] (promulgated and implemented by the EIBC on Feb. 14, 2000), art. 6, *available at* http://www.gsfzb.gov.cn/FLFG/ShowArticle.asp?ArticleID=36119.

[9] JONATHAN WESTON ET AL., CHINA'S FOREIGN ASSISTANCE IN REVIEW: IMPLICATIONS FOR THE UNITED STATES 12 (U.S.-China Economic and Security Review Commission Staff Research Backgrounder, Sept. 1, 2011), http://www.uscc.gov/researchpapers/2011/9_1_%202011_ChinasForeignAssistanceinReview.pdf.

[10] The foreign aid is as reported in the Guanyu 2010 Nian Zhongyang Benji Juesuan de Shuoming (关于2010年国家中央本级决算的说明) [Explanation of the 2010 State-Level Final Account Report], available on the official website of the MOF, *at* http://yss.mof.gov.cn/2010juesuan/201107/t20110720_578455.html. GNI is cited from World Bank's statistics, http://siteresources.worldbank.org/DATASTATISTICS/Resources/GNI.pdf (last visited Jan. 30, 2012).

B. Private Contribution Figures

The Chinese government leads the management of foreign aid projects and programs. Private donations to foreign countries are generally concentrated in humanitarian aid provided through legally formed institutions, mainly the Red Cross Society of China (RCSC), whose administration and operation are subject to the supervision of the government and to the Law of the Red Cross Society of the People's Republic of China promulgated by the Standing Committee of the National People's Congress (NPC).[11] The RCSC reported humanitarian aid in the 2011 Financial Balance Report as follows:

(1) The RCSC received donations from organizations and individuals at home and abroad equivalent to RMB558.48 million (approximately US$88.23 million), RMB79.41 million (approximately US$12.54 million) of which was designated by the donors to aid Japan's recovery from the earthquake and tsunami.

(2) The RCSC donated RMB88.86 million (approximately US$14.04 million) for the purpose of foreign aid by donating

- RMB72.08 million (approximately US$11.39 million) to the Japanese Red Cross for earthquake and tsunami rescue work;

- RMB10.2 million (approximately US$1.61 million) to Kenya, Somalia, and Ethiopia for fighting drought and famine;

- RMB300 million (approximately US$47.4 million) to Pakistan for recovering from floods; and

- RMB3.58 million (approximately US$0.57 million) to Haiti and Chile for earthquake and tsunami rescue work, as well as aftermath recovery.[12]

C. Snapshot of Foreign Aid Activity

1. Development of China's Foreign Aid System

China initiated foreign assistance in 1950 by providing materials to neighboring socialist countries and soon extended this to other developing countries in Asia and Africa following the Bandung Conference in 1955.[13] Foreign aid expenditure was first categorized in the national

---

[11] Zhonghua Renmin Gongheguo Hongshizihui Fa (中华人民共和国红十字会法) [Law of the People's Republic of China on the Red Cross] (promulgated by the Standing Comm. of the NPC on Oct. 31, 1993, effective on the same day), *translated in* LAWS OF PEOPLE'S REPUBLIC OF CHINA [P.R.C. LAWS] 247–54 (Legislative Affairs Commission of the Standing Committee of the NPC, Beijing, 1995), *available in Chinese at* http://www. moh.gov.cn/publicfiles/business/htmlfiles/mohzcfgs/pfl/200804/18254.htm.

[12] RCSC, 2011 NIAN SHOUZHI QINGKUANG BAOGAO (中国红十字总会2011年收支情况报告) [FINANCIAL BALANCE REPORT OF THE RCSC OF 2011] (approved by the Board of Directors of the RCSC on Dec. 8, 2011), http://www.redcross.org.cn/ xxfb/gg/201112/t20111209_43462.html.

[13] White Paper, *supra* note 4, at 2.

budget for the approval of the NPC as early as 1958 and soared by 118% in 1959, accounting for 1.2% of the total national budget, without defining "foreign aid" or indicating its scope.[14]

In 1964, then Prime Minister Zhou En'lai on behalf of the Chinese government declared the Eight Principles for Economic Aid and Technical Assistance to Other Countries (Eight Principles) during an official tour to Africa, highlighting that China's foreign aid policy is based upon equality, mutual benefit, no strings attached, respect for sovereignty, and no requests for privileges.[15]

After China resumed its legal seat in the United Nations (UN) in 1971, its foreign aid spread to infrastructure projects, for example, assisting in the construction of the Tanzania-Zambia Railway.[16] Since 1978, along with adopting the policy of Reform and Opening-up, China gradually transferred its unilateral supply of aid to mutual cooperation, including managing projects on behalf of the recipient states, lease management, and joint ventures.[17] Currently, China provides eight forms of foreign aid: complete projects, goods and materials, technical cooperation, human resource development cooperation, medical teams, emergency humanitarian aid, debt relief, and an overseas volunteer program.[18]

2. Financing Source

At the beginning of the 1990s, in accordance with the gradual transformation of its previously planned economy into a socialist market economy, China diversified the sources and means of funding for foreign aid. In addition to grants and interest-free loans provided by state finance through a unified government budget system, concessional loans are mainly invested by the Export-Import Bank of China (EIBC) with market capital.[19]

3. International Cooperation

Although China has traditionally provided foreign assistance through bilateral agreements, it has greatly enhanced dialogue, cooperation, and assistance through multinational platforms since 2000, including the following:

---

[14] Guanyu 1957 Nian Guojia Yusuan de Zhixing Qingkuang he 1958 Nian Guojia Yusuan Cao'an de Shencha Baogao (关于1957年国家预算的执行情况和1958年国家预算草案的审查报告) [Report on Examining the Implementation of State Budget of 1957 and Draft of State Budget of 1958] (Reported by the Budget Committee of the first NPC on Feb. 1, 1958), *available at* http://www.npc.gov.cn/wxzl/gongbao/2000-12/23/content_5000462. htm; Guanyu1958 Nian Guojia Yusuan he 1959 Nian Guojia Yusuan Cao'an de Baogao (关于1958年国家决算和1959年国家预算草案的报告) [Report on Final State Account of 1957 and Draft of State Budget of 1958] (Reported by the Vice Premier Li Xiannian on behalf of the State Council on the first meeting of the second NPC on Apr. 21, 1959), *available at* http://www.gov.cn/test/2008-03/07/content_912734.htm.

[15] White Paper, *supra* note 4, at 2. The Eight Principles are available in English *at* http://news.xinhuanet. com/english 2010/china/2011-04/21/c_13839683_17.htm (last visited Jan. 30, 2012).

[16] White Paper, *supra* note 4, at 2.

[17] *Id.*

[18] *Id.* at 5–9.

[19] *Id.* at 2, 4.

- Forum on China-Africa Cooperation (FOCAC)
- UN High-Level Meeting on Financing for Development
- UN High-Level Meeting on the Millennium Development Goals
- Forum on China-Africa Cooperation
- Shanghai Cooperation Organization
- China-ASEAN Leaders Meeting
- China-Caribbean Economic and Trade Cooperation Forum
- China-Pacific Island Countries Economic Development and Cooperation Forum
- Forum on Economic and Trade Cooperation between China and Portuguese-Speaking Countries[20]

4. Distribution of Foreign Aid

Geographic Dimension. The Chinese government reported that, by the end of 2009, China's foreign aid had extended to 123 developing countries in Asia, Africa, Latin America, the Caribbean, Oceania, and Eastern Europe with the largest proportion in Africa.[21] China also provided funding to more than thirty international and regional organizations.[22]

Sectoral Dimension. China's foreign aid projects cover agriculture, industry, economic infrastructure, public facilities, education, medical and health care, clean energy, and responsive solutions to climate change.[23] By 2009, 61% of the concessional loans were invested to construct transportation, communications, and electricity infrastructures, with 8.9% allocated to energy and resources, such as oil and minerals.[24]

II. Legal Framework

As noted above, as a non-DAC state, China does not necessarily conduct global assistance in strict adherence to ODA standards, but instead has developed a unique domestic concept of foreign aid.[25] However, China's comprehensive foreign affairs policies, in addition to over sixty years of global aid practice, have incorporated substantial ODA elements, particularly in terms of purposes and instruments, such as aiming to promote the economic growth and social progress of the recipient states and through the instruments of grants and concessions.[26] By and

---

[20] *Id.* at 3.

[21] *Id.* at 9,10.

[22] *Id.*

[23] *Id.* at 11–14.

[24] *Id.* at 5.

[25] Measures for Administration of Budgetary Disbursement for Foreign Aid, *supra* note 8.

[26] White Paper, *supra* note 4, at 2.4.

large, China regulates international assistance on a more flexible and broader basis than standard ODA approaches.

A. Regulation of ODA

1. Overview

Constitutional Foundation

The Chinese Constitution proclaims that China carries out an independent foreign affairs policy underpinned by five principles: (1) mutual respect for sovereignty and territorial integrity, (2) mutual nonaggression, (3) noninterference in each other's internal affairs, (4) equality and mutual benefit, and (5) peaceful coexistence in developing diplomatic relations and economic and cultural exchanges with other countries.[27] The Constitution underlies the footing of Chinese foreign affairs policy with noninterference and equality.

Policy Guidelines

The Eight Principles referred to above are regarded as the fundamental guidelines for the legal framework for China's foreign aid, which is given (1) for the purpose of self-reliance and independent economic growth of the recipient countries, such as increased income and capital accumulation; (2) with no attached conditions and no requests for privileges; and (3) based upon mutual development rather than unilateral aid.[28]

The Eight Principles also address the modalities and applicable standards for foreign aid, including (1) economic aid with a deferrable repayment date; (2) Chinese equipment and materials of the best quality at negotiable prices, based upon international market prices; (3) assistance to local construction projects of the recipient countries; (4) technical assistance with the guarantee of ensuring that local staff fully master the techniques; and (5) the deployment of experts without special demands.[29]

Outline of Current Policy

The White Paper elaborated the Chinese government's most recent principles of foreign aid policy, including the following:

- Aid is to be provided under South-South Cooperation and on the footing of equality, mutual benefit, and common development, to fit with both China's actual conditions and the needs of the recipient countries.

---

[27] XIANFA (宪法) [Constitution of the People's Republic of China] (1982, *last amended* Mar. 14, 2004), Preamble, *translated in* 2004 P.R.C. LAWS 4.

[28] White Paper, *supra* note 4, at 3; Eight Principles, *supra* note 15.

[29] Eight Principles, *supra* note 15.

- Aid should be undertaken with the aim of helping develop aided countries' self-development capacity.

- No political conditions to be attached to aid, no interference with others' internal affairs, and no political privileges sought.

- Aid should not exceed the government's capability. China provides foreign aid in line with its national conditions and applicable comparative advantages, to meet the needs of the aided countries.

- Aid reflects adjustable policy making, meaning that there should be an innovative approach to the form of aid and reform of administrative mechanisms in order to keep pace with the development of domestic and international situations.[30]

2. Implementing Agencies

The State Council is the highest executive organ to administer foreign affairs and enact related regulations, as authorized by the Constitution and the Legislation Law of China.[31]

The Ministry of Commerce (MOFCOM) is designated as the lead agency to (1) draw up the foreign aid plan, (2) map out and implement foreign aid policy and programs, (3) update the pattern of foreign aid, (4) determine aid programs and organize implementation, and (5) manage Chinese government funds for foreign aid.[32] The MOFCOM divides the above functions among the following departments:

- The Department of Aid to Foreign Countries (Department of Aid) takes charge of drawing up and implementing the foreign aid plan, policy, and programs; supervising foreign aid projects; handling intergovernmental issues and negotiations related to foreign aid; and signing relevant documents.[33]

- The Executive Bureau of International Economic Cooperation (Cooperation Bureau) mainly takes responsibility for administering the implementation of complete foreign aid projects (CFAP).[34]

---

[30] White Paper, *supra* note 4, at 3–4.

[31] Constitution of the People's Republic of China, *supra* note 27, art. 89(9); Lifa Fa (立法法) [Legislation Law of the People's Republic of China] (promulgated by the NPC on Mar. 15, 2000), art 56(2), 2000 P.R.C. LAWS 17.

[32] Shangwubu ZhuyaoZhize Neishe Jigou he Renyuan Bianzhi de Guiding (商务部主要职责内设机构和人员编制规定) [Provisions on the Main Functions, Internal Bodies and Staffing of the Ministry of Commerce] (promulgated by the General Office of the State Council on July 11, 2008; effective on the same day), art. 2(13), *available at* http://news.xinhuanet.com/fortune/2008-08/23/content_9651733.htm.

[33] *Id.* art. 3(16).

[34] Shangwu Bu Bangong Ting Tiaozheng Yuanwai Xiangmu Guanli Gongzuo Zhineng Fengong de Tongzhi (商务部办公厅提整援外项目管理工作职能分工的通知) [Notice of the General Office of the Ministry of Commerce on Adjusting the Division of Work Functions in Connection with the Administration of China Foreign Aid Projects] (promulgated by the General Office of the MOFCOM on Mar. 5, 2007; effective on the same day), http://www.mofcom.gov.cn/aarticle/b/bf/200811/20081105910006.html?3352970973=3287115492.

- The China International Center for Economic and Technical Exchanges (Exchange Center) administers the implementation of China's foreign aid materials projects (FAMP).[35]

- The Training Center of MOFCOM (Training Center) runs foreign aid training projects.[36]

- The Department of Finance of the MOFCOM manages the foreign aid fund and compiles relevant budget documents and final accounts.[37]

The Cooperation Bureau, along with the Exchange Center and the Training Center, conducts the tender invitation and negotiation processes under the supervision of the Department of Aid.[38]

The EIBC is responsible for accepting and reviewing loan applications, signing relevant agreements, issuing the loans, and supervising post-lending and repayment processes.[39] As a policy bank founded in 1994 and solely owned by the Chinese government, the EIBC is under the direct administration of the State Council.[40]

The MOF takes charge of the administration of the foreign aid fund through exclusive responsibility for drawing up the foreign aid budget and managing final accounts. It also administers Chinese donations to other countries.[41]

The economic and commerce divisions of embassies and consulates of China shoulder a portion of the functions relating to foreign aid, such as assisting the EIBC with collecting outstanding debt from end-borrowers of concessional loans, assisting the MOFCOM in handling intergovernmental affairs, and supervising and administering the CFAP abroad.[42]

---

[35] *Id.*

[36] *Id.*

[37] Provisions on the Main Functions, Internal Bodies and Staffing of the Ministry of Commerce, *supra* note 32, art. 3(6).

[38] Notice of the General Office of the Ministry of Commerce on Adjusting the Division of Work Functions in Connection with the Administration of China Foreign Aid Projects, *supra* note 34.

[39] Interim Measures of the Export-Import Bank on Concessional Loans to Foreign Countries, *supra* note 8, art. 3.

[40] An introduction to the EIBC is available in English on its official website, http://english.eximbank.gov.cn /profile/intro.shtml# (last visited Jan. 30, 2012).

[41] Measures for Administration of Budgetary Disbursement for Foreign Aid, *supra* note 8, art. 3.

[42] Zhongguo JinchukounYinhang Duiwai Youhui Daikuan Daihou Guanli Guiding (Jinchu Yin Youdai Fa [2000] No.3), (中国进出口银行对外优惠贷款管理规定(进出银优贷发(2000)第338号)) [Provisions of Export-Import Bank of the People's Republic of China on Post-Credit Management of Concessional Loans to Foreign Countries] (promulgated by the EIBC on Oct. 31, 2000), art. 26, http://www.gsfzb.gov.cn/FLFG/Show Article. asp?ArticleID=36366.

3. Restrictions

The three types of financial resources that the Chinese government provides, which are grants, interest-free loans, and concessional loans, are oriented to different types of projects under distinct restrictive conditions.

Grants mainly support medium and small projects related to social welfare in recipient countries, such as hospitals, schools, low-cost housing, and water supply projects.[43] Grants also flow to human resources development projects, technical cooperation, and emergency humanitarian aid.[44] They are not subject to the economic conditions of the recipient.

Interest-free loans are granted to public facilities and projects to improve people's livelihood in aided states, generally conditioned upon the economic conditions of the developing countries.[45]

The term "concessional loans" refers to the medium- or long-term, low-interest credit basically targeted to profitable projects for the aided states aligned with the purpose of stimulating the export of Chinese mechanical and electrical products.[46] Concessional loans provided by the EIBC are tied to all of the following requirements:

- The recipient must have a stable political status, relatively strong economy, and the ability to repay.

- Mutual approval by China's government and the aided country's government.

- Profitable projects, a borrower with good credit, and a guarantor with the ability to repay.

- The amount of Chinese RMB borrowed is generally no less than an amount equivalent to US$2 million

- Materials, techniques, and services purchased or imported from China are in general not less than 50% of the total amount of the loans.[47]

According to statistical data compiled by the Chinese government, by the end of 2009, China had provided concessional loans for 325 projects in seventy-six foreign countries.[48]

Although the Chinese government insists that China's foreign aid should not be attached to political conditions, reports from a number of institutions allege that China uses foreign aid to

---

[43] *Id.* at 4.

[44] *Id.*

[45] *Id.*

[46] Interim Measures of the Export-Import Bank on Concessional Loans to Foreign Countries, *supra* note 8, art. 6.

[47] *Id.* art. 7.

[48] White Paper, *supra* note 4, at 5.

trade off for diplomatic objectives, market access, natural resources, foreign investment advantages, and other benefits.[49]   A report on China's aid to Africa by the International Monetary Fund (IMF) optimistically assessed the situation as a healthy transformation to mutual benefit upon a trading basis other than mere unilateral aid, i.e., satisfying the export and market demands of China, as well as the infrastructure and export-import needs of African nations.[50]

4. Discretionary Aid

Chinese law does not encompass a particular legal term or concept that is comparable to "discretionary aid." The budget for foreign aid projects could be regarded as discretionary since each competent department subordinate to the State Council controls and manages its own budget account within its authority.[51] However, such discretion is subject to certain principles and rules.

The annual budget for foreign aid, formulated by the MOF upon intergovernmental agreement, follows the principle of "a fixed sum for a fixed purpose," which requires foreign aid funding to be accounted and managed separately by the MOF.[52]

The foreign aid budget is subject to the following uses by law:

- Expenditure for complete foreign aid projects, general supplies of goods and materials, military supplies, catastrophic expenditures, training staff from aided countries, wages of dispatched experts, and interest subsidies for concessional loans

- Budgetary funds allocated to Chinese enterprises cooperating or in joint ventures with aided countries

- Management fees and agency fees for enterprises and institutions embarking on foreign aid as delegated by the competent departments

- Other costs approved by the State Council or the MOF, and incurred during foreign aid projects or the implementation of agreements[53]

No definition for "other cost" is provided, thus the scope and standard could be subject to the discretion of the State Council and the MOF.

---

[49] THOMAS LUM ET AL., CONG. RESEARCH SERVICE, R40361, CHINA'S FOREIGN ACTIVITIES IN AFRICA, LATIN AMERICA AND SOUTHEAST ASIA 9 (Feb. 25, 2009).

[50] Jian-Ye Wang & Abdoulaye Bio-Tchané, *Africa's Burgeoning Ties with China*, 45(1) FINANCE & DEVELOPMENT (Mar. 2008), http://www.imf.org/external/pubs/ft/fandd/2008/ 03/wang.htm#author.

[51] Measures for Administration of Budgetary Disbursement for Foreign Aid, *supra* note 8, ch. 3.

[52] *Id.* art. 4.

[53] *Id.* art. 7.

5. Oversight

China offers foreign aid through both financial and project channels, and the relevant oversight mechanisms are separated accordingly.

Oversight of Finance

The foreign aid budget falls into the category of the state budget,[54] which is supervised by the NPC and the Standing Committee of the NPC (SCNPC).[55] The NPC and SCNPC have the power to conduct investigations of the major issues or specific questions concerning the budget or final accounts.[56]

The MOF is a specific central agency able to inspect the utilization of the foreign aid budget and punish illicit delay, occupancy, and embezzlement of an appropriation in accordance with the Interim Provisions on Penalties for Violations of Fiscal Regulations promulgated by the State Council.[57]

The EIBC exercises supervision over concessional loans, including the management of loan projects, loan outflows, and repayment of the principal and interest.[58] It reports to the MOFCOM on the implementation of loans on a regular basis.

Oversight of Projects

The MOFCOM has promulgated specific regulations related to the supervision of various aspects of the CFAP and the provision of aid materials. These relate to the quality of the projects and their management, the qualification and classification of the enterprises implementing FAMP, the work safety system for CFAP, and the inspection of materials.[59] The Department of

---

[54] Yusuan Fa (预算法) [Budget Law of the People's Republic of China] (adopted by the Standing Committee of the NPC on Mar. 22, 1994; effective on Jan. 1, 1995), art. 46, 1994 P.R.C. LAWS 20.

[55] *Id.* art. 66.

[56] *Id.* art. 67.

[57] Measures for Administration of Budgetary Disbursement for Foreign Aid, *supra* note 8, art. 25. The Interim Provisions on Penalties for Violations of Fiscal Regulations was repealed after the Regulations on Penalties and Sanctions for Fiscal Violations were promulgated by the State Council (effective Feb. 1, 2005), *available at* http://www.gov.cn/zwgk/2005-05/23/content_261.htm.

[58] Provisions of Export-Import Bank of the People's Republic of China on Post-Credit Management of Concessional Loans to Foreign Countries, *supra* note 42, art. 2.

[59] These regulations include Duiwai Yuanzhu Chengtao Xiangmu Guanli Banfa (Shixing) (对外援助成套项目管理办法(试行)) [Measures for the Administration of Complete Foreign-Aid Projects (Trial)] (promulgated by the Ministry of Commerce on Dec. 31, 2008; effective on Jan. 1, 2009), art. 9, XIN FAGUI HUIBIAN, Feb. 2009, at 169; Measures for the Administration of Work Safety of Complete Set of Foreign Aid Projects (Trial), *available at* http://www.gov.cn/flfg/2009-01/05/content_1196170.htm; Measures for Administration of Qualifications of Enterprises for Implementing Foreign Aid Complete Projects, *available at* http://www.gov.cn/fwxx/bw/swb/content_447921.htm; Measures for the Administration of Foreign Aid Materials Projects (Trial), *available at* http://www.gov.cn/flfg/2011-06/15/content_1884564.htm.

Finance of MOFCOM is responsible for managing financial accounts and supervises use of the CFAP budget.[60]

The economic and commerce divisions of the Chinese embassies and consulates also assist the MOFCOM with financial supervision and guidance relating to the foreign technology groups in CFAP.[61]

No separate anti-corruption legislation or special mechanism regarding foreign aid was found. The investigation and penalty for embezzlement and bribery are basically governed by criminal laws and administrative regulations.

6. Policy Considerations

On a variety of occasions the Chinese government has emphasized that China must build its foreign aid policy under the framework of South-South Cooperation (SSC) because it is still a developing country dependent on ODA to eradicate poverty and enhance social development. In 2010, China's GNI per capita was as low as US$4,260, merely 10% of the United States and with a ranking of 121 among all 215 listed countries.[62]

SSC pursues the objectives of fostering self-reliance and technological capacities, as well as enabling and expanding international communication of the developing countries through cooperation in the forms of sharing knowledge and experience, training, technology transfer, financial and monetary cooperation, and in-kind contributions.[63]

In the most recent Resolution on the Outline of the Twelfth Five-Year Plan for National Economic and Social Development (Resolution) released by the NPC, in addition to affirming the goal of increasing economic and technical aid to developing countries with respect to civil welfare projects, public utilities, and self-development capabilities, the NPC reaffirmed that SSC is the core attribute and long-term goal of China's foreign aid.[64]

---

[60] Shangwubu Duiwai Yuan Chengtao Xiang Caiwu Guanli Banfa (商务部对外援助成套项目财务管理办法) [Measures of the Ministry of Commerce on the Financial Management of Complete Foreign Aid Projects] (promulgated by the MOFCOM on Jan. 20, 2010; effective on Apr. 1, 2010), art. 3, http://jjhzj.mofcom.gov.cn/aarticle/huiyuanzl/201108/20110807719593.html.

[61] *Id.* art. 27.

[62] World Bank (World Development Indicators Database), Gross National Income Per Capita 2010 (July 1, 2011), http://siteresources.worldbank.org/DATASTATISTICS/Resources/GNIPC.pdf.

[63] *What Is South-South Cooperation?*, UNDP SPECIAL UNIT FOR SOUTH-SOUTH COOPERATION, http://ssc.undp.org/content/ssc/about/what_is_ssc.html (last visited Jan. 30, 2012).

[64] Quanguo Renmin Daibiao Dahui Guanyu Guomin Jingji he Shehui Fahzhan Di shi'erge Wunian Guihua Gangyao de Jueyi (全国人民代表大会关于国民经济和社会发展第十二个五年规划纲要的决议) [Resolution of the NPC on the Outline of the Twelfth Five-Year Plan for National Economic and Social Development] (promulgated by the NPC on Mar. 14, 2011, effective on the same day), ch. 5, 2011 STANDING COMM. NAT'L PEOPLE'S CONG. GAZ. 248.

Mutual Respect and Non-interference

The guiding principles of SSC require respect for national sovereignty, national ownership and independence, equality, non-conditionality, and noninterference in domestic affairs between developing countries.[65] It is reflected in both China's foreign affairs and foreign aid policies, the latter providing that China respects recipient countries' rights to independently select their own path and model of development, and takes their actual needs into account when marking out assistance schemes. Chinese citizens are legally required to observe local customs and traditions when engaging in aid projects.[66]

The non-interference approach has been criticized by some researchers under the assumption that it has enabled China to be more welcomed by corrupt governments or abusive regimes than ODA contributors, who require commitments from those aided governments relating to improving human rights, democratization, and transparent governance, while other researchers consider such an assumption a "misplaced exaggeration" because some countries that are perceived as relatively corrupt actually show significant improvements through China's engagement of aid and investment.[67]

Mutual Benefit and Mutual Interest

It is noteworthy that mutual benefit, as a critical principle of SSC, has been strongly highlighted by the Chinese government to justify the gains China obtained from its foreign assistance practice, because SSC encourages extensive cooperation between South-South countries to achieve mutual development other than unilateral benefit.[68] While SSC includes private funding and private donors with commercial tools in development assistance, both the UN and the OECD have admitted that the SSC mechanism is a departure from traditional ODA in terms of goals, scope, and delivery patterns, and have separately formed their own task units working on forging a more effective global aid architecture based upon merging positive indicators from the SSC practice.

The SSC model plays an important role in China's assistance to African countries so as to satisfy needs and provide benefits to both sides. In the Sharm El Sheikh Action Plan (2010–2012) (Action Plan), agreed upon by China and forty-nine African countries at the Forum on China-Africa Cooperation in 2009, China made commitments as follows: (1) to relieve certain debts owed by all heavily-indebted poor countries and the Least Developed Countries (LDCs) in Africa to the extent that they have diplomatic relations with China; (2) to increase investment and promote infrastructure development in Africa by not only providing free assistance and US\$10 billion concessional loans within the following three consecutive years but also encouraging investment from Chinese enterprises; (3) to provide RMB500 million (about US\$79.51 million) worth of medical equipment to thirty hospitals, which will be built by

---

[65] *What Is South-South Cooperation?*, *supra* note 63.

[66] Measures for the Administration of Complete Foreign-Aid Projects (Trial), *supra* note 59, art 9, at 169.

[67] Helmut Reisen, *Is China Actually Helping Improve Debt Sustainability in Africa?*, G-24 Policy Brief No. 9, OECD, at 1, 3, *available at* http://www.oecd.org/dataoecd/21/20/39628269.pdf.

[68] *What Is South-South Cooperation?*, *supra* note 63.

Chinese enterprises; and (4) to increase the China-Africa Development Fund to US$3 billion to support the expansion of investment from Chinese businesses to Africa.[69] This Action Plan also mentioned that both sides have noted China's fast growth of investment in Africa since the 2006 forum, "which is welcomed by the African countries."[70]

B. Regulation of Private Contributions

China does not have a law that specifically governs private contributions relating to international aid. Donations for domestic aid are primarily regulated by the Law on Donation for Public Welfare Undertakings (Donation Law). An array of tax incentives have been provided to encourage private enterprises' contributions to public welfare in accordance with the Donation Law.

Administrative Measures for the Donations for Disaster Relief (Measures), as a derivative law under the Donation Law, has distinguished foreign aid donations from nationwide aid donations and provides that, "where catastrophic natural disasters occur and result in the need for foreign aid, the Civil Affairs Department under the State Council shall organize and carry out social donations and coordinate foreign aid by reference to the Measures."[71] Therefore, while it remains uncertain whether foreign aid falls within the above definition of "public welfare undertakings," many private foreign aid donations go to a portion of programs run by the Chinese government.

Donations to the RCSC for the purpose of international humanitarian aid may trigger a full deduction for the purposes of corporate income tax or personal income tax, provided that the RCSC meets the qualifications to accept the donations directly given or transferred to it.[72]

---

[69] Zhongfei Hezuo Luntan Shamu Shayihe Xingdong Jihua (2010–2012) (中非合作论坛—沙姆沙伊赫行动计划 (2010至2012年)) [Forum on China-Africa Cooperation Sharm El Sheikh Action Plan (2010–2012)], arts. 4.2.3, 4.3.3, 4.4.3 and 5.6.4, http://www.focac.org/eng/dsjbzjhy/hywj/t626387.htm.

[70] *Id.* art. 4.2.1.

[71] Jiuzai Juanzeng Guanli Banfa (救灾捐赠管理办法) [Administrative Measures for the Donations for Disaster Relief] (promulgated by the Ministry of Civil Affairs on Apr. 28, 2008, effective on the same day), art. 36, XIN FAGUI HUIBIAN (June 19, 2008) at 24.

[72] Caizhengbu Guojia Shuiwu Zongju Guanyu Qiye deng Shehui Liliang Xiang Hongshizi Shiye Juanzeng Youguan Wenti de Tongzhi (财政部、国家税务总局关于企业等社会力量向红十字事业捐赠有关问题的通知) [Notice of the Issues on Donations of the Enterprises and Civil Entities to the Red Cross Undertaking] (promulgated by the MOF and State Administration of Taxation on Mar. 8, 2001; effective on the same day), arts. 1(7), 2(1), 2(2), http://www.whgs.gov.cn/cms/whgs03/laws/05/030205/200103080202.html.

III. Foreign Aid Appropriations Process

A. Bilateral Aid

The state budget is a key financial source for bilateral aid. As noted in the White Paper, the central government directly finances grants and interest-free loans, along with other budgetary foreign aid disbursements.[73] Such budgetary disbursements are subject to (1) the purpose of implementing China's aid commitment under intergovernmental protocols that China has concluded, or (2) government approval.[74] Another important source of bilateral aid results from the EIBC's provision of concessional loans with a lower interest rate, which therefore necessitates interest subsidies from the government.[75]

The White Paper summarized the legal approval procedure for the foreign aid budget as follows:

> [F]oreign aid expenditure is part of the state expenditure, under the unified management of the Ministry of Finance in its budgets and final accounts system. The Ministry of Commerce and other departments under the State Council that are responsible for the management of foreign aid handle financial resources for foreign aid in their own departments in accordance with their respective jurisdictions. Each of these departments draws up a budget for foreign aid projects every year and submits it to the Ministry of Finance for examination, and then to the State Council and the National People's Congress for approval and implementation. Each department controls and manages its own funds for foreign aid projects in its budget.[76]

B. Multilateral Aid

The DAC has observed that China is a high-share donor through bilateral channels but a low-share contributor in the area of multilateral aid, except for China's key role in International Development Association (IDA) replenishment by making an additional voluntary prepayment of US$1.0 billion in outstanding IDA credits.[77]

However, according to the Chinese government's view of multilateral aid, China has provided multilateral-level assistance, including comprehensive training and teaching programs, joint construction projects, and the deployment of technical personnel in cooperation with many international institutions, as demonstrated below:

---

[73] *See* White Paper, *supra* note 4, at 4.

[74] This summary is compliant with the provisions of the Measures for Administration of Budgetary Disbursement for Foreign Aid, *supra* note 8, art. 2.

[75] White Paper, *supra* note 4, at 4.

[76] *Id.*

[77] OECD, 2011 DAC REPORT ON MULTILATERAL AID, at 31, 33, *available at* http://www.oecd.org/dataoecd/5/61/49014277.pdf.

- Allocated US$8 million to the World Health Organization for use in Africa.[78]

- Donated US$200,000 to developing countries between February 2008 and September 2010, many of which are least-developed nations, as part of the WTO's "Aid for Trade" initiative.[79]

- Pledged a total of US$30 million to the Food and Agricultural Organization (FAO) to help improve food production and rural people's livelihoods, and donated US$10 million in 2009 and 2010 respectively.[80]

- Trained more than 6,000 technicians for other developing countries over a period of more than twenty years in implementing the Technical Cooperation among Developing Countries (TCDC) program and by the end of 2009 had sent more than 700 agricultural experts and technicians to Africa, the Caribbean, and the Asia-Pacific area.[81]

Donations on behalf of the government and cooperative programs managed by the competent authorities may fall within the state budget.

IV. Other Types of 'Aid'

As noted above, to date China has officially acknowledged eight official forms of foreign aid, some of which have obvious features that are "made-in-China" and may not fit the category of ODA as defined by the DAC.

A. Complete Foreign Aid Projects

As the main form of foreign aid, CFAPs are referred to as productive or civil projects constructed in recipient countries that are:

- financed by the Chinese government through grants, interest-free loans, or low-interest loans;

- carried out with the assistance of enterprises selected by the Chinese government to provide materials, equipment, and technical personnel, and to inspect, survey, design, and guide the construction, installation, and production of the projects; and

- subject to the administration of the MOFCOM.[82]

---

[78] JONATHAN WESTON ET AL., *supra* note 9, at 7.

[79] Ministry of Foreign Affairs of the People's Republic of China & United Nations System in China, China's Progress towards the Millennium Development Goals (2010 Report) at 60, http://www.un.org. cn/cms/p/resources/30/1539/content.html.

[80] *Id.* at 54–55.

[81] White Paper, *supra* note 4, pt. IV, "International Cooperation in Foreign Aid," at 14, 15.

[82] Measures for the Administration of Complete Foreign-Aid Projects (Trial), *supra* note 59, art. 2, 6, at 168–69.

By the end of 2009, China had completed over 2,000 CFAPs involving a wide range of industry, agriculture, culture and education, health care, communication, power supply, energy, and transportation projects.[83]

B. Technical Cooperation

Unlike under the standard ODA definition, technical cooperation provided by China mainly refers to a post-CFAP aid program that involves the deployment of experts to recipient countries where the CFAP has been completed. Deployed personnel give technical guidance on the production, operation, or maintenance of the CFAP and provide managerial and consultant skills. Technical cooperation also comprises education and training in agriculture skills, handicrafts, and sports, and usually lasts one or two years on an extendable basis, upon request of the aided partner. [84]

C. Medical Teams

Medical teams represent a locally-based program launched as early as 1963, when China dispatched the first medical team to Algeria. Since then, China has continued sending medical teams and provides free medical devices and medicines to recipient countries. This program also takes into account the need for training local staff and helping to improve local medical and health services. So far, there are sixty-nine beneficiary countries spread over Asia, Africa, Europe, Latin America, the Caribbean, and Oceania.[85]

D. Debt Relief

China maintains a strong commitment to debt relief. By the end of 2009, China had signed debt relief protocols with fifty countries throughout Africa, Asia, Latin America, the Caribbean, and Oceania, writing off 380 mature debts amounting to RMB25.58 billion (about US\$ 4.08 billion).[86]

E. Overseas Volunteer Program and Scholarships

The Overseas Volunteer Program was initiated in 2002. Volunteers designated and managed by the Chinese Young Volunteers Association, under the delegation and supervision of the MOFCOM, are sent to other developing countries to serve the local people in the field of education, medical treatment, health care, and any other aspect beneficial to the development of local public welfare.[87] Youth volunteers and Chinese language teachers constitute the majority of this group.[88]

---

[83] White Paper, *supra* note 4, at 6.

[84] *Id.* at 7.

[85] *Id.*, at 7, 8.

[86] *Id.* at 9.

[87] Yuanwai Qingnian Zhiyuanzhe Xuanpai he Guanli Zanxing Banfa (援外青年志愿者选派和管理暂行办法) [Interim Measures for Designation and Administration of Foreign Aid Youth Volunteers] (promulgated by the

China also made a commitment to increase the number of scholarships and on-the-job masters' degree programs for people from developing countries at the 2010 UN High-Level Meeting.[89]

Prepared by Rong Xiang
Foreign Law Intern
Supervised by Kelly Buchanan
Chief, Foreign, Comparative, and
International Law Division I
February 2012

MOFCOM on Nov. 2, 2004; effective on Dec. 2, 2004), art. 3, *available at* http://www.gov.cn/gongbao/content/2005/content_64311.htm.

[88] White Paper, *supra* note 4, at 8.

[89] Six Measures for Foreign Aid Pledged by the Chinese Government at the 2010 UN High-Level Meeting on the Millennium Development Goals, art. 6, *available at* http://news.xinhuanet.com/english2010/china/2011-04/21/ c_13839683_22.htm.

LAW LIBRARY OF CONGRESS

FINLAND

REGULATION OF FOREIGN AID

Executive Summary

Finland is one of the Nordic countries that give the least in aid. Lagging behind Denmark, Sweden, and Norway, which all give close to 1% of gross national income (GNI) in aid, Finland gives some 0.55%. As a member of the European Union (EU), Finland has pledged to meet the 0.7% United Nations Millennium Goal threshold by 2015.

I. Introduction

A. Official Development Assistance Figures

Finland is currently not meeting the United Nations' Millennium Development Goals of 0.7% of GNI in aid but has pledge to meet the threshold by 2015.[1] As of 2010, Finland donates some €966 million (approximately US$1,328 million) in official development assistance (ODA), which is equivalent to 0.55% of Finland's GNI.[2] This figure is just 0.01% short of the "collective" EU goal of 0.56% for 2010,[3] yet it is a sharp increase from 2004 when the total official figures only totaled 0.36% of GNI.[4]

For the fiscal year of 2012, the suggested figures are €290 million (approximately US$398 million) for multilateral development cooperation, and close to €255 million (approximately US$350 million) for bilateral development cooperation.[5] In addition, Finland has appropriated €58.9 million (approximately US$81 million) for the European Development Fund, another €57.7 million (approximately US$79 million) for unspecified development cooperation, and €91 million (approximately US$125 million) for humanitarian aid. The 2012

---

[1] *Finlands utrikespolitik 2020, utrikesministeriets framtidsöversikt, available at* http://formin.finland.fi/public/download.aspx?ID=69699&GUID={579DB143-06DF-4DC1-893A-76CCF3E7BE0E}(last visited Oct. 12, 2011).

[2] *Id.*

[3] European Commission, *Monterrey Consensus*, Aug. 30, 2011, http://ec.europa.eu/europeaid/how/delivering-aid/monterrey_en.htm.

[4] *See* Valtiovarainministeriö [Treasury], Stadsbudgetten 2012 – 30 Internationellt utvecklingssamarbete [Proposed Budget Bill 2012 – expense 30 International Development Cooperation], at 2, http://budjetti.vm.fi/indox/indoxservlet?documentrole=taefop&t3_param=string:year:2012&t3_param=string:lang:sv&fullpathxpointer=/2012/TAE/ruotsi/pl24/pl24ml30.xml%23/1&documentrole=taerp2012 (last visited Oct 17, 2011).

[5] *Id.* at 3.

budget includes some €11 million (approximately US$15 million) in administrative costs associated with planning, evaluating, and revising development aid.[6]

B. Private Contribution Figures

According to Organisation for Economic Co-operation and Development (OECD) figures from 2009, the Finnish private contribution to Finland's total aid was US$1,741 million.[7]

There is also an umbrella organization for all Finnish organizations that work with international development issues called KePa,[8] also known as the Service Centre for Development Cooperation, but it does not provide an official figure for private contributions to development cooperation.

C. Snapshot of Foreign Aid Activity

Finland gives both multilateral and bilateral aid. The three largest recipients of aid in 2010 were Mozambique, Tanzania, and Vietnam.[9] The Foreign Ministry maintains oversight of development projects, which include bilateral, multilateral, and nongovernmental organization (NGO) projects, as well as the granting of concessional credits (i.e. export credits).[10] These projects include budget support as well as more specific activities, e.g., a district heating project in a Chinese province.[11]

II. Legal Framework

A. Regulation of ODAs

1. Overview

The appropriation of development assistance is governed by Finland's annual budget legislation.[12] The implementing agency is the Ministry of Foreign Affairs of Finland. The agency may enter into bilateral and multilateral agreements that bind Finland but only as specified in the annual budget. In addition to the annual budget, Finland, through decisions by Parliament, may legally bind itself to foreign aid pledges.

---

[6] Id.

[7] OECD, *Table 5. Total Net Private Flows^a by DAC Country*, http://www.oecd.org/dataoecd/31/38/47452671.xls (last visited Oct. 12, 2011).

[8] Kepa, *Vad är kepa?* [*What is Kepa?*], http://www.kepa.fi/svenska/vad-ar-kepa (last visited Oct. 17, 2011).

[9] Utrikesministeriet, *Utvecklingssamarbete 2010* [Development cooperation 2010], at 7, http://www.formin.fi/public/download.aspx?ID=79041&GUID={CA0CBD8F-B95D-4B3B-97D5-60ADDE76CB43} (last visited Oct. 12, 2011).

[10] Ministry of Foreign Affairs of Finland, *Development Projects*, http://formin.finland.fi/public/default.aspx?nodeid=38721&contentlan=2&culture=en-US (last visited Oct. 17, 2011).

[11] *Id.*

[12] (Författningssamling [Förfs] 11.6.1999/731) FINLANDS GRUNDLAG [FINNISH CONSTITUTION], ch. 7:83-85, *available in Swedish at* http://www.finlex.fi/sv/laki/ajantasa/1999/19990731.

2. Implementing Agencies

The Finnish Ministry of Foreign Affairs distributes Finland's foreign aid. The Ministry operates a webpage dedicated to development cooperation issues.[13] The Ministry has a special department for development policy which, in turn, is divided into various units (e.g., general development policy and planning, sectoral policy, NGOs, UN development, financing institutions, international environmental policy, and humanitarian assistance).[14] The Ministry of Foreign Affairs provides an annual report to Parliament on all its activities and expenses.[15]

Finnish foreign aid policy is also carried out through a range of public-private partnerships, including Finnfund and Finnpartnership, as well as through concessional credits for exports.

Finnfund is a development finance company that is largely (89%) owned by the Finnish state.[16] The main purpose of Finnfund is to provide financing for projects in developing countries that involve risks that prevent the project from receiving financing from other sources.[17] The oversight and mission of Finnfund is regulated by the Finnfund Act.[18]

Finnpartnership is a trade promotion agency with a "mission to increase commercial cooperation between Finland and developing countries" and it also distributes *de minimis* aid (aid that, within a three-year period, is less than €200,000 (approximately US$275,000).[19]

3. Restrictions

Because ODA is regulated in the annual budget, there are no permanent restrictions on ODA other than that any assistance must be made in accordance with Finnish export laws. In addition, sums appropriated as transferable appropriations may only be used for the following:

1) Payment of costs that are incurred for use as specified by the disposition plan;

2) Payment of costs for the management of development cooperation, when used for educating employees; business travel the employees within the development cooperation department make to or within the recipient countries, or to international multilateral organizations and financial institutions that focus on issues related to these countries as

---

[13] *Available at* http://global.finland.fi/public/default.aspx?culture=sv-FI&contentlan=3 (last visited Oct. 12, 2011).

[14] *See* Ministry of Foreign Affairs, *Utvecklingspolitiska avdelningen* [Development Policy Department], http://formin.finland.fi/public/default.aspx?nodeid=15871&contentlan=2&culture=en-US (last visited Oct. 17, 2011).

[15] FINNISH CONSTITUTION, *supra* note 12, ch. 4:46.

[16] Finnfund, *Finnfund in brief*, http://www.finnfund.fi/yritys/en_GB/brief/ (last visited Oct. 17, 2011).

[17] *Id.*

[18] Finnfund Act 291/79, *available at* http://www.finnfund.fi/yritys/en_GB/ffact/ (last visited Oct. 17, 2011).

[19] Ministry of Foreign Affairs of Finland, *Finnpartnership offers new business cooperation opportunities*, Mar. 6, 2011, http://formin.finland.fi/public/default.aspx?nodeid=31479&contentlan=2&culture=en-US.

well as to the EU; purchase of office automation; and payment of experts in connection with development cooperation projects;

3) Humanitarian aid; the appropriation may be used for aid to countries other than developing nations only if an exceptionally extensive humanitarian crisis requires it and the aid award is based on the country's request for assistance, and only if the Finnish government makes such decision; or

4) Payment of costs for cooperation projects between the Ministry and the Austrian Development Agency (ADA), the Nordic Development Fund (NDF), Norway's Foreign Ministry, Luxemburg's Foreign Ministry, and the German development cooperation agency (GIZ).[20]

4. Discretionary Aid

Finland uses so-called framework appropriations when it allocates resources for international development cooperation. This means that the budget is divided among countries, regions, and types of development cooperation, but does not specify any particular project that must be supported.[21] The budget also provides some discretionary funds to be used for new development cooperation agreements.[22] For example, some €201,773,000 (approximately US$277,480,000) are to be used for new agreements; although an estimated future appropriation is provided, it need not be followed.[23] There are three types of appropriations: "estimated appropriations," which may be exceeded; "transferrable appropriations," which may not be exceeded but may be transferred to a coming year; and "fixed appropriations," which cannot be transferred or exceeded.[24]

5. Oversight

The main agency for review of development cooperation spending is the National Audit Office of Finland, which reports directly to Parliament.[25] The National Audit Office checks compliance with the budget and oversees the state finances.[26] Also, as noted above, the Ministry of Foreign Affairs must provide an annual report on its expenses to Parliament, which

---

[20] Valtiovarainministeriö [Treasury], *Stadsbudgeten 2012*, *supra* note 4, at 3 (translation by author).

[21] *See id.* (generally).

[22] *Id.*

[23] *Id.*

[24] FINNISH CONSTITUTION, *supra* note 12, ch. 7:85 §1 (translation by author).

[25] National Audit Office, *National Audit Office of Finland*, http://www.vtv.fi/en/?lang=2&menu_id=1 (last visited Oct. 12, 2011).

[26] FINNISH CONSTITUTION, *supra* note 12, ch. 7:90 §1.

includes development cooperation expenditures.[27] A recent evaluation of Finnish aid in relation to trade determined that there was a need for a "more strategic approach and fewer projects."[28]

6. Policy Considerations

The Finnish government's overriding policy is that it should aim at reaching the United Nations' Millennium Development Goals by focusing aid on "climate and environment, prevention of crises, [and] support for peace-building processes."[29] In this work, special focus is placed on gender equality, children's rights, and the fight against HIV/AIDS.[30]

B. Regulation of Private Contributions

1. Legislative Regulations

There are no legislative restrictions in Finnish law that prevent private donors or corporations from contributing to charitable organizations or international development cooperation efforts. However, "technical support" to developing countries that includes technology that may have dual uses is regulated by the Export Controls Act and its amendments.[31] These regulations include license requirements for export of products that may have dual uses.[32] Even if not on the specified EU list of products that require licenses, the Finnish government may require licenses for products that can be used in connection with "chemical, biological or nuclear" powers.[33] Moreover certain dual products may not be exported due to military embargoes on individual countries.[34]

2. Tax Incentives for Charitable Contributions

Finland, together with Austria and Sweden, are the only remaining Development Credit Authority (DCA) countries that do not allow any tax deductions for private donations to development cooperation or humanitarian aid efforts.[35] However, Finland did allow tax

---

[27] *Id.* ch. 4:46.

[28] Utrikesministeriet, *Evaluering visar: Handelsfrämjande bistånd kräver finslipning*, [Trade-promoting aid requires some fine-tuning] (Sept. 5, 2011), http://www.formin.fi/public/default.aspx?contentid=227959&nodeid= 15148&contentlan=3&culture=sv-FI (translation by author).

[29] Ministry of Foreign Affairs of Finland, *Finland's Development Policy Programme*, Feb. 22, 2008, http://www.formin.fi/public/default.aspx?nodeid=15319&contentlan=2&culture=en-US.

[30] *Id.*

[31] The most recent amendment, Lag 226/2011 *om ändring av lagen om kontroll av export av produkter med dubbel användning* [change in the legislation of control of export of products with multiple uses], is available in Swedish *at* http://www.finlex.fi/sv/laki/alkup/2011/20110226, and in Finnish *at* http://www.finlex.fi/fi/laki/ alkup/2011/20110226 (both last visited Oct. 18, 2011).

[32] *Id.* at 3 §.

[33] *Id.* at 4 §1.

[34] *Id.* at 4 §2.

[35] Utrikesministeriet (Finland), Bred utvecklingsfinansiering –utökad finansiering av utvecklingssamarbete i samverkan med den offentliga och privata sektorn samt civilsamhället [Broad Development Financing – Increased

deductions during a short period in the 1980s.[36] At present, there are no indications that such a tax incentive will be reintroduced, despite lobbying from the Finnish UNICEF, the Finnish Red Cross, and the Finnish Church Aid.[37] The Finnish government is instead discussing a tax deduction for corporate costs associated with education of local workers in developing countries.[38] The measure is intended to stimulate Finnish corporations' activities and corporate responsibility in developing countries.[39]

III. Foreign Aid Appropriation Process

The foreign aid budget, together with all other State expenses, is appropriated annually in the annual budget bill that is approved by the Finnish Parliament.[40]

There is no legislative act other than the current budget that mandates the percentage of aid given. However, Finland, as a member of the EU, has made commitments to increase its foreign aid budget to 0.7% of GNI by 2015.[41] In addition, the Finnish government has pledged to keep development cooperation for the least developed nations at 0.15% of GNI as the overall percentage of foreign aid increases to 0.7%.[42] Finland has also pledged some €110 million (approximately US$151 million) in foreign aid between 2010 and (through) 2012 as part of the EU's pledge at the 15th Conference of the Parties (COP15) meeting in 2009.[43]

The procedure for enacting the budget is regulated by "Parliament's Working Order."[44] Generally, budget preparations (and the appropriations process) start in January with the Ministers Committee.[45] In March, the Treasury Department approves the overall figure that should be spent in the budget, a sum that is later divided among the departments.[46] The Minister of each department allocates the sum for the department, and a joint discussion of the

---

Financing of Development Cooperation in Conjunction with the Public and Private Sector as well as Civil Society] (U002:00/2010) at 9, available at http://formin.finland.fi/public/download.aspx?ID=74524&GUID={B4345E70-FE19-443C-88CE-E6F5E5E414AD} (last visited Oct. 13, 2011).

[36] *Id.* at 11.

[37] *Id.* at 11–12.

[38] *Id.* at 14.

[39] *Id.*

[40] FINNISH CONSTITUTION, *supra* note 12, ch. 7:83.

[41] European Commission, *Monterrey Consensus*, (Aug. 30, 2011), http://ec.europa.eu/europeaid/how/delivering-aid/monterrey_en.htm.

[42] Valtiovarainministeriö [Treasury], *Stadsbudgetten 2012*, *supra* note 4, at 1.

[43] *See id.*

[44] FINLEX, (Författningssamling [Förfs] 40/2000) RIKSDAGENS ARBETSORDNING [THE PARLIAMENT WORKING ORDER] at 59, http://www.finlex.fi/sv/laki/ajantasa/2000/20000040 (last visited Oct. 18, 2011) (translation from Swedish by the author).

[45] Ministry of Finance, *Budgeten* [The Budget], http://www.vm.fi/vm/sv/09_statsfinanserna/01_budgeten/index.jsp (last visited Oct. 18, 2011).

[46] *Id.*

appropriations is held in August.[47] The final draft budget is passed in Parliament in December.[48] Generally the budget also includes references to expenditures outside of the current budget year.[49] If a budget is not agreed upon, the Treasury must suggest to the Parliament how the draft budget should be interpreted in the short-term.[50]

IV. Other Types of 'Aid'

Remittances from Finland are recognized as an internationally vital source of development cooperation.[51] However, Finnish official figures for remittances have been low, with "compensation of employees" for 2006 at US$251 million for outward and US$698 million for inward remittance.[52] In 2005, Finland had twice the number of emigrants as immigrants.[53] The numerical difference between immigrants and emigrants corresponds to the discrepancies in the figures above and explains why, in 2008, the Finns ranked "third to last" on total contributions to developing nations in a study comparing twenty-two major donor countries despite a sizeable official ODA contribution.[54] Although the Finnish government provides no tax incentive to promote remittances, it has discussed increasing competition on the market among financial institutions to make remittance payments easier and less expensive.[55]

Prepared by Edith Palmer, Chief
Foreign, Comparative and International Law Division II
Global Legal Research Center
and Elin Hofverberg
Law Library Intern
October 2011

---

[47] Finnish Government, *Stadsbugeten*, http://www.vn.fi/toiminta/talousarvio/sv.jsp (last visited Oct. 18, 2011).

[48] *Id. See also* FINNISH CONSTITUTION, *supra* note 12.

[49] *See* for instance Valtiovarainministeriö [Treasury], *Statsbudget 2012*, *supra* note 4 (freezing the total foreign aid appropriation at 0.56% of GNI for 2013 through 2015).

[50] FINLEX, Riksdagens arbetsordning, *supra* note 44.

[51] *See* Utrikesministeriet (Finland), *Bred utvecklingsfinansiering*, *supra* note 35, at 7.

[52] World Bank, *Migration and Remittances in Finland*, Migration and Remittances Factbook – Development Prospect Group, http://siteresources.worldbank.org/INTPROSPECTS/Resources/334934-1181678518183/Finland.pdf (last visited Oct. 12, 2011).

[53] *Id.*

[54] *See* Utrikesministeriet (Finland), *Bred utvecklingsfinansiering*, *supra* note 35, at 8.

[55] *Id.* at 7.

LAW LIBRARY OF CONGRESS

FRANCE

REGULATION OF FOREIGN AID

Executive Summary

France is strongly committed to supporting development assistance and uses a broad range of approaches to achieve its objectives. France was the second largest donor in the world after the United States in 2009 and the third largest donor in 2010. It provides aid at the bilateral, European, and multilateral levels. Bilateral agreements are seen as a key component of France's development assistance. Its five priority sectors are education, health, sustainable development, agriculture and food security, and economic growth. France concentrates its aids on two priority regions: sub-Saharan Africa and the Mediterranean Basin.

The strategic guidelines, objectives, and geographical focus of French foreign aid are set forth by the Inter-ministerial Committee on International Development Cooperation, as France does not have a single ministry in charge of foreign aid. France's four main objectives are: foster sustainable shared growth, fight against poverty and inequality, preserve global public goods, and ensure global stability and the rule of law.

The Ministry of Foreign and European Affairs and the Ministry of Economy, Finance and Industry play major roles in the coordination and management of development aid. The main implementing agency is the French Development Agency. It is both a public establishment in charge of implementing French policy in matters of development assistance and a development bank.

France's budget is presented in the form of major public policies called "missions." Each mission comprises a set of programs with their own specific objectives and performance targets. Programs are further divided into subprograms. Each program has a clearly identified coordinator. The program coordinator may reallocate appropriations between subprograms within a program for a more flexible management of appropriations. The Official Development Assistance Mission comprises twenty-three programs for 2011. Finally, France is very active in the development of innovative sources of financing to supplement traditional development aid.

I. Introduction

A. Official Development Assistance Figures

France reported to the Development Assistance Committee (DCA) of the Organization for Economic Co-operation and Development (OECD) a net Official Development Assistance (ODA) of US$12,600 million in 2009 that comprised US$7,019 million in bilateral ODA, 56% of the total; US$2,900 million in European ODA, 23% of the total; and US$2,681 million in multilateral ODA, 21% of the total.[1] France was the second largest donor in the world after the United States and Europe's largest donor, closely followed by Germany and the United Kingdom. The French ODA was 0.47% of its Gross National Income (GNI).[2] Africa was the largest recipient of French ODA, in particular, sub-Saharan Africa. In 2010, France achieved its objective of 0.50% of its GNI with a net ODA of US$12,915 million.[3] It was the third largest donor after the United States and the United Kingdom.

France's next objective is 0.70% of its GNI by 2015.[4] This objective was adopted for the first time in 1970 by the United Nations and has been reaffirmed on numerous occasions.[5] The European Council of Ministers repeated this commitment in June 2010. However, it may be difficult to achieve this goal as stated in a recent parliamentary report.[6]

B. Private Contribution Figures

A recent report prepared by the General Finance Inspection of the Ministry of Economy evaluates private aid at around €600 to €800 million (approximately US$840 million to US$1,120 million) a year. The report notes that France does not have nongovernmental organizations (NGOs) or foundations similar in size to their British or American counterparts. Some organizations are recognized at the international level—for example, Doctors Without Borders—but they generally are smaller organizations. French foundations are generally

---

[1] *ODA by Donor*, OECD.STATEXTRACTS, http://stats.oecd.org/Index.aspx?DatasetCode=ODA_DONOR (select France in "Donor" field, then select Net Disbursements in "Flow type" field) (last visited Aug. 8, 2011); STRATEGY 2011–DEVELOPMENT COOPERATION: A FRENCH VISION, MINISTÈRE DES AFFAIRES ETRANGÈRES ET EUROPÉENNES 61, 62, http://www.diplomatie.gouv.fr/fr/IMG/pdf/Doc_Cadre_ANG_2011.pdf (last visited Aug. 8, 2011).

[2] GNI is "the Gross Domestic Product (GDP) less net taxes on production and imports, less compensation of employees and property income payable to the rest of the world plus the corresponding items receivable from the rest of the world." *Glossary of Statistical Terms: Gross National Income (GNI)*, OECD, http://stats.oecd.org/ glossary/detail.asp?ID=1176 (last updated Mar. 5, 2003).

[3] *ODA by Donor*, OECD.STATEXTRACTS, *supra* note 1; STRATEGY 2011–DEVELOPMENT COOPERATION: A FRENCH VISION, *supra* note 1.

[4] *Enjeux Internationaux*, MINISTÈRE DES AFFAIRES ETRANGÈRES ET EUROPÉENNES, http://www.diplomatie. gouv.fr/fr/entrees-thematiques_830/index.html (last visited Aug. 8, 2011).

[5] Rapport 2857 fait au nom de la COMMISSION DES FINANCES, DE L'ECONOMIE GENERALE ET DU CONTROLE BUDGETAIRE sur le projet de loi de finances pour 2011 at 11,12 (Oct. 14, 2010), http://www.assemblee-nationale.fr/13/pdf/budget/plf2011/b2857-tIII-a5.pdf.

[6] *Id.*

undercapitalized and less oriented towards international actions.[7] The report further states that an estimated €650 million (US$910 million) came from individual donors and €150 million (US$ 210 million) from companies.[8]

C. Snapshot of Foreign Aid Activity

France is strongly committed to supporting development assistance and uses a broad range of approaches to achieve its objectives. The 2011 framework document on France's Cooperation and Development Policy states that

> [t]o respond to the challenge of sustainable globalization and guarantee the major balances of our planet over the long run, French cooperation strategy focuses on four overarching objectives: foster sustainable and equitable growth for the poorest populations; combat poverty and inequality; preserve global public goods;[9] and ensure global stability and the rule of law.
>
> In its search for comprehensive responses, France is working with all the resources at its disposal. It is one of the few countries in the world to use not only the traditional tools of official development assistance but also long-term financial instruments, as well as an expanding array of innovative financing mechanisms.[10]

France provides aid at the bilateral, European and multilateral levels. Bilateral agreements are seen as a "key component of France's development cooperation."[11] They are flexible tools that permit the targeting of geographic areas and sectors that are viewed as priorities. In addition, they may be entered into with a broad diversity of parties such as states, local authorities, foundations etc.[12]

In 1998, France created a "Priority Solidarity Zone" (*Zone de Solidarité Prioritaire*, ZSP) in order to focus French aid more closely on a limited number of countries. The ZSP comprises fifty-five countries, including primarily the former French African colonies and other countries

---

[7] Rapport 2009-M.089-02, LA PHILANTHROPIE PRIVÉE ORIENTÉE VERS L'AIDE AU DÉVELOPPEMENT, Synthèse (Feb. 2010), https://www.igf.minefi.gouv.fr/sections/les_rapports_par_typ/les_enquetes_portant/ international_et_eu/la_philanthropie_pri/downloadFile/attachedFile/2009-M-089-02_final_au_19_mai_ 2010.pdf?nocache=1274257664.75.

[8] *Id.* at 4.

[9] "Global public goods include peace and security, fair international trade rules, control of communicable diseases, financial stability, prevention of climate change, and information and knowledge." UMA LELE ET. AL, THE CHANGING AID ARCHITECTURE: CAN GLOBAL INITIATIVES ERADICATE POVERTY?, http://www.oecd.org/data oecd/47/13/24482500.pdf (last visited Aug. 18, 2011). For additional information, *see Global Public Goods*, GLOBAL POLICY FORUM, http://www.globalpolicy.org/social-and-economic-policy/global-public-goods-1-101.html (last visited Aug. 18, 2011); *Global Economy: Global Public Goods*, THE WORLD BANK, http://web.worldbank. org/WBSITE/EXTERNAL/EXTABOUTUS/0,,contentMDK:20627295~pagePK:51123644~piPK:329829~theSiteP K:29708,00.html (last visited Aug. 18, 2011).

[10] STRATEGY 2011–DEVELOPMENT COOPERATION: A FRENCH VISION, *supra* note 1, at 4.

[11] *Id.* at 27.

[12] *Id.* at 27, 28.

of sub-Saharan Africa, the Middle East, Indochina, the Caribbean, and the Pacific, plus Afghanistan on a provisional basis. France concentrates most of its bilateral aid on these countries.[13] In 2004 France introduced a new tool, the Framework Partnership Document (*document cadre de partenariat*, DCP), that is designed to take into account the realities in the field in order to program aid. The DCP is prepared for countries of the ZSP and aims at providing guidance for French cooperation over a period of five years. Each DCP is negotiated locally under the authority of the ambassador and is cosigned by the local authorities and thereby "ensures greater predictability and facilitates more effective ownership by the partner country of cooperation actions."[14] The DCP specifies a limited number of sectors of concentration (generally two to three) that must normally account for 80% of the aid earmarked for the country.[15]

The French contribution to European aid represents more than half of its multilateral aid. Half of this amount goes to the European Development Fund, which provides aid to countries from Africa, the Caribbean, and the Pacific. The other half goes to other European aid programs including programs for emergency aid and other developing countries. France substantially contributes to many non-European institutions, including the World Bank, other regional development banks, and the Global Fund to Fight AIDS, Tuberculosis and Malaria. It also provides support to many other international institutions that fight climate change and famine, or promote education.[16]

France's five priority sectors are education, health, sustainable development, agriculture and food security, and economic growth. These sectors accounted for 56% of France's total net ODA in 2008: education accounted for 17%, health 10%, agriculture and food security 7%, sustainable development 9%, and support for growth 13%.[17]

France concentrates its aid on two priority regions: sub-Saharan Africa and the Mediterranean Basin. Africa was the largest recipient of French ODA with 58% of net bilateral aid in 2009, and more specifically sub-Saharan Africa with 47%. This aid reflects France's strong historic ties with that continent. In 2010, sub-Saharan Africa received €2.2 billion (US$ 3.08 billion) of aid. The following fourteen priority poor countries—Benin, Burkina Faso, Central African Republic, Chad, Comoros, Democratic Republic of Congo, Ghana, Guinea, Madagascar, Mali, Mauritania, Niger, Senegal and Togo—received €467 million (US$654 million) of the overall amount.[18]

---

[13] *Aide au Développement et Gouvernance Démocratique: Zone de Solidarité Prioritaire*, MINISTÈRE DES AFFAIRES ETRANGÈRES ET EUROPÉENNES, http://www.diplomatie.gouv.fr/fr/actions-france_830/aide-au-developpement_1060/zone-solidarite-prioritaire_6119.html (last visited Aug. 8, 2011).

[14] STRATEGY 2011–DEVELOPMENT COOPERATION: A FRENCH VISION, *supra* note 1, at 56.

[15] *Id.*

[16] *Dispositifs et enjeux de l'aide au développement: Politique française et européenne pour le développement*, MINISTÈRE DES AFFAIRES ETRANGÈRES ET EUROPÉENNES, http://www.diplomatie.gouv.fr/fr/actions-france_830/aide-au-developpement_1060/aide-au-developpement_20515/politique-francaise-europeenne-pour-developpement_13129.html (last visited Aug. 8, 2011).

[17] STRATEGY 2011–DEVELOPMENT COOPERATION: A FRENCH VISION, *supra* note 1, at 62.

[18] *Id.* at 7, 8, 62, 63.

Aid is principally distributed to economic and social sectors—in particular education, water, and sanitation—in Africa. In February 2008, at Cape Town, President Sarkozy announced a new initiative to support economic growth in Africa. This initiative supports the private sector and agricultural development, job-creating companies, the financial services sector, transportation and energy infrastructure, and regional integration.[19]

Aid to countries on the southern coast of the Mediterranean Sea constitutes approximately 20% of the budgetary amount appropriated.[20] It focuses on the economy, employment, transportation, energy infrastructure, urban development, and water use policies. Water issues have been especially critical due to its scarcity in that region. France also assists its overseas territories in economic and social development.[21]

Fragile and crisis countries, in particular the Sahel (the transition zone along the southern Sahara Desert), the Middle East, and Afghanistan are also of concern to France. In these countries, assistance focuses on crisis prevention. Finally, France provides some assistance to emerging countries of systemic importance. This assistance is geared towards cooperation, which is viewed as a "key to strengthening dialogue and preparing together international negotiations on common concerns."[22]

II. Legal Framework

A. Regulation of ODAs

1. Overview

Institutional Organization

The strategic guidelines, objectives, and geographic focus of French foreign aid are set by the Inter-ministerial Committee on International Development Cooperation (*Comité interministériel de la coopération internationale et du développement*, CICID) as France does not have a single ministry in charge of foreign aid. This Committee was created in 1998.[23] It is chaired by the Prime Minister and comprises the twelve ministers more directly concerned with

---

[19] Speech by M. Nicolas Sarkozy, President of the Republic, to the Parliament of the Republic of South Africa (Cape Town, Feb. 28, 2008), *available at* http://www.ambafrance-uk.org/President-Sarkozy-s-speech-to-the.

[20] STRATEGY 2011–DEVELOPMENT COOPERATION: A FRENCH VISION, *supra* note 1, at 8.

[21] *Id.*

[22] *Id.*

[23] Décret 98-66 du 4 février 1998 portant création du comite interministériel de la coopération internationale et du développement [Decree 98-66 of February 4, 1998, creating the Inter-Ministerial Committee on International Development Cooperation], *available at* LEGIFRANCE, http://legifrance.gouv.fr/affichTexte.do;jsessionid=F2CC352458333EDC6AF17FB3EB974465.tpdjo12v_2?cidTexte=JORFTEXT000000753609&dateTexte=20110729.

development assistance issues. A representative of the President of the Republic attends the Committee meetings.[24]

Since its creation, the CICID has met nine times. Its last meeting took place in June 2009.[25] At that meeting, it was decided that France would give priority to five sectors: health, education and professional training, agriculture and food security, sustainable development and climate, and economic growth. In addition, it was decided that an objective of 60% of France's budgetary effort would be concentrated on the Sub-Saharan African countries. A new geographic prioritization was also defined that resulted in four categories: priority poor countries comprising fourteen poor countries, intermediary income countries having specific relations with France, emerging countries with a global or regional dimension, and crisis or post-crisis countries.[26]

The CICID Secretariat is run jointly by the three ministries more specifically involved in setting forth and implementing cooperation policy: the Ministry of Foreign and European Affairs (more specifically by the Minister responsible for cooperation attached to the Ministry of Foreign Affairs); the Ministry of Economy, Finance and Industry; and the Ministry of Immigration, Integration, National Identity and Solidarity Development.[27]

The General Directorate for Global Affairs, Development and Partnership (*Direction Générale de la Mondialisation, du Développement et des Partenariats*, DGM) co-leads the CICID on behalf of the Ministry of Foreign and European Affairs. It is in charge of the strategic coordination and management of aid and is responsible for the following sectors: governance, global public good, research, higher education, United Nations multilateral funds, and some health funds.[28]

The General Directorate of the Treasury (*Direction Générale du Trésor et des Politiques Economiques*) co-leads for the Ministry of Economy, Finance and Industry. It is responsible for issues relating to debt and monetary cooperation, relations with international financial

---

[24] *Id.* art. 2.

[25] *Le Dispositif Institutionnel Français: CICID Juin 2009–Relevé de Conclusions*, MINISTÈRE DES AFFAIRES ETRANGÈRES ET EUROPÉENNES, http://www.diplomatie.gouv.fr/fr/actions-france_830/aide-au-developpement_1060/politique-francaise_3024/dispositif-institutionnel_5155/cicid_5171/cicid-juin-2009_74507.html (last visited Aug. 8, 2011).

[26] *Id.*

[27] Décret 98-66 du 4 février 1998 art. 6.

[28] *Le Dispositif Institutionnel Français: Introduction*, MINISTÈRE DES AFFAIRES ETRANGÈRES ET EUROPÉENNES, http://www.diplomatie.gouv.fr/fr/actions-france_830/aide-au-developpement_1060/institutions-francaises_19758/dispositif-institutionnel-francais_19759/index.html (last visited Aug. 8, 2011).

institutions, cooperation with countries belonging to the Franc zone,[29] and financial cooperation and trade policies.[30]

The CICID secretariat meets about once a month with the French Agency for Development (*Agence Française de Développement*, ADF), which is France's major implementing agency.[31]

Foreign Aid Objectives

French foreign aid policy has four main objectives:

- To promote sustainable and equitable growth for the poorest countries

- To cooperate with emerging countries—for example, Brazil and China—in order to better position France's economic and strategic interests

- To participate in the financing of European and multinational actions aimed at better dealing with global challenges

- To help countries face crises resulting from either natural catastrophes or political and/or military conflicts[32]

In addition, regarding developing countries, France's aid is geared towards meeting four additional challenges:

- To promote growth that creates jobs and improves living standards

- To fight poverty and reduce inequality in line with France's commitments to the United Nations Millennium Development Goals (eradicate extreme poverty and hunger; achieve universal primary education; promote gender equality and empower women; reduce child mortality; improve maternal health; combat HIV/AIDS, malaria and other diseases; ensure environmental sustainability and develop a global partnership for development)

- To help the preservation of global public goods by managing climate change, biodiversity loss, and the spread of infectious diseases, and by improving financial stability

---

[29] After they attained their independence from France, many Saharan and sub-Saharan African countries retained the name "Franc" for their own monetary units. These countries became members of the Franc Zone as their currencies were linked to the French Franc. Since France adopted the Euro, these currencies have been linked to the Euro. *See* "Franc Zone," ENCYCLOPÆDIA BRITANNICA (online academic ed. 2011), http://www.britannica .com/EBchecked/topic/215756/Franc-Zone.

[30] *Le Dispositif Institutionnel Français: Introduction, supra* note 28.

[31] *Id.*

[32] *Dispositifs et enjeux de l'aide au développement: Politique Française et Européenne pour le Développement*, MINISTÈRE DES AFFAIRES ETRANGÈRES ET EUROPÉENNES, http://www.diplomatie. gouv.fr/fr/actions-france_830/aide-au-developpement_1060/aide-au-developpement_20515/politique-francaise-europeenne-pour-developpement_13129.html (last visited Aug. 8, 2011).

- To promote stability and the rule of law[33]

Limits on Recipients

The principles that guide French external action, such as "the right of peoples to self-determination, respect for human rights and democratic principles, [and] respect for the rule of law and cooperation among nations," bar transactions with hostile states.[34] In addition, as a member of the European Union (EU), France is bound by the Treaty of Lisbon. The Treaty sets forth similar principles guiding the external action of the EU on the international scene. These principles include democracy, the rule of law, the universality and indivisibility of human rights and fundamental freedoms, respect for human dignity, equality and solidarity, and respect for the principles stated in the United Nations Charter and by international law. The Treaty further states that the EU must seek to develop relations with third countries that share the principles listed above, therefore, discouraging development aid to hostile states that do not foster such principles.[35]

2. Restrictions

In 2001, the OECD Development Assistance Committee recommended that bilateral aid to the least developed countries (LCDs) be "untied." OECD defines "tied aid" as "official grants or loans that limit procurement to companies in the donor country or in a small group of countries."[36] In 2006, the Paris Declaration reaffirmed this recommendation on the ground that it increases aid efficiency, particularly by significantly reducing its cost and improving country ownership. Country ownership is one of the five principles of the Paris Declaration. The OECD 2001 recommendation was amended in 2008 to include the heavily indebted poor countries (HIPCs).[37]

France has untied aid beyond the OECD recommendations. It extended the recommendation to non-LCD countries and to food aid. It has now untied up to 91% of its total aid.[38] This percentage is higher in the case of ADF, France's leading implementing agency for ODA, which untied 100% of its aid for all sectors and countries.[39]

---

[33] *Id.*

[34] *France's Foreign Policy: Principles*, MINISTÈRE DES AFFAIRES ETRANGÈRES ET EUROPÉENNES, http://www.diplomatie.gouv.fr/en/france_159/france-in-the-world_6820/france-foreign-policy_6904/principles_1403.html (last visited Aug. 8, 2011).

[35] Consolidated Versions of the Treaty on European Union and the Treaty on the Functioning of the European Union art. 21, 2010 O.J. (C 83) 1, http://eur-lex.europa.eu/LexUriServ/LexUriServ.do?uri=OJ:C:2010:083:FULL:EN:PDF (last visited Aug. 8, 2011).

[36] *Untying Aid: The Right to Choose*, OECD, DEVELOPMENT CO-OPERATION DIRECTORATE, http://www.oecd.org/document/50/0,3746,en_2649_33721_46345330_1_1_1_1,00.html (last visited Aug. 8, 2011).

[37] *Id.*

[38] *Id.*

[39] *L'aide publique au développement dispensée par l'ADF est déliée*, AGENCE FRANÇAISE DE DÉVELOPPEMENT, http://www.afd.fr/site/afd/lang/fr/DeliementAidePublique (last visited Aug. 8, 2011).

3. Policy Considerations

France gives priority to development aid to countries that organize democratic elections on a regular basis, respect human rights, fight corruption, and have public policies that benefit their most needy populations. It views a sound political base as a prerequisite for successful development programs and promotes democratic governance through cooperation actions in many developing countries while respecting the sovereignty of these countries. France's strategic cooperation priorities include promoting democratic governance at the state, regional, and local authority levels; the rule of law and individual freedoms; gender equality; and the transparency of public actions.[40] The 2011 framework document on France's Cooperation and Development Policy reiterates the above in the following statement:

> France makes the promotion of individual rights, the rule of law and governance a core strand of its cooperation policy and considers them to be part and parcel of the political dialogue on the formulation and implementation of development strategies. This priority is grounded on the fact that governance is a critical dimension of the political fate of societies and their economic emergence. However, support for good governance comes up against the limits, encountered by any outside party, of noninterference in the political and social balance of a sovereign country.[41]

In addition, it is France's policy to jointly explore with the recipient state what its needs and priorities are and, if possible, to involve the population at large as further stated in the 2011 framework document:

> The effectiveness of cooperation policies and actions strongly depends on their responsiveness to citizens' needs. Inter-state dialogue is naturally the prime framework for government cooperation policy, but the population at large must also become increasingly involved. France will thus systematically mainstream the participation of partner countries' citizens and civil society into its bilateral actions and promote this at [the] European and multilateral level, whether it is translated by the partner government involving citizens upstream in the framing of public policies, or in the management, monitoring and evaluation of the actions supported.[42]

4. Discretionary Aid

As described in details in Part III of this report ("Foreign Aid Appropriations Process"), appropriations allocated to a program listed in France's annual budget law may be reallocated between subprograms within a program by its managers for a more flexible management of appropriations. These managers are accountable to their Ministry, which in turn is accountable

---

[40] *Gouvernance Democratique: L'approche française*, MINISTÈRE DES AFFAIRES ETRANGÈRES ET EUROPÉENNES, http://www.diplomatie.gouv.fr/fr/entrees-thematiques_830/aide-au-developpement-gouvernance-democratique_1060/gouvernance-democratique_1053/index.html (last visited Aug. 8, 2011); MINISTÈRE DES AFFAIRES ETRANGÈRES ET EUROPÉENNES, GOVERNANCE STRATEGY FOR FRENCH DEVELOPMENT ASSISTANCE (2007), http://www.diplomatie.gouv.fr/en/IMG/pdf/StrategieAngMAE.pdf.

[41] STRATEGY 2011–DEVELOPMENT COOPERATION: A FRENCH VISION, *supra* note 1, at 33.

[42] *Id.* at 34.

to Parliament. The management of each program must respect the set of objectives and performance indicators set forth in the Annual Performance Plans prepared for each programs.[43]

5. Oversight

Oversight of the Budget by Parliament and the National Audit Court

Once the budget is passed, Parliament has some supervisory control over its implementation. The National Assembly and Senate Finance Committees monitor the efficiency of public expenses and evaluate any public finance issue. The National Assembly has also set forth a monitoring and evaluation task force charged to control the use of public funds. Parliamentary control also takes the form of a budget review law that needs to be adopted by June 1 of the year following the applicable budget year. An Annual Performance Plan is provided to Parliament for each program. In addition, the National Audit Court publishes two important public reports for Parliament each year: the annual report on the situation of public finances and the annual report on performance. Parliament may also request that France's National Audit Court conduct specific investigations.[44]

Efficiency Requirements

The concept of ODA effectiveness emerged within the context of the adoption of the United Nations Millennium Development Goals in September 2000[45] and the substantial increase in ODA pledges made during the International Conference on Financing for Development held in March 2002 in Monterrey.[46] Further steps to promote ODA effectiveness were taken during the Paris Conference in 2005.[47] It was recognized that fragmentation of aid impairs aid effectiveness, whereas a pragmatic approach to burden sharing increases complementarity and can reduce transaction costs. A Declaration referred to as the Paris Declaration was adopted during the Conference. It lays out five core principles aimed at improving effectiveness. They are as follows:

---

[43] Loi de Finance et Lois de Financement à l'Assemblée Nationale (updated as of Aug. 31, 2010), http://www.assemblee-nationale.fr/connaissance/lois_finances_lois_financement/lois_finances_financement_actualisee.pdf.

[44] *L'évaluation des politiques publiques*, ASSEMBLÉE NATIONALE (Nov. 2009), http://www.assemblee-nationale.fr/connaissance/fiches_synthese/fiche_51.asp.

[45] *We Can end Poverty 2015: Millennium Development Goals*, UNITED NATIONS, http://www.un.org/millenniumgoals/ (last visited Aug. 24, 2011).

[46] *International Conference on Financing for Development* (Mar. 18–22, 2002, Monterrey, Mexico), UNITED NATIONS, http://www.un.org/esa/ffd/ffdconf/.

[47] *Cohérence et efficacité de l'aide: Introduction*, MINISTÈRE DES AFFAIRES ETRANGÈRES ET EUROPÉENNES, http://www.diplomatie.gouv.fr/fr/actions-france_830/aide-au-developpement_1060/dispositifs-enjeux-aide-au-developpement_20515/enjeux-du-developpement_19986/coherence-efficacite-aide_19988/index.html (last visited Aug. 8, 2011); Ministère des Affaires Etrangères et Européennes, Déclaration de Paris sur l'éfficacité de L'aide au développement (Feb. 28–Mar. 2, 2005), http://www.diplomatie.gouv.fr/fr/IMG/pdf/Declaration_de_Paris_2005.pdf.

- **Ownership:** *Developing countries set their own strategies for poverty reduction, improve their institutions and tackle corruption.*

- **Alignment:** *Donor countries align behind these objectives and use local systems.*

- **Harmonisation:** *Donor countries coordinate, simplify procedures and share information to avoid duplication.*

- **Results:** *Developing countries and donors shift focus to development results and results get measured.*

- **Mutual accountability:** *Donors and partners are accountable for development results.*[48]

In 2007, France transposed the Paris Declaration into a French Action Plan, which encompasses the different fundamental principles of the Declaration. The Action Plan is built around twelve priorities that focus on capacity building, the expanded role of Partnership Framework Documents, and the improvement of the practices of French cooperation, in particular with regard to the predictability and complementarity of donor interventions. Each priority is further broken down into actions and implementation modalities.[49] In 2008, the Ministry of Economy published an evaluation of the implementation of the Paris Declaration by France. It showed that the levels of implementation varied depending on the principle evaluated.[50] In 2009, the CICID made recommendations for updating the Action Plan structure to take into account the renewed commitments undertaken at the European and international levels (i.e., adoption of the EU Code of Conduct on Division of Labor and the ACCRA Agenda for Action, discussed below) and their operational implications for the French cooperation system.[51]

The EU Code of Conduct on Complementarity and Division of Labour in Development Policy, adopted in 2007, is expected to improve the implementation of the EU Cooperation policy. The Code sets forth "eleven principles designed to reduce the administrative formalities, to use the funds where they are most needed, to pool aid and to share the work to deliver more, better and faster aid."[52] The Code is voluntary, flexible and self-policing.[53]

---

[48] *Paris Declaration and Accra Agenda for Action*, OECD, DEVELOPMENT CO-OPERATION DIRECTORATE, http://www.oecd.org/document/18/0%2C3340%2Cen_2649_3236398_35401554_1_1_1_1%2C00.html (last visited Aug. 8, 2011).

[49] AGENCE FRANÇAISE POUR LE DÉVELOPPEMENT, PLAN D'ACTION FRANÇAISE POUR L'EFFICACITÉ DE L'AIDE (June 2007), http://www.afd.fr/jahia/webdav/site/afd/shared/ELEMENTS_COMMUNS/AFD/Efficacite%20 Aide/PlanAction-EfficaciteAide.pdf.

[50] MINISTÈRE DE L'ECONOMIE, EVALUATION OF THE IMPLEMENTATION OF THE DECLARATION OF PARIS BY FRANCE–2008/2, http://www2.economie.gouv.fr/directions_services/dgtpe/publi/eval_declar_paris0809_en.pdf (last visited Aug. 8, 2011).

[51] *Le Dispositif Institutionnel Français: CICID Juin 2009–Relevé de Conclusions*, *supra* note 25.

[52] *European Union Code of Conduct on Division of Labour in Development Policy*, EUROPA, http://europa.eu/legislation_summaries/development/general_development_framework/r13003_en.htm (last visited Aug. 8, 2011).

[53] *Id.*

Finally, at a Third High Level Forum on Aid Effectiveness organized by OECD and hosted by the Government of Ghana in Accra, developed and developing countries agreed on the Accra Agenda for Action (AAA). AAA calls on both countries and donors to continue their efforts to reduce fragmentation and improve the division of labor.[54]

B. Regulation of Private Contributions

The General Tax Code provides for a number of tax incentives for private contributions. Donations by individuals made to certain officially approved institutions, public interest institutions, and charitable organizations, if these donees are located in the EU, Norway, or Iceland, give rise to a tax credit equal to 66% of the donations within a limit of 20% of the taxpayer's total income.[55] In addition, donations to organizations providing care for persons in hardship (food, lodging, and health care) may give rise to a tax credit equal to 75% of the donation with a maximum of €521 (US$730) for donations made in 2011. Where the donations exceed 20% of the taxpayer's income in a given year, the excess is carried forward over the next five years and gives rise to a tax credit under the same conditions.[56]

If the taxpayer is subject to the net wealth tax, he can deduct 75% of his donation within a limit of €50,000 (US$70,000).[57] In addition, donations are not subject to estate tax.

Donations made by corporations to nonprofit organizations benefit from a tax reduction of up to 60% of the amount of the donation, up to a maximum of 0.05% of their French-source revenues.[58] Donations exceeding the above limitation may be carried forward for five years. Foreign organizations similar to French nonprofit organizations located within the EU or the EU Economic Area have been entitled to such donations since January 1, 2010. An approval from the French tax authorities is required, however.

The report prepared by the General Finance Inspection of the Ministry of Economy, mentioned above, lists several recommendations for promoting private contributions to development assistance. They include clarification of the existing tax rules, an evaluation of the effectiveness of such rules, providing better information to private donors using the German model, acquiring a greater knowledge of private aid and better monitoring it, rethinking the help the state can provide to private donors, politically valorizing private assistance, accelerating the integration of the various European policies on foreign aid, establishing a legal framework for European associations and foundations, and facilitating new ways of giving.[59]

---

[54] *The Accra High Level Forum (HLF3) and the Accra Agenda for Action*, OECD, DEVELOPMENT CO-OPERATION DIRECTORATE, http://www.oecd.org/document/3/0,3343,en_2649_3236398_41297219_1_1_1_1,00.html (last visited Aug. 8, 2011).

[55] CODE GENERAL DES IMPOTS art. 200, *available at* LEGIFRANCE, http://legifrance.gouv.fr/ (*Les codes en vigueur*).

[56] *Id.*

[57] *Id.* art. 885-0 V bis A.

[58] *Id.* art. art. 238 bis.

[59] Rapport 2009-M.089-02, *supra* note 7.

III. Foreign Aid Appropriations Process

Each autumn, the government presents its draft Finance Law (*projet de loi de finances*) for the upcoming year. Part one of this document summarizes the state's resources and authorizes the raising of taxes while part two states the amounts appropriated for each of the state policy missions.[60] Following a recent reform, expenditure-oriented budgets have been replaced by a budget presented in the form of major public policies called "missions."[61] Each mission comprises a set of programs with their own specific objectives and performance targets. Programs are further broken down into subprograms (*actions*). This breakdown into subprograms is only advisory and for guidance only. Parliament debates and votes on the missions and the programs within the mission.[62] Each program has a clearly identified coordinator(s). The program coordinator may reallocate appropriations between subprograms or types of expenditures within a program (with the exception of personnel expenditures) for a more flexible management of the appropriations.[63] The draft budget law is examined by Parliament and approved within seventy days of its submission.[64]

The Official Development Assistance Mission comprises twenty-three programs for 2011 with three of them accounting for most of the budget appropriations regarding the cooperation policy. They are as follows:

- **Program 110: Economic and Financial Aid for Development, under the Ministry of Economy and Finance**. This program is the major financial instrument to fight poverty in the world. Most of the funds are directed to multinational development institutions, primarily the International Development Association, which is the World Bank fund for the poorest and the African Fund for Development. Other funds that receive some aid include the Asian Development Fund, the Inter-American Development Bank's Multilateral Investment Fund, and the Inter-American Development Bank's Fund for Special Operations. The program also comprises macroeconomic aids and partly deals with the treatment of the debt of poor countries.

- **Program 209: Solidarity with Developing Countries, under the Ministry of Foreign and European Affairs**. This program covers bilateral and multilateral aid. Multilateral aid mainly covers contributions to the European Development Fund, the Global Fund to Fight Aids, and voluntary contributions to various United Nations bodies.

---

[60] Loi de Finance et Lois de Financement à l'Assemblée Nationale at 12–14 (updated as of Aug. 31, 2010), http://www.assemblee-nationale.fr/connaissance/lois_finances_lois_financement/lois_finances_financement_actualisee.pdf.

[61] *Id.*

[62] *Id.* at 129, 130.

[63] *Id.*

[64] *Id.* at 88.

- **Program 301: Co-development and Migration, under the Ministry of Immigration, Integration, National Identity and Solidarity Development.** The aim of this program is to link migration and development policy in order to facilitate the management of migratory flows. France promotes a policy of supportive development with countries of origin within the framework of agreements for the concerted management of migratory flows. Countries that agree to enter into such agreements with France receive ODA preferential treatment. This program also covers aid granted to encourage immigrants to leave France and voluntarily return to their countries of origin. Program 301 represents a small part of the total aid for the Official Development Assistance Mission.[65]

There are some other ODA expenditures that can be found in the budget outside of the Official Development Assistance Mission. They are part of other missions and programs whose resources are only partly earmarked for development assistance. They include budget missions such as External Action of the State, Research and Higher Education, Immigration, Asylum and Integration, and Defense and Security. The training of police or gendarmerie forces in developing countries, for example, accounts for a small percentage of the program for the gendarmerie, which is under the Defense and Security Mission.[66]

Parliament receives a great deal of information on the expenditure determinants. Annual Performance Plans for each mission are attached to the budget proposal. For each program in a mission they set forth the amount to be appropriated, the targets to be met, a cost analysis, the performance indicators, and results obtained in the previous year and expected for the following year.[67] A crosscutting policy document entitled "France's Policy for Development" is also attached to the draft budget. This document presents a synthesis of all the programs that contribute to France's cooperation policy, its coherence, a comprehensive strategy for performance improvement, and the budgetary resources required. The policy document identifies the programs and the ministries that contribute fully or partly to France's cooperation policy.[68]

IV. Implementing Agencies

A. French Development Agency

The main implementing agency for foreign aid is the French Development Agency (*Agence Francaise de Developpement*, AFD), a public establishment created in 1998. Its status is defined by the Monetary and Financial Code.[69] It replaces the Central Fund for Economic Cooperation, which operated as a bank and provided loans. AFD is both a public establishment

---

[65] STRATEGY 2011–DEVELOPMENT COOPERATION: A FRENCH VISION, *supra* note 1, at 57, 58; Rapport 2857, *supra* note 5.

[66] STRATEGY 2011–DEVELOPMENT COOPERATION: A FRENCH VISION, *supra* note 1, at 58.

[67] *Id.* at 55, 56.

[68] *Id.*

[69] CODE MONÉTAIRE ET FINANCIER arts. R.516-3 to R.516-20.

in charge of implementing France's policy in matters of development assistance and a development bank. It is principally monitored by the Ministry of Foreign and European Affairs and the Ministry of Economy. In fact, the Ministry of Economy plays a particularly important role due to the financial establishment status of the AFD. The French State owns AFD capital.[70]

The Ministry of Foreign and European Affairs is also directly responsible for the allocations of development funds in some areas. There is a division of tasks between AFD and the Ministry of Foreign and European Affairs. AFD concentrates on reducing poverty, promoting economic development, and preserving public global goods. The Ministry of Foreign and European Affairs is directly responsible for promoting the rule of law, institutional reform, education, and cultural and scientific cooperation.[71]

AFD employs approximately 1,900 persons. Most of its activity is exercised abroad through its network of in-country field offices and bureaus located in developing countries, emerging countries, and the French Overseas Territories.[72] Its governing board of directors comprises sixteen members including six representatives from the French state; two deputies from the National Assembly; one senator; five members chosen for their expertise in economic, financial, or environmental and sustainable issues; and two employee-elected members.[73]

To fulfill its missions, AFD receives public development funds from its supervisory ministries, the Ministry of Foreign and European Affairs, the Ministry of Economy, and the Ministry of Immigration. In addition, AFD finances itself through bonds issued in international capital markets and private placement.[74] AFD has a subsidiary, PROPARCO (*Promotion et Participation pour la Cooperation Economique*), that encourages private sector investment to promote growth and sustainable development.[75]

AFD uses a broad range of financial instruments to meet the specific needs of the receiving countries. They include, for example, subsidized long-term loans, grants, and environmental credit lines to banks to encourage them to make loans that will benefit the environment. The French State mandates the geographic areas where AFD operates, mainly sub-Saharan Africa, Asia, and South America.[76] Finally, AFD manages the French Global Environment Fund on behalf of the Ministry of Foreign and European Affairs.[77]

---

[70] COUR DES COMPTES, LA PLACE ET LE RÔLE DE L'AGENCE FRANÇAISE DE DÉVELOPPEMENT (AFD) DANS L'AIDE PUBLIQUE AU DÉVELOPPEMENT, http://www.ccomptes.fr/fr/CC/documents/divers/58_2_agence_francaise_developpement.pdf (last visited Aug. 8, 2011).

[71] *Le Dispositif Institutionnel Français: Introduction, supra* note 28.

[72] AGENCE FRANÇAISE DE DÉVELOPPEMENT, ADF 2010 ANNUAL REPORT 6, http://www.afd.fr/webdav/site/afd/shared/PUBLICATIONS/Colonne-droite/Rapport-annuel-AFD-VA.pdf.

[73] Code Monetaire et Financier art. R 516-13.

[74] AGENCE FRANÇAISE DE DÉVELOPPEMENT, *supra* note 72, at 17.

[75] *Id.* at 20.

[76] *Id.* at 4.

[77] *Le Dispositif Institutionnel Français: Introduction, supra* note 28.

B. France Expertise Internationale

France Expertise Internationale (FEI) was created by Law 2010-873 of July 27, 2010, on External Action of the State[78] and an implementing Decree of February 25, 2011.[79] It replaces *France Cooperation Internationale*, which was established by the Ministry of Foreign and European Affairs in 2002. FEI is a public agency that promotes French technical assistance and expertise abroad. It is supervised by the Ministry of Foreign and European Affairs. It carries out the engineering and management of projects financed by the state, local authorities, the EU, multilateral donors, and foreign states in this field. FEI acts either as an implementing agency or in support of a contracting authority for projects its donors or clients have entrusted to it by direct agreement or following a competitive bidding process.[80]

V. Other Types of 'Aid'

A. Emergency Aid

The main financial instrument used to meet emergency humanitarian situations is the Emergency Humanitarian Fund (*Fonds d'urgence humanitaire*). In addition to the funds appropriated by the annual Finance Law, the Fund may receive additional contributions from local authorities, individuals, and corporations.[81] It finances various types of actions:

- Direct actions, including shipments of food, medicine, shelter, etc.

- Funding actions implemented through the French Embassy and/or Consulates

- Funding actions implemented by NGOs

- Exceptional contributions to international bodies (e.g., UNICEF, WHO)[82]

Humanitarian action is also indirectly funded through France's contributions to the EU budget, which support the activities of the European Commission–Humanitarian Aid and Civil Protection.[83]

---

[78] Loi 2010-873 du 27 juillet 2010 relative a l'action exterieure de L'Etat [Law 2010-873 of July 27, 2010, on External Action of the State], LEGIFRANCE, http://legifrance.gouv.fr/affichTexte.do?cidTexte=JORFTEXT0000 22521532&fastPos=1&fastReqId=1217444084&categorieLien=id&oldAction=rechTexte.

[79] Décret n° 2011-212 du 25 février 2011 relatif à France expertise internationale [Decree 2011-212 of February 25, 2011 on France Expertise Internationale], LEGIFRANCE, http://legifrance.gouv.fr/affichTexte. do?cidTexte=JORFTEXT000023631691&fastPos=1&fastReqId=1810359409&categorieLien=id&oldAction=rechT exte.

[80] *Id.* art. 2.

[81] *L'Etat: Le Fonds d'urgence humanitaire*, MINISTÈRE DES AFFAIRES ETRANGÈRES ET EUROPÉENNES, http://www.diplomatie.gouv.fr/fr/actions-france_830/action-humanitaire-urgence_1039/acteurs-francais_2379/etat_2389/fonds-urgence-humanitaire_4241.html (last visited Aug. 8, 2011).

[82] *Id.*

[83] *Background & Mandate*, EUROPEAN COMMISSION–HUMANITARIAN AID AND CIVIL PROTECTION, http://ec.europa.eu/echo/about/what/history_en.htm (last visited Aug. 8, 2011).

B. College Scholarships to Foreign Students

Supporting education for developing countries is a major priority for France.[84] Approximately 260,000 foreign students receive higher education at almost no charge in France each year.[85] France also has decided to promote universal primary education and equal access to education for girls and boys between 2010 and 2015, as 75% of illiterate persons worldwide are women.[86] It contributes to the Fast Track Initiative, a partnership of donors and developing countries, multilateral institutions, the private sector, and civil society organizations that want all children around the world to receive a quality education.[87]

France concentrates its education aid on the fourteen priority poor countries and some moderate income African countries with which it has close ties.[88]

C. Foreign Remittances

France supports migrant remittances to developing countries. France took several actions to facilitate these transactions, including lowering transfer costs, promoting more flexible regulations for the transfers, and creating certain types of savings accounts benefiting from a favorable tax treatment where the migrants invest in productive development in their country of origin.[89]

D. Debt Relief

In the highly indebted countries (HIPCs), France uses a debt reduction process by signing Debt-reduction and Development Contracts (*contrats de désendettement-développement*, C2D), which make it possible for beneficiary states to channel budgetary savings from debt cancellation into spending aimed at reducing poverty.[90] This approach concerns the bilateral ODA debt that is owed to France even after France's assistance under the enhanced HIPC initiative. This initiative was launched by the World Bank and the International Monetary Fund to ensure that no poor country faces a debt it cannot manage.[91]

---

[84] MINISTÈRE DES AFFAIRES ETRANGÈRES ET EUROPÉENNES, FRENCH INTERNAL ACTION FOR EDUCATION IN DEVELOPING COUNTRIES 2010–2015, http://www.diplomatie.gouv.fr/en/IMG/pdf/Education_in_developing_countries_en.pdf (last visited Aug. 8, 2011).

[85] STRATEGY 2011–DEVELOPMENT COOPERATION: A FRENCH VISION, *supra* note 1, at 36.

[86] MINISTÈRE DES AFFAIRES ETRANGÈRES ET EUROPÉENNES, *supra* note 84.

[87] *Id.*

[88] *Id.*

[89] STRATEGY 2011–DEVELOPMENT COOPERATION: A FRENCH VISION, *supra* note 1, at 22, 36.

[90] *Mettre en place les contrats de désendettement et de développement: Présentation*, MINISTÈRE DES AFFAIRES ETRANGÈRES ET EUROPÉENNES, http://www.diplomatie.gouv.fr/fr/entrees-thematiques_830/aide-au-developpement_1060/gouvernance-democratique_1053/gouvernance-financiere_17823/mettre-place-les-contrats-desendettement-developpement_20473/index.html (last visited Aug. 8, 2011).

[91] *The Enhanced HIPC Initiative – Overview*, THE WORLD BANK, http://web.worldbank.org/WBSITE/EXTERNAL/TOPICS/EXTDEBTDEPT/0,,contentMDK:21254881~menuPK:64166739~pagePK:641666 89~piPK:64166646~theSitePK:469043~isCURL:Y,00.html (last visited Aug. 8, 2011).

Under a C2D the debtor continues to service the remaining ODA debt, but France refinances the same amount through grants. The grant money is then allocated to poverty reduction programs that have been selected by joint agreement between France and the receiving country—generally basic education, primary health care, infrastructure, rural development, and natural resource management.[92]

E. Innovative Financing

In December 2010, the United Nations General Assembly adopted resolution A/RES/65/146 on innovative mechanisms of financing for development. Innovative financing is aimed at supplementing traditional ODA. The international community has been urged to develop new sources of financing to achieve the Millennium Development Goals. France has been involved in this debate from its beginning. It hosts the permanent secretariat of the Leading Group on Innovative Financing. This group is the main forum for the discussion of innovative financing. It comprises fifty-nine countries and works with the main international organizations, including the World Bank, World Health Organization, United Nations International Children's Emergency Fund, and nongovernmental organizations.[93]

Some of the main proposals that have been implemented are as follows:

- **UNITAID**: This international drug purchase facility was created in 2006 by Brazil, Chile, France, Norway, and the United Kingdom. It is funded in particular by a tax on airline tickets adopted by eleven countries including France. UNITAID's mission is to centralize the purchase of medicines to obtain the best possible price primarily for people located in poor countries in order to treat HIV/AIDS, malaria, and tuberculosis.[94]

- **International Finance Facility for Immunization (IFFIm)**: IFFIm was created in 2006 by France and the United Kingdom. It is an initiative that raises capital to be managed by the Global Alliance for Vaccines and Immunization (GAVI) in order to increase access to immunization in developing countries.[95]

- **Advance Market Commitment (AMC)**: An Advanced Market Commitment is a binding agreement between a government or a financial institution and a pharmaceutical company under which a certain amount of funding is given to such

---

[92] *Mettre en place les contrats de désendettement et de développement: Présentation*, *supra* note 90.

[93] *Innovative Financing for Development-France ONU*, PERMANENT MISSION OF FRANCE TO THE UNITED NATIONS, http://franceonu.org/spip.php?article4365 (last visited Aug. 8, 2011); *Innovative Ways to Fund Development*, MINISTÈRE DES AFFAIRES ETRANGÈRES ET EUROPÈENNES, http://www.diplomatie.gouv.fr/en/france-priorities_1/development-and-humanitarian-action_2108/innovative-ways-to-fund-development_2109/index.html (last visited Aug. 8, 2011).

[94] *Mission*, UNITAID, http://www.unitaid.eu/en/about/mission-mainmenu-89.html (last visited Aug. 8, 2011).

[95] *Overview*, IFFIM, http://www.iffim.org/about/overview/ (last visited Aug. 8, 2011).

company to finance research for vaccines against specific diseases causing high mortality in developing countries.[96]

Additional initiatives are being considered or are already underway. France, for example, supports a tax of 0.005% on financial transactions to fund either food security, education, health, or the fight against climate. Another available mechanism, referred to as Debt2Health, allows a donor to cancel publicly-held debt if the recipient government transfers to the Global Fund to Fight AIDS, Tuberculosis and Malaria an equivalent amount, which is then used by the Fund to increase its health spending in that country.[97]

Prepared by Nicole Atwill
Senior Foreign Law Specialist
September 2011

---

[96] *Advanced Market Commitments for Vaccines*, WORLD HEALTH ORGANIZATION (July 19, 2006), http://www.who.int/immunization/newsroom/amcs/en/index.html.

[97] *Debt2Health*, THE GLOBAL FUND TO FIGHT AIDS, TUBERCULOSIS AND MALARIA, http://www.theglobal fund.org/en/innovativefinancing/debt2health/?lang=en (last visited Aug. 8, 2011).

LAW LIBRARY OF CONGRESS

GERMANY

REGULATION OF FOREIGN AID

Executive Summary

Germany is one of the largest donors of developmental aid, having ranked in the second and fourth places in overall donations in recent years. Germany's contribution, however, ranks below twelve other countries when measured in terms of a percentage of its Gross National Income (GNI). In 2010, Germany contributed 0.38% of its GNI, yet Germany promises that by 2015 it will meet the 0.7 percent goal that European countries have stipulated.

Germany is engaged in bilateral development cooperation with about fifty countries; among these are poor yet well-governed countries, fragile states that are troubled by conflicts, and some emerging economies that still qualify for aid. Germany aims to make its aid an effective tool for lasting improvements in the partner countries.

German bilateral aid focuses on good governance, education, rural development, climate control, sustainable development, and a strengthening of the private sector. To enhance these goals, the German Federal Ministry for Economic Cooperation and Development reviews cooperation agreements for effectiveness and partner countries are reviewed for compliance with standards of good government. Germany is reluctant to grant budget support to countries that have not proven their ability to use it wisely.

Germany donates its largest multilateral aid contribution to the European Union but is also a sizable contributor to institutions of the United Nations and the World Bank. In international efforts, Germany often takes a leadership role on the linking of climate control to developmental cooperation.

I. Introduction

A. Official Development Assistance Figures

For the year 2010, Germany reported net distributions of US$12,723 million in official development assistance (ODA) to the Development Cooperation Directorate (DCD-DAC) of the Organisation for Economic Co-operation and Development (OECD).[1] For 2009, Germany reported US$12,079 million, and for 2008, it reported US$13,981 million.[2] In 2008, Germany

---

[1] *Statistics, ODA by Donor*, OECD, http://stats.oecd.org/Index.aspx?DatasetCode=ODA_DONOR (last visited Oct. 18, 2011) (select Germany in "donor" box, then select Net Disbursements under "Flow type").

[2] *Id.*

was the second largest donor of net ODA, exceeded only by the United States.[3] In 2009 and 2010, Germany placed fourth among net ODA donors, after the United States, Great Britain, and France.[4]

Germany ranked lower, however, when comparing percentages of Gross National Income (GNI)[5] that were disbursed as ODA. During the period 2008 through 2010, Germany ranked in thirteenth place, having contributed 0.38% of GNI in 2008 and 2010, and 0.35% in 2009.[6] These percentages placed Germany below many European countries, among them several Scandinavian countries and the Netherlands, which had already exceeded the 0.7% of GNI that European countries are expected to meet by 2015.[7] Nevertheless, Germany is hopeful that the goal will be met by 2015, albeit with reliance on private-public partnerships and innovative financing methods to supplement the contribution from tax revenues.[8]

During the period 2008 through 2010, Germany disbursed 60 to 65% of its net ODA in the form of bilateral assistance.[9] Of the remaining 35 to 40% of ODA that Germany disbursed multilaterally, close to 60% consisted of contributions to institutions of the European Union (EU), and another 25% to World Bank institutions, with the bulk going to the International Development Association (IDA), the World Bank's fund for the poorest countries.[10] Germany's overall multilateral contribution during this period made it the largest donor of multilateral aid worldwide.[11]

---

[3] *Deutschland zweitgrösster Geber bei der Entwicklungshilfe*, DEUTSCHE WELLE (Apr. 4, 2008), http://www.dw-world.de/dw/article/0,,3244957,00.html.

[4] *Geber im Vergleich 2010 – Veränderungen gegenüber 2009*, BUNDESMINISTERIUM FÜR WIRTSCHAFTLICHE ZUSAMMENARBEIT UND ENTWICKLUNG [BMZ], http://www.bmz.de/de/ministerium/zahlen_fakten/Geber_im_Vergleich-Veraenderung_2010_gegenueber_2009.pdf (last visited Aug. 17, 2011).

[5] GNI is the Gross Domestic Product (GDP) less primary income payable to nonresident units plus primary income receivable from nonresident units. *See Glossary of Statistical Terms: Gross National Income (GNI)*, OECD, http://stats.oecd.org/ glossary/detail.asp?ID=1176 (last updated Mar. 5, 2003).

[6] *Geber im Vergleich 2010, supra* note 4.

[7] *The 0.7% Target: An In-Depth Look,* UN MILLENNIUM PROJECT, http://www.unmillenniumproject.org/press/07.htm (last visited Oct. 7, 2011).

[8] Press Release, BMZ, Deutschland steigerte 2010 seine öffentliche Entwicklungszusammenarbeit um 10 Prozent im Vergleich zu 2009 (Apr. 6, 2011), http://www.bmz.de/de/presse/aktuelleMeldungen/2011/april/20110406_pm_49_oda/index.html; Press Release, Deutscher Bundestag, Finanzmarktsteuer und Regulierung der Spekulation stehen auf Agenda des G20-Gipfels in Cannes, http://www.bundestag.de/presse/hib/2011_10/2011_433/01.html (last visited Nov. 8, 2011).

[9] *Statistics, supra* note 1. Germany finds this division between bilateral and multilateral aid appropriate. *See Soll Deutschland die multilaterale ODA stärken? Argumente und Evidenz*, BMZ, http://www.bmz.de/de/publikationen/reihen/strategiepapiere/spezial155pdf.pdf (last visited Nov. 1, 2011).

[10] Id.

[11] DEUTSCHLAND ENTWICKLUNGSAUSSCHUSS (DAC) PEER REVIEW 2010 [hereinafter PEER REVIEW] 62, OECD, http://www.oecd.org/dataoecd/5/43/46270433.pdf (last visited Oct. 11, 2011).

B. Private Contribution Figures

Germany has many nongovernmental organizations (NGOs) and philanthropic foundations that provide aid to developing countries.[12] For the year 2010, the German Statistical Office reported a total of €1,105 million (about US$1,461 million) in nongovernmental developmental aid. Thirty-one percent of this private aid went to Africa, 27% to Asia, and 28% to the Americas.[13] The Statistical Office compiles these figures on the basis of voluntary reports of the donors. Only aid that lives up to international standards is included. Disbursements that private parties channel through governmental organizations are not captured as private aid but are included in the ODA report to DCD-DAC.[14]

C. Snapshot of Foreign Aid Activity

Germany began giving assistance to the developing world in the 1950s,[15] after Germany itself had been the recipient of massive aid in the form of the Marshall Plan.[16] Germany's commitment to foreign aid is rooted in historic, political, economic, ecological, and moral considerations. Of these, the moral argument—the desire to help those in need—is the most prevalent justification in the eyes of the German population.[17]

From a historical perspective, Germany feels some responsibility to provide aid to its former colonies, particularly to the country of Namibia,[18] where German forces committed genocide in the first decade of the twentieth century.[19] Aside from this historic motive, Germany currently does not have any specific foreign policy consideration in its developmental aid program.[20] In Germany, as elsewhere, foreign aid's potential to enhance stability, deter terrorism, and reduce migratory movements is appreciated.[21] To promote these goals, Germany

---

[12] Rolf Rosenkranz, *Organization Profile, Top German Global Development NGOs: A Primer*, DEVEX (June 7, 2011), http://www.devex.com/en/articles/top-german-global-development-ngos-a-primer.

[13] *Entwicklungszusammenarbeit – Leistungen von Nichtregierungsorganisationen: Ihr Beitrag zur Statistik*, BMZ, http://www.destatis.de/jetspeed/portal/cms/Sites/destatis/Internet/DE/Content/Publikationen/Fach veroeffentlichungen/FinanzenSteuern/InfoblattEntwicklungZusammenarbeit,property=file.pdf (last visited Nov. 25, 2011).

[14] Id.

[15] *Die Geschichte des Ministeriums*, BMZ, http://www.bmz.de/de/ministerium/50JahreBMZ/ geschichte/index.html (last visited Nov. 14, 2011).

[16] Der Marshall-Plan und ein Blick zurück, VERSICHERUNGSWIRTSCHAFT 820 (1987).

[17] Uwe Andersen, *Deutschlands Entwicklungspolitik im Internationalen Vergleich*, BUNDESZENTRALE FÜR POLITISCHE BILDUNG at 1, http://www.bpb.de/publikationen/HWWQD2,0,0,Deutschlands_Entwicklungspolitik_ im_internationalen_Vergleich.html (last visited Oct. 11, 2011).

[18] *Id.* at 2.

[19] Mechthild Küpper, *Eine Geste des Bedauerns*, FRANKFURTER ALLGEMEINE ZEITUNG [FAZ], Oct. 1, 2011, at 9.

[20] Until 1990, West Germany used developmental aid to influence recipient countries to refuse international law recognition to East Germany. *See* Andersen, *supra* note 17, at 2.

[21] *Id.*

encourages the political participation of the populations of partner countries in both local and national matters. In addition, German developmental policy aims to strengthen civil society, improve laws, and make governments more accountable in the partner countries.[22]

From an economic perspective, Germany adheres to the belief that economic development is essential to overall sustainable development[23] and therefore promotes the development of the private sector in partner countries.[24] Germany has in the past concentrated on cooperating with countries that show some prospect for improvement. This has led the OECD Peer Review of 2005 to suggest that Germany did not focus enough on the least developed countries and recommended giving more aid to sub-Saharan Africa.[25] It appears that Germany heeded these admonitions and increased its involvement in sub-Saharan Africa,[26] sending it about 26% of German bilateral ODA in 2009.[27]

Germany is engaged in development cooperation with over fifty partner countries. Included among these are poor yet well-governed, developing countries; fragile states that are troubled by conflict; and some emerging economies that still qualify for aid.[28] In choosing partner countries, Germany considers whether German cooperation would be useful from a global perspective and whether the government in the potential partner country is willing to reform. Other criteria are the poverty of the country and any historical or political links to Germany.[29]

Bilateral assistance is given in the form of financial aid, technical cooperation, and/or personal consultation. Germany refers to its developmental aid as "developmental cooperation," thus stressing the partnership aspect of the relationship. Germany feels strongly that developmental cooperation should have lasting effects in the partner country,[30] as envisioned by the Paris Declaration.[31]

---

[22] DIE FÖRDERUNG KONSTRUKTIVER STAAT-GESELLSCHAFT-BEZIEHUNGEN – LEGITIMITÄT, TRANSPARENZ, RECHENSCHAFT, BMZ (Jan. 2010), http://www.bmz.de/de/publikationen/reihen/strategiepapiere/Strategie papier298_01_2010_de.pdf.

[23] BMZ, GERMAN DEVELOPMENT POLICY AT A GLANCE 7 (Feb. 2011), http://www.bmz.de/en/publications/ type_of_publication/special_publications/BMZ_Policy_at_a_glance.pdf.

[24] Growth. Education. Unity. The Coalition Agreement Between the CDU, CSU and FDP for the 17th Legislative Period [hereinafter Coalition Agreement] 182–85 (Oct. 26, 2009), http://www.cdu.de/doc/pdfc/091215-koalitionsvertrag-2009-2013-englisch.pdf.

[25] PEER REVIEW, *supra* note 11, at 56 (referring to the 2005 Peer Review).

[26] *Afrika südlich der Sahara*, BMZ, http://www.bmz.de/de/was_wir_machen/laender_regionen/ subsahara/index.html (last visited Oct. 11, 2011).

[27] *Bilaterale ODA nach Instrumenten und Ländern 20109 im Detail*, BMZ, http://www.bmz.de/de/ ministerium/zahlen_fakten/Bilaterale_ODA_nach_Instrumenten_und_Laendern_2010_im_Detail.pdf (last visited Jan. 9, 2012).

[28] GERMAN DEVELOPMENT POLICY, *supra* note 23, at 8.

[29] *Id.*

[30] Coalition Agreement, *supra* note 24.

[31] OECD, Development Co-operation Directorate, The Paris Declaration on Aid Effectiveness and the Accra Agenda for Action, Paris, Feb. 28–Mar. 2, 2005, at 1, http://www.oecd.org/dataoecd/ 30/63/43911948.pdf.

German cooperation projects focus on good governance, education, health, rural development, climate protection, environmental protection, resource management, and encouragement of business and the private sector.[32] Germany devotes considerable resources to projects that have a favorable effect on climate control.[33] In addition, Germany has taken the lead in international efforts that link development aid with climate control and other environmental issues.[34]

II. Legal Framework

A. Regulation of ODAs

1. Overview

In Germany, the granting of ODA is a matter of policy formulated by the executive branch of government.[35] Some experts have decried the lack of a statutory basis for developmental aid, yet have conceded that the existing parliamentary oversight of the executive branch is sufficient to meet constitutional requirements.[36]

German policy on developmental cooperation professes to be based on adherence to the principles of

- the United Nations Millennium Goals of 2000,[37]

- the Monterrey Consensus of the International Conference on Financing for Development,[38]

- the Paris Declaration of 2005,[39] and

---

[32] Coalition Agreement, *supra* note 24.

[33] Id.

[34] DIE BUNDESREGIERUNG, AKTIONSPLAN ANPASSUNG DER DEUTSCHEN ANPASSUNGSSTRATEGIE AN DEN KLIMAWANDEL 36 (Aug. 31, 2011), http://www.bmu.de/files/pdfs/allgemein/application/pdf/aktions plan_anpassung_klimawandel_bf.pdf.

[35] The Constitution grants the Federal Chancellor (head of the executive branch of government) broad powers to shape the general policy for the government, GRUNDGESETZ FÜR DIE BUNDESREPUBLIK DEUTSCHLAND [BASIC LAW], May 23, 1949, BUNDESGESETZBLATT [BGBL.] 1, *as amended*, art. 65, thus eliminating the need for legislation for matters that fall within the power of the executive branch.

[36] Hannes Grimm, Parlamentarische Kontrolldefizite der Deutschen Entwicklungszusammenarbeit, DIE ÖFFENTLICHE VERWALTUNG 24 (1992).

[37] *The 0.7% Target: An In-Depth Look*, UN MILLENNIUM PROJECT (Commissioned by the Secretary General and Supported by the UN Development Group), http://www.unmillenniumproject.org/press/07.htm (last visited Oct. 7, 2011).

[38] Monterrey Consensus of the International Conference on Financing for Development, Final Text of Agreements and Commitments Adopted at Monterrey, Mexico, Mar. 18–22, 2002, http://www.un.org/esa/ffd/monterrey/MonterreyConsensus.pdf.

- the Accra Agenda for Action of 2008.[40]

Germany, however, is not entirely in agreement with the preference for budget support over other modalities of aid that is expressed or implied in the Paris Declaration[41] and the Accra Agenda.[42] Germany favors a more differentiated approach to minimize the risks inherent in budgetary assistance.[43]

German policy on developmental aid was most recently formulated in the coalition agreement of October 26, 2009, of the parties forming the government during the seventeenth legislative period.[44] These principles stress

- applying minimum standards regarding the rule of law and the observance of human rights;

- sustaining the fight against hunger and structural deficiencies in the spirit of the UN Millennium Goals;

- strengthening good governance, self-determination, and self-help capabilities through strengthening civil society; and

- harnessing business and industry to foster sustainable economic development.[45]

German policy on developmental aid appears to be supported by a broad consensus of the political powers.[46] Nevertheless, criticism has often been expressed from both the right and the left. Whereas some domestic critics find German developmental policy inefficient and its implementation wasteful,[47] humanitarian aid organizations deplore the recent German emphasis on cooperation with the private sector.[48]

---

[39] Paris Declaration on Aid Effectiveness, Paris, Feb. 28 – Mar. 2, 2005, *reprinted in* OECD, THE PARIS DECLARATION ON AID EFFECTIVENESS AND THE ACCRA AGENDA FOR ACTION 1, http://www.oecd.org/dataoecd/11/41/34428351.pdf.

[40] Accra Agenda for Action, Sept. 4, 2008, *reprinted in* OECD, THE PARIS DECLARATION ON AID EFFECTIVENESS AND THE ACCRA AGENDA FOR ACTION 15, http://www.oecd.org/dataoecd/30/63/43911948.pdf.

[41] BMZ, DIE IMPLEMENTIERUNG DER PARISER ERKLÄRUNG: FALLSTUDIE DEUTSCHLAND. KURZFASSUNG DER EVALUIERUNG 3 (July 2008), http://www.bmz.de/de/publikationen/reihen/evaluierungen/evaluierungs berichte_ab_2006/EvalBericht040.pdf.

[42] BUDGETHILFE ALS INSTRUMENT DER ENTWICKLUNGSZUSAMMENARBEIT 21 (Gerhard Wahlers ed., 2007), http://www.kas.de/wf/doc/kas_15210-544-1-30.pdf.

[43] *See infra* notes 93–95 and accompanying text.

[44] Coalition Agreement, *supra* note 24.

[45] GERMAN DEVELOPMENT POLICY, *supra* note 23, at 6.

[46] PEER REVIEW, *supra* note 11, at 39.

[47] Manfred Neumann, BAYERISCHE VERWALTUNGSBLÄTTER 587 (2005).

[48] TERRE DES HOMMES, THE REALITY OF AID 2010: A CRITICAL ASSESSMENT OF GERMAN DEVELOPMENT POLICY 1 (18th Report, 2010), http://www.welthungerhilfe.de/fileadmin/media/pdf/Wirklichkeit_Entwicklungshilfe/ Wirklichkeit_englisch-Kurzfassung_18_2010_Internet.pdf.

2. Implementing Agencies

The Federal Ministry for Economic Cooperation and Development (*Bundesministerium für wirtschaftliche Zusammenarbeit und Entwicklung*, BMZ) shapes developmental policy for approval by the Federal Cabinet.[49] The BMZ also decides on the bilateral developmental projects that will be undertaken. These, however, are implemented by government-owned corporations that act on a private law basis, although subordinated to the BMZ.[50]

The BMZ is not the only federal ministry that makes and implements policy on developmental cooperation. The Federal Ministry of Finance is instrumental in the budget process (see discussion, *infra*). Other ministries are involved through consultations and oversight.[51] Among these is the Federal Ministry for Environment, Nature Conservation, and Nuclear Safety[52] on projects and issues relating to the environment. The Federal Foreign Office (*Auswärtiges Amt*) administers humanitarian aid.[53] Even the Federal Ministry of Defense cooperates at times with civilian developmental aid organizations when the participation of the military is needed for a project that provides humanitarian and developmental aid.[54]

The BMZ is staffed by about 600 civil servants. About fifty of these serve in the field, on a rotating basis, either in partner countries or with international organizations.[55] The BMZ is structured into four directorates. One of these is in charge of administrative tasks and cooperation with NGOs, private companies, the German states and municipalities, and other contributors to developmental aid. The other three directorates specialize in geographic areas. In addition, the BMZ has a special auditing and evaluation unit, and a Scholarly Council (*Wissenschaftlicher Beirat beim BMZ*) that advises the BMZ on policy issues and publishes many of its findings.[56]

Developmental aid is implemented by government-owned companies that provide either technical or financial assistance. These, in turn, have contractual relationships with the relevant

---

[49] For information on the structure and organization of the Federal Ministry for Economic Cooperation and Development, BMZ, *see* http://www.bmz.de/en/index.html (last visited Nov. 7, 2011).

[50] German Development Policy, *supra* note 23, at 9.

[51] Andersen, *supra* note 17, at 3.

[52] BUNDESMINISTERIUM FÜR UMWELT, NATURSCHUTZ UND REAKTORSICHERHEIT, http://www.bmu.de (last visited Nov. 7, 2011).

[53] ORGANISATIONSPLAN DES AUSWÄRTIGEN AMTS ¶ VN 05 (updated through Jan. 9, 2012), http://www.auswaertiges-amt.de/cae/servlet/contentblob/382698/publicationFile/160910/Organisationsplan-Druckversion.pdf.

[54] Stephan Löwenstein, *Zivil-militärisches Herbstmanöver*, FAZ, Sept. 22, 2011, at 10.

[55] *Ministry, Structure and Organization*, BMZ, http://www.bmz.de/en/ministry/structure/ index.html (last visited Nov. 7, 2011).

[56] BMZ, ORGANISATIONSPLAN DES BUNDESMINISTERIUMS FÜRWIRTSCHAFTLICHE ZUSAMMENARBEIT UND ENTWICKLUNG (updated through Sept. 1, 2011), http://www.bmz.de/de/ministerium/dokumente/organisations plan.pdf.

organizations in the partner countries. The BMZ supervises the aid work of the German implementing companies.[57]

Recently, Germany reformed its implementing organizations for technical cooperation by merging three companies into one: the newly created German Company for Technical Cooperation (*Deutsche Gesellschaft für internationale Zusammenarbeit*, GIZ).[58] The GIZ commenced operations on January 1, 2011. Through the merger, Germany hopes to streamline operations, avoid duplication, and increase efficiency and transparency.[59]

GIZ works not only for the BMZ but also on behalf of other German ministries, and cooperates with German states and municipalities as well as with public and private sector clients in Germany and abroad. It appears that compared to the former companies, GIZ functions more like a business and puts more emphasis on involving the private sector, both in Germany and in the partner countries.[60]

The implementing company for financial assistance is KfW Development Finance (*KfW Entwicklungsbank*), one of the banks in the government-owned KfW bank group.[61] Financial cooperation with private parties in the partner countries is carried out by the German Investment and Development Company.[62]

In addition to these major players in developmental cooperation, there are many other actors. There are some highly specialized agencies along with development programs of states and municipalities. Moreover, much partnering occurs between the governmental agencies and private organizations.[63]

3. Restrictions – Tied Aid

Germany has not entirely lived up to the recommendations on untying aid that were made by the OECD/DAC and the Accra Action Plan.[64] Especially with respect to technical

---

[57] *Ministry, Players – Implementing Organisations*, BMZ, http://www.bmz.de/en/what_we_do/ approaches/bilateral_development_cooperation/players/implementing_organisations/index.html (last visited Nov. 7, 2011).

[58] *Deutsche Gesellschaft für internationale Zusammenarbeit (GIZ)*, BMZ, http://www.bmz.de/en/what_ we_do/approaches/bilateral_development_cooperation/players/selection/giz/index.html (last visited Nov. 7, 2011).

[59] Id.

[60] *About GIZ*, http://www.giz.de/en/profile.html?PHPSESSID=d630390644ef748e9e183a36c1584434 (last visited Nov. 7, 2011).

[61] KfW ENTWICKLUNGSBANK, http://www.kfw-entwicklungsbank.de/EN_Home/index.jsp (last visited Nov. 7, 2011). Other members of the KfW group carry out domestic subsidies and provide export banking services. *Id.* (click on KfW Group).

[62] *Deutsche Investitions – und Entwicklungsgesellschaft*, BMZ, http://www.bmz.de/en/what_we_do/ approaches/bilateral_development_cooperation/players/selection/deg/index.html (last visited Nov. 7, 2011).

[63] Andersen, *supra* note 17, at 3.

[64] *Untying Aid: The Right to Choose*, OECD, DEVELOPMENT CO-OPERATION DIRECTORATE, http://www.oecd.org/document/50/0,3746,en_2649_33721_46345330_1_1_1_1,00.html (last visited Nov. 7, 2011).

cooperation, Germany often insists on the use of German equipment.[65] Moreover, the federal budget often specifies that technical assistance is to be provided directly by German services.[66] According to some critics, German equipment is costly, even though there is general agreement on its high quality. In 2008, 41% of German technical assistance was provided in the form of tied aid.[67] Germany, however, has promised reform.[68]

4. Discretionary Aid

Expenditures for developmental cooperation are authorized through the annual budget.[69] It appears that, from a budgetary point of view, these expenditures are generally discretionary. Budgetary law provides that appropriations enable an agency to disburse funds and to incur obligations, without requiring that the appropriated funds be spent.[70] Instead, the law requires that appropriated funds be used economically, in accordance with budgetary principles.[71] To provide flexibility, the annual budget allows for the transfer of some unused funds to other designated appropriations.[72] Generally, it appears, however, that the authorized funds have been expended in recent years.[73]

The budget process takes into consideration that agencies incur obligations or adopt plans that need to be funded over several years and spells out what funds will be allocated over the required period. Such multiyear appropriations are particularly common for developmental aid.[74] The appropriation for contributions to international organizations often spans several years.[75] For some appropriations, however, the budget explains that the Federal Cabinet may decide to withhold promised contributions if other contributor countries are not living up to their obligations.[76]

---

[65] PEER REVIEW, *supra* note 11, at 87.

[66] Bundeshaushaltsplan für das Haushaltsjahr 2011 [hereinafter Budget 2011] at 19 (2011), ch. 23, tit. 896.03, Erläuterungen 2.2, *available at* http://www.bundesfinanzministerium.de/bundeshaushalt2011/html/vsp20.html.

[67] PEER REVIEW, *supra* note 11, at 87.

[68] Id.

[69] Budget 2011 ch. 23. Although the law allows for annual or biannual budgets, Haushaltsgrundsätzegesetz [HGrG], Aug. 19, 1969, BGBL. I, 1273 *as amended*, § 9, the budget until now has been an annual budget.

[70] HGrG § 3.

[71] *Id.* § 6.

[72] Haushaltsgesetz 2011, Dec. 22, 2010, BGBL. I at 2228, § 5, http://www.bundesfinanzministerium.de/bundeshaushalt2011/pdf/haushaltsgesetz.pdf.

[73] This is indicated by the figures for the actual budget expenditures for ch. 23 in 2007, 2008, and 2009 as shown in the budgets for the years 2008–2010.

[74] Budget 2011 at 19 (2011).

[75] *Id.* ch. 23, tit. 687.01.

[76] *Id.* tit. 836.02, Erläuternungen 2.2.

In the appropriations for both financial and technical bilateral aid the budget often spells out that contributions must be made in accordance with specified guidelines. For measures that do not fall within the framework of these guidelines, individual approval by parliamentary committees is often required.[77] Specific parliamentary approval is also required for each grant of budget support and engagement in a silent partnership.[78]

5. Oversight

The developmental policy of the Federal Cabinet and the work of the BMZ are subject to parliamentary oversight exercised in various ways, including committee hearings, reports of the executive branch of government, and the parliamentary right of questioning the Federal Cabinet on any issue.[79] In the Federal Diet (*Deutscher Bundestag*), the representative chamber of the bicameral federal legislature, the Committee on Economic Cooperation and Development (*Ausschuss für wirtschaftliche Zusammenarbeit und Entwicklung*), is primarily responsible for overseeing developmental policy and its implementation.[80]

As with all governmental spending, the implementation of developmental cooperation policy is subject to the scrutiny of the Federal Court of Audit,[81] an independent quasi-judicial body charged with examining the efficient administration of public funds.[82] The Federal Court of Audit monitors all governmental spending through spot-checks. In addition, the Court may study problems in depth and make recommendations to the legislative and executive branches of government.

Within the BMZ, an internal but independent unit continuously monitors German developmental policy and implementation for effectiveness.[83] This subdivision of the BMZ provides the guidelines for internal and external evaluations in observance of the criteria provided by OECD/DAC. The German implementing organizations carry out the evaluations for their spheres of operation, and these evaluations involve a great deal of monitoring of the participating organizations and companies in the partner countries.[84]

In addition, the BMZ has a program of evaluations. These focus periodically on specific topics and also provide biannual reviews of relations with individual partner countries.[85] In

---

[77] *Id.* tit. 896.01, Haushaltsvermerk 7 & 8.

[78] *Id.* tit. 896.03, Haushaltsvermerk 8 & 9.

[79] MEDIENHANDBUCH ENTWICKLUNGSPOLITIK 2008/2009 at 48, http://www.entwicklungsdienst.de/fileadmin/Redaktion/Publik_ext/Medienhandbuch2008_2009.pdf.

[80] Deutscher Bundestag, Ausschuss für wirtschaftliche Zusammenarbeit und Entwicklung, http://www.bundestag.de/bundestag/ausschuesse17/a19/index.jsp.

[81] Bundesrechnungshof, http://bundesrechnungshof.de/.

[82] BASIC LAW art. 114; Bundesrechnungshofgesetz, July 11, 1985, BGBL. I at 1445, http://www.gesetze-im-internet.de/bundesrecht/brhg_1985/gesamt.pdf.

[83] MEDIENHANDBUCH, *supra* note 79, at 102–03.

[84] *Id.*

[85] *Id.*

addition to its own evaluations, the BMZ also relies on external appraisers.[86] Evaluations are made public.[87] They serve to inform the German people on how effective aid has been. The published evaluation reports range from a description of German aid to a specific country (such as a report on aid to Burkina Faso in 2006)[88] to an evaluation in 2007 on how effectively the Paris Declaration had been implemented by Germany at that time.[89]

In March 2009, the BMZ published an updated operational plan for its implementation of the Paris Declaration and the Accra Action Plan[90] in which Germany reiterated its commitment to monitoring and evaluating aid effectiveness. German implementation of these international instruments focuses on accountability, both domestically and at the level of the partner countries, and envisions the development of international accountability mechanisms.

6. Policy Considerations of the Partner Countries

The German system of developmental cooperation seems sufficiently flexible to adjust to acceptable legal or political requirements in a partner country while at the same time being well-equipped to identify and reject policies of a partner country that are at odds with German principles. Germany designs most of its cooperation projects individually, in negotiations with the partner country. Moreover, every second year, the BMZ meets with each partner country and addresses any lingering concerns on issues such as good governance or human rights. The overall plan for assistance for the partner country is then agreed upon, and details are then further negotiated between the German implementing organizations and the involved organizations of the partner country.[91] Under this detailed approach, Germany appears to have control over any objectionable policies or wasteful procedures of the partner country with respect to how German aid will be used, and is able to identify and reject them.

This German attention to detailed supervision may explain why Germany is somewhat skeptical about budget support.[92] In 2009, only 9% of German ODA fell into this category, and the conditions that Germany imposes for this type of aid specify a high degree of democratization in the recipient country. Germany is apprehensive that this type of general aid may foster corruption and encourage centralization in countries that lack a stable political

---

[86] *Mandate of the Ministry*, BMZ, http://www.bmz.de/en/ministry/mandate/index.html#t5 (last visited Nov. 7, 2011).

[87] A list of published evaluations is *available at* http://www.bmz.de/en/what_we_do/approaches/evaluation/pdf/zep_en_20100127.pdf (last visited Oct. 11, 2011).

[88] LÄNDERPROGRAMM BURKINA FASO, BMZ EVALUIERUNGSBERICHTE 041 (2006), http://www.bmz.de/de/publikationen/reihen/evaluierungen/evaluierungsberichte_ab_2006/EvalBericht041.pdf.

[89] DIE IMPLEMENTIERUNG DER PARISER ERKLÄRUNG, *supra* note 41.

[90] German Ministry of Economic Cooperation and Development, Plan of Operations for Implementing the Paris Declaration of 2005 and the Accra Agenda for Action of 2008 to Increase Aid Effectiveness (Apr. 2009), http://www.oecd.org/dataoecd/46/2/42632678.pdf.

[91] GERMAN DEVELOPMENT POLICY, *supra* note 23, at 9.

[92] Coalition Agreement, *supra* note 24, at 185.

climate and do not practice a reasonable degree of transparency.[93] The German Federal Court of Audit reviewed this type of aid in 2008 and recommended that it be given only to countries with which Germany is already cooperating and that have a reasonable level of good governance.[94]

Germany has given much thought to advancing democratization and encouraging the participation of recipient countries' populations in decision-making processes. To achieve these goals, Germany encourages the recipient countries to enact and enforce laws that give the population substantive rights of participation safeguarded by procedural rules. In addition, Germany encourages governments that function and are transparent. Germany is well aware of the complexity and difficulty of the task and the need for a varied and flexible approach that involves nongovernmental actors in addition to governmental aid.[95]

B. Regulation of Private Contributions

1. Taxation

German law exempts nonprofit corporations, associations, and foundations from corporate income tax liability[96] and allows individuals and corporations to deduct up to 20% of their annual income for qualifying nonprofit purposes.[97] Alternatively, corporations and individual business owners can elect to be limited in their qualifying nonprofit spending by an amount that equals 0.04% of the sum of their annual turnover plus the total of wages paid.[98] In addition, individual taxpayers may deduct up to €1 million (about US$1.28 million) over a one- to ten-year period if they donate funds toward the establishment of a charitable foundation.[99]

Developmental cooperation qualifies as a tax-favored nonprofit purpose[100] provided that it lives up to the general criteria for beneficial tax treatment of charitable purposes. These require that the benevolent activities that a German developmental aid organization carries out abroad serve to enhance the image of Germany[101] and that the donor organization is not

---

[93] Stefan Leiderer, *Budgethilfe in der Entwicklungszusammenarbeit – weder Teufelszeug noch Allheilmittel*, DEUTSCHES INSTITUT FÜR ENTWICKLUNGSPOLITIK (Oct. 2009), http://www.die-gdi.de/CMS-Homepage/openwebcms3.nsf/(ynDK_contentByKey)/ANES-7WTFWU/$FILE/AuS%2010.2009.pdf.

[94] Id.

[95] BMZ, DIE FÖRDERUNG KONSTRUKTIVER STAAT-GESELLSCHAFT-BEZIEHUNGEN – LEGITIMITÄT, TRANSPARENZ, RECHENSCHAFT (Jan. 2010), http://www.bmz.de/de/publikationen/reihen/strategiepapiere/Strategiepapier298_01_2010_de.pdf.

[96] Körperschaftssteuergesetz [KStG], *repromulgated* Oct. 15, 2002, BGBL. I at 4144, *as amended*, § 5(1), no. 5. The exemption, however, does not extend to commercial enterprises owned by nonprofit corporations. *Id.*

[97] Einkommensteuergesetz [EStG], *repromulgated* Oct. 2, 2002, BGBL. I at 4210, *as amended*, § 10b; KStG § 9 (2).

[98] EStG § 10b; KStG § 9(2).

[99] EStG § 10b(1a).

[100] Abgabenordnung [AO], *repromulgated* Oct. 1, 2001, BGBL. I at 3866, *as amended*, § 52(2) no. 15.

[101] AO § 51(2)

subversive or extremist and does not engage in such conduct.[102] EU law appears to require that donations to charitable organizations located in other EU member states also qualify for the German tax exemptions.[103]

Until 2007, the law clearly indicated that tax-exempt nonprofit organizations had to be located in Germany to enjoy tax-exempt status and for donors to qualify for tax deductions. Changes in the law in 2007 and 2009 have opened the possibility of a tax deduction for donations to nonprofit organizations located abroad, as long as they benefit either German residents or Germany's image.[104] This new rule, however, is controversial; the tax authority is challenging its constitutionality and its application is uncertain.[105]

2. Subsidies and Cooperation with Government

Germany has many NGOs that provide developmental assistance.[106] Among them are medical associations and other providers of health services, associations assisting a particular country, and religious communities that operate schools and hospitals (see section IV.B, below for the differentiation between the religious and nonreligious activities of religious communities). These organizations may obtain subsidies for developmental aid projects and also engage in cooperative projects with the BMZ.[107] Under either of these circumstances, the private donor organizations are bound by any governing guidelines and directives that the BMZ may have issued.[108]

Political foundations also partner with government developmental aid organizations and are eligible for subsidies.[109] Political foundations are civic associations that have a close relationship with a political party. In developing countries, they provide civic education and encourage democratization.[110] Despite their relationship with a particular political party, political foundations may be recipients of governmental subsidies for their work in civic education, as long as certain safeguards are met that guarantee their independence from the political party.[111]

---

[102] AO § 51(3).

[103] Franz Klein et al., Abgabenordnung Kommentar § 51 n.7 (10th ed. 2009).

[104] AO § 51, *as amended by* Jahressteuergesetz 2009, Dec. 19, 2008, BGBL. I at 2026.

[105] Sebastian Unger, Steuerbegünstigung grenzüberschreitender Gemeinnützigkeit im Binnenmarkt – Vorgaben des Gemeinnützigkeits- und Spendenrechts im Lichte der unionalen Grundfreiheiten, DEUTSCHE STEUERZEITUNG 154 (2010).

[106] *NRO Verzeichnis*, ENGAGEMENT GLOBAL, http://www.engagement-global.de/nro-liste.html (last visited Jan. 9, 2012).

[107] Budget 2011, ch. 23, tit. 687 06.

[108] Id.

[109] *Id.* tit. 687 11.

[110] Roland Kress, Die politischen Stiftungen in der Entwicklungspolitik 3 (1985).

[111] Bundesverfassungsgericht, decision of July 14, 1986, *reprinted in* NEUE JURISTISCHE WOCHENSCHRIFT 2487 (1986).

German NGOs may also request assistance from the EU's developmental aid office.[112] Such cooperation is governed by EU policies, as expressed in EU Regulation 1905/2006.[113]

III. Foreign Aid Appropriations Process

Federal developmental aid is appropriated in the course of the annual budgetary process of the Federation. Each Ministry prepares a budget for its sphere of competence, and the Federal Ministry of Finance reviews the ministerial budgets and compiles them into one draft budget.[114] After the Federal Cabinet approves the draft budget, it is submitted to both chambers of the bicameral federal legislature.

The Federal Council, the Chamber representing the states, notifies the Federal Diet of any comments it may have. In the Federal Diet, the Budget Committee reviews the draft budget.[115] After the Federal Diet approves the draft budget,[116] the Federal Council is asked for its consent. Disagreements are resolved through a conciliation committee. After the Parliament approves the budget, the Federal President signs and promulgates it as a federal law.[117]

Although the budget generally lists annual expenditures, the law permits the inclusion of expenditures for future years to cover long-term obligations.[118] The appropriations for developmental aid frequently employ such commitment plans.[119] These may span periods of three to five years or may be open-ended.

Commitment plans are used for obligating developmental funds to the EU[120] and to international organizations. These plans may include reservations allowing the Federal Cabinet to block funds if other contributor countries do not live up to their obligations.[121] They may also require the consent of parliamentary committees to unblock funds.[122]

---

[112] *2010 Annual Action Programmes*, EUROPEAN COMMISSION, DEVELOPMENT AND COOPERATION – EUROPEAID, http://ec.europa.eu/europeaid/work/ap/aap/2010_en.htm (last visited Nov. 17, 2011).

[113] Regulation (EC) No. 1905/2006 of the European Parliament and of the Council of 18 December 2006 establishing a financing instrument for development cooperation, OFFICIAL JOURNAL OF THE EUROPEAN UNION [O.J.] (L 378) 41, http://eur-lex.europa.eu/LexUriServ/LexUriServ.do?uri=CELEX:32006R1905:EN:NOT.

[114] Bundeshaushaltsordnung [BHO], Aug. 19, 1969, BGBl. I at 1284, *as amended*, § 28.

[115] *Haushaltsausschuss*, DEUTSCHER BUNDESTAG,http://www.bundestag.de/bundestag/ausschuesse17/a08/index.jsp (last visited Nov. 7, 2011).

[116] BHO § 29.

[117] *See Entstehung des Bundeshaushalts*, DEUTSCHER BUNDESTAG, http://www.bundestag.de/bundestag/aufgaben/haushalt/entstehung.html (last visited Aug. 19, 2011).

[118] BHO § 6.

[119] Budget 2011, ch. 23, Übersicht 1, Verpflichtungsermächtigungen.

[120] *Id.* tit. 896 02.

[121] Such blockages are foreseen in the appropriations for the International Development Association and the Asian Development Bank. *Id.* tits. 836 02 & 836 03.

[122] *Id.* tit. 687 01.

IV. Other Types of 'Aid'

A. Emergency Aid

The federal budget contains an allocation for emergency aid to be granted in conflicts, catastrophes, and crises. This allocation serves to finance food, infrastructure, water, sewage services, social services, housing, transportation, encouragement of self-help, and assistance for refugees.[123] The BMZ administers this appropriation. It may act on its own or make contributions through the UN Central Emergency Response Fund. To the extent that cash grants are given, guidelines must be observed.[124]

In addition, Germany provides humanitarian assistance through the Federal Foreign Office.[125] The appropriation for this assistance allocates funds for catastrophes and also for human rights efforts, and to help other countries become more democratic.[126]

B. Religious Ministries

In Germany, the largest nongovernmental foreign aid donors are religious ministries, particularly the Roman Catholic Church and the Evangelical Church in Germany.[127] Germany, however, does not categorize religious activities as developmental aid. According to German statistical guidelines, expenditures incurred to propagate or observe a faith or religious belief, build churches or sanctuaries, and train clergy cannot be included in the statistics for private foreign aid contributions.[128] Only to the extent that religious communities provide developmental aid or humanitarian assistance may the expenditures incurred by such activities be reported to the Federal Statistical Office as private foreign aid.[129]

Moreover, the budget appropriation for subsidizing developmental aid provided by religious ministries clearly specifies that religious activities are not subsidized in this context, and that BMZ guidelines must be observed for expenditures and commitments.[130] The subsidization of church-sponsored developmental aid is not surprising in Germany, given the fact that domestically, partnerships between the government and religious communities are not unusual in matters relating to education, health, and social services.[131]

---

[123] *Id.* tit. 687 20.

[124] Id.

[125] Press Release, Auswärtiges Amt, Dank an alle, die helfen (Aug. 18, 2011), http://www.auswaertiges-amt.de/DE/Infoservice/Presse/Meldungen/2011/110818-MRHH_Welttag_HH.html.

[126] Budget 2011, ch. 5, tit. 07.

[127] Andersen, *supra* note 17, at 7.

[128] *Entwicklungszusammenarbeit*, *supra* note 13.

[129] *Id.*

[130] Budget 2011, ch. 23, tit. 896 04.

[131] SOZIALRECHTSHANDBUCH 1040 (Bernd Baron von Maydell et al. eds., 2008).

C. Scholarships for Foreign Students

The German states grant scholarships for higher education to students from developing countries.[132] This type of aid is included in ODA in the German report to OECD/DAC.[133] In fact, the educational expenditures of the states for students from developing countries constitute a substantial contribution to German ODA. In 2006 such aid amounted to 9% of German ODA for the year.[134]

D. Remittances

Germany is aware of the importance of remittances sent home by foreign workers to developing countries.[135] To make such money transfers less expensive, GIZ maintains a website that lists the costs of transfers and describes the terms of doing business offered by banks and transfer services.[136]

Prepared by Edith Palmer, Chief
Foreign, Comparative and International Law Division II
Global Legal Research Center
November 2011

---

[132] *Die Entwicklungszusammenarbeit der Bundesländer*, BMZ, http://www.bmz.de/de/was_wir_machen/wege/bilaterale_ez/akteure_ez/laendergemeinden/laender/index.html (last visited Nov. 17, 2011).

[133] Id.

[134] MEDIENHANDBUCH, *supra* note 79, at 52.

[135] In 2008, remittances from Germany to countries outside of the European Union amounted to €3.1 billion (about US$3.96 billion). *See Tipps für Zahlungen ins Ausland*, FAZ (Dec. 16, 2009), *available at* http://www.geldtransfair.de/presse.php.

[136] GELDTRANSFAIR.DE, http://www.geldtransfair.de/about-us.php (last visited Nov. 7, 2011).

LAW LIBRARY OF CONGRESS

INDIA

REGULATION OF FOREIGN AID

Executive Summary

In the last decade India has increasingly transitioned toward becoming an "emerging donor" country. As part of its "South-South" strategy, India seeks to use its foreign aid programs as a tool to further its own economic, political, and strategic interests, while also taking into account the needs of the recipient country. Its foreign assistance spending consists of grants, preferential loans, contributions to international organizations and international financial institutions, and subsidies for preferential bilateral loans. However, rather than organizing its aid programs under one unified aid agency, India's development assistance is channeled through a variety of ministries and government departments, including the Ministry of External Affairs and the Ministry of Finance.

I. Introduction

A. Official Development Assistance Figures

Although traditionally considered largely as a recipient of foreign aid, India in the last decade has increasingly transitioned toward becoming an "emerging donor" country. The Indian government does not release official figures on the amount it spends on foreign development assistance or "report its aid flows to the Organization for Economic Cooperation and Development (OECD) Development Assistance Committee (DAC)."[1] Therefore, most figures are approximate, based on how foreign assistance activities are allocated in India's annual budget.

The OECD estimates that India spent US$539 million in 2009–10 on foreign assistance.[2] In 2010, according to its annual budget, the Indian government allocated US$785 million for aid-related activities.[3] An analysis by the Real Instituto Elcan found that budget allocations for aid-

---

[1] C.R. Bijoy, *India: Transitioning to a Global Donor*, *in* THE REALITY OF AID, SOUTH-SOUTH COOPERATION: A CHALLENGE TO THE AID SYSTEM? 68 (Special Report on South-South Cooperation 2010), http://www.realityofaid.org/userfiles/roareports/roareport_3ce2522270.pdf.

[2] HOUSE OF COMMONS INTERNATIONAL DEVELOPMENT COMMITTEE, THE FUTURE OF DFID'S PROGRAMME IN INDIA, 2010-12, H.C. 616-I, http://www.publications.parliament.uk/pa/cm201012/cmselect/cmintdev/616/61608.htm.

[3] Dweep Chanana, *India's Transition to Global Donor: Limitations and Prospects* (Real Instituto Elcan, ARI No. 123/2010, July 23, 2010), http://www.realinstitutoelcano.org/wps/portal/rielcano_eng/Content?WCM_GLOBAL_CONTEXT=/elcano/elcano_in/zonas_in/cooperation+developpment/ari123-2010.

related activities have grown at "a compound annual growth rate (CAGR) of 6.9% from 2004 to 2010."[4]

B. Private Contribution Figures

Data could only be found in relation to government-related foreign assistance programs. No information could be found on private contributions.

C. Snapshot of Foreign Aid Activity

India has been providing significant economic and military aid to neighboring countries in South Asia since the 1950s, soon after its independence.[5] It is only in the last decade, however, that India has relied on foreign assistance as an increasingly important foreign policy tool to further its own economic, political, and strategic interests.

According to economist Dweep Chanana, there are three parts to India's foreign assistance spending: "grants and preferential bilateral loans to governments, contributions to international organisations (IOs) and financial institutions (IFIs), and subsidies for preferential bilateral loans provided through the Export Import (EXIM) Bank of India."[6]

As mentioned above, India has traditionally given foreign aid mainly to neighboring countries. Even today a large proportion of its foreign aid goes to surrounding countries like Bhutan, Afghanistan, Nepal, and Burma. According to experts, India is "one of the five largest donors to Afghanistan with commitments of over $1 billion since 2001."[7]

In the last decade, however, India has increasingly attempted to broaden its influence through its aid programs. In particular, aid to Africa has grown at a "compound annual growth rate of 22% over the past ten years" from 1998–1999.[8] In 2007, in a joint initiative with the African Union (AU), India helped set up "a pan-African e-network to connect schools and hospitals in Africa with top institutions in India."[9] Moreover, in 2008, after an India-Africa Business Summit, India "pledged $500 million in concessional credit facilities to eight resource

---

[4] *Id.*

[5] Dweep Chanana, *India as an Emerging Donor*, 44 ECON. & POL. WKLY. 11 (Mar. 21–27, 2009), *available at* http://papers.ssrn.com/sol3/papers.cfm?abstract_id=1410508&#.

[6] Chanana, *supra* note 3.

[7] Chanana, *supra* note 5, at 12.

[8] Vijaya Ramachandran & Julie Waltz, *India Emerges as an Aid Donor*, CENTER FOR GLOBAL DEVELOPMENT (Oct. 5, 2010), http://blogs.cgdev.org/globaldevelopment/2010/10/india-emerges-as-an-aid-donor.php.

[9] Chanana, *supra* note 5, at 12.

rich West-African nations."[10]   In May 2011, at the second annual Africa-India forum summit, India announced a $5 billion credit line for African countries over the next three years.[11]

Besides awarding development aid in the form of grants, loans, and project assistance, India also operates programs for training and technical assistance. The Indian Technical and Economic Cooperation (ITEC) Programme has operated as India's flagship foreign assistance program. It primarily provides technical assistance and training to scholars and leaders of other developing countries. According to the Ministry of External Affairs (MEA) website:

> Under ITEC and its corollary SCAAP (Special Commonwealth Assistance for Africa Programme), 158 countries in Asia & the Pacific, Africa, Latin America & the Caribbean and East & Central Europe are invited to share in the Indian development experience, acquired since its Independence. It has six components, viz. (i) Training (civilian and defence) in India of nominees from ITEC partner countries; (ii) Projects and project related activities such as feasibility studies and consultancy services; (iii) Deputation of Indian experts abroad; (iv) Study tours; (v) Gifting/Donation of equipment; and (vi) Aid for Disaster Relief.[12]

In the last decade, India's contributions to multilateral organizations have also increased significantly. According to Chanana,

> [i]n 2004, India lent over $400 million in hard currency to Brazil, Burundi, and Indonesia under the International Monetary Fund's (IMF) financial transactions plan (FTP). In 2005, India became the 15th largest donor to the World Food Programme. And last year India's voting share in the IMF increased slightly, addressing a long-standing demand.[13]

II. Legal Framework

A. Regulation of ODA

1. Overview

According to an International Development Research Centre report, India "does not adhere to any standard definition of development assistance. What the country calls 'overseas development assistance' is often a mixed bag of project assistance, purchase subsidies, lines of credit, travel costs, and technical training costs incurred by the Indian government."[14]

---

[10] Ramachandran & Waltz, *supra* note 8.

[11] Dr. Manmohan Singh, Address by PM at the Plenary Session of the 2nd Africa-India Forum Summit (May 24, 2011), http://www.indiaafricasummit.nic.in/pdfs/PMPlenarySessionof2ndafrica.pdf.

[12] *Introduction*, ITEC MINISTRY OF EXTERNAL AFFAIRS, http://itec.mea.gov.in/ (last visited Sept. 15, 2011).

[13] Chanana, *supra* note 5, at 12.

[14] SUBHASH AGRAWAL, EMERGING DONORS IN INTERNATIONAL DEVELOPMENT ASSISTANCE: THE INDIA CASE 5 (Int'l Dev. Res. Centre, Dec. 2007), http://publicwebsite.idrc.ca/EN/Documents/Case-of-India.pdf.

2. Restrictions

Although under its 2003 new aid policy[15] India refuses to accept tied aid from other donor countries, much of its own development assistance is tied. According to Chanana, the development assistance India provides is "unconditional but often tied, with a substantial part spent in India. For instance, the flagship ITEC programme provides training in India for visiting delegates, while many EXIM bank lines of credit (LOCs) require the purchase of Indian goods or services."[16] A Chatham House working paper notes that "India's new aid policy was far from unique in that it was driven not by pure altruism, but primarily from the domestic and international political and economic benefits that would accrue from it."[17]

3. Policy Considerations

One could attribute a number of political, economic, and strategic objectives to India's foreign assistance programs. According to Chanana, "India has increasingly sought to expand its activities as a donor, both to reposition itself as an emerging power and to use aid as an instrument for engaging with other developing countries."[18]

India has traditionally seen its development assistance as "a component of a South-South cooperation in which countries interact with each other as partners at an equal level."[19] The First Secretary of the Permanent Mission of India to the United Nations Office at Geneva, speaking on a joint initiative between India and the AU, stated that "South-South cooperation has always been an important policy plank for India, and as part of this objective we are building a relationship of partnership for mutual benefit with Africa, not one of donor-recipient."[20] Therefore, India is not shy in acknowledging that the development assistance it provides can be to "further Indian interests abroad and to promote its *own* economic situation."[21] According to a briefing paper by the Friedrich Ebert Stiftung Foundation,

> [t]he "Indian Development Assistance Scheme" (IDEAS), a successor-programme to the 2003 "Indian Development Initiative," covers the large part of India's donor activities, and is explicitly designed to increase Indian exports, to promote economic relations to other developing countries and to support India's strategic interests abroad. Development assistance, as a complementary foreign policy tool, is intended here especially to

---

[15] Budget Speech, Ministry of Finance, Union Budget 2003–2004, http://www.indiabudget.nic.in/ub2003-04/bs/speecha.htm.

[16] Chanana, *supra* note 3.

[17] Gareth Price, *India's Aid Dynamics: From Recipient to Donor?* (Chatham House, Asia Programme Working Paper, Sept. 2004), http://www.chathamhouse.org/sites/default/files/public/Research/Asia/wp200904.pdf.

[18] Chanana, *supra* note 3.

[19] Matthias Jobelius, *New Powers for Global Change? Challenges for the International Development Cooperation: The Case of India* (Friedrich Ebert Stiftung, Briefing Paper 5, Mar. 2007), *available at* http://www.basas.org.uk/projects/Jobelius.pdf.

[20] *South-South Trade,* INTERNATIONAL TRADE FORUM, http://www.tradeforum.org/m/fullstory.php/aid/1187/South_96South_Trade.html (last visited Sept. 15, 2011).

[21] Jobelius, *supra* note 19, at 4.

- open up new markets for Indian companies,

- guarantee energy security,

- strengthen India's negotiating position in international fora,

- further diversify the country's alliance and partner structure, and

- strengthen regional security, suppress separationist movements and terrorist activities in South Asia and thereby also guarantee the security of the nation itself.[22]

The other side of India's South-South strategy is to also take into account the needs and interests of the aid recipient. Chanana states that "India attaches far fewer conditionalities to its grants and also gives beneficiaries a greater voice in the process."[23] Moreover, he states, "India focuses on smaller interventions, allows recipient countries to define their own priorities and encourages mutual economic growth and long-term trade linkages rather than purely a development impact."[24] Therefore, the overall objective is focused on "promoting goodwill" and "local capacity." However, some experts, like Bijoy, believe that "there are indications that India is moving from exerting soft to hard power. The goodwill generated could very well get diluted with India emerging as a major donor."[25]

4. Discretionary Aid

India's foreign development assistance programs may be characterized as discretionary aid because spending is determined through a budget appropriation process every year.

5. Oversight

It appears that there are very few oversight mechanisms and safeguards against corruption. According to Vijaya Ramachandran, a senior fellow at the Center for Global Development, "[n]o official records of aid disbursements are kept, either by the Ministry of External Affairs or the Ministry of Finance."[26]

B. Regulation of Private Contributions

There does not appear to be any regulation of private contributions.

---

[22] *Id.*

[23] Chanana, *supra* note 5, at 12.

[24] Chanana, *supra* note 3.

[25] Bijoy, *supra* note 1, at 74.

[26] Ramachandran & Waltz, *supra* note 8.

III. Foreign Aid Appropriations Process

India's annual budget proposal is prepared by the Ministry of Finance (MoF) on the basis of proposals from each ministry of the Indian government. Each department and ministry submits an expenditure proposal known as a "demand of grants." After the MoF presents the Budget proposal to the Indian Parliament for discussion and scrutiny, all demands of grants must be passed by the Indian Parliament. Subsequently an appropriations bill is introduced to authorize the Indian government to draw funds from government revenue.

Funding for foreign assistance programs is channeled through multiple ministries of the Indian government. For example, in the Ministry of External Affairs' expenditure proposal, foreign assistance is allocated under the title of "Technical and Economic Cooperation With Other Countries." According to the Notes on Demand of Grants 2011-2012, "[t]his budget head caters to India's multilateral and bilateral aid and assistance programmes to neighbouring and other developing countries."[27]

As will be discussed below, foreign assistance is also channeled through the MoF. The MoF's expenditure proposal for 2011-2012 includes a separate allocation for contributions to IFIs (the World Bank and IMF). Also, a separate budget is allocated for contributions to the United Nations Development Programme (UNDP). Other multilateral assistance is under the heading of "International Cooperation," which represents India's contribution to the following entities:

- International Fund for Agricultural Development (IFAD)

- Commonwealth Fund for Technical Co-operation (CFTC)

- Technical Assistance Scheme of the Asian Development Bank (ADB)

- Organisation for Economic Co-operation and Development (OECD)

- Network on Fiscal Relations

- Technical Cooperation with African Development Bank (AfDB)[28]

India has also entered into numerous bilateral cooperation agreements for the provision of foreign aid, including the following:

- Line of Credit Agreement worth $1 billion was signed in Dhaka on August 7, 2010, between EXIM Bank of India and Government of Bangladesh.[29]

---

[27] Ministry of External Affairs, *Notes on Demand of Grants 2011-2012*, http://indiabudget.nic.in/ ub2011-12/eb/sbe31.pdf.

[28] Id.

[29] Ministry of External Affairs, *India-Bangladesh Relations* (Aug. 2011), http://mea.gov.in/mystart.php? id=50042439.

- In December 2009, twelve MoUs were signed in the areas of hydropower, narcotics, IT, medicine, agriculture, civil aviation, and environment between India and Bhutan.[30]

- In Nepal, India contributes to various development projects in the areas of health, infrastructure, rural development, and education.[31]

IV. Implementing Agencies

Although India does not have a dedicated aid agency, most aid work is conducted through multiple programs operating within different ministries of the Indian government. According to Dweep Chanana, "the Ministry of External Affairs plays a coordinating function" while the other "individual ministries have their own objectives and budgets both for bilateral programmes and for the funding of International Organisations."[32]

The MEA plays the principal role in providing development aid through grants and project assistance. According to the German Development Institute (DIE), "MEA has various institutional arrangements under its wings, such as the Indian Technical and Economic Cooperation (ITEC) Programme, Aid to African countries through Special Commonwealth Assistance Programme for Africa (SCAAP), [and] Bilateral Aid to neighboring and other developing countries."[33]

Budget allocations for development assistance are also channeled through the MoF. According to the 2011-2012 Annual Budget, India provides development assistance to both Sri Lanka and Cambodia through the Finance Ministry.[34] Moreover, the MoF's Department of Economic Affairs has been extending Lines of Credit to other developing foreign countries. According to the MoF website, one of the Department's major functions is "Government of India Supported Lines of Credit (LOCs) routed through EXIM Bank of India to countries of Asia (Excluding Bangladesh, Nepal, Bhutan) Africa, CIS region and Latin American region[,] which are being extended under the Indian Development and Economic Assistance Scheme (IDEAS)."[35]

---

[30] Ministry of External Affairs, *India-Bhutan Relations* (Aug. 2011), http://mea.gov.in/mystart.php?id=50042442.

[31] Ministry of External Affairs, Embassy of India: Kathmandu, *India-Nepal Relations* (July 31, 2011), www.mea.gov.in/mystart.php?id=50044504.

[32] Chanana, *supra* note 3.

[33] *India's Development Cooperation – Opportunities and Challenges for International Development Cooperation* (Deutsches Institut für Entwicklungspolitik/German Development Institute Briefing Paper, Mar. 2009), http://www.die-gdi.de/CMS-Homepage/openwebcms3_e.nsf/(ynDK_contentByKey)/ANES-7QAGRV/$FILE/BP%203.2009.pdf.

[34] Ministry of Finance (MoF), *Notes on Demand of Grants 2011-2012*, http://indiabudget.nic.in/ub2011-12/eb/sbe32.pdf.

[35] *Commercial Imports and Exports (CIE) – II Section*, MINISTRY OF FINANCE (MoF), http://finmin.nic.in/the_ministry/dept_eco_affairs/cie2sec/cie2sec_index.asp (last visited Sept. 15, 2011).

The size of contributions to the World Food Programme is decided by the Ministry of Agriculture.[36] However, the MEA still determines which countries should be recipients of the assistance.[37]

Under the 2007–2008 Budget, the Indian government proposed the creation of a unified aid agency called the India International Development Cooperation Agency (IIDCA), "which would consolidate Indian aid and allow for larger projects."[38] However, progress has stalled and the agency has yet to be established. Consequently, according to the German Development Institute, "India's development cooperation policy remains fragmented in the responsibility of various ministries."[39]

V. Other Types of 'Aid'

India also provides scholarships to overseas students through the Indian Council for Cultural Relations (ICCR) scholarship scheme.[40]

Prepared by Tariq Ahmad
Foreign Law Specialist
September 2011

---

[36] Chanana, *supra* note 3.

[37] Gareth Price, *Diversity In Donorship: The Changing Landscape of Official Humanitarian Aid: India's Official Aid Programme* 14 (Humanitarian Policy Group, HPG Background Paper No. 20, Sept. 2005), *available at* http://www.odi.org.uk/resources/download/302.pdf.

[38] GARETH PRICE, FOR THE GLOBAL GOOD: INDIA'S DEVELOPING INTERNATIONAL ROLE 14 (Chatham House, Sept. 2004), http://www.chathamhouse.org/sites/default/files/public/Research/Asia/r_indiarole0511.pdf.

[39] *India's Development Cooperation*, *supra* note 33, at 1.

[40] *The Many Scholarship Schemes of ICC*, INDIAN COUNCIL FOR CULTURAL RELATIONS (ICCR), http://www.iccrindia.net/scholarshipschemes.html (last visited Sept. 20, 2011).

LAW LIBRARY OF CONGRESS

ISRAEL

REGULATION OF FOREIGN AID

Executive Summary

Israel's official development assistance (ODA) in 2010 amounted to 0.065% of its gross national income (GNI). Israel's ODA has traditionally focused on the agricultural sector, rural regional planning, youth programs, women's empowerment, and medical assistance.

Israel's ODA budget is allocated to a number of government agencies, including Bank of Israel, the Ministry of Foreign Affairs through MASHAV (the Department for International Cooperation), the Ministry of Finance, and the Ministry of Industry, Trade, and Labor. The total budget allocation of each ministry is based on parliamentary approval of the government request for budget allocations. The amounts that are subsequently spent on foreign aid by each ministry and by Bank of Israel are subject to the government's discretion.

Israeli foreign assistance to developing countries is managed mainly by MASHAV, the department dedicated for this purpose at the Ministry of Foreign Affairs. MASHAV's activities focus on areas in which Israel has a comparative advantage and/or has acquired expertise. In exercising its responsibilities MASHAV cooperates with local partners and targets grassroots community-driven development in recipient countries. MASHAV also engages in cooperation with other development organizations and funds numerous training projects in Israel as well as in developing countries. The administration and financial management of MASHAV's activities are handled by a government company called Igud. The activities of both MASHAV and Igud are subject to oversight by the office of the State Comptroller.

Although no specific restrictions regarding tied aid were identified in current Israeli legislation, some general restrictions on trade with enemy countries or entities and cooperation with organizations that are viewed as supporting activities against principles of the state may apply to transactions involving foreign aid.

Having first started five decades ago, Israel's ODA, in particular its bilateral aid budget, has fluctuated over time. The shifts in both the amounts as well as the recipient countries reflect geopolitical trends relating to changing alliances in the context of the Arab-Israeli conflict. Israel is committed to the UN Millennium Development Goals, which were reaffirmed at the MDG Summit held in New York in September 2010.

I. Introduction

A. Official Development Assistance Figures

Israel joined the Organisation for Economic Co-operation and Development (OECD) on May 10, 2010,[1] and has made a commitment to pursue[2] the United Nations Millennium Development Goals that were reaffirmed at the New York MDG Summit in September 2010.[3]

As an OECD member-state Israel is expected to reach the target goal of contributing 0.7% of its gross national income (GNI) to official development assistance.[4] According to OECD statistics, Israel's gross as well as net disbursement figures were US$140.55 million for 2010 (net disbursements reported by the OECD as $123.75 million for bilateral aid and $16.79 million for multilateral aid) and US$123.9 million for 2009 (both net and gross disbursements reported by the OECD as $107.52 million for bilateral aid and $16.38 million for multilateral aid).[5] This latter amount constituted 0.065% of Israel's GNI in 2009.[6] A Tel Aviv University study published in June 2009 suggested that this small budget, as compared with the strong Israeli contribution to foreign aid in Israel's early days, reflects the weak public and political support for Israeli foreign aid in recent years.[7]

---

[1] *Accession: Estonia, Israel and Slovenia Invited to Join OECD*, OECD, http://www.oecd.org/document/57/0,3343,en_2649_201185_45159737_1_1_1_1,00.html (last visited July 28, 2011). For implementation, *see* Implementation of the Agreement Between the State of Israel and the Organization for Cooperation and Economic Development Regarding Privileges, Immunities and Exemptions Granted to the Organization, Law 5770-2010, SEFER HAHUKIM No. 2250, p. 580 (July 22, 2010), *available at* NEVO LEGAL DATABASE, http://www.nevo.co.il/law_word/law01/500_344.doc (in Hebrew; by subscription).

[2] *See* Ministry of Foreign Affairs, *MASHAV Highlights: Spotlight on 2010*, *available at* http://mashav.mfa.gov.il/mfm/Data/197168.pdf; *see also Millennium Development Goals*, THE WORLD BANK, http://web.worldbank.org/WBSITE/EXTERNAL/EXTABOUTUS/0,,contentMDK:20104132~menuPK:250991~pagePK:43912~piPK:44037~theSitePK:29708,00.html (both last visited Aug. 23, 2011).

[3] *Keeping the Promise: United to Achieve the Millennium Development Goals*, U.N. GAOR, 65th Sess., 9th plen. mtg. at 12–19, U.N. Doc. A/RES/65/1, http://www.un.org/en/mdg/summit2010/pdf/outcome_document N1051260.pdf.

[4] This objective was first adopted by the United Nations in a 1970 General Assembly Resolution, and has been reaffirmed in many international agreements over the years. *See The 0.7% target: An In-depth Look*, UN MILLENNIUM PROJECT (Commissioned by the Secretary General and Supported by the UN Development Group) http://www.unmillenniumproject.org/press/07.htm (last visited Aug. 18, 2011).

[5] *ODA By Donor*, OECD.STATEXTRACTS, http://stats.oecd.org/Index.aspx?DatasetCode=ODA_DONOR (click on Israel, down the list between Iceland and Poland) (last visited Sept. 13, 2011))(please note that the figures noted by the OECD for 2010 net disbursements vary slightly from the figure reached by adding net bilateral and multilateral aid figures); *see also Israel: Donor View – Official Development Assistance, AidFlows*, THE WORLD BANK, http://siteresources.worldbank.org/CFPEXT/Resources/299947-1266002444164/index.html (click on Israel on the list of countries on the left side of the screen) (last visited Aug. 18, 2011).

[6] Information provided by the Knesset Center for Research and Information to the author (Aug. 16, 2011) (on file with author).

[7] ALIZA BELMAN INBAL & SHACHAR ZAHAVI, THE RISE AND FALL OF ISRAEL'S BILATERAL AID BUDGET 1958–2008 at 12 (Tel Aviv University, the Harold Hartog School of Government and Policy, June 2009), *available at* http://spirit.tau.ac.il/government/downloads/Aliza%20Belman%20Inbal%20Bl.pdf. The Study quoted a slightly different figure for Israel's total ODA for 2009: $101.1 million, constituting merely 0.068% of its GNI for that year.

B. Private Contribution Figures

Although no specific figures for private contributions have been identified, one of the recommendations of the 2009 Tel Aviv University study was to develop a nonprofit, private sector in Israel that would bring Israeli expertise to assist the developing world.[8] To encourage such development the report further suggested supporting the establishment of

> "development-technology incubators" that would provide seed money for Israeli entrepreneurship in the field of development and professional support for Israeli consultants and companies interested in submitting bids for beneficiary and aid organization funding.[9]

In addition, the report proposes to accord Israeli nongovernmental organizations (NGOs) that engage in foreign aid activities abroad the same tax-exempt status currently enjoyed by similar organizations that are active within Israel.[10]

C. Snapshot of Foreign Aid Activity

General Principles and Focus

Israel's aid to developing countries began ten years after its independence, when Israel itself was a developing country. Its assistance to other developing countries is said to have been based on the Jewish principle of *Tikun Olam*—literally, "repair of the world", or the obligation to make the world a better place—and on the belief that Israel, as a member of the world community, had the obligation to help other countries.[11]

Israel's foreign aid assistance in its early days was characterized by its "unique form of socialism, which was welcomed as a 'third force' between Western and Communist models."[12] As an example, researchers have highlighted the emphasis on "bottom-up collectivization, empowerment of local government and community development structures, private-public sector partnership, and dominant labour unions," which played a key role both in Israel in the 1960s and '70s, and in liberation movements in Africa and Asia at that time.[13]

Scholars have found that the focus of Israel's training and technical assistance programs generally differed from that of OECD countries, in that Israeli programs were designed to

---

[8] *Id.* at 57.

[9] *Id.* at 58.

[10] *Id.*

[11] Israel Ministry of Foreign Affairs, The Moral-Ethical Duty, Extend a Hand, Share Knowledge: Fifty Years of Assistance and International Cooperation of the State of Israel, *available at* http://www.mfa.gov.il/NR/rdonlyres/A35F16D0-A8C0-4E81-B0FE-DC941A06C011/0/MashavDec2008.pdf (in Hebrew; last visited Aug. 2, 2011).

[12] INBAL & ZAHAVI, *supra* note 7, at 29.

[13] *Id.*

contribute more for "grassroots capacity-building" rather that in an effort to support the absorption of capital inflows.[14]

Israel's aid programs have traditionally focused on the agricultural sector by providing training on the utilization of better irrigation techniques and crop varieties, establishing agricultural collectives, and extending financial and distribution services.[15] Additional areas of foreign aid include rural regional planning, youth programs, training rural women in nutrition and early childhood education, providing medical assistance, etc.

According to MASHAV (the Department for International Cooperation), the Ministry of Foreign Affairs' department that handles foreign aid, in its fifty years of operation the department has provided training to more than 80,000 persons in Israel and about 120,000 persons overseas.[16] MASHAV has been instrumental in providing courses that empowered women from African developing countries to engage in the development process in their countries, preparing doctors and nurses, establishing the first hospital in Zaire, and providing medical assistance and knowledge to Latin American and Asian countries.[17] Israeli scholars have concluded that by the late 1960s and early 1970s, Israel's aid contribution had become "per capita, one of the most extensive technical assistance programs in the western world."[18]

According to its 2010 annual report, MASHAV engaged in a wide variety of international partnerships and development programs, involving 2,459 professionals from ninety-seven countries who participated in 114 courses offered in Israel, and 3,979 professionals in courses overseas. The 2010 report further notes that

> MASHAV experts were dispatched throughout the world on 128 short-term consultancies and humanitarian medical missions to 42 countries, and eight long-term experts were serving on MASHAV demonstration projects around the world in a total of six countries. MASHAV hosted 17 professional delegations, and organized and participated in an impressive number of international conventions.[19]

Evolution of Foreign Aid

Israeli aid and cooperation with the developing world was greatly reduced following the severance of relationships with Israel by all but four African countries in the wake of the October 1973 Yom Kippur War. This led to an immediate 50% drop in MASHAV's operational budget as well as to a shift in the target of aid from Africa to Latin American and Asian countries.

---

[14] *Id.* at 32.

[15] *Id.* at 28.

[16] *MASHAV – The National Assistance Agency of Israel*, MINISTRY OF FOREIGN AFFAIRS, http://www.mfa.gov.il/MFAHeb/General+info/departments+and+sections/mashav+Israels+Agency+for+Internation al+Development+Cooperation.htm (in Hebrew; last visited July 28, 2011).

[17] *Id.*

[18] INBAL & ZAHAVI, *supra* note 7, at 9.

[19] MASHAV ANNUAL REPORT 2010, *available at* http://mashav.mfa.gov.il/mfm/Web/main/document. asp?DocumentID=45172&MissionID=16210&tem (last visited July 28, 2011).

Africa's severance of ties with Israel is said to have significantly reduced Israeli public and political support for its aid program.[20]

A partial reversal of the continued decline of MASHAV budgets occurred in the mid-to late-1990s, "when MASHAV was used during the Oslo process to help solidify newly-established relations with countries from the Middle East, Eastern Europe, and the former Soviet Union."[21] Thus, after signing the Peace Treaty with Egypt, MASHAV operated an agricultural demo farm and provided training for Egyptians. Similarly, following the signing of the Peace Treaty with Jordan MASHAV cooperated with Jordan on agricultural as well as medical projects.[22]

In the late 1990s, following the signing of the 1993 Oslo Accords, MASHAV was also active in providing training to Palestinians. In late 2004 Israel engaged in regional cooperation projects with Jordan, Egypt, and the Palestinian Authority, under the auspices of the Government of Denmark, that have not ceased even in periods of political and security tensions.[23] Scholars have noted, however, that "when prospects for the development of a 'new Middle East' foundered with the demise of the peace process, Israel's foreign aid budget once again shrank considerably."[24]

II. Legal Framework

A. Regulation of ODAs

1. Overview

Israel's official development assistance, as described above, is handled by MASHAV within the Ministry of Foreign Affairs. MASHAV's declared objectives are as follows:

- Assistance for economic and social development
- Assistance for growth and for eliminating poverty and illiteracy in developing countries
- Promotion of state and political contacts
- Strengthening of trade and economic contacts
- Improvement of Israel's image in a recipient state and among other donor countries and in international institutions[25]

---

[20] INBAL & ZAHAVI, *supra* note 7, at 9.

[21] *Id.* at 9-10.

[22] Israel Ministry of Foreign Affairs, *supra* note 11, at 19.

[23] *Id.*

[24] INBAL & ZAHAVI, *supra* note 7, at 10.

[25] The State Comptroller and Ombudsman, Annual Report 55B for 2004 and Accounting for Fiscal Year 2003 [State Comptroller Annual Report] at 603, *available at* http://www.mevaker.gov.il/

MASHAV has declared the following principles as guiding Israel's ODA activities:

1) MASHAV activities focus on areas in which Israel has a comparative advantage and/or accumulated expertise. MASHAV believes that our greatest possible contribution can be made in fields where Israel has expertise directly relevant to emerging nations. The list of such fields is extensive, including: water resource management and irrigation, desert agriculture and combat of desertification, early childhood education, community development, emergency and disaster medicine, refugee absorption and employment programs, and many, many others.

2) MASHAV believes in active consultation with local partners. For development cooperation to work, it is not enough to help the South learn new technologies and methodologies which have had positive effect elsewhere. The solutions that may work in one culture or geographical area often can be inappropriate or even harmful in another environment. Thus, we understand the importance of developing solutions in partnership with local organizations, asking them to help us adapt ideas to local needs rather than just blindly adopt them.

3) MASHAV is committed to cooperation throughout the developing world. We do not limit our activities to a small number of target countries: our focus is on areas of expertise rather than on geographical areas. We extend our hand in partnership wherever Israel's experience is relevant.

4) MASHAV prefers small-scale activities aimed at "bottom-up," community-driven development. MASHAV endeavors to identify relevant micro-project activities that can serve as a catalyst for wider-scale development, targeting the grassroots in many of our activities.

5) MASHAV's focus is on human capacity building and training. Our belief is that training of trainers and other capacity building activities is the best way to achieve maximum impact in development activity. Education leads to empowerment—the surest guarantee of sustainable growth.

6) MASHAV seeks cooperative projects with other development organizations. MASHAV offers partnership in subjects in which Israel has comparative advantage, to all development agencies, governmental as well as non-governmental, international agencies and development banks. MASHAV's experience with such joint projects, often on a cost-sharing basis, has been very positive, broadening the impact of MASHAV's potential contribution and the efficacy of the projects undertaken.

---

serve/contentTree.asp?bookid=426&id=57&contentid=7940&parentcid=undefined&bctype=7939&sw=1024&hw=6 98 (in Hebrew; click on report corresponding to page number 603) (translation by the author, R.L.).

7) MASHAV believes that development cooperation can and should be used to forge bonds of peaceful cooperation with Israel's neighbors. Consequently, MASHAV endeavors to be active throughout the Middle East, regardless of the political climate.[26]

Although MASHAV has declared the above as its guiding principles, it has not established any predefined criteria for the allocation and distribution of resources for their implementation. Moreover, according to Israel's State Comptroller report, MASHAV has not developed any clear action plan that integrates the international agenda into its own activities.[27]

2. Implementing Agencies

MASHAV

The Ministry of Foreign Affairs provides aid to developing countries through MASHAV by transferring knowledge and technology, establishing and operating local projects, and providing humanitarian aid. Aid services are provided by MASHAV's three fully funded professional satellites as well as by independent institutions, including universities, research centers, and the Ministry of Health, on the basis of independent contracts.[28]

According to the State Comptroller's annual report, the three fully funded MASHAV professional satellites are the following:[29]

- *The Golda Meir Mount Carmel International Training Center*. The Center deals with four major areas: advancement of women, preschool education, community development, and development of small factories.

- *The Aharon Ofri International Training Center*. The Ofri Center was established in cooperation with the Ministry of Education, Culture and Sports, and focuses mainly on scientific and technological education, community projects, and absorption of immigrants.

- *The Center for International Agricultural Development Cooperation (CINADCO)*. CINADCO operates as the professional affiliate of MASHAV and implements Israel's cooperation policies with developing nations in the fields of agriculture and rural development.

In 2003, the year for which the most recent State Comptroller's Annual Report on MASHAV's activities is available, two-thirds of MASHAV's training courses for persons from developing countries were in agriculture and the remainder in health, education, and community

---

[26] *Guiding Principles, About MASHAV: Our Mission*, ISRAEL DIPLOMATIC NETWORK, http://mashav.mfa. gov.il/mfm/web/main/document.asp?SubjectID=17267&MissionID=16210&LanguageID=0&StatusID=0&Docume ntID=-1 (last visited Aug. 3, 2011; emphasis in original).

[27] State Comptroller Annual Report, *supra* note 25, at 607.

[28] *MASHAV Highlights: Spotlight on 2010*, *supra* note 2; *See also* State Comptroller Annual Report, *supra* note 25, at 605.

[29] *See* State Comptroller Annual Report, *supra* note 25, at 607.

development. All training, except in the health area, is usually managed by the MASHAV satellites.[30] Training is provided both in Israel for longer periods of time, as well as abroad for two-week periods each. Training abroad usually involves sending a team of two Israeli experts, with the local partner paying for the daily costs and for the use of facilities in which the training takes place, and MASHAV paying all remaining costs.[31]

According to the State Comptroller's Annual Report for 2003 and 2004, MASHAV's budget included both an authorization for net expenses as well as an authorization for an expense that depends on funding from joint projects with foreign governments, with nongovernmental organizations, and with international organizations.[32]

Igud, Company for Technology Transfer

The administration and financial management of MASHAV's satellites and its local training activities are handled by *Igud, the Company for Technology Transfer* (hereinafter *Igud*). *Igud* was established in 1963 as a government company. As a government company, *Igud* must submit an annual financial report to the Agency for Government Companies.[33] *Igud* is managed by and composed of public as well as government representatives, a general manager (who is Deputy Head of MASHAV), a deputy, a representative of the agency for government companies, an accountant, a legal advisor, and an auditor.[34]

Igud operates exclusively for the purpose of implementing plans that have been approved by MASHAV. According to the State Comptroller's Annual Report for 2003–2004, the *Igud* enables MASHAV to overcome various restrictions that apply to government ministries, "especially with regard to signing cooperation agreements with entities that are not interested in direct contact with the government."[35]

Igud's major areas of activities include management of training for MASHAV as well as the independent organizations in Israel, personnel management in CINADCO, contracting with research institutions in Israel and in developing countries, fundraising abroad and creating partnerships with both Israeli as well as foreign institutions, and promoting Israeli exports while achieving a political dividend.[36]

---

[30] Id.

[31] *Id.* at 609.

[32] *Id.* at 614.

[33] Government Companies Law, 5733-1975, § 33, 29 LAWS OF THE STATE OF ISRAEL [LSI] 162 (5735-1974/75), *as amended.*

[34] *See* The Igud – Company for Technology Transfer Financial Reports for December 31, 2007 [Igud Financial Reports], The Agency for Government Companies, *available at* http://www.gca.gov.il/ NR/rdonlyres/43202B73-9446-4000-835F-4B85989E1BB2/0/igud2007.pdf (in Hebrew).

[35] *See* State Comptroller Annual Report, *supra* note 25, at 618.

[36] Igud Financial Reports for 2007, *supra* note 34, at 31.

Igud's budget is composed of both MASHAV and foreign funding sources.[37] In its latest financial report *Igud*'s income is reported as composed of an allocation by MASHAV, proceeds from training courses, as well as from "other [unspecified] income."[38]

3. Restrictions

Israeli law does not contain any specific regulation of foreign assistance. Foreign aid is managed by the MASHAV division of the Ministry of Foreign Affairs and is guided by the objectives and principles discussed above.[39]

Israeli aid does not seem to be tied to procurement by companies either in Israel or in any group of countries. Similarly, although promoting Israel's image and political interests are among the objectives of MASHAV, these objectives are regarded as merely guiding principles and not as legal conditions for assistance.

Foreign aid, however, is subject to certain limitations. Generally, any transactions with countries that are at war with the State of Israel, with individuals who reside in those countries, or with corporations that were incorporated or supervised by residents of such countries are prohibited in accordance with the Trading with the Enemy Ordinance, 1939.[40]

In addition, based on a March 2011 amendment to the Budget Foundations Law, 5745-1985, it appears that MASHAV's foreign aid allocation to specific projects may be reduced if it involves cooperation with organizations that are determined by the Minister of the Treasury to be involved with specific activities, as follows:[41]

Addition of section 3B.

… Reduction of Budget or Support Because of Activity Against the Principles of the State….

b. When the Minister of the Treasury has found that a body has incurred an expense that is in its substance one of the following (in this provision an unfunded expense) he is authorized, with the approval of the minister who is in charge of the budget provision according to which that body is budgeted or funded, after hearing the body, to deduct from the amounts that should be transferred from the State budget to that body according to any law:

---

[37] State Comptroller Annual Report, *supra* note 25, at 603.

[38] IGUD FINANCIAL REPORTS FOR DECEMBER 31, 2010, http://www.gca.gov.il/NR/rdonlyres/A0D36741-D9E6-406D-8D6C-1A158A1860FD/0/haigud.pdf.

[39] *See* Section II.A.1. of this report.

[40] ITON RISHMI [Official Gazette] 923 p. 79 (1939), *available at* the TAKDIN LEGAL DATABASE, http://www.takdin.co.il (by subscription, last visited Aug. 15, 2011). This is a British Ordinance that was applied to Palestine before the establishment of the State of Israel. It is still in force today.

[41] Budgetary Principles Law, 5745, 39 LSI 61 (5745-1984/85), *as amended in* the Budgetary Principles Law (Amendment No. 40), 5761-2011, *available at* THE KNESSET WEBSITE, http://www.knesset.gov.il/privatelaw/data/18/3/315_3_2.rtf (last visited Aug. 3, 2011) (in Hebrew; translation by the author, R.L.).

(1) Negation of the existence of Israel as a Jewish and Democratic state;
(2) Incitement of racism, violence, or terrorism;
(3) Support for armed struggle or a terrorist act of an enemy state or terrorist organization against the State of Israel;
(4) Marking Independence Day, or the date of the establishment of the State as a day of mourning;
(5) An act of vandalism or physical disgrace that harms the State's flag or emblem.[42]

4. Discretionary Aid

Israel's foreign aid budget is allocated to a number of agencies, including the Bank of Israel; the Foreign Affairs Ministry (through MASHAV); the Finance Ministry; and the Ministry of Industry, Trade, and Labor. Whereas the total budget allocation of each ministry is subject to parliamentary approval of the government request for the annual (or biannual) budget allocations, the amount allocated by each ministry or by Bank of Israel to foreign aid is subject to the government's discretion.[43] In that sense, the budget allocated by various governmental ministries is discretionary and spent based on ministerial decisions.

5. Oversight

As a government company, *Igud* must submit its financial reports to the Government Companies Authority.[44] In addition, in accordance with Basic Law on the State Comptroller,[45] the Ministry of Foreign Affairs, including MASHAV, and *Igud* as a government company are both subject to regular audits by the State Comptroller's office.

6. Policy Considerations

The declared objectives of MASHAV's ODA, listed above, reflect Israel's policy considerations and its intention to use Israel's foreign aid to build bilateral as well as multilateral relations. According to the 2009 Tel Aviv University study, "attempts to use MASHAV to build bilateral relationships, both during the 1960s and more recently with Arab states during the Oslo peace process, have led only to short-term diplomatic gains, and longer-term disillusionment with the program."[46]

Citing historical evidence, the study similarly suggested that, while development cooperation might have had some impact on emerging relations with recipient states, "it was unlikely to substantially influence the course of those relations when larger political issues were

---

[42] *Id.* § 3B.

[43] According to information in a statement by the Knesset Center for Research and Information, *supra* note 6, the foreign aid budget "is set up according to a government plan and is not fixed."

[44] Government Companies Law, 5735-1975-29 LSI 162 (5735-1974/75), *as amended.*

[45] Basic Law: the State Comptroller, 42 LSI 24 (5748-1987/88), *available at* the KNESSET WEBSITE, http://www.knesset.gov.il/laws/special/eng/basic9_eng.htm.

[46] INBAL & ZAHAVI, *supra* note 7, at 53.

at stake."[47]   The study proposed, however, that Israeli foreign aid activity may still have a positive effect by "enhancing Israel's standing among United Nations agencies and other development organizations,"[48] and by helping build demand for its services in areas in which it has highly specialized knowledge and experience, such as semiarid agriculture and disaster preparedness.[49]

B. Regulation of Private Contributions

Israel's Income Tax Ordinance recognizes tax credits for individuals or corporations that donated an amount that exceeds NIS 310 (approximately US$84) to national or public institutions as determined by the Minister of the Treasury and authorization of the Knesset Finance Committee, as long as the credit does not exceed 30% of the taxable income for the year or NIS 7.64 million (approximately US$2.08 million), whichever is less.[50]   The Ordinance defines a public institution as follows:

> A group of at least seven persons, or a trust, whose members are not related to each other, that exist and operate for a public purpose and whose assets and income are used exclusively for obtaining the public purpose and who submit a yearly report regarding their assets, income, and expenses, to the satisfaction of the tax assessor in accordance with regulations . . . .[51]

It appears that private contributions may give rise to tax credits in Israel only if they are received by institutions that report their financial activities to Israel's tax authorities. Therefore private donations to MASHAV, to *Igud*, or to other organizations that engage in foreign aid would appear to qualify as a basis for tax credits; direct contributions to foreign organizations, however, do not.

III. Foreign Aid Appropriations Process

As noted above, Israel's foreign aid budget is allocated to a number of government agencies, including the Bank of Israel, the Foreign Ministry (MASHAV), the Ministry of Finance, the Ministry of Industry and Trade, and the Ministry of Labor, among others. The budget is set according to a government plan and is not fixed.[52]   MASHAV's budget, for example, is composed of both appropriated money from the Ministry of Foreign Affairs as well as funding originating from foreign sources.[53]

---

[47] *Id.* at 10.

[48] *Id.* at 11.

[49] *Id.* at 12.

[50] The Income Tax Ordinance, 1 LSI (New Version) 145 (1967) § 46(a), *as amended.*

[51] *Id.* § 9(2)(b) (translated by the author, R.L.).

[52] *See* Information from Knesset Center for Research and Information, *supra* note 6.

[53] State Comptroller Annual Report, *supra* note 25, at 616.

A budget report posted on the Ministry of the Treasury website provides information on foreign aid budget allocations. The report cited the Ministry of Foreign Affairs' budget for MASHAV for fiscal year 2011 as NIS 36.4 million (approximately US$10.118 million). According to the same report, MASHAV spent only 37.07% of its budget for 2011 by August 4, 2011.[54] A similar report for 2012 specifies that the total approved expenses by MASHAV for fiscal year 2012 is NIS 47 million (about US$13.5 million).[55] In allocating funding for its projects MASHAV does not distinguish between bilateral and multilateral agreements, and financial resources seem to come from its general budget.

MASHAV has coordinated various multiyear projects with foreign countries and agencies (such as USAID) as well as with international organizations and development banks. In its 2003 report, Israel's State Comptroller's Office held that multiyear agreements undertaken by the Ministry of Foreign Affairs through MASHAV require authorization by the Ministry of the Treasury because of their budget implications.[56]

Israel has entered numerous bilateral and multilateral cooperation agreements for the provision of foreign aid. Among its bilateral agreements are the following:

- An agreement to pursue a program of development cooperation directed toward alleviating the disastrous effects of the tsunami that hit Sri Lanka in December 2005[57]

- A two-year Cooperation Agreement in the field of aquaculture between the Israeli Ministry of Foreign Affairs and the Ministry of Fisheries of Ghana[58]

- A January 18, 2010, Israeli-German agreement to enhance cooperation in the Middle East, Africa, and Central Asia, with particular emphasis on water management, agricultural development, and public health[59]

Among multilateral cooperation agreements entered into by MASHAV are the following:

- An agreement between Israel and the Joint United Nations Programme on HIV/AIDS signed on April 13, 2011[60]

---

[54] *Search Results for 2011 Performance Data as registered in Ministries' Books 04/08/2011*, ISRAEL MINISTRY OF THE TREASURY, DEPARTMENT OF BUDGET, http://147.237.72.152/magic94scripts/mgrqispi94.dll?APPNAME=budget&PRGNAME=doc3&ARGUMENTS=-N2011,-A09 (last visited Sep. 6, 2011).

[55] *Id.*

[56] State Comptroller Annual Report, *supra* note 25, at 617.

[57] Israel Ministry of Foreign Affairs, *MASHAV Highlights: Spotlight on 2006, available at* http://mashav.mfa.gov.il/mfm/Data/119412.pdf.

[58] *Id.*

[59] *Israel and Germany Sign Memorandum of Understanding*, MASHAV- DEVELOPMENT NEWS (Jan. 24, 2010), http://mashavdevelopmentnews.blogspot.com/2010/01/israel-and-germany-sign-memorandum-of.html.

[60] *Israel Signs First Agreement of Cooperation with UNAIDS*, UNAIDS (April 13, 2011), http://www.unaids.org/en/resources/presscentre/featurestories/2011/april/20110413israel/.

- A 2006 Memorandum of Understanding (MOU) between MASHAV, the Japan International Cooperation Agency (JICA), and the Ministry of Agriculture and Land Reclamation (MALR) of the Arab Republic of Egypt on a Japan–Israel joint training program for Egypt in arid and semiarid areas[61]

- A Regional Agricultural Program, in partnership with Egypt, Jordan, and the Palestinian Authority, with Denmark as the initiator and main supporter[62]

- A Memorandum of Cooperation between the UN World Food Program (WFP) and MASHAV signed in February 2010 in the field of water management, including irrigation and drinking water systems, and specifically relating to Nepal's development strategies[63]

- An MOU between Israel and the Organization of American States (OAS) signed in May 2010, pledging to advance existing collaboration on the issues of education, the environment, economic and social development, poverty, gender equity, disaster prevention and relief, agriculture, security and combating terrorism, and crisis management[64]

In addition to MASHAV's budget, additional funding from foreign independent sources "that are not interested in acting openly with the Israeli government"[65] are being used by *Igud* to further MASHAV's objectives. In its review of both MASHAV and *Igud*'s activities, Israel's State Comptroller found fault with *Igud*'s handling of cooperation with Israeli companies in comparison to foreign companies with regard to opportunities for involvement in MASHAV's projects. The State Comptroller recommended, accordingly, that *Igud* adopt criteria that would provide equal opportunities to Israeli companies that are interested in engaging in joint projects involving assistance to developing countries.[66] It is unclear whether the company has addressed this criticism to date.

IV. Other Types of 'Aid'

Emergency Aid

Emergency aid is provided by the Ministry of Foreign Affairs through MASHAV, by the government company *Igud*, as well as by other organizations through both public and private

---

[61] Israel Ministry of Foreign Affairs, *Middle East and North Africa*, http://mashav.mfa.gov.il/mfm/Data/158512.pdf (last visited Sept. 13, 2011).

[62] According to a MASHAV report for 2008, "[t]he Regional Agricultural Program, in which Egypt, Jordan, Israel, and the Palestinian Authority participate, with Denmark as the initiator and main supporter, is well into its second five-year phase." These agreements are cited due to their importance, in particular in view of the recent regime changes in the Middle East. *See* Israel Ministry of Foreign Affairs, *MASHAV Highlights: Spotlight on 2008*, http://mashav.mfa.gov.il/mfm/Data/158502.pdf.

[63] *MASHAV Highlights: Spotlight on 2010*, *supra* note 2.

[64] *Id.*

[65] State Comptroller Annual Report, *supra* note 25, at 619.

[66] *Id.*

funding. *Igud* has launched disaster relief donation campaigns, including, e.g., for humanitarian aid to Haiti,[67] to supplement its ODA budget. Donations for Japan following the tsunami, however, were collected by the Israeli Red David Shield emergency organization.[68]

Following the devastating earthquake in Haiti, MASHAV funded an Israeli delegation in 2010 composed of medical and search-and-rescue personnel that set up a field hospital and provided medical treatment to over 500 patients a day in addition to performing surgeries.[69] MASHAV also established a Trauma and Emergency Unit in a hospital in Cap-Haïtien, provided medical equipment, and trained the local medical staff.[70] In addition, it built a primary care clinic in the city of Leogane and took part in the efforts to stop the cholera epidemic in Haiti, in cooperation with Sheba Medical Center and the Israeli NGO IsraAID.[71]

Other emergency aid in 2010 included assistance to Colombia after its severe winter floods, assistance to Uzbekistan following recent conflicts between two ethnic communities, and assistance to Albania after the devastating floods that hit the country in December 2010.[72] In 2011 Israel sent medical as well as general assistance to Japan following the tsunami disaster.[73]

Religious Ministries

Israel's state budget allocation for Jewish education overseas is relatively small. In a hearing before the Knesset's Immigration and Absorption Committee conducted almost three years after the 2008 deadly terrorist attack at the Mumbai Chabad House,[74] members of the Knesset discussed Israel's cooperation with programs for outreach and education of overseas Jewry. They "called on the government to increase funding for Chabad educational institutions worldwide, and to restore the budget for Jewish education in the Diaspora, which has been reduced by nearly 80% in recent decades."[75] According to Deputy Education Minister Menahem Eliezer Moses of the political party United Torah Judaism, the state's budget for overseas Jewish

---

[67] *Israel Sending an Assistance Unit to Haiti*, ISRAEL'S MINISTRY OF FOREIGN AFFAIRS WEBSITE, http://www.mfa.gov.il/MFAHeb/Spokesman/2010/Israeli_aid_to_Haiti_140110.htm (in Hebrew; last visited Aug. 8, 2011).

[68] *In Israeli Red David Shield Organization they are Getting Ready to Assist the International Red Cross*, MAGEN DAVID ADOM IN ISRAEL, http://www.mdais.org/316/11532.htm (in Hebrew; last visited Aug. 23, 2011).

[69] *MASHAV Highlights: Spotlight on 2010*, *supra* note 2, at 12.

[70] *Id.*

[71] *Id.* at 13.

[72] *Id.*

[73] *Israel Sending an Assistance Unit to Japan*, ISRAEL MINISTRY OF FOREIGN AFFAIRS, http://www.mfa.gov.il/MFAHeb/Spokesman/2011/Israel_aid_Japan_210311.htm (in Hebrew; last visited Aug. 8, 2011).

[74] *See* News Agencies and Anshel Pfeffer in Mumbai, *9 Dead in Mumbai Chabad House Attack; Israel to Help Identify Bodies*, HAARETZ.COM (Nov. 28, 2008), http://www.haaretz.com/news/9-dead-in-mumbai-chabad-house-attack-israel-to-help-identify-bodies-1.258454.

[75] Rebecca Anna Stoil, *MKs Call for State to Help Fund Chabad Houses*, THE JERUSALEM POST (Mar. 3, 2011), http://www.jpost.com/JewishWorld/JewishNews/Article.aspx?id=210702.

education had plummeted since 1987, when it stood at NIS 48 million (approximately US$13.36 million), to NIS 8 million (US$2.2 million) by 2003.[76] According to data for 2009 published by Israel's Ministry of Education, however, the budget allocation to "Jewish Education Overseas" is NIS 23.18 million (US$6.3 million).[77]

College Scholarships to Foreign Students

Foreign students may obtain scholarships for professional training from Israeli government sources such as MASHAV as well as directly from academic institutions. Government scholarships may be given to students enrolled in the following types of courses:

- Agriculture and related sciences

- Industrial development and management

- Rural and urban economic development

- Medicine and public health[78]

In addition to scholarships from government sources, foreign students may obtain various types of academic scholarships. Some university departments (generally in experimental sciences) offer scholarships and fellowships to individual students and postdoctoral students based on academic merit. Additionally, the Weizmann Institute of Science has a special summer program for undergraduate students as well as for graduate school students.[79]

Other scholarships for foreign students are available from international organizations, including from the International Association for the Promotion of Co-operation with Scientists from the Newly Independent States of the Former Soviet Union (INTAS).[80] While not necessarily targeting students from developing countries, these scholarships certainly may be awarded to qualified students from such countries.

Prepared by Ruth Levush
Senior Foreign Law Specialist
September 2011

---

[76] *Id.*

[77] *Current Budget (2009), Freedom of Information Law,* MINISTRY OF EDUCATION, http://cms.education.gov.il/EducationCMS/Units/Hofesh/DeenVeHeshbon/2009/2009/taktsiv_nohehi.htm (in Hebrew; updated to Dec. 2009).

[78] *Scholarships for Foreign Students for Training in Israel,* ISRAEL SCIENCE AND TECHNOLOGY HOMEPAGE, http://www.science.co.il/Scholarships-international.asp (last visited Aug. 18, 2011).

[79] *Kupcinet-Getz International Summer Science School, Feinberg Graduate School,* WEIZMANN INSTITUTE OF SCIENCE, http://www.fgs.org.il/en/article.php?id=221 (last visited Aug. 18, 2011).

[80] Scholarships for Foreign Students for Training in Israel, *supra* note 78.

LAW LIBRARY OF CONGRESS

JAPAN

REGULATION OF FOREIGN AID

Executive Summary

Japan was the biggest official development assistance (ODA) donor in the 1990s, but its contribution has declined in the 2000s as the national economy has worsened and the national deficit has grown extraordinarily.

There is no law that directly regulates ODA. The Ministry of Foreign Affairs, Ministry of Finance, and Japan International Cooperation Agency are the biggest players in Japan's ODA, but many other ministries are also involved. The lack of comprehensive management of ODA nationwide has been a problem in the past, but this has improved through recent reforms. Still, it is hard to determine ODA, especially with regard to aid that is not approved by the Diet (Japan's Parliament).

I. Introduction

A. Official Development Assistance Figures

Japan reported to the Development Assistance Committee (DAC) of the Organization for Economic Co-operation and Development (OECD) net official development assistance (ODA) of US$9,457 million in 2009, which comprised US$6,167 million in bilateral ODA and US$3,290 million in multilateral ODA.[1] Japan was the fifth largest donor in the world in net disbursements. In gross disbursements, Japan was the second largest donor (US$16,440 million) in 2009, next to the United States.[2] Japan's net ODA for 2009 represented 0.18% of its gross national income (GNI).[3]

While Japan's ODA was the largest in the world during the 1990s, its ODA contributions have declined in the 2000s due to a poor economy and huge national budget deficits.[4] Japan has

---

[1] *ODA by Donor*, OECD.STATEXTRACTS, http://stats.oecd.org/Index.aspx?DatasetCode=ODA_DONOR (select Japan in "Donor" field, then select Net Disbursements in "Flow type" field) (last visited Oct. 19, 2011).

[2] *Id.* (select Gross Disbursements in "Flow type" field).

[3] GNI is "the Gross Domestic Product (GDP) less net taxes on production and imports, less compensation of employees and property income payable to the rest of the world plus the corresponding items receivable from the rest of the world." *Glossary of Statistical Terms: Gross National Income (GNI)*, OECD, http://stats.oecd.org/glossary/detail.asp?ID=1176 (last updated Mar. 5, 2003).

[4] Editorial, *Japan's ODA Strategy*, ASAHI NEWSPAPER (Jan. 27, 2010), http://www.asahi.com/english/TKY201001260328.html

been the fifth largest donor since 2007.[5]   After Japan was devastated by a massive earthquake and subsequent tsunami in March 2011, the ruling party proposed a 20% reduction in ODA contributions because the damage from the earthquake is huge and there would be no room for Japan to help other countries.[6] There were arguments both for and against the reduction. After the earthquake and tsunami, the ODA budget was reduced by about 500 billion yen,[7] or by about 10% of the ODA budget provided by the general budget.[8]

B. Private Contribution Figures

No information on private contribution figures was located.

C. Snapshot of Foreign Aid Activity

Japan's ODA net disbursements in 2009 included 63.4% to bilateral ODA and 36.6% to international organizations.[9] Historically, Asia was the geographic focus of its bilateral ODA, but recently the portion of aid allocated for the Middle East and Africa has increased.[10]

Among the bilateral ODA disbursement, grant aid totaled US$2,208.94 million (23.3% of overall ODA in 2009). Of this amount, debt relief accounted for US$68.33 million at roughly 0.7%; grant aid through international organizations accounted for around 7.0% at US$660.49 million; and funds for other grant aid accounted for about 15.6% at US$1,480.12 million. Additionally, technical cooperation accounted for approximately 32.9% at roughly US$3,118.40 million, and loan aid accounted for approximately 7.1% at US$673.90 million.[11]

The character of Japan's ODA is often described as follows:

> Although it has a traditionally strong focus on infrastructure and industrial production, Japan is gradually engaging with issues including governance and human security, even if such engagements remain limited. Japan is also beginning to emphasize poverty

---

[5] *Nihon no ODA, zennen to onaji sekai 5i, 16.8% zōgaku* [*Japan's ODA, Same No. 5 as Previous Year, Increased 16.8%*], Asahi Newspaper (Apr. 6, 2011), http://www.asahi.com/international/update/0406/ TKY201104060393.html. The Ministry of Foreign Affairs (MOFA) provides main donors' contribution charts for 2001 to 2010. Shuyō enjokoku no ODA jisseki no suii [Changes in ODA Contributions by Main Donors], MOFA, http://www.mofa.go.jp/Mofaj/gaiko/oda/ shiryo/jisseki.html (last visited Oct. 19, 2011).

[6] "ODA sakugen shi fukkō zaigen ni" Minshutō, naikaku ni mousi ire ["Providing a financial source for the reconstruction by reducing ODA," Democratic Party of Japan, proposed to the Cabinet], Asahi Newspaper (Apr. 7, 2011), http://www.asahi.com/politics/update/0406/TKY201104060573.html.

[7] At the October 19, 2011, exchange rate, US$1 is about 77 yen.

[8] National Diet Library, Heisei 23 nendo daiji hosei yosan to kongo no kadai [Issues of the First Amended Budget of 2011 from Now On], Issue Brief No. 711 at 1 (May 24, 2011), http://www.ndl.go.jp/jp/data/ publication/issue/pdf/0711.pdf.

[9] MOFA, Japan's ODA White Paper 2010: Japan's International Cooperation, pt. III, ch. 1, at 39 http://www.mofa.go.jp/policy/oda/white/2010/index.html (click "Part III, Chapter 1").

[10] *Id.* at 41, Chart III-2.

[11] *Id.* at 39.

reduction as a key objective of aid, to be achieved through economic growth rather than the provision of basic services.[12]

II. Legal Framework

A. Regulation of ODAs

1. Overview

The philosophy and principles of Japan's current ODA policies are set forth in the Official Development Assistance Charter (ODA Charter). The current Charter was adopted in 2003.[13] The Charter states, "[t]he objectives of Japan's ODA are to contribute to the peace and development of the international community, thereby helping to ensure Japan's own security and prosperity."[14] Based on the Charter, the Medium-Term Policy on Official Development Assistance and Country Assistance Programs was formulated.[15] Country Assistance Programs that explicitly set out priorities are drawn up for major recipient countries.[16] In addition, the Sector-Specific Development Policies, the Priority Issues for International Cooperation, and the Rolling Plans were formulated.[17]

Country-based ODA Task Forces that are made up of overseas diplomatic missions participate in the formulation of assistance policies like Country Assistance Programs and Rolling Plans. ODA Task Forces also hold policy consultations with the governments of developing countries and offer suggestions on possible collaborations. They review aid schemes and engage in the formation and selection of candidate assistance projects.[18]

---

[12] Event Report summarizing Alina Rocha Menocal's speech, *in The Future of Japan's ODA: Defining Donor Identity in a Crowded Marketplace*, OVERSEAS DEVELOPMENT INSTITUTE (July 14, 2011), http://www.odi.org.uk/events/details.asp?id=2705&title=future-japans-oda-defining-donor-identity-crowded-marketplace#report.

[13] MOFA, Economic Co-operation Bureau, Japan's Official Development Assistance Charter [hereinafter Japan's ODA Charter] (Aug. 29, 2003), http://www.mofa.go.jp/policy/oda/reform/revision0308.pdf.

[14] *Id.* at 1.

[15] *Id.* at 5. ODA policies are available on MOFA's website *at* http://www.mofa.go.jp/policy/oda/policy.html (last visited Oct. 19, 2011).

[16] Japan's ODA Charter, *supra* note 13, at 5–6.

[17] WHITE PAPER 2010, *supra* note 9, pt. III, ch. 2, § 1, at 45–48.

[18] *Id.* pt. III, ch. 2, § 5, at 121.

2. Implementing Agencies

According to the Ministry of Foreign Affairs (MOFA), "[i]n Japan, the Cabinet Office and the 12 ministries and agencies are involved in development assistance."[19] Because many agencies are involved, there have been criticisms of the lack of an overall national policy[20] and of inefficiencies arising from overlapping projects.[21] The Cabinet established the Overseas Economic Cooperation Related Cabinet Members Council within its jurisdiction in 1988,[22] and again in 1993,[23] and the Overseas Economic Cooperation Council in 2006, to tactically and efficiently implement overseas economic cooperation.[24] However, it seems that a lack of leadership is still a problem; calls for a strong headquarters for ODA persist.[25] For the collaboration between related government ministries and agencies, there are the Inter-Ministerial Meeting on ODA, the Experts Meeting on Technical Cooperation, and the Experts Meeting on ODA Evaluation.[26] MOFA was identified as the center for the coordination of the entire government in terms of overall ODA planning since Central Government Reform in 2001.[27]

In the bilateral aid arena, MOFA has a central role in ODA policymaking. MOFA set up the International Cooperation Bureau in 2006, which comprehensively plans and drafts policies relating to ODA and coordinates with other agencies.[28] While MOFA makes policies, the Japan International Cooperation Agency (JICA) is responsible for aid implementation. JICA has undertaken "the integrated management of three modalities of assistance—technical cooperation, ODA loans, and grant aid"—since October 2008.[29] There are also grants that ministries

---

[19] *Id.* at 121.

[20] Seisaku Koso [Policy Building] Forum, Teigen [Suggestion] No. 43, *Seifu Kaihatsu enjo (ODA) no kokka senryaku o tsukure* [Make ODA National Strategy] at 1–2 (July 17, 2001), http://www.grips.ac.jp/forum/pdf01/odasenryaku.pdf.

[21] Keidanren, ODA kaikaku ni kansuru teigen [Proposal on ODA Reform] § 3(2) (Oct. 16, 2001), http://www.keidanren.or.jp/japanese/policy/2001/049.html.

[22] Statement of Kimio Fujita, Gaikō·sōgō anzen hoshō ni kansuru chōsakai kokusai keizai·shakai shō iinkai uchiawase kai [International Economy, Public Affairs, Small Committee Under Foreign Affairs Security Committee], Minutes, No. 1 (Mar. 8, 1989), House of Councilors, 114th Diet Session, http://kokkai.ndl.go.jp/SENTAKU/sangiin/114/1489/main.html.

[23] Kakuryō kaigi no kaisai ni tsuite [Regarding Having Cabinet Member Meeting], Cabinet Oral Agreement (Aug. 24, 1993), http://www.kantei.go.jp/jp/singi/oda/konkyo.html. Though all Cabinet member meetings were abolished in 1993, some of them were reestablished.

[24] Kaigai keizai kyōryoku kaigi no secchi ni tsuite [Regarding Establishment of Overseas Economic Cooperation Council], Cabinet Decision (Apr. 28, 2006), http://www.kantei.go.jp/jp/singi/kaigai/konkyo.html.

[25] Izumi Ohno, ODA kaikaku: 5tsu no teigen [Five Recommendations for Future Development Cooperation], slide 5 (Dec. 13, 2010), http://www.devforum.jp/bbl/pdf/20101213_02.pdf.

[26] WHITE PAPER 2010, *supra* note 9, pt. III, ch. 2, § 5, at 120.

[27] Chūō shōchō tō kaikaku kihon hō [Basic Act on Central Government Reform], Law No. 103 of 1998, art. 19, item 4.

[28] WHITE PAPER 2010, *supra* note 9, pt. III, ch. 2, § 5, at 120.

[29] Strategy 1: Integrated Assistance, *Mission Statement*, JICA, http://www.jica.go.jp/english/about/mission/index.html#vision (last visited Oct. 19, 2011).

implement by themselves.[30]   Regarding ODA loans, MOFA consults with the Ministry of Economy, Trade and Industry (METI) and the Ministry of Finance (MOF).[31]   Faster implementation of ODA loans was discussed and measures to achieve this were implemented among them.[32]

JICA had a more limited role until recently. JICA was reorganized from 2006 to 2008. The former JICA carried out only technical cooperation and promotion of executing grant aid. The Overseas Economic Cooperation operation under the former Japan Bank for International Cooperation (JBIC) was in charge of providing ODA loans. JICA has now merged with JBIC. Also at that time, some of the actual implementation duties for grant aid that had previously belonged to MOFA were transferred to the new JICA.[33]

3. Restrictions

Japan's ODA Charter states that any use of ODA for military purposes or to provoke international conflicts should be avoided.[34]

With regard to the procurement system, in 2007, the ratio of Japan's untied ODA worldwide was 95.1%.[35]   Tied aid "often prevents recipient countries from receiving good value for money for services, goods, or works."[36]   Japan has untied ODA beyond the requirements of the Recommendation to Untie Official Development Assistance to the Least Developed Countries that was adopted by the DAC High Level Meeting in April 2001.[37]

---

[30] *Enjo jisshi taisei [Aid Implementation System]*, MOFA, http://www.mofa.go.jp/mofaj/gaiko/oda/about/ keitai/taisei.html (see notes on the bottom illustrated chart) (last visited Oct. 20, 2011).

[31] There appears to be no particular legal basis for this three-ministry consultation system. The consultation system is mentioned casually in various documents, but no explanation is provided. *E.g., Enjo jisshi taisei [Aid Implementation System]*, MOFA, http://www.mofa.go.jp/mofaj/gaiko/oda/about/keitai/taisei.html (see bottom illustrated chart) (last visited Oct. 20, 2011).

[32] Press Release, MOFA, En shakkan no jinsokuka ni tsuite [Faster Process of Yen Loan] (June 18, 2007), http://www.mofa.go.jp/mofaj/press/release/h19/6/1174072_806.html; Press Release, MOFA, MOF, METI & JICA, En shakkan no jinsokuka ni tsuite [Faster Process of Yen Loan] (July 15, 2010), http://www.mof.go.jp/international_ policy/economic_assistance/press_release/enshaku-jinsokuka-honbun.pdf.

[33] WHITE PAPER 2010, *supra* note 9, pt. III, ch. 2, § 5, at 121.

[34] Japan's ODA Charter, *supra* note 13, at 5.

[35] Q2, *ODA Q&A*, EMBASSY OF JAPAN IN THE PHILIPPINES (July 2010), http://www.ph.emb-japan.go.jp/bilateral/oda/qa.htm.

[36] *Untying Aid: The Right to Choose*, OECD, http://www.oecd.org/document/50/0,3746,en_2649_ 33721_46345330_1_1_1_1,00.html (last visited Oct. 21, 2011).

[37] *Id.*

4. Oversight

MOFA primarily focuses on evaluations of policies and programs. JICA, as the implementer of individual projects, mainly takes on project evaluations. ODA-related ministries and agencies also conduct evaluations of their ODA activities. MOFA holds the Inter-Ministerial Liaison Meeting on ODA Evaluation and collects results of ODA evaluations conducted by each government ministry.[38] Policy evaluations by Japanese ministries expanded when the Government Policy Evaluations Act was enforced in 2002.[39]

Regarding MOFA's policy and program-level evaluations, "evaluations are conducted from the perspectives of the relevance of the policy, the effectiveness of the results, and the appropriateness of the process."[40] To guarantee the objectivity and transparency of the evaluations, many MOFA ODA evaluations are carried out by third parties. Joint evaluations with partner country governments and organizations are also carried out.[41]

JICA developed a common, post-project evaluation method for all three forms of ODA: Technical Cooperation, ODA Loans, and Grant Aid. "Each project is evaluated on (1) relevance, (2) effectiveness (impact), (3) efficiency, and (4) sustainability."[42]

5. Policy Considerations

Japan provides ODA "taking into account developing countries' need for assistance, socio-economic conditions, and Japan's bilateral relations with the recipient country."[43] In addition, Japan pays attention to recipient countries' environmental conservation and development, military expenditures and activities against international peace and stability, efforts to promote democratization, introduction of a market-oriented economy, and protection of basic human rights and freedoms.[44]

It is important that the developing countries' development policies and assistance needs are aligned with Japan's assistance policies. The Japanese government engages in dialogue and policy consultations with developing countries. It carries out policy consultations with governmental parties from the partner country prior to the aid request from the country.[45]

---

[38] ODA EVALUATION DIVISION, INTERNATIONAL COOPERATION BUREAU, MOFA, ODA EVALUATION GUIDELINES 11 (6th ed., Feb. 2009), http://www.mofa.go.jp/policy/oda/evaluation/basic_documents/guideline.pdf.

[39] Gyōsei kikan ga ukonau seisaku no hyōka ni kansuru hōritsu [Government Policy Evaluations Act], Law No. 86 of 2001.

[40] WHITE PAPER 2010, *supra* note 9, pt. III, ch. 2, § 5, at 132.

[41] ODA EVALUATION DIVISION, *supra* note 38, at 10.

[42] JICA, ANNUAL EVALUATION REPORT 2010 at 18, http://www.jica.go.jp/english/operations/evaluation/reports/2010/pdf/part2-1.pdf (last visited Oct. 20, 2011).

[43] Japan's ODA Charter, *supra* note 13, at 5.

[44] *Id.*

[45] WHITE PAPER 2010, *supra* note 9, pt. III, ch. 2, § 5, at 121.

B. Private Contributions

There are ways for individuals and companies to deduct or reduce taxable income through charitable contributions.[46] Private contributions to qualified organizations in Japan that engage in development assistance in developing countries may be tax deductible. Individuals' donations to designated trusts for public purposes may be tax deductible. To qualify for tax-deductible contributions, a trust's purpose must reflect one of those purposes specified in the law. One such purpose is monetary donations for economic cooperation in developing countries.[47]

III. Foreign Aid Appropriations Process

According to MOFA's chart in the ODA White Paper, "Budgetary Financing Sources for the ODA Project Budget and Expenditure by Type of Assistance," Japan uses four financing sources for ODA: the General Account, the Special Account, issuance of government bonds, and fiscal loans and investments.[48]

A. Complexities of Japanese Public Finance

The word "budget" is sometimes confusing when used to describe Japan's public finances. As the Ministry of Internal Affairs and Communications stated, "Japan's national budget consists of the general account, special accounts, and the budget for government-affiliated agencies."[49] Although it is separate from the national budget, the Fiscal Investment and Loan Program (FILP) is sometimes described as part of the budget. FILP "uses various interest-bearing public funds, such as the Fiscal Loan Fund, which issues FILP bonds in the financial market to implement various public policies such as social infrastructure and policy-based loans."[50] FILP is "so large as to earn the appellation 'the second budget.' "[51] The financial source of Japan's ODA includes FILP.

---

[46] Income Tax Law, Law No. 33 of 1965, *last amended by* Law No. 6 of 2010, arts. 78 & 120; Corporation Tax Law, Law No. 34 of 1965, *last amended by* Law No. 65 of 2010, art. 37; Tax Special Measures Law, Law No. 29 of 1957, *last amended by* Law No. 65 of 2010, arts. 41-18, 41-18-3, 41-19 & 66-11-2, and related regulations.

[47] Income Tax Law Enforcement Order, Order No. 96 of 1965, *last amended by* Order No. 50 of 2010, art. 217-2, para. 3, item 7.

[48] WHITE PAPER 2010, *supra* note 9, pt. IV, ch. 1, § 1, at 139, Chart IV-7.

[49] STATISTICS BUREAU, MINISTRY OF INTERNAL AFFAIRS AND COMMUNICATIONS (MIC), STATISTICAL HANDBOOK OF JAPAN, ch. 4.1, "National and Local Government Finance," http://www.stat.go.jp/english/ data/handbook/index.htm (last visited Oct. 20, 2011).

[50] *Understanding the Japanese Budget 2004*, pt. I.4.1, BUDGET BUREAU, MINISTRY OF FINANCE (MOF), http://www.mof.go.jp/english/budget/budget/fy2004/brief/2004b_01.htm#2 (last visited Oct. 20, 2011).

[51] Tanaka, Hideaki, *Postal Reform and the Fiscal Investment and Loan Program: Toward Democratic Control of Government Finances (1)*, TOKYO FOUNDATION (June 23, 2010), http://www.tokyofoundation.org/ en/articles/2010/postal-reform-and-the-fiscal-investment-and-loan-program-toward-democratic-control-of-government-finances-1.

In the national budget, the General Account may be the most important category because, using revenues from general sources such as taxes, it covers core national expenditures such as social security, education, and national defense.[52]　Special Accounts are "established by legislation under specific conditions.　The accounts may be instituted when the government needs to carry out specific projects, to administer and manage specific funds, or to administer revenues and expenditures separately from the General Account."[53]　Government-affiliated agencies are "entities established by special laws and are entirely funded by the government."[54] JICA's Loan Aid Section is one such agency.

B. General Account Budget Process

The Cabinet prepares the budget and presents it to the Diet.[55]　First, the Cabinet issues the Guidelines for Budget Requests that set initial expenditure ceilings for major programs such as public works and social security for the next fiscal year's budget to ministries and agencies. "These ceilings are usually expressed in terms of absolute or percentage increase (decrease) vis-à-vis the previous fiscal year's amount."[56]　Each ministry must prepare its budget request within the limits of these guidelines.　About a month later, each ministry submits its budget request to the MOF.[57]　Following the submission of budget requests, budget examiners of the Budget Bureau in MOF begin a series of hearings with each ministry and agency on the details of their budget requests.　After the discussion between MOF and the Cabinet, the Cabinet releases guidelines for formulation of the budget.[58]　Following this decision, a draft of the draft budget is finalized by MOF and presented to each ministry and agency.[59]　After final negotiations on the budget requests between the MOF and each ministry and agency, the draft budget is approved by the Cabinet.[60]　The Cabinet first submits it to the House of Representatives.[61]　After approval by the House of Representatives the budget is sent to the House of Councilors. Following its passage in the House of Councilors, the budget becomes effective on April 1, the beginning of the Japanese fiscal year.[62]

---

[52] STATISTICS BUREAU, MIC, *supra* note 49.

[53] BUDGET BUREAU, MOF, *supra* note 50, pt. I.2.2.

[54] STATISTICS BUREAU, MIC, *supra* note 49.

[55] NIHONKOKU KENPŌ [CONSTITUTION OF JAPAN] (1946), art. 73, item 5.

[56] BUDGET BUREAU, MOF, *supra* note 50, pt. I.7.1 (click "next page" at the bottom of the page).

[57] *Id.*; Zaisei hō [Public Finance Law], Law No. 34 of 1947, *last amended by* Law No. 152 of 2002, art. 17, para. 2.

[58] Public Finance Law, art. 18, para. 1.

[59] BUDGET BUREAU, MOF, *supra* note 50, pt. I.7.2.

[60] The Minister of Finance drafts the budget and the Cabinet approves it.　Public Finance Law, art. 21.

[61] The budget must first be submitted to the House of Representatives. CONSTITUTION OF JAPAN, *supra* note 55, art. 60, para. 1.

[62] BUDGET BUREAU, MOF, *supra* note 50, pt. I.7.3.

C. Procedure for FILP

The FILP process is basically the same as the budget process. Government ministries and agencies submit their requests for FILP to MOF. MOF holds hearings with related organizations, reviews requests, negotiates changes, and then finalizes the FILP plan at the same time as the draft budget is formed. The FILP plan is not subject to Diet approval but is submitted to the Diet as an attachment to the Special Account Budget.[63]

D. ODA Budget Sources

The General Account is the main source of funding for grant aid, technical cooperation, and contributions through the United Nations (UN) or UN-related organizations. Government bonds are the main source of funding for contributions through multilateral development banks (MDBs). FILP is mainly used for *yen* loans.[64] It was not possible to locate a comprehensive explanation of the entire ODA budget of Japan.

Regarding the General Account ODA budget, each ministry and agency includes its ODA budget in the budget request, as stated above. The General Account ODA budget consisted of 35% of the gross ODA project budget in 2010. Two-thirds of that amount was under MOFA jurisdiction.[65] One percent of the ODA gross project budget is from a Special Account.[66]

Issuance of government bonds constitutes 16.6% of the ODA gross project budget.[67] It was not possible to locate an explanation as to why MDB contributions are outside of the General Account. Matters regarding MDBs are under the jurisdiction of MOF.[68]

FILP provides 47.3% of the ODA gross project budget. This is mainly used for *yen* loans. A *yen* loan is decided after several processes. First, a developing country government requests consideration of a loan. Then, MOFA conducts a preliminary investigation at its office in the developing country. If necessary, an investigator is dispatched from Japan. Next, JICA examines the case, and MOFA drafts a plan. MOFA discusses the proposed loan with MOF, METI, other relevant ministries (if any), and JICA. If the loan is approved by them, a draft of the exchange note for the *yen* loan is sent to the Cabinet. The Cabinet makes the final decision.[69]

---

[63] MOF, FILP REPORT 2010 pt. I.4 (Aug. 2010), http://www.mof.go.jp/english/filp/filp_report/ zaito2010/zaito2010-1-04.html.

[64] *Hayawakari ODA* [*Quick View of ODA*], MOFA, http://www.mofa.go.jp/mofaj/gaiko/oda/nyumon/ hayawakari/hayawakari_4.html (last visited Oct. 20, 2011); MOFA, Heisei 20 nendo ODA jigyō yosan no gaiyō to sono zaigen [Budget Source and Summary of 2008 ODA], http://www.mofa.go.jp/mofaj/gaiko/oda/shiryo/yosan/ pdfs/20_gai_zai.pdf (last visited Oct. 20, 2011).

[65] WHITE PAPER 2010, *supra* note 9, pt. IV, ch. 1, § 1, at 139, Chart IV-7.

[66] *Id.*

[67] *Id.*

[68] Zaimusho secchi hō [Law Concerning Establishment of MOF], Law No. 95 of 1999, *last amended by* Law No. 74 of 2011, art. 4, item 52.

[69] MOFA, 2009 nen ban sankō shiryō shū [2009 Reference Materials], at 73, http://www.mofa.go. jp/mofaj/gaiko/oda/shiryo/hakusyo/09_hakusho_sh/pdfs/s2-7.pdf.

IV. Other Types of 'Aid'

The following are examples of different types of development assistance provided by the Japanese government that are outside of the general ODA framework described above.

A. Emergency Aid

"Japan has three tools for emergency assistance for overseas disasters: (i) Dispatch of Japan Disaster Relief Team; (ii) Provision of Emergency Relief Goods; and (iii) Emergency Grant Aid."[70] Depending on "the magnitude of the disaster and requests from the affected country," one or more of these tools are chosen.[71] Japan began dispatching emergency medical teams abroad in 1979. Since then, a Japan Disaster Relief Team (JDR) was expanded to include a rescue team and other post-disaster experts.[72] The Law Concerning Dispatch of the Emergency Relief Team was enacted in 1987.[73]

B. Funding Assistance for Japanese NGOs

The Japanese government has a program, Grant Assistance for Japanese NGO Projects, for providing government funds for economic and social development projects undertaken by Japanese NGOs in developing countries and regions. In Japan's fiscal year 2006, approximately 2,000 million yen (about US$26 million) was provided as Grant Assistance for Japanese NGO Projects. The assistance was used for eighty-eight projects in twenty-six countries conducted by about thirty-nine organizations.[74]

C. Cooperation Among Trade, Investment, and Other Official Flows

In addition to ODA, Japan uses Other Official Flows (OOFs)[75] to support promotion of small- and medium-size enterprises in developing countries, the transfer of industrial technology, and other economic policies.[76]

---

[70] *Humanitarian Assistance/Emergency Assistance*, MOFA, http://www.mofa.go.jp/policy/emergency/index.html (last visited Oct. 20, 2011).

[71] *Id.*

[72] Kokusai kinkyū enjotai hossoku no keii to enkaku [Establishment of JDR and JDR History], JICA, http://www.jica.go.jp/jdr/history.html (last visited Oct. 20, 2011).

[73] Kokusai kinkyū enjotai no haken ni kansuru hōritsu [Law Concerning Dispatch of Emergency Relief Team], Law No. 93 of 1987, *last amended by* Law No. 118 of 2006.

[74] MOFA, International Cooperation Bureau, Non-Governmental Organizations Cooperation Division, International Cooperation and NGOs: Partnership Between the Ministry of Foreign Affairs and Japanese NGOs 7 (Nov. 2007), http://www.mofa.go.jp/policy/oda/category/ngo/partnership/english.pdf.

[75] OOFs are "Transactions by the official sector with countries on the List of Aid Recipients which do not meet the conditions for eligibility as Official Development Assistance or Official Aid, either because they are not primarily aimed at development, or because they have a Grant Element of less than 25 per cent." Definition, Other Official Flows (OOFS), Glossary of Statistical Terms, OECD, http://stats.oecd.org/glossary/detail.asp?ID=1954 (last visited Jan. 10, 2012).

[76] WHITE PAPER 2010, *supra* note 9, pt. III, ch. 2, § 2, at 58.

Regarding access to Japanese markets, Japan adopts lower tariff rates than the general rates for exports of products from developing countries. According to a MOFA White Paper, "Duty-Free and Quota-Free measures are also taken for Least Developed Countries (LDCs). Japan also actively promotes Economic Partnership Agreements (EPAs), and supports economic growth in developing countries through the liberalization of trade and investment."[77]

Prepared by Sayuri Umeda
Senior Foreign Law Specialist
October 2011

---

[77] *Id.* at 58.

LAW LIBRARY OF CONGRESS

KUWAIT

REGULATION OF FOREIGN AID

Executive Summary

Kuwait is one of the leading providers of official development assistance to developing countries, averaging 1.5% of its gross national income (GNI) for the period between 1973 and 2008, according to a study conducted by the World Bank. Kuwait implements its development assistance program through the Kuwait Fund for Arab Economic Development. Kuwait is also a major donor of humanitarian assistance and a participant in a number of regional and international development institutions.

I. Introduction

A. Official Development Assistance Figures

According to a study conducted by the World Bank, Kuwait, along with Saudi Arabia and the United Arab Emirates, played a major role in assisting developing countries in the financing of their development projects. The official development assistance (ODA) amounts provided by the three countries during the last four decades averaged 1.5% of their gross national incomes (GNIs), a rate much higher than the United Nations target of 0.7% or the actual average provided by the Organization for Economic Co-operation and Development (OECD) member states.[1]

B. Private Contribution Figures

Contributions from Kuwaiti private donors to developing countries are generally assumed to be substantial given the country's wealth but no reliable figures are available in this respect.

C. Snapshot of Foreign Aid Activity

For the fiscal year ending March 31, 2010, Kuwait's foreign aid activities through official development assistance covered the financing of twenty-three projects in twenty-two countries, distributed as follows:

- Seven Arab countries
- Seven African countries
- Five countries in Southeast Asia and the Pacific

---

[1] Mustapha Rouis, *Arab Development Assistance: Four Decades of Cooperation*, MENA KNOWLEDGE AND LEARNING QUICK NOTES SERIES (World Bank), Aug. 2010, at 1, http://siteresources.worldbank.org/INTMENA/Resources/QuickNote28-ArabODA.pdf.

- Three Asian and European countries

- One Latin American and Caribbean countries[2]

The percentage share of the total aid was distributed among these countries as follows: 53.94% to the Arab countries, 14.55% to the African countries, 19.33% to the Southeast Asian and Pacific countries, 9.97% to the Asian and European countries, and 2.21% to the Latin American and Caribbean countries. The sectors benefiting from these projects included energy, water and sewage, and agriculture,[3] at a total cost of 199 million Kuwaiti dinars.[4]

II. Legal Framework

A. Regulation of ODAs

1. Overview

The Kuwait Government is a major donor of humanitarian aid. From 2000 to 2008 it gave a total of US$221 million, ranking as the fourth highest non-Development Assistance Committee (DAC) contributor for this period.[5]

2. Implementing Agencies

Kuwait channels its official development assistance to other countries through the Kuwait Fund for Arab Economic Development (KFAED or Fund), which is a Kuwaiti public institution whose Charter was first established by a decision issued by the Prime Minister pursuant to Law No. 35 of 1961. Originally the mandate of the Fund was limited to assist Arab countries only. However, the mission and scope of the Fund's activities was broadened in 1974 to include all developing countries when Law No. 35 of 1961 was replaced by Law No. 25 of 1974.[6]

The objective of the Fund, as provided for in article 2 of Law No. 25 of 1974, is to assist the Arab and other developing countries in the development of their economies, and to provide them with loans necessary for the implementation of their development programs, in a manner consistent with the regulations issued by the Prime Minister that serves the national interests of the State of Kuwait and supports its regional and international foreign policy.

---

[2] KUWAIT FUND FOR ARAB ECONOMIC DEVELOPMENT [THE FUND], FORTY EIGHTH ANNUAL REPORT, 2009/2010 at 16, http://www.kuwait-fund.org/images/annual48_english/2%20-%2019.pdf. The number and geographic areas of the recipient countries change from year to year.

[3] *Id.*

[4] At the current exchange rate, one Kuwaiti dinar is equal to about US$3.67. *See* http://coinmill.com/KWD_USD.html#KWD=1 (last visited Aug. 26, 2011).

[5] *Kuwait: Introduction*, GLOBAL HUMANITARIAN ASSISTANCE, http://www.globalhumanitarianassistance.org/countryprofile/kuwait (last visited Aug. 26, 2011).

[6] Arabic copies of Law No. 25 of 1974 and the Fund Charter are available on the Fund's website, http://www.kuwait-fund.org/publications/general/law_and_basic_info_a.pdf (in Arabic; last visited Aug. 26, 2011).

3. Restrictions

The assistance provided by the Fund is not subject to any specific restrictions concerning the types of projects that it finances or participates in financing. However, due to the needs of the beneficiary countries, the focus of the assistance has been concentrated primarily on agriculture, irrigation, transport, communications, water and sewage, and energy.[7]

There is also no restriction as to which entities within the beneficiary countries can seek the Fund's assistance. Pursuant to article 17 of the Charter, the Fund may extend its assistance to any entity that has juridical personality, public or private, that contributes to the economic development of the beneficiary country as long as the objectives of such entities are not limited to for-profit activities only. However, the Fund may request the beneficiary countries to be a guarantor for the implementation by the recipient entities of their obligations and the loan agreements.

The Fund's Charter requires in particular that the agreement contain a commitment on the part of the borrowing country not to tax the assets of the Fund, to keep such assets and income free from exchange control, and not to give other foreign debt priority over the Fund's debt.[8] The Fund may of course impose whatever other restrictions it deems necessary as conditions in the loan agreement on a case-by-case basis.

4. Discretionary Aid

There are no provisions in the Law that established the Fund or in its Charter that allow it to give discretionary aid outside the norms described in the Law.

5. Oversight

As a public institution that enjoys an independent juridical personality, the Fund is subject to the oversight of its Board of Directors and auditors, and the general oversight of the Kuwaiti Government.

6. Policy Considerations

Law No. 25 of 1974 authorizing the establishment of the Fund as well as its most recent Charter issued by the Prime Minister in 1981 give the board of directors of the Fund a wide discretionary power to set the conditions of the loans as it deems desirable. Even the provision that requires the loan not to exceed 50% of the total cost of the project can be overlooked if the Board of Directors so decides.[9]

---

[7] FORTY EIGHTH ANNUAL REPORT, *supra* note 2, at 1.

[8] Fund Charter, *supra* note 6, art. 20.

[9] *Id.* arts. 18, 21.

B. Regulation of Private Contributions

It appears that private contributions are not regulated by the Kuwaiti Government. Rather, its policy, according to a World Bank report dating from 1990, is to not be involved in such activities.[10]

III. Foreign Aid Appropriations Process

In addition to the disbursement processes established by the Board of Directors of the Fund, Kuwait is a participant in a number of regional and international development institutions, such as the Arab Fund for Economic and Social Development, each of which appropriates development funds according to its own rules and processes.

IV. Other Types of 'Aid'

No information was found as to whether Kuwait provides or regulates other types of aid in addition to its official development assistance program.

Prepared by Issam M. Saliba
Senior Foreign Law Specialist
October 2011

---

[10] Nural Abdulhadi, *The Kuwaiti NGOs: Their Role in Aid Flows to Developing Countries*, para. 4 (World Bank, Working Paper No. 524, Oct. 1990), http://www-wds.worldbank.org/external/default/WDSContentServer/WDSP/IB/1990/10/01/000009265_3960930001418/Rendered/PDF/multi_page.pdf.

LAW LIBRARY OF CONGRESS

NEW ZEALAND

REGULATION OF FOREIGN AID

Executive Summary

The New Zealand government provides a separate appropriation for the majority of its official development assistance activities. In 2010, the amount of aid provided equated to about 0.26% of GNI. The appropriation includes funding for bilateral, regional, and multilateral programs, with a particular focus on the Pacific region. A recent policy document sets out the overarching objectives, policy considerations, and approaches relating to the provision of development assistance. Aid is untied and there is an emphasis on partnerships with recipient countries and with international organizations in terms of establishing joint priorities as well as in implementing the aid program. New Zealand's development assistance activities also include scholarships, a guest worker program, and initiatives aimed at improving the remittance system. The aid program is managed by the Ministry of Foreign Affairs and Trade, which also works with other government agencies and with New Zealand nongovernmental organizations involved in foreign aid activities. Oversight mechanisms include mandatory annual reports to Parliament as well as external peer reviews and evaluations.

I. Introduction

A. Official Development Assistance Figures

The most recent OECD figures available show that New Zealand's official development assistance (ODA) funding was US$352.83 million in 2010, which equated to 0.26% of Gross National Income (GNI).[1] The New Zealand government sought an ODA budget for the 2011/12 financial year of NZ$586.17 million (about US$491.55 million), which is made up of the following:

- Over NZ$61 million for the "Management of New Zealand Official Development Assistance (ODA)"

- Over NZ$94 million for contributions to international organizations

- Nearly NZ$33 million for contributions to nongovernmental organizations (NGOs)

---

[1] *ODA by Donor*, OECD.STATEXTRACTS, http://stats.oecd.org/Index.aspx?DatasetCode=ODA_DONOR (last visited Aug. 17, 2011) (select "New Zealand" in "Donor" box and "Net Disbursements" from "Flow type" box).

- Nearly NZ$129 million from an existing multiyear appropriation for Global Development Assistance

- Nearly NZ$269 million from an existing multiyear appropriation for Pacific Development Assistance[2]

The OECD has noted that "New Zealand plans to achieve an ODA level of $NZ 600 million by 2012-13 and appears on track to meet this."[3] The New Zealand government did not provide GNI percentage figures in its ODA budget documentation for the current financial year and also stated that the planned increases had been deferred:

> From 2002 to 2009, New Zealand increased Vote ODA [ODA appropriations] progressively to achieve ODA:GNI targets. Since 2009/10, budget increases for Vote ODA are based on performance and delivery of outcomes, rather than ODA:GNI targets, resulting in New Zealand committed [sic] to increases of $25 million in 2011/12 and $50 million 2012/13 and outyears.

> However due to current fiscal pressures, the commitment to further increases in Official Development Assistance has been deferred over four years rather than two. This results in a decrease of $100 million spent on Official Development Assistance over 2012/13 to 2014/15.

> As 2011/12 is the final year of the Pacific and Global multiyear appropriations, it includes the reforecast of funds unspent in the first two years. This results in an increase in expenditure in 2011/12, compared to the original forecast in Budget 2009. A multiyear appropriation has this flexibility to allow for the time to develop activities over the three year period.[4]

B. Private Contribution Figures

In its 2009/10 Annual Report, the Council for International Development (CID), an umbrella organization for ninety-five nongovernmental organizations (NGOs) working in the area of international development, stated that income generated through fundraising by the NGOs for the 2009/10 financial year amounted to NZ$130 million (about US$107 million) received from an estimated 750,000 New Zealanders.[5] The Council reported that there had been

---

[2] New Zealand Government, The Estimates of Appropriations for the Government of New Zealand for the Year Ending 30 June 2012: Vote Official Development Assistance (May 2011), available at http://www.treasury. govt.nz/budget/2011/estimates/est11offdev.pdf.

[3] *Development Aid Reaches an Historic High in 2010*, OECD DEVELOPMENT CO-OPERATION DIRECTORATE (DCD-DAC), http://www.oecd.org/document/35/0,3746,en_2649_34447_47515235_1_1_1_1,00.html (last visited Aug. 17, 2011).

[4] New Zealand Government, Information Supporting the Estimates of Appropriations for the Government of New Zealand for the Year Ending 30 June 2012, External Sector, Performance Information for Appropriations: Vote Official Development Assistance 137 (May 2011), available at http://www.treasury.govt.nz/budget/ 2011/ise/v4/ise11-v4-pia-offdev.pdf.

[5] Council for International Development, *CID Annual Report 2009-10* at 1 (2010), *available at* http://www.cid.org.nz/assets/About/2010annual-report.pdf. This was a reduction from the previous year when the NGOs received NZ$144.18 million (about US$119.5 million) from private contributions. Council for International

a significant reduction in the funding that it received from the New Zealand government for the year, as well as challenges faced by members arising from a number of natural disasters in the region.[6]

C. Snapshot of Foreign Aid Activity

In March 2011, the New Zealand government published an "International Development Policy Statement" that sets out its "overarching policy" on international development assistance.[7] The document followed a number of structural and funding changes and policy adjustments relating to New Zealand's aid program that were introduced in early 2009 by the incoming government. This included establishing the following mission statement:

> The mission of the New Zealand Aid Programme is to support sustainable development in developing countries, in order to reduce poverty and to contribute to a more secure, equitable, and prosperous world.[8]

Specific themes and approaches that contribute to achieving this overarching goal are discussed in the sections below.

In terms of the geographic focus of New Zealand's aid program, priority has historically been accorded to the Pacific region, where there are unique challenges as well as historical ties between New Zealand and the various countries within the region. The current government has clearly stated that this focus should be maintained and that "there will be close cooperation with Australia and other donors on development in the Pacific, in line with our commitment in the Cairns Compact, the Paris Declaration and the Millennium Development Goals."[9] Over half of New Zealand's total aid spending goes to countries in the Pacific region.[10]

Development, *CID Annual Report* 11 (2009), *available at* http://www.cid.org.nz/assets/About/2009Annual reportweb.pdf.

[6] *Id.* (2009-10 Annual Report) at 1-2.

[7] New Zealand Ministry of Foreign Affairs & Trade Aid Programme [NZ Aid Programme], *International Development Policy Statement* (Mar. 2011), *available at* http://www.aid.govt.nz/what-we-do/Int_Dev_Policy_Statement_Supporting_Sustainable_Development.pdf.

[8] New Zealand Government, *Cabinet Paper: New Zealand Agency for International Development: Mandate and Policy Settings* (Apr. 2009), *available at* http://www.aid.govt.nz/library/publications/corporate/cabinet-papers-mandate-policy-cabpaper3.html; New Zealand Government, *Cabinet Minute of Decision: CAB Min (09) 13/3C – New Zealand Agency for International Development: Mandate and Policy Settings (Paper Three)* (Apr. 20, 2009), *available at* http://www.aid.govt.nz/library/publications/corporate/cabinet-papers-mandate-policy-cabmin3.html.

[9] *Id.* at 3. *See also The Millennium Development Goals,* NZ AID PROGRAMME, http://www.aid.govt.nz/what-we-do/international-targets.html (last visited Aug. 17, 2011). Note that New Zealand's relationship with Australia is an important component of the broader approach and policies relating to ODA. In 2009, the two countries signed the Australia-New Zealand Partnership for Development Cooperation, which "sets out the shared vision and high-level objectives for cooperation." *Australia: Overseas Development Assistance,* MINISTRY OF FOREIGN AFFAIRS AND TRADE [MFAT], http://www.mfat.govt.nz/Foreign-Relations/Australia/2-Political-links/0-ODA.php (last visited Aug. 18, 2011).

[10] *About the New Zealand Aid Programme,* NZ AID PROGRAMME, http://www.aid.govt.nz/about/ (last visited Aug. 18, 2011).

In addition to the Pacific region, the government has stated that there will be a "targeted approach" to providing development assistance to countries in Asia, Africa, and Latin America. This is due to New Zealand's relative size, with the government therefore stating that New Zealand's "comparative advantage" in a selection of areas should guide the program.[11] This means that, in Africa and Latin America, a significant focus of the aid program will be support for agriculture, while in Asia "New Zealand will focus on complementing ASEAN's (Association of South East Asian Nations) community building goals through the agreed flagship areas of scholarships, agriculture, disaster risk management, and fostering young business leaders."[12] The education and economic linkages with Asian countries is also reflected in New Zealand's support for tourism, renewable energy, and English language training in that region.[13]

Documents published by the Ministry of Foreign Affairs and Trade (MFAT), which manages the New Zealand Aid Programme, provide more specific information about its activities and approaches in different areas. The overall program was previously made up of thirty-three programs in a range of countries and sectors.[14] However, starting from the 2011–12 year, a new program framework has been adopted that will reduce the number of programs to twenty-four.[15] These programs include bilateral support, involving direct assistance to twenty countries;[16] regional programs aimed at contributing to "the reduction of poverty by focusing on thematic issues such as growth and livelihoods, education, health, governance";[17] and partnerships with and contributions to multilateral agencies and programs.[18] In terms of this latter area, a significant proportion—around one third—of New Zealand's ODA budget is spent on working with multilateral agencies. Following a review, ten agencies have been prioritized for increased engagement.[19]

This engagement with multilateral agencies, as well as with New Zealand NGOs, is an important aspect of New Zealand's approach to responding to humanitarian needs and natural

---

[11] *International Development Policy Statement*, *supra* note 7, at 12.

[12] *Id.* at 4.

[13] *Id.*

[14] *New Zealand Aid Programme Activities*, NZ AID PROGRAMME, http://www.aid.govt.nz/what-we-do/ (last visited Aug. 17, 2011). *See also Where New Zealand's Aid is Focused*, NZ AID PROGRAMME, http://www.aid.govt.nz/programmes/ (last visited Aug. 17, 2011).

[15] *See* MFAT, *Statement of Intent 2011–2014* (April 2011), *available at* http://mfat.govt.nz/Media-and-publications/Publications/Statement-of-Intent/index.php (last visited Aug. 17, 2011).

[16] *Country and Regional Aid*, NZ AID PROGRAMME, http://www.aid.govt.nz/what-we-do/bilateral-aid.html (last visited Aug. 17, 2011).

[17] *New Zealand Aid Programme Activities*, *supra* note 14.

[18] *Id.*

[19] *Multilateral Aid*, NZ AID PROGRAMME, http://www.aid.govt.nz/what-we-do/multilateral-aid.html (last visited Aug. 17, 2011). The top ten agencies are: United Nations Development Programme, United Nations Children's Fund, United Fund for Population Activities, United Nations High Commissioner for Refugees, World Food Programme, United Nations Office of the High Commissioner for Human Rights, United Nations Office for the Coordination of Humanitarian Affairs, World Bank International Development Association, Asian Development Bank – Asia Development Fund, and OECD Development Assistance Committee.

disasters, particularly outside of the Pacific region. The MFAT New Zealand Aid Programme division provides advice to Ministers on responses to specific emergencies. Broadly, however, beyond the Pacific, "New Zealand's response is generally part of a broader international effort with support provided through United Nations (UN) multilateral agencies specialising in humanitarian assistance, the Red Cross movement and New Zealand nongovernmental organisations (NGOs) with partners in the affected country."[20]

The New Zealand Aid Programme also partners with other New Zealand government agencies in order to plan and implement some of its activities. The involvement of such agencies in the program is discussed further below.

II. Legal Framework

A. Regulation of ODAs

1. Overview

The overarching policies relating to the development and implementation of New Zealand's aid program are established by executive branch decision-making processes (i.e., involving the responsible Minister and the Cabinet) with funding and agency activities overseen by Parliament, which must approve appropriations. MFAT, as the relevant executive agency, is responsible for implementing these policies and for providing information and advice to the government to assist its decision-making, as well as developing the accountability documents required by law.[21] In this context, the government in March 2011 established the mission statement set out above along with four "priority themes" that "will guide the New Zealand Aid Programme in stimulating sustainable development."[22] These are

- investing in economic development,
- promoting human development,
- improving resilience and responding to disaster, and
- building safe and secure communities.[23]

These themes, and the types of activities that fall within them, are explained in further detail in the policy document. In addition, the document sets out a number of approaches related to the development and delivery of the aid program that are intended to:

---

[20] *Humanitarian and Emergency Assistance*, NZ AID PROGRAMME, http://www.aid.govt.nz/what-we-do/humanitarian-assistance.html (last visited Aug. 17, 2011).

[21] Under the State Sector Act 1988, the chief executive of each government department is responsible to the appropriate Minister for: "carrying out the functions and duties of the department (including those imposed by Act or by government policy); providing advice to Ministers; the good conduct of the department; and the efficient, effective and economical management of the activities of the department." *State Sector Act 1988*, STATE SERVICES COMMISSION, http://ssc.govt.nz/node/8408 (last visited Aug. 17, 2011).

[22] *International Development Policy Statement, supra* note 7, at 5.

[23] *Id.*

- Make aid more effective;

- Improve efficiency and value for money;

- Enhance accountability for results;

- Integrate cross-cutting and thematic issues;

- Increase responsiveness and flexibility;

- Ensure consistency of development assistance and foreign policy;

- Focus on New Zealand's comparative advantage; and

- Work through partnerships.[24]

Some of the approaches that relate to these goals are drawn from or include references to international objectives, commitments, and best practices, while others reflect domestic values and interests.

The above policies are also reflected in Ministry of Foreign Affairs and Trade's Statement of Intent for 2011–2014. The international development assistance mission statement is set out as "Outcome 4" in this document, which also sets out intermediate outcomes for the period covered.[25] The themes and approaches established by the government are then included to demonstrate how the agency intends to achieve those outcomes.

In terms of the legislative regime, MFAT, including its management of the aid program, is governed by the range of statutes that apply to all government agencies. These include the New Zealand Bill of Rights Act 1990 and Human Rights Act 1993, Official Information Act 1982, the Public Finance Act 1989, and the State Sector Act 1988.[26] In addition, the terms of United Nations sanctions relating to countries, individuals, or entities, as implemented in New Zealand through individual regulations, need to be adhered to by New Zealand government agencies and NGOs.[27]

2. Implementing Agencies

Twice in the past ten years the structural arrangements relating to the agency responsible for New Zealand's ODA program have been changed significantly. Prior to 2002, the program

---

[24] *Id.* at 10–12.

[25] *Statement of Intent 2011–2014*, *supra* note 15, Outcome 4, http://mfat.govt.nz/Media-and-publications/Publications/Statement-of-Intent/0-operating-intentions-cont.php (last visited Aug. 17, 2011).

[26] *See Core State Sector Legislation*, STATE SERVICES COMMISSION, http://ssc.govt.nz/legislation (last visited Aug. 25, 2011).

[27] For lists of current sanctions implemented in New Zealand, including links to the relevant regulations, *see Recent United Nations Security Council Sanctions Implementation*, MFAT, http://www.mfat.govt.nz/Treaties-and-International-Law/09-United-Nations-Security-Council-Sanctions/index.php; *United Nations Security Council Sanctions: Assets Freeze Measures,* MFAT http://www.mfat.govt.nz/Treaties-and-International-Law/09-United-Nations-Security-Council-Sanctions/Assets-freeze-measures.php (last visited Aug. 17, 2011).

was managed by MFAT. Then, in 2002, the government established a semi-autonomous agency within MFAT called the New Zealand Agency for International Development (NZAID).[28] This agency operated until 2009 when the incoming government rescinded the semi-autonomous status of NZAID and reintegrated the management of the program back into MFAT, with the program renamed as the New Zealand Aid Programme.[29] The rationale for the change in status explained that it would

- normalise institutional arrangements within MFAT by bringing NZAID into line with standard management and accountability arrangements for Public Service departments;

- be enabling in nature with regard to future developments. Subsequent questions around whether, what, how and when actual changes may occur in terms of any integration of NZAID and its operations in MFAT would be a matter for the Secretary of Foreign Affairs and Trade to determine in his or her capacity as chief executive of the department. The onus would be on the chief executive to consult with relevant Ministers and others, to ensure that the institutional arrangements for MFAT including NZAID are fit for purpose to deliver on all the goals and priorities across the Foreign Affairs Portfolio.[30]

MFAT's mandate with respect to the management of the ODA program was also amended in 2009 in order to "reflect the Government's priorities as set out in the pre-election manifesto."[31] In particular, the central focus of the program shifted from the elimination of poverty to "sustainable economic development."[32] The government's decisions also included the geographic focus, development approaches, and thematic issues discussed above.[33] An overview of the political context for the policy directions and institutional arrangements was also considered by the Cabinet and this information made publicly available.[34]

MFAT is the lead agency for New Zealand's external relations and works closely with, and is consulted by, other agencies that are involved in work that impacts this area. Government

---

[28] *About the New Zealand Aid Programme*, NZ AID PROGRAMME, http://www.aid.govt.nz/about/ (last visited Aug. 18, 2011).

[29] *See* New Zealand Government, *Cabinet Paper: New Zealand Agency for International Development: Institutional Arrangements* (Apr. 2009), *available at* http://www.aid.govt.nz/library/publications/corporate/cabinet-papers-institutional-arrangements-cabpaper2.html; New Zealand Government, *Cabinet Minute of Decision: CAB Min (09) 13/3A – New Zealand Agency for International Development: Institutional Arrangements (Paper Two)* (Apr. 20, 2009), *available at* http://www.aid.govt.nz/library/publications/corporate/cabinet-papers-institutional-arrangements-cabmin2.html.

[30] *Cabinet Paper: New Zealand Agency for International Development: Institutional Arrangements*, *supra* note 29, ¶ 5.

[31] *Cabinet Paper: New Zealand Agency for International Development: Mandate and Policy Settings*, *supra* note 8, ¶ 1.

[32] *Id.* ¶ 2.

[33] *Id.* ¶ 10.

[34] New Zealand Government, *Cabinet Paper: Pacific Island Forum Countries: NZ Policy on Aid, Trade and Economic Development Overview Paper* (Apr. 2009), *available at* http://www.aid.govt.nz/library/publications/corporate/cabinet-papers-pifc-nz-policy-cabpaper1.html.

agencies may receive ODA-related funding, either directly through their own appropriations for specific activities or through arrangements that form part of the New Zealand Aid Programme. For example, the New Zealand Police and the New Zealand Defence Force receive some direct funding for the operation of international programs aimed at improving law and order and security, particularly in the Pacific.[35] These agencies may also receive funding through the New Zealand Aid Programme for activities such as assisting with responses to natural disasters.

In terms of other funding for government agency initiatives, the New Zealand Aid Programme operates the State Sector Development Partnerships Fund, which "provides a contestable funding source for New Zealand state sector organisations to work in partnership with New Zealand's development partners to achieve sustainable development outcomes in their areas of expertise."[36]

3. Restrictions

The policy context, discussed above, includes specific reference to the need to align the aid program with New Zealand's broader approach to foreign and trade policy. In fact, MFAT's Statement of Intent for 2011–2014 states that:

> Development cooperation advances New Zealand's well-being by contributing to New Zealand's relationships with partner countries and the building of a secure, equitable and prosperous world. It is a core pillar of New Zealand's wider foreign and trade policy.[37]

However, this focus on the country's broader interests and policies does not include any requirements relating to the use of New Zealand products and contractors in delivering the program. The International Development Policy Statement includes the following statements in explaining the approaches that will be used to improve efficiency and value for money in the aid program:

- Development interventions, approaches and practices will represent the best value for money for New Zealand and country partners.

---

[35] *See FAQ About New Zealand Police Overseas*, NEW ZEALAND POLICE, http://www.police.govt.nz/ service/overseas/faq.html (last visited Aug. 18, 2011), stating that "Most of the short-term deployments the New Zealand Police undertake are commissioned and funded by the Government's international aid and development agency NZAID. The agency has a Pacific focus that is aligned with the Government's responsibility to be a good neighbour. Other long-term operations, such as Operation Tuiatuia in the Solomons are funded as part of the police budget." In addition, the Defence Act 1990 "allows the Armed Forces to be made available for the performance of public services and assistance to the civil power in time of emergency, either in New Zealand or elsewhere. The NZDF also undertakes or supports a range of tasks, including maritime resource protection, humanitarian assistance and disaster relief, and search and rescue, as part of a whole-of-government effort directed by civil authorities." New Zealand Defence Force, *Statement of Intent 2011-2014* at 7 (2011), *available at* http://www.nzdf.mil.nz/downloads/ pdf/public-docs/2011/soi/nzdf-soi-2011-14.pdf.

[36] *New Zealand State Sector Development Partnerships Fund (SSDPF)*, NZ AID PROGRAMME, http://www.aid.govt.nz/what-we-do/dpf.html (last visited Aug. 18, 2011).

[37] *Statement of Intent 2011–2014*, *supra* note 15, Outcome 4.

- Value for money will continue to be evaluated at the inception of new initiatives, during design and during procurement. Increased efforts will be made to ensure that this can be demonstrated.

- New Zealand will engage in a strategic dialogue with partner country governments to ensure that both aid resources and partners' domestic resources are used as effectively as possible to achieve development outcomes.[38]

The New Zealand Aid Programme's contracting processes follow the government's procurement guidelines.[39] These guidelines focus on value for money and include requirements relating to "open and effective competition" among suppliers from any country, while also seeking to ensure "full and fair opportunity for domestic suppliers."[40] MFAT's guidance for contractors clearly describe a nondiscriminatory approach, stating that "[t]here are no restrictions in relation to who may submit a tender. Consultants are not required to be resident in New Zealand or be New Zealand citizens."[41]

The contracting processes include open tenders as well as an Approved Contractor Scheme, which "provides MFAT with a pool of pre-tendered, pre-selected consultants to undertake short-term assignments."[42] This scheme is currently under review to ensure that contracting aligns with the strategic direction of the program.[43]

Among other situations, the open tender process is applied where MFAT "wishes to outsource the implementation of an in-country New Zealand Aid Programme project."[44] A particular model is used in these cases, involving the contractor assuming responsibility for the management of the project's implementation in conjunction with the relevant agency in the partner country. This is seen as promoting "partner ownership, achieving more sustainable outcomes, delivering good results efficiently, and flexibility to meet changing and emerging needs."[45]

In terms of the use of goods manufactured in New Zealand, MFAT has recently provided information to the body that represents manufacturers (ManufacturingNZ) regarding why New Zealand's aid spending cannot be tied to New Zealand suppliers. This information was aimed at

---

[38] *International Development Policy Statement, supra* note 7, at 10.

[39] *Contracts,* NZ AID PROGRAMME, http://www.aid.govt.nz/contracts/ (last visited Aug. 18, 2011).

[40] *See* New Zealand government procurement website, http://www.business.govt.nz/procurement/for-agencies/government-policy (last visited Aug. 18, 2011).

[41] *Contracting Guidelines*, NZ AID PROGRAMME, http://www.aid.govt.nz/contracts/contracting-guidelines.html (last visited Aug. 18, 2011). For a list of awarded contracts, *see Awarded Contracts*, NZ AID PROGRAMME, http://www.aid.govt.nz/contracts/awarded-contracts.html (last visited Aug. 18, 2011).

[42] Id.

[43] *Approved Contractor Scheme*, NZ AID PROGRAMME, http://www.aid.govt.nz/contracts/acs.html (last visited Aug. 18, 2011).

[44] *Management Services Contracts (MSC)*, NZ AID PROGRAMME, http://www.aid.govt.nz/contracts/msc.html (last visited Aug. 18, 2011).

[45] Id.

supporting MFAT's view that "there are bigger benefits to New Zealand companies if aid is not tied to local suppliers but is put out to tender to all comers, as this allows NZ companies to tender in a much bigger international aid pool than if we were just tendering for the NZ aid spend."[46] It included figures showing that New Zealand suppliers and contractors had benefited from contracts arising from Asian Development Fund and World Bank projects.

4. Discretionary Aid

The New Zealand Aid Programme includes contestable funding opportunities for government agencies, NGOs, private entities, and individuals.[47] The guidelines for these funds set out particular objectives, criteria, and documentation requirements that must be met before funding can be granted, with funding decisions made at the discretion of MFAT. In addition to the State Sector Development Partnerships Fund referred to above, the following funds are available:

- Asia Development Assistance Facility-Partnerships for Sustainable Development (ADAF-PSD), which is targeted at government agencies and private entities that have established a partnership with an organization from an eligible country in Asia.[48]

- Latin American Development Assistance Facility-Partnerships for Sustainable Development, which is similar to the ADAF-PSD fund but focused on projects relevant to development priorities that involve partnerships with organizations in Latin America.[49] This fund is currently under review.

- South Africa Fund for Exchange (SAFE), which was established to "assist in building people-to-people links between the Eastern Cape Province of South Africa and New Zealand by facilitating opportunities for people-to-people interaction and exchange."[50] Applications must be submitted jointly by the New Zealand and Eastern Cape based parties.

---

[46] Press Release, ManufacturingNZ, International Aid Spend and Opportunities for NZ Suppliers (June 24, 2011), http://www.manufacturingnz.org.nz/news-and-info/latest/international-aid-spend-and-opportunities-for-nz-suppliers.

[47] *See Funding Opportunities,* NZ AID PROGRAMME, http://www.aid.govt.nz/what-we-do/funding-opportunities.html (last visited Aug. 25, 2011).

[48] *Asia Development Assistance Facility*, NZ AID PROGRAMME, http://www.aid.govt.nz/adaf/ (last visited Aug. 25, 2011). For eligibility requirements and criteria *see* NZAID (NZ Aid Programme), *ADAF-PSD Guidelines* (Feb. 2006), *available at* http://www.aid.govt.nz/adaf/docs/adaf-psd-guidelines.pdf.

[49] *Latin America Development Assistance Facility*, NZ AID PROGRAMME, http://www.aid.govt.nz/ladaf/ (last visited Aug. 25, 2011). For eligibility requirements and criteria, *see* NZAID (NZ Aid Programme), *LADAF-PSD Guidelines* (Feb. 2006), *available at* http://www.aid.govt.nz/ladaf/docs/ladaf-psd-guidelines.pdf.

[50] *South Africa Fund for Exchange (SAFE)*, NZ AID PROGRAMME, http://www.aid.govt.nz/what-we-do/safe.html (last visited Aug. 25, 2011). For eligibility requirements and criteria, *see* NZ Aid Programme, *South Africa Fund for Exchange ("SAFE")* (June 2010), *available at* http://www.aid.govt.nz/what-we-do/docs/safe-guidelines-june-2010.pdf.

- Pacific Island Countries Participation Fund, which supports attendance by Pacific Islanders at regional and international conferences.[51]

- International Development Research Fund (IDRF), which assists New Zealand-based researchers to carry out research likely to improve development policy and practice in partnership with researchers from developing countries.[52] This program is also currently under review.[53]

- Postgraduate Field Research Awards, which are available to students from New Zealand universities seeking to undertake field research in developing countries. This program, along with the IDRF, is currently under review.[54]

5. Oversight

MFAT, including the New Zealand Aid Programme, are subject to the standard oversight mechanisms applicable to New Zealand government agencies. These include Ombudsman investigations and reviews,[55] Auditor-General processes,[56] and parliamentary oversight by way of appropriations and accountability requirements, such as the mandatory annual reporting system.[57] The government's International Development Policy Statement states that MFAT

---

[51] *Pacific Island Countries Participation Fund,* NZ AID PROGRAMME, http://www.aid.govt.nz/pic/ (last visited Aug. 25, 2011).

[52] *International Development Research Fund,* NZ AID PROGRAMME, http://www.aid.govt.nz/what-we-do/idrf.html (last visited Aug. 25, 2011).

[53] *International Development Research Fund: Application Guidelines,* NZ AID PROGRAMME, http://www.aid.govt.nz/what-we-do/idrf-application-guidelines.html (last visited Aug. 25, 2011).

[54] *Postgraduate Field Research Awards,* NZ AID PROGRAMME, http://www.aid.govt.nz/what-we-do/postgraduate-awards.html (last visited Aug. 25, 2011).

[55] MFAT comes under the jurisdiction of the Office of the Ombudsmen, a legislative branch agency that investigates complaints about government agencies, receives reports of serious wrongdoing under the Protected Disclosures Act, and undertakes investigations on its own initiative. *See What We Do,* OFFICE OF THE OMBUDSMEN, http://www.ombudsmen.govt.nz/index.php?CID=100005 (last visited Aug. 25, 2011). *See also* Ombudsmen Act 1975 sch 1, *available at* http://www.legislation.govt.nz/act/public/1975/0009/latest/DLM431204.html, which lists the agencies to which the Act applies.

[56] See, e.g., Performance Audits from 2008: Follow-up Report – New Zealand Agency for International Development: Management of Overseas Aid Programmes, OFFICE OF THE CONTROLLER AND AUDITOR-GENERAL, http://www.oag.govt.nz/2010/performance-audits/overseas-aid-programmes.htm (last visited Aug. 25, 2011).

[57] Annual reports of government agencies are required by section 43 of the Public Finance Act 1989, *available at* http://www.legislation.govt.nz/act/public/1989/0044/latest/DLM160809.html. *See also Performance Information for Appropriations: Vote Official Development Assistance, supra* note 4, at 143, stating that "[t]he four appropriations are managed through 24 programmes (such as the Samoa programme, the Humanitarian & Disaster Response programme, or the multilateral agencies programme), each of which has a strategic framework that specifies appropriate objectives and development outcomes. Progress towards these programme objectives and the contribution of New Zealand's ODA is monitored and rated annually, with results printed in the MFAT Annual Report. Each of the programmes consists of a number of ODA activities, of which there are around 700 in total. Each of these activities has its own objectives and monitoring and evaluation arrangements. There are extensive reporting obligations for MFAT's implementing partners and a requirement that MFAT regularly assess progress and quality of the activities it administers. Results, including from MFAT's reviews and evaluations of activities, are reported in aggregate in the MFAT Annual Report."

"will use its Annual Report to monitor and report on progress, including the fit of the New Zealand Aid Programme with the themes and approaches set out in this policy."[58]

The policy document also includes reference to the need for "robust monitoring and evaluation procedures" to ensure that the program is accountable and to improve practices as well as mitigating future risks.[59] The New Zealand Aid Programme defines evaluation as "the assessment of planned, ongoing or completed development projects."[60] The program is also subject to reviews, "which take place at key points during the lifetime of a development activity."[61] Reviews and evaluations are managed by divisions within MFAT's New Zealand Aid Programme and involve commissioning reports from external providers. An Evaluation and Research Committee provides "oversight of evaluative activities and research studies" and "ensure[s] close feedback between evaluative activities and programme planning and development."[62] An Evaluation Policy Statement and Evaluation Guidelines explain how evaluations are to be carried out.[63]

New Zealand is a member of the OECD Development Assistance Committee (DAC) Network on Development Evaluation[64] and is subject to periodic peer reviews under the OECD processes. The most recent peer review report was published in 2005.[65]

6. Policy Considerations

As part of its approach to the aid program, New Zealand has made clear moves towards greater coordination with other donors and with recipient countries in terms of focusing assistance on jointly identified areas of need. The International Development Assistance Policy includes a statement that aid activities "will be closely aligned to partner country needs, and support will be provided to partners to develop sound plans, seek innovative ideas and jointly monitor implementation."[66] In addition, the document states that "New Zealand will engage in a strategic dialogue with partner country governments to ensure that both aid resources and partners' domestic resources are used as effectively as possible to achieve development

---

[58] *International Development Policy Statement*, *supra* note 7, at 13.

[59] *Id.* at 11.

[60] *New Zealand Aid Programme Evaluation*, NZ AID PROGRAMME, http://www.aid.govt.nz/what-we-do/evaluation-at-nzaid.html (last visited Aug. 18, 2011).

[61] Id.

[62] Id.

[63] *Evaluation Policy Statement*, NZ AID PROGRAMME, http://www.aid.govt.nz/what-we-do/evaluation-policy-statement.html (last visited Aug. 18, 2011). Links to the Evaluation Guidelines for different types of evaluations are available on the *New Zealand Aid Programme Evaluation* page, *supra* note 60.

[64] *Members of the DAC Network on Development Evaluation*, OECD-DAC, http://www.oecd.org/document/62/0,3746,en_21571361_34047972_34518718_1_1_1_1,00.html (last visited Aug. 18, 2011).

[65] OECD Development Assistance Committee, *DAC Peer Review: New Zealand* (2005), *available at* http://www.aid.govt.nz/library/docs/dac-peer-review-report.pdf.

[66] *International Development Policy Statement*, *supra* note 7, at 10.

outcomes."[67]   There is also to be increased focus on mutual accountability for results and on greater accountability on the part of recipient governments.[68]

These concepts were also reflected in the Cairns Compact on Strengthening Development Coordination in the Pacific,[69] signed in 2009 by New Zealand and Australia together with other members of the Pacific Islands Forum.[70] This compact was based on a number of principles, including reference to the need to draw on international best practices as expressed in the Paris Declaration on Aid Effectiveness and an acknowledgment that "country leadership, mutual accountability and mutual responsibility between Forum Island countries and their development partners are fundamental to successful development outcomes."[71]

The agreed approaches set out in the compact include annual reporting by Forum Island countries, with assistance from New Zealand and Australia, on the implementation of a process of regular peer reviews of national development plans; annual reporting by the Forum Secretariat on progress towards the Millennium Development Goals and the effectiveness of development efforts in the region; and "directing the Forum Secretariat to coordinate with relevant development partners to develop a 'road map' aimed at progressive strengthening of Forum Island countries' public expenditure management, procurement, accountability and monitoring systems so they are the best delivery mechanisms for official development assistance."[72]   In addition, the countries agreed that there should be close alignment of regional aid efforts with regional priorities.

In July 2011, within the context of the principles of the Cairns Compact and other international declarations, New Zealand entered into joint development agreements with Samoa,[73] Tonga,[74] and the Cook Islands.[75] These agreements set out mutually agreed goals and investments in priority sectors in order to guide New Zealand's development assistance efforts in those countries. They also establish commitments from the recipient countries, including the development of long-term sector plans and the reflection of these in national planning and

---

[67] Id.

[68] *Id.* at 11.

[69] The Cairns Compact on Strengthening Development Coordination in the Pacific (Aug. 2009), *available at* http://www.forumsec.org/resources/uploads/attachments/documents/Cairns%20Compact%202009.pdf.

[70] *See generally*, PACIFIC ISLAND FORUM SECRETARIAT, http://forum.forumsec.org/ (last visited Aug. 18, 2011).

[71] Id.

[72] Cairns Compact, *supra* note 69.

[73] Samoa-New Zealand Joint Commitment for Development (July 2011), *available at* http://www.aid.govt. nz/programmes/samoa-joint-commitment-development.pdf; *see generally Samoa,* NZ AID PROGRAMME, http://www.aid.govt.nz/programmes/c-samoa.html (last visited Aug. 18, 2011).

[74] Tonga-New Zealand Joint Commitment for Development (July 2011), *available at* http://www.aid. govt.nz/programmes/tonga-joint-commitment-development.pdf; *see generally Tonga,* NZ AID PROGRAMME, http://www.aid.govt.nz/programmes/c-tonga.html (last visited Aug. 18, 2011).

[75] New Zealand-Cook Islands Joint Commitment for Development (July 2011), *available at* http://www.aid.govt.nz/programmes/cooks-joint-commitment-development.pdf; *see generally Cook Islands,* NZ AID PROGRAMME, http://www.aid.govt.nz/programmes/c-cook-islands.html (last visited Aug. 18, 2011).

budgeting processes, and the provision of clear guidance on areas each country wishes New Zealand to invest in. Under the agreements, discussions on performance and progress towards the goals are to be held annually.

B. Regulation of Private Contributions

New Zealand NGOs and private entities operating in the area of foreign aid must comply with the relevant registration and reporting requirements that apply to companies,[76] charitable organizations,[77] or incorporated societies,[78] depending on their organizational arrangements.[79] Entities with a "charitable purpose" that are registered by the Charities Commission may receive tax benefits.[80] Such entities are required to submit annual returns to the Commission.[81] Charitable organizations that are assessed by the Inland Revenue Department as being fully exempt from tax do not need to file income tax returns unless requested, but are required to maintain accurate records.[82]

If an entity's own rules permit funds to be spent on a charitable purpose overseas it can still register as a charity in New Zealand. The Charities Commission states that

1. New Zealand entities will not fail the charitable purpose test simply because they have an overseas purpose or their public benefit is directed overseas—for example, a New Zealand entity established with the purpose of relieving poverty in another country.

---

[76] *See* Companies Act 1993, *available at* http://www.legislation.govt.nz/act/public/1993/0105/latest/DLM319570.html.

[77] *See* Charitable Trusts Act 1957, *available at* http://www.legislation.govt.nz/act/public/1957/0018/latest/DLM308796.html; Charities Act 2005, *available at* http://www.legislation.govt.nz/act/public/2005/0039/latest/DLM344368.html.

[78] *See* Incorporated Societies Act 1908, *available at* http://www.legislation.govt.nz/act/public/1908/0212/latest/DLM175775.html.

[79] *See generally, Setting Up a Development Sector Group or Project*, GLOBAL FOCUS AOTEAROA, http://www.globalfocus.org.nz/?page=DevelopmentSector!PracticeGuides!SettingUpADevelopmentSectorGroupOrProject#Establishing%20your%20NGO%20as%20a%20legal%20entity (last visited Aug. 24, 2011).

[80] Under the Charities Act 2005, charitable entities registered under the Charitable Trusts Act 1957, Companies Act 1993, or the Incorporated Societies Act 1908, must also register with the Charities Commission in order to "access certain tax benefits on the grounds of charitable purpose." Charities Commission, *How the Charities Act Affects Charitable Trusts, Incorporated Societies and Companies* (June 2009), *available at* http://www.charities.govt.nz/Portals/0/docs/infosheet_trusts_societies.pdf. Under section 5 of the Charities Act 2005, "charitable purpose" includes "the relief of poverty, the advancement of education or religion, or any other matter beneficial to the community." In order to qualify for exemptions, the organizations aims must be "exclusively charitable" and no income or funds may be used "to benefit any of its members, trustees or associates." *Charitable Organisations*, INLAND REVENUE DEPARTMENT (IRD), http://www.ird.govt.nz/charitable-organisations/chart-orgs-intro/ (last visited Aug 24, 2011).

[81] Charities Act 2005 s 42.

[82] *Charitable Organisations*, *supra* note 80.

2. To be eligible for registration under the Charities Act, overseas entities must either be 'established in New Zealand' or have a 'very strong connection' to New Zealand so that we are able to monitor them and carry out our enforcement functions.[83]

Donations to charitable entities that meet the criteria for "donee status" may entitle the donor to a tax credit under the Income Tax Act 2007.[84] The Inland Revenue Department administers the process for entities to be treated as a donee organization, including receiving information from the Charities Commission.[85] However, there are limitations on the ability for entities involved in charitable work overseas to qualify for donee organization status. The Inland Revenue Department states

[d]onations to organisations that apply most of their funds overseas will not qualify for donee organisation status, unless the organisation:

- has been approved as a donee organisation by the New Zealand Parliament, or

- sets up a separate fund maintained exclusively for providing money for charitable, benevolent, philanthropic, or cultural purposes within New Zealand.[86]

New Zealand government funding for New Zealand-based NGOs is primarily distributed through contestable funding programs.[87] Organizations that wish to apply for funding must be accredited by MFAT. Two funds are available: the Sustainable Development Fund, which focuses on activities relating to sustainable economic development, and the Humanitarian Response Fund. Eligibility criteria and conditions of funding, including reporting requirements, are set out in guidelines provided for each fund.[88]

In conducting their activities, NGOs and other private entities must comply with all relevant New Zealand legislation, including the regulations that implement U.N. sanctions.

---

[83] *Compliance FAQs,* CHARITIES COMMISSION, http://charities.govt.nz/FAQs/Compliance/tabid/188/Default.aspx (last visited Aug 24, 2011).

[84] Tax credits for charitable or other public benefit gifts are governed by Income Tax Act 2007 ss LD1 to LD3, *available at* http://www.legislation.govt.nz/act/public/2007/0097/latest/DLM1512301.html. *See also Non-profit Organisations: Donee Organisations,* IRD, http://www.ird.govt.nz/non-profit/np-donee/ (last visited Aug. 24, 2011); *Individual Income Tax: Donations, Childcare and Housekeeper Tax Credits*, IRD, http://www.ird.govt.nz/income-tax-individual/tax-credits/dch-taxcredits/iit-dch-taxcredits.html (last visited Aug. 24, 2011).

[85] See *Compliance FAQs*, *supra* note 83.

[86] *Donee Organisations*, IRD, http://www.ird.govt.nz/donee-organisations/donee-organisations-index.html (last visited Aug. 24, 2011). *See also* Income Tax Act 2007 s LD3(2)

[87] *New Zealand Government Partnership with Non-Government Organisations,* NZ AID PROGRAMME, http://www.aid.govt.nz/what-we-do/nz-ngo-contestable-funds.html (last visited Aug. 24, 2011).

[88] MFAT, *Sustainable Development Fund Guidelines* (July 2010), *available at* http://www.aid.govt.nz/what-we-do/docs/sustainable-development-fund-guidelines-final-jul10.pdf; MFAT, *Sustainable Development Fund: Grant Funding Arrangement* (Apr. 2011), *available at* http://www.aid.govt.nz/what-we-do/docs/SDF-GFA-template.pdf; MFAT, *Humanitarian Response Fund Guidelines* (July 2010), *available at* http://www.aid.govt.nz/what-we-do/docs/humanitarian-response-fund-guidelines-fina-jul10l.pdf.

III. Foreign Aid Appropriations Process

In 2002, when the New Zealand government decided to establish NZAID as an autonomous agency, it also determined that there should be a separate appropriation ("Vote") for New Zealand ODA.[89] The current government decided to maintain this arrangement when it moved responsibility for the aid program back into MFAT in 2009, stating that

> [a] separate Vote provides transparency and accountability around the funding, objectives and outcomes of New Zealand's ODA programme and the performance measures and standards for delivery of the programme. These would be explicit in the context of the range of outcomes that MFAT as a whole seeks.[90]

The New Zealand government budget process involves advice and submissions by executive agencies to Ministers and Cabinet. Following review of these submissions and proposals, the Cabinet makes final budget decisions in line with the government's budget strategy. The government's Budget Policy Statement is tabled in Parliament in May and this is considered by a parliamentary committee. Once the committee has reported, by July 31 the government must introduce an Appropriation (Estimates) Bill and other Budget documents required by the Public Finance Act 1989.[91] Passage of the Bill must be completed within three months of the delivery of the Budget. Any changes to appropriations after the passage of the Bill are included in an Appropriation (Supplementary Estimates) Bill that must be passed by the end of the financial year.[92]

The New Zealand ODA budget includes funding for multilateral and bilateral aid activities, including membership dues for international organizations.[93] As noted above, other agencies may receive ODA-related funding as part of their own appropriations, particularly the New Zealand Police and New Zealand Defence Force.

IV. Other Types of 'Aid'

A. Scholarships

The New Zealand aid program includes the provision of scholarships "to citizens of some developing countries to undertake vocational training or tertiary level study in their home

---

[89] *Cabinet Paper: New Zealand Agency for International Development: Institutional Arrangements*, *supra* note 29, at ¶ 35.

[90] *Id.*

[91] The Appropriation (2011/12 Estimates) Act 2011, *available at* http://www.legislation.govt. nz/act/public/2011/0055/latest/DLM3744702.html. Schedule 1 of this Act includes the appropriations for Vote ODA for that year (note that funding for particular areas was also available for the current year as a result of multiyear appropriations passed in previous years).

[92] *Budget Process*, THE TREASURY, http://www.treasury.govt.nz/budget/process (last visited Aug. 24, 2011).

[93] *See* Vote Official Development Assistance estimates of appropriations 2011–12, *supra* note 2; Vote Official Development Assistance performance information for appropriations 2011–12, *supra* note 4.

country, in New Zealand or in the Pacific region."[94] The scholarships offered are currently under review, although there is a commitment to continuing the approach. The following scholarships are listed as being available as of August 2011:

- New Zealand Pacific Scholarships, which are open to candidates from a number of Pacific Island countries to support both undergraduate and graduate study;[95]

- New Zealand Development Scholarships, which "provide the opportunity for individuals from targeted developing countries to undertake studies at tertiary education institutions in New Zealand" with the purpose of applying knowledge and skills in particular subject areas to assist development in their home country;[96]

- New Zealand ASEAN Scholar Awards, which are open to postgraduate applicants from Cambodia, Indonesia, the Philippines, Laos, Burma/Myanmar, and Vietnam to undertake development-related studies in New Zealand.[97]

- Commonwealth Scholarships, which "provide the opportunity for individuals from selected developing Commonwealth countries to undertake postgraduate study or research at one of the eight universities in New Zealand."[98]

- Short Term Training Awards, which are available for applicants from selected developing countries to undertake short-term vocational and/or skills courses in New Zealand for up to one year.[99]

- New Zealand Regional Development Scholarships, which are open to eligible postgraduate students from the Cook Islands, Kiribati, Samoa, Solomon Islands, Tonga, Tuvalu, and Vanuatu for "full-time, multiyear study at undergraduate or graduate level."[100]

B. Seasonal Guest Worker Program

Following the completion of a pilot program, in 2006 the New Zealand government announced the establishment of the Recognised Seasonal Employer (RSE) Policy, which

---

[94] *Scholarships*, NZ AID PROGRAMME, http://www.aid.govt.nz/scholarships/ (last visited Aug. 24, 2011).

[95] *New Zealand Pacific Scholarships*, NZ AID PROGRAMME, http://www.aid.govt.nz/scholarships/nzps/pacific-scholars.html (last visited Aug. 24, 2011).

[96] *New Zealand Development Scholarships*, NZ AID PROGRAMME, http://www.aid.govt.nz/scholarships/nzds/dev-scholars.html (last visited Aug. 24, 2011).

[97] *New Zealand ASEAN Scholarships*, NZ AID PROGRAMME, http://www.aid.govt.nz/scholarships/nzds/asean-scholars.html (last visited Aug. 24, 2011).

[98] *Commonwealth Scholarships Scheme*, NZ AID PROGRAMME, http://www.aid.govt.nz/scholarships/nzds/commonwealth-scholars.html (last visited Aug. 24, 2011).

[99] *Short Term Training Awards*, NZ AID PROGRAMME, http://www.aid.govt.nz/scholarships/nzds/stta.html (last visited Aug. 24, 2011).

[100] *New Zealand Regional Development Scholarships*, NZ AID PROGRAMME, http://www.aid.govt.nz/scholarships/nzrds/nzrds-scholarships.html (last visited Aug. 24, 2011).

commenced in 2007.[101] This policy is aimed at facilitating "the temporary entry of additional workers from overseas to plant, maintain, harvest and pack crops in the horticulture and viticulture industries" in order to meet labor shortages.[102] The program is targeted at the recruitment of nationals from specified Pacific countries, although employers can recruit workers from other countries in limited circumstances.[103] Under the policy, foreign workers may be granted "RSE limited visas" to work for approved employers in those industries for a defined period. There is currently a limit of 8,000 RSE limited visas available per year.[104]

C. Remittances

New Zealand undertakes a range of activities related to improving the remittance system, particularly between workers in New Zealand and their home countries in the Pacific region.[105] This includes

- A joint project with the Australian aid agency, AusAID, and a private development company to create the www.sendmoneypacific.org website. This website provides information on providers and fees in relation to remittances from New Zealand and Australia to different countries with the aim of encouraging competition among providers and bringing down costs.[106]

- The development of financial education material for Pacific households in New Zealand as part of the New Zealand-Pacific Remittance Project.[107] This includes a project run by the Ministry of Pacific Island Affairs, in partnership with the New Zealand Aid Programme and the Reserve Bank of New Zealand, to produce financial awareness calendars (MoneyPACIFIC Calendars) in different Pacific languages.[108]

---

[101] Press Release, Hon. David Benson-Pope & Hon. David Cunliffe, Seasonal Work Scheme for Pacific Workers (Oct. 26, 2006), http://www.beehive.govt.nz/Documents/Files/Seasonal%20work%20background.pdf.

[102] *Recognised Seasonal Employer (RSE) Policy*, DEPARTMENT OF LABOUR, http://www.dol.govt. nz/initiatives/strategy/rse/index.asp (last visited Aug. 12, 2011); Immigration New Zealand, Operational Manual WH1.1, http://www.immigration.govt.nz/opsmanual/i34413.htm (last visited Aug. 12, 2011).

[103] *Requirements for an Agreement to Recruit,* IMMIGRATION NEW ZEALAND, http://www.immigration.govt.nz/employers/employ/temp/rse/ATRrequirements.htm (last visited Sept. 13, 2011).

[104] *Recognised Seasonal Employers*, IMMIGRATION NEW ZEALAND, http://www.immigration.govt.nz/employers/employ/temp/rse/default.htm (last visited Sept. 13, 2011).

[105] *See generally* Australian Government & New Zealand Government, *Trends in Remittance Fees and Charges* (Oct. 2010), *available at* http://www.rbnz.govt.nz/research/4229162.pdf. This report was presented at the Pacific Islands Forum Ministers' meeting in October 2010 and sets out figures and activities relating to remittances between New Zealand and Australia and Pacific Island countries.

[106] Press Release, Hon. Georgina Te Heuheu, Faster and Cheaper Remittance to the Pacific (March 19, 2011), http://www.beehive.govt.nz/release/faster-and-cheaper-remittance-pacific.

[107] *Trends in Remittance Fees and Charges*, RESERVE BANK OF NEW ZEALAND, http://www.rbnz.govt. nz/research/4229796.html (last visited Aug. 25, 2011).

[108] *See Pacific Calendar Receives International Interest*, MINISTRY OF PACIFIC ISLAND AFFAIRS, http://www.mpia.govt.nz/pacific-calendar-receives-international-interest/ (last visited Aug. 24, 2011).

- A pilot training program that includes financial literacy for Pacific workers in New Zealand under the Recognised Seasonal Employer policy.[109]

- Regulatory changes that allow financial institutions to offer a "two-card remittance facility." This means that banks and other financial institutions can provide a card that allows funds to be loaded by a New Zealand-based remitter, up to a particular limit each year, and a second card that can be used by a second person to access money in another country though ATM and point of sale transactions. This means that the normally stringent verification of the person receiving the funds is not necessary.[110]

Prepared by Kelly Buchanan
Foreign Law Specialist
September 2011

---

[109] *See Review of the Recognised Seasonal Employer (RSE) Worker Pilot Training Programme: Report Summary* (Feb. 2011), NZ AID PROGRAMME, http://www.aid.govt.nz/what-we-do/review-and-evaluation-report-summaries/review-and-evaluation-report-summary-eva11-06sum-1.html.

[110] *Id. See* Anti-Money Laundering and Countering Financing of Terrorism (Exemptions) Regulations 2011 reg 10, *available at* http://www.legislation.govt.nz/regulation/public/2011/0223/latest/DLM3844341.html. *See also* Press Release, Hon. Helen Clark, Law Change Paves Way for Lower Remittance Costs (Sept. 28, 2008), http://www.beehive.govt.nz/node/34779.

LAW LIBRARY OF CONGRESS

NORWAY

REGULATION OF FOREIGN AID

Executive Summary

Without any tied aid and with its foreign aid contributions expected to exceed 1% of GNI, Norway is one of the world leaders in international development cooperation. It gives most of its aid to Afghanistan, Tanzania, and Palestinian Territories. Norway has stepped up its efforts over the last ten years by doubling the amount of aid given, refocusing its bilateral efforts and encouraging private donations by granting tax deductions for charitable contributions. In addition, Norway is the only European nation that provides free university education to any student regardless of nationality or permanent residence, including citizens of developing countries.

I. Introduction

A. Official Development Assistance Figures

For the first time, Norway's preliminary official development assistance (ODA) figures for 2010 supersede neighboring Sweden in actual numbers, at US$4,582 million compared to Sweden's US$4,527 million.[1] This is an increase in Norwegian aid compared to 2008 and 2009, and more than a 100% increase compared to 2004, when the corresponding value was US$2,198 million.[2] Calculated in the local Norwegian currency (NOK), there has been a sharp increase from NOK 14,814.9 million in 2004 to NOK 27,681.2 million in 2010.[3] Even compared to as recently as 2007, Norwegian aid for 2010 has increased by NOK 5,872.7 million (approximately US$1,015.4 million), which reflects an increase of more than 20%. In 2007, Norway was ranked as the world's greatest donor of aid, with 0.95 of gross national income (GNI) dispersed.[4] However, despite the sharp 20% increase in aid from 2007, the increase as a percentage of GNI "only" translated to a 15% increase; thus, part of the increase was a result of Norway becoming

---

[1] OECD, Net Official Development Assistance (measured in U.S. dollars), DOI 10.1787/20743866-table 1 (Apr. 13, 2011), http://www.oecd-ilibrary.org/development/development-aid-net-official-development-assistance-oda_20743866-table1.

[2] *Id.*

[3] Norad, *Norsk bistand i tal* [*Norwegian Aid Statistics*], http://www.norad.no/norskbistanditall/statistikkvisning (last visited Sept. 22, 2011).

[4] OECD, Norway (2008) DAC Peer Review of Norway – Main Findings and Recommendations, http://www.oecd.org/document/43/0,3746,en_2649_34603_41833003_1_1_1_1,00.html. (last visited Sept. 22, 2011).

richer.[5] Norway has since 2007 consistently pledged 1% of GNI and provided for at least 0.89% of GNI since 2003.[6] Despite the financial crisis of 2008, Norway even increased its aid in 2009, both as a percentage of GNI and in actual value.[7]

The government appropriates sums for both bilateral and multilateral aid that are then earmarked to certain uses. In 2010, the NOK 4,522 million (approximately US$781.9 million) assigned to bilateral development was divided up regionally between Africa, Asia, the Middle East, and Latin America.[8]

Most of Norway's net ODA is given as bilateral aid (US$3,620.35 million out of US$4,582.23 million in 2010).[9]   Budget support to developing countries accounts for approximately 7% of the Norwegian aid budget.[10] For the year 2010, for example, the proposed allocation was NOK 4,522.1 million (approximately US$781.9 million) for bilateral development cooperation and NOK 6,264.42 million (approximately US$1,083.98) for multilateral development cooperation.[11]

B. Private Contribution Figures

The total private contribution to foreign aid by Norwegians is unclear. The Organisation for Economic Co-operation and Development (OECD) has no figures available.[12] However, the Norwegian Red Cross, Røde Kors,[13] received some NOK 105 million (approximately US$18 million) in donations during 2010 and spent some NOK 61 million (approximately US$10.5 million) on their international human rights efforts alone.[14] Another NOK 570 million (approximately US$98 million) was spent on emergency relief and efforts connected with aid to victims of catastrophes (primarily natural disasters and civil wars) and the prevention of such

---

[5] *See* OECD, *ODA by Donor, Norway, Current Prices, Net Disbursements*, http://stats.oecd.org/ Index.aspx?DatasetCode=ODA_DONOR (last visited Sept. 22, 2011).

[6] *Id.*

[7] *See* Dagen, *Norge ökar sitt bistånd nästa år - trots krisen* [*Norway Increases Its Aid Despite the Financial Crisis*], http://www.dagen.se/dagen/ article.aspx?id=195066.

[8] *Id.* at 114. For further discussion *see* "Discretionary Aid," section II.A.4, *infra.*

[9] See OECD, ODA by Donor, Norway, Current Prices, Net Disbursements, *supra* note 5.

[10] Norad, *Budsjettstøtte - den nye bistanden* [*Budget Support, the New Foreign Aid*], http://www.norad.no/satsingsomr%C3%A5der/samfunns% C3%B8konomi-og-offentlig-forvaltning/budsjettst%C3%B8tte/budsjettst%C3%B8tte-den-nye-bistanden (last visited Sept. 26, 2011). Recipient countries include "Mozambique, Tanzania, Zambia, Malawi, Uganda and Nicaragua." *Id.*

[11] *Proposisjon [Prop.]. S 1 (2009-2010) til Stortinget (forslag til stortingsvedtak) for budsjettåret 2010 Utgiftskapitler*: 100–172 [*Proposed Budget Bill for 2010 Expenses Accounts 100-172*], at 114, 212, *available at* http://www.regjeringen.no/pages/2251401/PDFS/ PRP200920100001_UDDDDPDFS.pdf.

[12] *See* OCD Table 5, Total Net Private Flows by DAC Country, http://www.oecd.org/dataoecd/ 31/38/47452671.xls.

[13] RØDE KORS, http://www.rodekors.no/ (last visited Sept. 22, 2011).

[14] *See* RØDE KORS ÅRSRAPPORT [ANNUAL REPORT] 2010 at 15, http://www.rodekors.no/Global/ HK/Media/Rapporter/110609%20aarsrapport%202010.pdf.

catastrophes.[15] Following the tsunami in Thailand, the Norwegians gave a total of NOK 2 billion (approximately US$345 million) to the Røde Kors alone, of which NOK 725 million (approximately US$125 million) was spent on emergency relief and long-term aid.[16] Statistics covering the year 2007 show that charitable organizations created an additional societal value of NOK 35 billion (approximately US$605 million, or about 1.15% of Norway's GNI) through their volunteer workers alone.[17] Charitable donations to organizations like the Røde Kors are tax deductible in Norway for both private persons and corporations.[18]

C. Snapshot of Foreign Aid Activity

The top three recipients of Norwegian aid are Afghanistan, Tanzania, and Palestinian Administered Areas.[19] Measured by region, Norway gives most aid to "unspecified' efforts, followed by sub-Saharan Africa and South and Central Asia.[20] As one of the largest contributors to Palestinian Administered Areas, the Norwegian government has been criticized for supporting, at least indirectly, terrorists who are imprisoned in Israel.[21]

In its budget for 2010, the Norwegian government increased its commitment to fighting AIDS by increasing its support to the Global Fund by 20%.[22] Other recent projects include "Tax for Development" aimed at improving the tax systems of recipient countries.[23] Norway also participates in "university cooperation."[24]

---

[15] *Id.*

[16] NTB, *Stort Røde Kors-overskudd i katastrofeår* [*Large Surplus for Norwegian Red Cross During Disaster Year*]*,* DN.NO (June 9, 2006, 12:30 p.m., updated 1:12 p.m.), http://www.dn.no/forsiden/politikkSamfunn/article800342.ece.

[17] Statistisk Sentralbyrå Norge, *Frivillighet-Norge skaper store verdier* [*Volunteers in Norway Are Creating Great Value*], *SSB.no*, http://www.ssb.no/_vis/magasinet/analyse/art-2010-01-11-01.html (last visited Sept. 28, 2011).

[18] For further discussion of Norwegian tax incentives for charity donations, *see* section II.B of this report, *infra.*

[19] OECD–DAC, Norway, Gross Bilateral ODA 2008-2009, http://www.oecd.org/dataoecd/42/48/44285266.gif (last visited Sept. 22, 2011)

[20] *Id.*

[21] Jørgen M. Gilbrant, *Norske bistandspenger går til å lønne terrorister* [*Norwegian Foreign Aid Given to Fund Terrorist*], DAGBLADET.NO (Sept. 4, 2011, 9:52 a.m.), http://www.dagbladet.no/2011/09/04/nyheter/israel/palestinske_selvstyremyndigheter/terrorisme/utenriks/17941848/.

[22] Press Release, Regjeringen, Norway to donate NOK 1.4 billion to the Global Fund to Fight AIDS, Tuberculosis and Malaria (Sept. 22, 2010), http://www.regjeringen.no/en/dep/ud/press/news/2010/fight_aids.html?id=614806.

[23] For more detailed information on the project, *see* Norad, *Skatt for utvikling* (Mar. 4, 2010), http://www.norad.no/satsingsomr%C3%A5der/samfunns%C3%B8konomi-og-offentlig-forvaltning/skatt-for-utvikling/skatt-for-utvikling.

[24] *See* Norad, Resultatrapport 2010 – Kapasitetsutvikling: Bygging av levedyktige samfunn [Building Capacity: Building Sustainable Societies], *available at* http://www.norad.no/en/tools-and-publications/publications/publication-page?key=207940 (translation by author).

II. Legal Framework

A. Regulation of ODAs

1. Overview

Norwegian ODA is regulated by the annual budget as well as any government appropriation letters given to the implementing agencies. Norwegian aid is also affected by Norway's United Nations (UN) and OECD commitments. There is no law that prohibits individuals from sending aid abroad; however, anything that is sent out of the country must comply with Norwegian export laws and regulations.[25]

2. Implementing Agencies

Norad

The Norwegian Agency for Development Cooperation (Norad)[26] is the main implementing agency for development cooperation in Norway. Norad receives its mandate from the Norwegian Ministry of Foreign Affairs. The mission of Norad is regulated in *Instruks for Norad.*[27] The Norad budget and short-term mandate are determined by the annual budget as well as an *årlige tildelingsbrev* (annual appropriations letter) and *Tillskottsbrev.*[28] For the government's instructions to Norad, see *Instruks for Norad.*[29] Norad has four main responsibilities: to provide "guidance" to the government, ensure quality, "initiate and carry through," and "manage grant schemes."[30] These responsibilities include entering into bilateral agreements with recipients of foreign aid.

Norfund

The Norwegian Investment Fund for Developing Countries (Norfund) is the Norwegian state-owned investment fund for commercial activity in developing countries. It receives most of its funding from the Ministry of Foreign Affairs in the development cooperation budget.[31] The main purpose of Norfund is to "develop and establish profitable and sustainable enterprises in

---

[25] *See, e.g.*, Lov 6 juni 1997 [June 6, 1997] nr 32 reglering av utførsel samt Lov 18 dec 1987 [Dec. 18, 1987] nr 93 utførsel av strategiske varer, tjenster og teknologi (Eksportkontrolloven).

[26] NORAD, http://www.norad.no/en/ (last visited Sept. 22, 2011).

[27] Forordning [FOR] 2004-03-26 nr 576: Instruks For Direktoratet For Utviklingssamarbeid (NORAD) (Instruks for NORAD [Instruction for NORAD]), *available at* http://www.lovdata.no/for/sf/in/xd-20040326-0576.html.

[28] Tillskottsbrev, *previously available at* http://www.bistandsnemnda.no/newsread/ReadImage.aspx?DOCID=325&QUALITY=10 (last visited Sept. 23, 2011) (copy on file with author).

[29] Instruks for NORAD, *supra* note 27.

[30] *Id.* § 2.

[31] Norfund, *About Norfund*, http://www.norfund.no/index.php?option=com_content&view=category&layout=blog&id=76&Itemid=260&lang=en (last visited Sept. 27, 2011). For an example of budget appropriations, *see also Prop. S 1 (2009-2010), supra* note 11.

poor countries. The objective is to promote business development and contribute to economic growth and "poverty alleviation."[32] Norfund is unique because it is designed to function as a high-risk investor, accepting risks others would not.[33] Its focus is thus on finding the investment opportunity that would have the greatest effects on development, not necessarily on profit alone.[34] Norfund enables these riskier investment ventures by providing guarantees as well as funds and loans to local enterprises and companies.[35]

Norfund is run by a board of appointed directors.[36] Norfund, like all other government institutions, must complete an annual financial report.[37] The report includes "income statements, balance sheet, cash flows, and notes."[38] The financial report for 2010 is available online.[39] Norfund is under the oversight of *Riksrevisjonen* (Office of the Auditor General of Norway), as described below.[40]

3. Restrictions

Legal and Regulatory Restrictions

Norway places no direct restrictions on its foreign aid through legislation. However, under the bilateral agreements and letters of allocation made by Norad and the Ministry for Foreign Affairs, aid is conditioned on the stipulation that (among other things) the funds be distributed in a "gender-equal" manner.[41] Moreover, all "civil society actors" who are recipients of financial support from Norad must follow and maintain "ethical guidelines."[42]

---

[32] *Id.*

[33] *See* Lov 9 mai 1997 [May 9, 1997] nr. 26 om Statens investeringsfond for næringsvirksomhet i utviklingsland § 1 (Nordfundloven).

[34] *See* Norfund, *Mandate*, http://www.norfund.no/index.php?option=com_content&view= category&layout=blog&id=78&Itemid=252&lang=en (last visited Sept. 27, 2011).

[35] Nordfundloven, *supra* note 33, § 1.

[36] *Id.* at § 9.

[37] *Id* at § 18. For a full list of those entities that must make an annual financial report, *see* Lov 17 juli 1998 [July 17, 1998] nr 56. om årsregnkap m.v.(Regnskapsloven) § 1-2.

[38] *Id.* § 3-2 (translation by author).

[39] NORFUND, ANNUAL REPORT 2010, http://www.nsd.uib.no/polsys/data/filer/aarsmeldinger/ AE_2010_4606.pdf (last visited Sept. 26, 2011).

[40] Regnskapsloven, *supra* note 37, § 20.

[41] See Norad, Bjørg Skotnes, Fremover i ujevn takt for kvinners rettigheter og likestilling i utviklingssamarbeidet [The Future in an Uneven Pace for Women's Rights and Equality in Development Cooperation], http://www.norad.no/en/132908/fremover-i-ujevn-takt-for-kvinners-rettigheter-og-likestilling-i-utviklingssamarbeidet (last visited Sept. 23, 2011).

[42] *See* Grant Scheme Rules for Research and Research Dissemination (Apr. 4, 2011), *available at* http://www.norad.no/en/support-and-tender/support/climate-and-forest-initiative-support-scheme/conditions-for-support-in-2010 (click on "Rules for Support to Civil Society Actors" on right side of screen) (last visited Sept. 23, 2011).

There are also certain restrictions on which countries aid may be given to; for example, Norfund may only invest in countries the OECD ranks as developing.[43] Also, the individual appropriations letter may place additional restrictions and conditions on the distribution of aid. Norwegian aid is often geared toward foreign policy objectives, such as democratization, women's rights, and access to health care (including the right to inexpensive or free abortions).[44]

Untied Trade and Aid

Norway is one of the few countries that has managed to "untie" all of its aid, meaning that the aid it provides is not tied to trade policy considerations.[45] However, trade in goods with Africa is still skewed, with exports outnumbering imports both in real values and in percentages, except for Botswana and South Africa. Norway exported NOK 4,540 million (approximately US$786 million) to the African continent from January through August 2011.[46] NOK 1 million of that total (approximately US$173,000) went to Botswana, NOK 488 million (approx US$84 million) to South Africa, and the remaining NOK 4,053 million (approximately US$701 million) to other unnamed African countries. In comparison, Norway imported NOK 6,380 million (approximately US$1103) from Africa; of that total, NOK 1,632 million (approximately US$282 million) came from Botswana and NOK 1,793 million (approximately US$310 million) came from South Africa. Thus, Norway imports NOK 2,954 million (approximately US$511.2) from Africa while it exports NOK 4,053 million (approximately US$701 million).[47]

4. Discretionary Aid

The budget for Norwegian development cooperation is divided into sectors in the annual budget, with a so-called framework appropriation that requires a total of NOK 4,522.1 million (approximately US$782 million) to be allocated to bilateral development aid. Out of that amount, NOK 2,808.5 million (approximately US$484 million) goes to Africa, NOK 993.1 million (approximately US$172 million) to Asia, NOK 500 million (US$86.5 million) to the Middle East, and NOK 220.5 million (approximately US$38 million) to Latin America.[48] A similar division is provided for under the sector of "Global Systems."[49] How the sums are to be divided (i.e., what projects they are to support) is not specified in the budget, although it does provide for earmarked sums for gender equality work.[50] Yet, funds appear to be transferable.[51]

---

[43] Nordfundloven, *supra* note 33, § 1.

[44] *See Prop. S 1 (2009-2010)*, *supra* note 11, at 200.

[45] *See* EDWARD J. CLAY, MATTHEW GEDDES, & LUISA NATALI, UNTYING AID: IS IT WORKING?, table 3.2 at 10 (Copenhagen, Dec. 2009), *available at* http://www.oecd.org/dataoecd/51/35/44375975.pdf (ISBN: 978-87-7605-352-9 e-ISBN: 978-87-7605-356-7); *Untied Aid*, OECD, http://www.oecd.org/document/16/0,3746,en_2649_33721_46890896_1_1_1_1,00.html (last visited Oct. 13, 2011).

[46] Statistisk Sentralbyrå [Statistics Norway], Tabell 18 Imports and exports, by country and groups of countries. Traditional commodities, Mill. kr., http://www.ssb.no/emner/09/05/muh/tab18-01.shtml (last visited Sept. 22, 2011).

[47] *Id.*

[48] *Prop. S 1 (2009-2010)*, *supra* note 11, at 5. *See also* programkategori 03.10 at 114f.

[49] *Id.* (03.20 Globale ordninger) at 148 (translation by author).

[50] *See Prop. S 1 (2009-2010)*, *supra* note 11, ch. 168; *kvinnior og likestillning* (post 70), at 200.

5. Oversight

Oversight of the development cooperation funds is chiefly maintained by the agencies themselves and other government agencies.

Riksrevisjonen

The supreme oversight organ in Norway is the *Riksrevisjonen* (Office of the Auditor General of Norway).[52] The main goal of *Riksrevisjonen* is to ensure that funds appropriated by the *Storting* (national parliament) are used as specified.[53] Because the development cooperation funds are appropriated by the *Storting* following a proposition by the government, *Riksrevisjonen* also oversees and evaluates development cooperation expenses. *Riksrevisjonen* is intended to function as an independent agency that has discretion to decide "how the work shall be carried out and organized."[54] The oversight shall be "objective and neutral."[55]

Norad

Norad has its own *evalueringsavdelning* (evaluation department).[56] The evaluation process from start ("mandate/terms of reference") to finish (the evaluation report) is described on Norad's website.[57] To facilitate efficiency and oversight, Norad has developed a special *Agreement Manual* and a *Cooperation Development Manual*, which it uses to avoid fraud, corruption, and other problems connected with bilateral foreign aid.[58] One example of an oversight measure is the field visit.[59]

---

[51] "Kan overføres" [transferable] is written following the budget appropriation. *See id.* at 115.

[52] RIKSREVISJONEN, http://www.riksrevisjonen.no/Sider/hovedside.aspx. (last visited Sept. 23, 2011) (official translation in brackets).

[53] Riksrevisjonen, *Om Riksrevisjonen* [*About the Office of the Audit General*] (Sept. 21, 2011, 8:48 p.m.), http://www.riksrevisjonen.no/ OmRiksrevisjonen/Sider/OmRiksrevisjonen.aspx.

[54] Lov 7 mai 2004 [May 7, 2004] nr 21 om Riksrevisjonen. (Riksrevisjonsloven) § 2; *see also* § 3, which provides that in addition to the legal statute on Riksrevisjonen, the *Storting* is also allowed to create an instruction for the Riksrevisjon.

[55] *Id.* § 10.

[56] *See* Norad, *Uavhengig evaluering av bistand* [*Independent Evaluation of Development Cooperation*], http://www.norad.no/evaluering/uavhengig-evaluering-av-bistand (last visited Sept. 23, 2011).

[57] Norad, *Evalueringsprosessen* [*The Evaluation Process*], http://www.norad.no/evaluering/ gjennomf%C3%B8 ring-av-evalueringer/evalueringsprosessen (last visited Sept. 26, 2011).

[58] NORAD, AGREEMENT MANUAL (Dec. 2006), http://www.norad.no/en/tools-and-publications/publications/publication-page?key=109586; NORAD, DEVELOPMENT COOPERATION MANUAL (2005), http://www.norad.no/en/tools-and-publications/publications/publication-page?key=109515.

[59] *See* DEVELOPMENT COOPERATION MANUAL, *supra* note 58, at 31.

General

The most recent report covering Norwegian aid was published in 2011 by *Riksrevisjonen.*[60] Most reports are commissioned by the Norwegian government or Norad; however, one recent report on the effectiveness of aid to Russia was initiated following a request from Norad's Russian counterpart.[61] Although Norwegian aid is overseen and thoroughly scrutinized by both implementing agencies and other government agencies, there is a lack of independent evaluation.[62]

6. Policy Considerations

Norway bases its policy goals on the UN millennium goals.[63] The Norwegian government believes that the way to meet these goals lies in focusing its aid on "climate change, conflict areas and the poorest countries."[64]

Norway gives what is known as "budget support," meaning it gives foreign governments additional income to be used in their annual budgets.[65] This support is mainly used to aid the creation of democratic election processes and relies on the 2008 Paris Declaration[66] as well as international coordination for implementation.[67]

---

[60] Riksrevisjonen, *Riksrevisjonens undersøkelse av resultatorienteringen i norsk bistand* [*The Auditor General's Investigation on the Effectiveness(Results Orientation) of Norwegian Development Cooperation*], Dokument 3:4 2010-2011, Dokument 3-serien (Jan. 13, 2011), *available at* http://www.riksrevisjonen.no/Rapporter/ Documents/2010-2011/Dokument%203/Dokumentbase_3_4_2010_2011.pdf.

[61] *Id.*

[62] Norad, *Vi trenger mer uavhengig forskning om norsk bistand* [*We Need More Independent Research on Norwegian Development Cooperation*] (Sept. 6, 2011), http://www.norad.no/evaluering/nyhetsarkiv-evaluering/vi-trenger-mer-uavhengig-forskning-om-norsk-bistand. For detailed analysis of the need for independent research on the effectiveness of aid, *see* SIPU INTERNATIONAL, EVALUATION OF RESEARCH ON NORWEGIAN DEVELOPMENT ASSISTANCE, Report 2/2011 – Evaluation (Norad, June 2011), *available at* http://www.norad.no/en/tools-and-publications/publications/publication-page?key=382864.

[63] Norad, *Norsk utviklingspolitikk* [*Norwegian Policy on Development*], http://www.norad.no/om-bistand/norsk-utviklingspolitikk (last visited Sept. 28, 2011).

[64] *Id.*

[65] Norad, *Budsjettstøtte - den nye bistanden* [*Budget Support – the New Foreign Aid*] http://www.norad.no/satsingsomr%C3%A5der/_samfunns%C3%B8konomi-og-offentlig-forvaltning/budsjettst%C3%B8tte/budsjettst%C3%B8tte-den-nye-bistanden (last visited Sept. 26, 2011).

[66] OECD, *Paris Declaration and Accra Agenda for Action,* http://www.oecd.org/document/18/0,3343, en_2649_3236398_35401554_1_1_1_1,00.html (last visited Sept. 27, 2011).

[67] Norad, *Budsjettstøtte – den nye bistanden, supra* note 65.

B. Regulation of Private Contributions

Private contributions to international aid organizations are tax deductible under Norwegian law.[68] The Norwegian Tax Authority (*Skatteetaten*) manages a list of approved organizations.[69] These organizations may include foreign organizations within the European Economic Area (EEA).[70] To be eligible as a recipient organization, the organization must provide or organize

> (a) care and health promotion for children and youth, or the elderly, sick, disabled, or other fragile groups; (b) child and youth programs on music, theater, literature, dance, sports or outdoor activity; or (c) religious or faith-based activity, (d) activit[ies] that benefit[] human rights or development aid; (e) catastrophe relief or activities that prevent accidents or injuries, (f) [or be an organization] that protects culture, the environment or animals. The [Foreign] Ministry may further regulate what areas of culture shall be covered [by this regulation].[71]

To be deductible, donations to an organization on the approved list must be at least NOK 500 (approximately US$74) per year, and amounts above NOK 12,000 (approximately US$2,090) are not eligible for tax deductions.[72]

There are no laws prohibiting the donation of aid by individuals. Donations by corporations are governed by the bylaws of the corporation. However, certain restrictions are indirectly in effect, as the use of "hawala systems" (informal money transfers) is outlawed.[73]

III. Foreign Aid Appropriations Process

All appropriations of State funds must be approved by the *Storting*.[74] As the first step in allocating funds to international development cooperation, the Department of Finance starts working on the budget "approximately a year in advance."[75] Six days after the *Storting* convenes

---

[68] Skatteetaten, Donations to certain voluntary organisations and religious and beliefs-based communities, Artikkel 9 (Feb. 9, 2011), http://www.skatteetaten.no/no/Artikler/Donations-to-certain-voluntary-organisations-and-religious-and-beliefs-based-communities/.

[69] *See* Skatteetaten, *Gaver til frivillige organisasjoner og tros-og livssynssamfunn – liste over godkjente organisasjoner* [*Gifts to Volunteer Organizations and Religious and Faith Based Organizations – List of Approved Organizations*], http://www.skatteetaten.no/frivillige (last visited Sept. 23, 2011).

[70] Skatteetaten, *supra* note 68.

[71] Taxation Act [Lov om skatt av formue og inntekt (skatteloven)] § 6-50 (1), *available at* http://www.lovdata.no/all/tl-19990326-014-028.html#6-50 (translation by author).

[72] *Id.*

[73] For further discussion, *see* section IV, "Other Types of 'Aid,' " *infra*.

[74] Lov 1814 May 17 nr 00: Kongeriget Norges Grundlov [Constitution] § 75 (d), *available at* http://www.lovdata.no/all/hl-18140517-000.html.

[75] Finansdepartementet, *Budsjettarbeidet* [*The Budget Process*],http://www.regjeringen.no/nb/dep/fin/tema/statsbudsjettet/budsjettarbeidet.html?id=439269 (last visited Sept. 23, 2011) (translation by author).

for the fall session, the budget is presented to the *Storting* by the Minister of Finance.[76] Afterwards, the Standing Committee on Finance and Economic Affairs presents its recommendations on the budget.[77] These recommendations include both ceilings and appropriations.[78] Once the *Storting* decides to adopt or amend these budget ceilings, they are final.[79] Before the *Storting* reaches a binding ceiling, each department that receives an allocation by the government may comment on the allocations, the timeline for which is set by the *Storting*.[80]

IV. Other Types of 'Aid'

A. Free Trade Agreements

Norway has a number of Free Trade Agreements.[81] Most of them are multilateral agreements with the European Free Trade Association (EFTA). Norwegian policy is focused on increasing free trade as a better resource than aid.

B. Tuition-free Universities

Norway is currently the only country in Europe that does not impose any tuition fees on any of its students, including international non-EEA (European Economic Area) students.[82] Although attempts are being made to investigate the possibility of introducing tuition for international students in a similar way as neighboring Sweden, the idea of tuition at Norwegian universities and colleges is still very controversial.[83]

C. Financing University Studies in Norway for Citizens of Developing Countries

In addition to providing tuition-free university study, the Norwegian government also provides a limited number of scholarships to students from developing countries under its "quota scheme."[84] Under the quota scheme, a student is given both grants and loans similar to those

---

[76] Stortinget, The Norwegian Parliament, Rules of Procedure § 21, para. 1, *available at* http://www.stort inget.no/Global/pdf/Diverse/StortingetsForretENGELSK.pdf.

[77] *Id.* para 2.

[78] *Id.*

[79] *Id.* § 21, para 4.

[80] *See id.* § 22.

[81] For full list, *see* Regjeringen, *Partnerland* (July 8, 2011), http://www.regjeringen.no/nb/dep/nhd/tema/ handelsavtaler/partner-land.html?id=438843.

[82] Högskoleverket, *Kraftig ökning av utländska sökande i Norge* [*Sharp Increase in Foreign Applicants in Norway*], Internationellt om högskolan nr 6, 2011 (Feb. 18, 2011), http://www.hsv.se/publikationerarkiv/ nyhetsbrev/2011/internationelltomhogskolan/internationelltomhogskolannr62011.5.4dfb54fa12d0dded89580008790 .html (Swed.).

[83] *See Students Flock to Free Universities*, NORWAY INTERNATIONAL NETWORK (Feb. 9, 2011), http://www.newsinenglish.no/2011/02/09/students-flock-to-free-universities/.

[84] University of Oslo, *The Quota Scheme* (May 15, 2010, 8:35 p.m., modified Sept. 2, 2011, 2:13 p.m.), http://www.uio.no/english/studies/admission/quota-scheme/index.html.

given to Norwegian students, but as long as the student returns home and does not "take up residence" in Norway within ten years of finishing his or her studies, the loan portion is converted into a scholarship.[85] This de-incentivizes "brain drain" from developing countries. A full list of countries that are on the development cooperation list and therefore eligible for the quota scheme is available on the University of Oslo website.[86] However, only students linked to university institutions in their home countries are eligible to apply, and only for master's and PhD programs.[87]

Norad provides funding for university education for the benefit of citizens of developing countries by sponsoring local institutions or Norwegian institutions with collaboration agreements.[88] The project targets education of public and civil servants of relevant countries.[89]

D. Health Care for Asylum Seekers and Children of 'Undocumented Immigrants'

Health care is provided to adults who permanently or temporarily reside in one of Norway's *kommuner* (municipalities).[90] Persons who have applied for asylum, as well as their families, also may seek medical care in a Norwegian *kommun*.[91] Non-asylum seekers and those whose asylum applications were denied are not covered. Consequently, only emergency care is provided for undocumented adults, at the cost of its current monetary value.[92] For example, a "non-complicated" delivery costs approximately NOK 30,000[93] (approximately US$5,192). However, a report by the *Bymisjon* (Norwegian Church City Mission) illustrates that current legislation and actual practice do not always coincide; some general practitioners treat undocumented immigrants while others do not.[94] Still, children under eighteen are legally

---

[85] Lånekassan, Financial Aid and Remission of Debt for Citizens from Developing Countries in Central and Eastern Europe and Central Asia (quota scheme) 2010-2011 (Jan. 11, 2011), http://www.lanekassen.no/Toppmeny/Languages/English/Rules/Rules-2010/Financial-Aid-and-Remission-of-Debt-for-Citizens-from-Developing-countries-and-countries-in-Central-and-Eastern-Europe-and-Central-Asia-quota-scheme-2010-2011/

[86] *See* University of Oslo, *Quota Cooperation by Country* (Sept. 30, 2010, 4:42 p.m., modified Aug. 31, 2011, 2:04 p.m.), http://www.uio.no/english/studies/admission/quota-scheme/cooperation-agreements/cooperation-by-country/index.html.

[87] *Id.*; Oslo University, *Quota Cooperation by Programme* (Sept. 30, 2010, 4:42 p.m. , modified Aug. 30, 2011, 3:46 p.m.), http://www.uio.no/english/studies/admission/quota-scheme/cooperation-agreements/cooperation-by-programme/index.html.

[88] Center for International Cooperation in Higher Education [SIU], *Norad's Programme for Master Studies*, http://siu.no/eng/Front-Page/Programme-information/Development-cooperation/NOMA (last visited Sept. 26, 2010).

[89] *Id.*

[90] Lov 19 nov 1982 [Nov. 19, 1982] nr 66 om helsetjenesten i kommunen (Kommunehelsetjenesteloven) kap 1-1.

[91] *Id.* kap 2-1a.

[92] Kirkens Bymisjon, *Rettigheter [Rights]*, http://www.bymisjon.no/Virksomheter/Helsesenteret-for-papirlose-migranter/Rettigheter-/ (last visited Sept. 26, 2011).

[93] *Id.* (translation by author).

[94] Solveig Holmedal Ottesen, *Papirløse migranter [Undocumented Immigrants]*, En rapport fra Stiftelsen Kirkens Bymisjon Oslo, Mangfold & Oppvekst, at 20

provided health care regardless of status as a result of Norway's efforts to uphold the UN Child Convention.[95]

The Norwegian Røde Kors provides health care for persons who are present in Norway without any form of identification.[96] The organization has also asked the government to take responsibility for providing free health care to asylum seekers whose applications are denied.[97] The Røde Kors argues that it is a matter of being a humane society to offer health care services to undocumented persons in the same manner as those who are documented.[98]

E. Foreign Remittances

There are no official figures on foreign remittances from Norway to developing nations. However, Ba-Musa Ceesay, Executive Officer at Norad, explains in an article in *Bistandsaktuellt* that "[almost] all Gambians living in Norway (about 1200) send back part of their earnings."[99] Still, remittances cannot be sent to all parts of the world. For example, the Norwegian government makes it impossible to legally "transf[er] [funds] from Norway to Somalia" and other countries where the hawala system is the transferor's only option.[100] However, that does not mean that the process is not used, only that it is more difficult to survey.[101]

Prepared by Edith Palmer, Chief
Foreign, Comparative and International Law Division II
Global Legal Research Center
and Elin Hofverberg
Law Library Intern
October 2011

---

http://www.bymisjon.no/PageFiles/4132/Pairl%c3%b8se%20migranter%20rapport.pdf (last visited Sept. 26, 2011) (translation by author).

[95] *See* Lov om pasientrettigheter (Pasientrettighetloven) kap 6.1. and 2-2, Kommunhelsetjensteloven *supra* note 90; Kirkens Bymisjon, *Rettigheter*, *supra* note 92.

[96] Røde Kors, *Helsesenter for papirløse migranter* [*Health Center for Undocumented Immigrants*], http://lokal.rodekors.no/oslo/papirlose (last visited Sept. 25, 2011).

[97] Jon Martin Larsen, *Helsehjelp til papirløse innvandrere* [*Health Care for Undocumented Immigrants*] (Oct. 29, 2009), http://lokal.rodekors.no/ Nyheter_og_presse/Nyheter/Helsehjelp_til_papirlose_innvandrere_/.

[98] *Id.*

[99] Ba-Musa Ceesay, *Remittances*, BISTANDSAKTUELT (Mar. 26, 2007, 2:01 p.m.), http://www.bistands aktuelt.no/debatt/kategorier/tr%C3%A5der?thread=117864.

[100] Ministry of Foreign Affairs, *Coherent for Development?* http://www.regjeringen.no/nb/dep/ud/dok/nou-er/2008/nou-2008-14-2/11/3/11.html?id=538508. For the full government report on the coherency of development cooperation and Norway's other policies, *see* COHERENT FOR DEVELOPMENT? HOW COHERENT NORWEGIAN POLICIES CAN ASSIST DEVELOPMENT IN POOR COUNTRIES, NOU [Official Norwegian Reports] 2008:14 (Oslo, 2008), *available at* http://www.regjeringen.no/pages/2134467/PDFS/NOU200820080014000EN_PDFS.pdf.

[101] *See* Jørgen Carling et al., *Legal, Rapid and Reasonably Priced? A Survey of Remittance Services in Norway* 5–6 (PRIO Publications, 2007), http://www.isn.ethz.ch/isn/Digital-Library/Publications/Detail/?ots591=0c54e3b3-1e9c-be1e-2c24-a6a8c7060233&lng=en&id=57403.

LAW LIBRARY OF CONGRESS

RUSSIAN FEDERATION

REGULATION OF FOREIGN AID

Executive Summary

　　Russian official development assistance (ODA) in 2010 amounted to US$472 million, which is about 0.07% of gross national income and is expected to stay at that level in the near future. Russian assistance is primarily provided indirectly by writing off debts of developing countries; through participation in various international programs; and by providing humanitarian aid, grants, and trade preferences. A regulatory and institutional framework for assistance has not been firmly established. While there is no single legislative act related to the provision of ODA, major principles of assistance are formulated in the government-approved International Development Assistance Concept. Creation of a federal agency responsible for implementation of assistance policies and coordination of assistance provided has been proposed. The existing Federal Agency for the Commonwealth of Independent States, Compatriots Living Abroad and International Humanitarian Cooperation is engaged in aid work. Presently, development assistance is conducted through multilateral mechanisms taking advantage of already established aid delivery channels. Specific amounts of aid are defined in the budget bills specifying activities of individual executive agencies and Russian funds designated to support the work of international organizations. Most of Russian ODA is provided as untied aid; however, the government supports the idea of lending tied assistance funds based on certain economic and policy considerations. The effectiveness of ODA is assessed by the Ministries of Finance and Foreign Affairs.

I. Introduction

A. Official Development Assistance Figures

Despite its increasing involvement in international cooperation programs, Russia is not a member of the Organisation for Economic Co-operation and Development (OECD) and does not report aid flows to the Development Assistance Committee (DAC).[1]

According to the Ministry of Finance, in 2010 Russia spent a total of US$472.32 million,[2] nearly meeting the annual target rate of US$500 million set by the Concept of Russia's

---

[1] Mark Rakhmangulov, *Establishing International Development Assistance Strategy in Russia*, INT'L ORGS. RES. J. No. 5(31) at 50, 57 (2010), *available at* http://www.ecsocman.edu.ru/data/2011/05/06/1268030701/9.pdf.

[2] Ministry of Finance of the Russian Federation, Statements of Director of the International Finance Affairs of Ministry of Finance of the Russian Federation A. Bokarev (May 20, 2011), http://www.minfin.ru/en/pressoffice/quotes/index.php?id4=12751.

Participation in International Development Assistance (IDA Concept).[3] Russia's contribution of US$785 million in 2009 was not a move to a new level of aid volume but was explained by aid allocation to main partners, especially Commonwealth of Independent States (CIS) member states, to help them cope with the worldwide economic crisis.[4] According to Russian officials, within the next few years Russia's Official Development Assistance (ODA) will remain at the level of about US$500 million.[5]

Russia's ODA/Gross National Income (GNI) ratio increased from 0.015% in 2004 to 0.065% in 2009 and was expected to reach 0.07% in 2010, which is well below the DAC members' levels.[6] The IDA Concept states that "as the necessary socioeconomic conditions are created, Russia will further increase provisions for aid, aiming to steadily move towards the achievement of the United Nations (UN) recommended target: allocation of at least 0.7% GDP for purposes of international development assistance."[7]

Given limited resources in the previous two decades and large debts under loans provided by the former Soviet Union, Russia contributed to development assistance mostly by writing off debts of developing countries, often within the framework of the International Monetary Fund (IMF) Heavily Indebted Poor Countries (HIPC) Initiative.[8] In 2003, Russia ranked first in the share of developing countries' debt relief to its Gross Domestic Product (GDP) and third in absolute value after Japan and France.[9] In 2006, Russia committed to canceling US$11.3 billion worth of debts owed by African countries, including US$2.2 billion of debt relief to the HIPC Initiative.[10] According to Russian officials, in 2009 the amount of write-offs in favor of African countries reached around US$20 billion.[11]

---

[3] Concept of Russia's Participation in International Development Assistance [IDA Concept] (June 14, 2007), *available at* http://www.minfin.ru/common/img/uploaded/library/2007/06/concept_eng.pdf.

[4] Rakhmangulov, *supra* note 1, at 55.

[5] A. Bokarev, *It Is Important to Reach New Quality Standards of Russia's Development Assistance Programmes*, International Organisations Research Institute [IORI] (May 3, 2011), http://www.hse.ru/en/org/hse/iori/news/29467387.html.

[6] Rakhmangulov, *supra* note 1, at 55.

[7] IDA Concept, *supra* note 3, at 10.

[8] *Id.* at 4.

[9] Rakhmangulov, *supra* note 1, at 59.

[10] Id.

[11] Interviu Zamestitelia Ministra Inostrannykh Del Rossii A.V. Saltanova, "Rossiia i Blizhnii Vostok" [Interview of the Deputy Foreign Minister of Russia A.V. Saltanov, "Russia and the Middle East"], MEZHDUNARODNAIA ZHIZN' No. 12 (2009), *available at* http://www.mid.ru/brp_4.nsf/0/44F5671485529C4 0C32576AA00491FA7 (in Russian).

B. Private Contribution Figures

Russian philanthropists are encouraged to invest domestically and be involved in resolving domestic problems. Most of their donations stay in Russia.[12] Even the large-scale catastrophes of the December 2004 Southeast Asia tsunami and the January 2010 Haiti earthquake did not engender substantial private Russian contributions to international humanitarian and relief operations.[13]

C. Snapshot of Foreign Aid Activity

The Soviet Union has been actively involved in international development assistance.[14] It spent around US$26 billion in 1986 alone on friendly poor countries in the communist world, South America, Asia, and Africa.[15] The economic crisis that followed the collapse of the Soviet Union seriously limited Russia's participation in development assistance[16] and resulted in Russia's inclusion on the list of aid recipient countries.[17] Recent economic revival has enabled Russia to widen the scope and types of its assistance to international development efforts and emerge as a donor.[18]

Russia expends significant resources to support primarily neighboring former Soviet republics through participation in various international programs and provision of humanitarian aid, grants, trade preferences, and other measures.[19] In recent years Russia mostly contributed to development assistance by writing off debts under loans provided by the former Soviet Union.[20]

Russia identified its main priorities in development cooperation and pledged a significant increase in external aid financing during its G8 Presidency in 2006.[21] While Russia aims to create a regulatory and institutional framework for assistance, currently it provides development assistance mainly in two ways: by individual executive agencies according to established bilateral treaties and through multilateral mechanisms, taking advantage of well-established aid

---

[12] Alexander Livshin & Richard Weitz, *Civil Society and Philanthropy Under Putin*, 8(3) INT'L J. NOT-FOR-PROFIT L. 6 (May 2006), *available at* http://www.icnl.org/research/ journal/vol8iss3/special_2.htm.

[13] *Id.*; Jose Milhazes, *Grazhdane Rossii ne Pozhertvovali ni Rublia na Pomosh' Gaiti* [*Russian Citizens Did Not Donate a Single Ruble to Help Haiti*], INOSMI.RU (Jan. 26, 2010), http://inosmi.ru/social/20100126/ 157806793.html.

[14] Rakhmangulov, *supra* note 1, at 50.

[15] Conor Humphries, *Russian Aims to Increase Clout with Soft-Power Campaign*, REUTERS (Feb. 10, 2011), http://in.reuters.com/article/2011/02/10/idINIndia-54800120110210?pageNumber=1.

[16] IDA Concept, *supra* note 3, at 3.

[17] Rakhmangulov, *supra* note 1, at 50.

[18] Id.

[19] Eurasia Heritage Foundation [EHF] & United Nations Development Programme [UNDP], Engagement of Russian Business in International Development Assistance in the CIS Countries (Kyrgyzstan, Tajikistan) 9 (Moscow, 2010), *available at* http://www.undp.ru/index.php?iso=ru&lid=_1&cmd=publications1&id=133.

[20] Rakhmangulov, *supra* note 1, at 58.

[21] *Id.* at 56.

delivery channels, additional coordination opportunities provided by international organizations, financial monitoring systems, and technical capacity and expertise.[22] This is consistent with the IDA Concept, which states that pending the establishment of a national development assistance system,

> Russia will provide international development assistance mainly on a multilateral basis, that is by making voluntary and earmarked contributions to the international financial and economic institutions, first of all, to UN programs, funds, and specialized agencies, regional economic commissions and other organizations participating in development programs; by participating in global funds; and by implementing special international initiatives of the Group of Eight, the World Bank, IMF, and UN agencies.[23]

Current sectoral priorities of Russia's development assistance were mainly formulated under the influence of the Russian G8 Presidency in 2006 and include energy, health and education, governance and public administration, conflict resolution, industrial development, and capacity building.[24]

Russian initiatives to help develop energy infrastructure in rural areas of African countries, including the construction of mini-power plants, mini-hydroelectric power plants, and power lines for electric energy access, are carried out under the Global Village Energy Partnership program. Russia was expected to contribute about US$30 million to this program over four years starting in 2007.[25]

In October 2008, Russia and the World Bank established the Russia Education Aid for Development (READ) Trust Fund aimed at enhancing education quality in low-income countries.[26] The Trust Fund money (US$32 million) is being allocated over five years among seven countries (four in Africa, two in Central Asia, and one in Southeast Asia).[27]

Health care has become a traditional area of development assistance for Russia.[28] In that sphere, Russian ODA has been allocated in recent years as follows:

2006 – US$20.35 million

2007 – US$102.17 million

2008 – US$110.29 million

2009 – US$90.72 million[29]

---

[22] IDA Concept, *supra* note 3, at 9.

[23] *Id.* at 8.

[24] *Id.* at 7.

[25] Rakhmangulov, *supra* note 1, at 60.

[26] Id.

[27] Id.

[28] Ministry of Finance of the Russian Federation, *supra* note 2.

[29] Rakhmangulov, *supra* note 1, at 60–61.

2010 – US$80 million[30]

2011 – US$26.47 million (as allocated)[31]

In 2006, Russia terminated its recipient status and compensated the Global Fund to Fight AIDS, TB, and Malaria (Global Fund) the US$217 million that the Fund had previously spent on its activities in Russia.[32] Payments to the Global Fund constituted more than half of the total contribution of US$430 million that Russia made to public health services worldwide from 2006 to 2011.[33] Russian contributions to the fight against tropical diseases amounted to RUB 157 million (US$4.9 million) in 2010 and RUB 240 million (US$7.8 million) in 2011.[34] In the past few years Russia contributed US$28 million in technical assistance to CIS countries to establish national systems for monitoring infectious diseases, and another US$5 million was appropriated in 2010.[35] Russia pledged to contribute US$75 million to the Muskoka Initiative on Maternal, Newborn and Under-Five Child Health from 2011–2014.[36]

In 2011, Russia's contribution to global food security efforts remained at the 2010 level (US$98.2 million), and the total sum of Russia's commitments to the L'Aquila Food Security Initiative in 2009–2011 amounts to US$330 million (humanitarian aid is excluded).[37] From January 2008 to June 2009, Russia allocated US$73 million to overcome the consequences of the food crisis and ensure food security, including through emergency aid programs.[38] Russian food aid is allocated through the World Food Programme of the United Nations (WFP) and by one-time emergency donations, such as US$3.5 million in food aid deliveries to Bangladesh, Guinea, and Zimbabwe in 2008.[39] Russian food assistance contributions reached about US$30 million in 2009.[40] Russian food aid is received by a relatively small number of countries. For example, in 2010, contributions were allocated to Afghanistan (US$5 million), Armenia (US$2.5 million), the Democratic Republic of the Congo (US$2 million), Kyrgyzstan (US$5 million), and Tajikistan (US$5.5 million).[41] An additional US$10 million was set aside for one-time emergency operations, with US$4.2 million from these funds dedicated to food aid to Haiti.[42] Russia also contributes to WFP infrastructure development by supporting logistical functions

---

[30] Ministry of Finance of the Russian Federation, *supra* note 2.

[31] Rakhmangulov, *supra* note 1, at 62.

[32] *Id.* at 61.

[33] *Id.* at 62.

[34] IORI, *supra* note 5.

[35] Rakhmangulov, *supra* note 1, at 62.

[36] IORI, *supra* note 5.

[37] Ministry of Finance of the Russian Federation, *supra* note 2.

[38] Rakhmangulov, *supra* note 1, at 62.

[39] *Id.*

[40] *Id.*

[41] *Id.* at 63.

[42] *Id.*

carried out by the WFP for the entire UN system.[43] The WFP and the Russian government are designing school meals programs for long-term projects in CIS countries, starting with Armenia, where such a program funded by a Russian contribution of US$8 million will be implemented in 2010–2012.[44] Russia plans to donate up to US$15 million for the development of agriculture in developing countries through the World Bank Global Food Crisis Response Program.[45] Tajikistan received US$6.75 million through this program in 2009 and 2010, and an allocation of US$6.8 million to Kyrgyzstan is being considered.[46] In 2010, Russia spent US$98.2 million to train farm specialists and to supply technology and resistant seed cultures to Africa, and it appears that in 2011 spending on food security stayed the same.[47]

Russia is expected to announce a decision to contribute up to US$200 million to the Green Climate Fund, established for mitigating the consequences of climate change.[48]

In April 2011, the Russian government decided to donate €5 million (US$6.8 million) to the Nuclear Safety Account in 2012 and €20 million (US$27.4 million) annually in 2011 and 2012 to the Chernobyl Shelter Fund. Russia provided US$27 million to these initiatives in 2005–2006 and 2009–2010.[49]

In the context of the ongoing financial crisis, Russia together with other countries of the Eurasian Economic Community (EurAsEC), which includes Belarus, Kazakhstan, Kyrgyzstan, and Tajikistan, has established a US$10 billion Anti-Crisis Fund, with Russia contributing US$7.5 billion. The proceeds of this fund will be used to support poor countries within the EurAsEC on terms and conditions comparable with ODA criteria.[50]

Russia also provides assistance in the sphere of good governance, such as the support provided by the Federal Service for Fiscal Monitoring to several CIS countries for developing fiscal monitoring systems.[51]

---

[43] *Id.*

[44] *Id.* at 64.

[45] *Id.* at 65.

[46] *Id.*

[47] Ministry of Finance of the Russian Federation, *supra* note 2.

[48] IORI, *supra* note 5.

[49] *Id.*

[50] Opening Address by Russia's Minister of Finance A.L. Kudrin at the International Conference on New Partnerships in Global Development Finance (Feb. 17, 2010), http://www.mgdf.ru/eng/press/speeches/ opening_kudrin.

[51] Rakhmangulov, *supra* note 1, at 59.

II. Legal Framework

A. Regulation of ODAs

1. Overview

Russian ODA legislation is still being developed. A number of important terms and concepts are not defined and some terms have different definitions from those in the DAC documents.[52] Russia is the only G8 country that does not include the concept of "official development assistance"[53] in its laws. Foreign aid provision concepts appear in certain laws, treaties, and strategic conceptual documents.[54]

The IDA Concept, approved in 2007, defines the major goals, objectives, principles, and priorities of Russia's international development assistance policy and aims at establishing a national development assistance system.[55] The purpose of the IDA Concept is to ensure that the federal government uses a systemic approach to Russia's participation in international development assistance.[56] The legal framework for the IDA Concept is provided by the Constitution of the Russian Federation, the Russian Foreign Policy Concept, the Russian Security Concept, and the Budget Code of the Russian Federation.[57] The IDA Concept is also based on the UN Charter, the Millennium Declaration, the Monterrey Consensus, the Johannesburg Plan of Implementation of the World Summit on Sustainable Development, the 2005 World Summit Outcome, the Paris Declaration, and other international instruments.[58] The IDA Concept provides that the creation of a national system of international development assistance will occur in several stages, but no time frames or terms have been set for the stages.[59]

The Plan of Measures to Implement the International Development Assistance Concept was adopted in November 2007 and provides for measures to create legal and institutional bases for Russia's development assistance.[60] The plan was to be implemented from 2008 to 2010, but institutional changes have not yet been made.[61] To date there is no document that would enable all concerned agencies to address the tasks set out by the IDA Concept in an integrated and step-by-step fashion.[62] There are individual acts issued by federal executive agencies, but they have

---

[52] *Id.* at 51.

[53] IDA Concept, *supra* note 3, at 3.

[54] Rakhmangulov, *supra* note 1, at 51.

[55] *Id.*

[56] IDA Concept, *supra* note 3, at 2.

[57] *Id.*

[58] *Id.*

[59] Rakhmangulov, *supra* note 1, at 52.

[60] *Id.*

[61] *Id.* at 53.

[62] EHF & UNDP, *supra* note 19, at 12.

narrow application and do not amount to a unified system of actions to promote and enhance the effectiveness of the ODA.[63]

Plans to establish a specialized governmental agency for development assistance were announced by the Russian Finance Ministry on August 26, 2011. It appears that a newly created federal agency "will contribute to international development, [and] assist other countries to advance economy and fight poverty."[64] According to the draft of the new agency's statute, it will "develop Russian assistance strategy and monitor its implementation."[65] The agency will be subordinated to the federal Ministry of Finance and will coordinate its activities with the Ministry of Foreign Affairs.[66]

2. Restrictions

Currently more than 75% of Russian ODA is provided as untied aid.[67] At the same time the Concept for the Long-Term Social and Economic Development of Russia through 2020, approved in November 2008, states that Russian businesses will be supported by tied loans and international development aid mechanisms with a view toward promoting Russian goods and services in the markets of developing countries.[68] In particular, Russian authorities consider humanitarian food supplies as a measure to support Russian grain exporters. For example, in April 2009 the Russian government made targeted "tied" contributions to the WFP and the International Civil Defense Organization of US$9.3 million and US$10.7 million, respectively, emphasizing that they will be used to purchase wheat and flour in Russia and to pay Russian organizations for their delivery.[69] The IDA Concept also states that "[o]ther conditions being equal, preference will be given to projects and programs involving the use of goods and services originating in Russia."[70]

3. Policy Considerations

The IDA Concept states that Russia's economic and political interests will be met by "strengthening Russia's international position and credibility; stabilizing [the] socioeconomic and political situation in the partner countries; establishing a belt of good neighborliness; prevent[ing] the occurrence of potential focal points of tension and conflict, primarily in the

---

[63] *Id.*

[64] Evgeniia Pismennaia & Ekaterina Kravchenko, Minfin Rossii Khochet Pomoch Drugim Stranam v Likvidatsii Bednosti (Russian Finance Ministry Wants to Help Other Countries to Eliminate Poverty), VEDOMOSTI (Aug. 26, 2011), http://www.vedomosti.ru/finance/news/1349485/agentstvo_pomoschi#ixzz1dzsrsxM4.

[65] *Id.*

[66] Id.

[67] MUSKOKA ACCOUNTABILITY REPORT, G8 MEMBER REPORTING: AID AND AID EFFECTIVENESS 8 (June 2010), *available at* http://canadainternational.gc.ca/g8/assets/pdfs/mar_annex51.pdf.

[68] Government Regulation No. 1662 of Nov. 17, 2008, SOBRANIE ZAKONODATELSTVA ROSSIISKOI FEDERATSII [SZ RF] [official gazette] 2008, No. 47, Item 5489.

[69] Rakhmangulov, *supra* note 1, at 64.

[70] IDA Concept, *supra* note 3, at 12.

regions neighboring Russia; [and] creating a favorable external environment for Russia's own development."[71] The IDA Concept emphasizes the importance of poverty reduction activities in countries with effective governance and anticorruption programs, and those interested in building a consistent bilateral relationship with Russia.[72]

The IDA Concept charges the Ministry of Foreign Affairs and the Ministry of Finance with joint coordination of expenditures on Russia's IDA, including the determination of priority countries and regions; the political advisability of aid provision; and the amount, delivery channels, types, and terms of such assistance.[73]

Given Russia's limited resources, the IDA Concept specifies the priority group of aid recipients. Russia's regional priorities are one of the main considerations in its IDA system.[74] The priority group includes the bordering countries—members of the Agreement on the Integrated Economic Space (IES) and the Eurasian Economic Community (EurAsEC)—and other CIS countries.[75] The CIS countries are perceived as a security belt around Russia, and social and political stability in these countries enables Russia to conduct more liberal policies and reduce its military expenditures.[76] The countries of sub-Saharan Africa also are given particular attention as the least developed and most in need of international aid.[77]

Another priority group consists of Russian compatriots living abroad. Russia provides support to compatriots in ninety-one countries, including through scholarships on equal terms with Russian citizens.[78]

4. Discretionary Aid

Federal executive agencies coordinate their proposals with the Ministry of Foreign Affairs and the Ministry of Finance for inclusion in the federal budget of spending items in connection with IDA. The IDA Concept lists the goals of Russia's development assistance, principles for avoiding corruption risks and ensuring transparency of decision making, and other factors that must be taken into account in supporting documents prepared by federal executive agencies. The law on the federal budget generally does not contain restrictions on spending funds appropriated for IDA.

---

[71] *Id.* at 5.

[72] *Russia: The Ministry of Foreign Affairs/The Ministry of Finance*, PARIS 21, http://www.paris21.org/globaldirectory/Bilaterals/id/170 (last updated 2008).

[73] IDA Concept, *supra* note 3, at 10.

[74] *National Strategies on Development Assistance: Russia*, RESEARCH CENTRE FOR INTERNATIONAL COOPERATION AND DEVELOPMENT [RCICD], http://en.rcicd.org/national-strategies-on-development-assistance/russia/ (last visited Nov. 16, 2011).

[75] IDA Concept, *supra* note 3, at 7.

[76] EHF & UNDP, *supra* note 19, at 8.

[77] IDA Concept, *supra* note 3, at 7.

[78] Rakhmangulov, *supra* note 1, at 65.

5. Oversight

The Accounting Chamber of the Russian Federation controls spending of appropriated funds.[79] Performance assessments of Russia's participation in specific development assistance projects is carried out in coordination with the authorities of the recipient country and/or the leadership of international organizations.[80] To avoid the risks of "nurturing" corruption, misuse of allocated funds, and conservation of inefficient public administration in the recipient countries, the IDA Concept includes a number of requirements that recipient countries must meet to be eligible for Russian development assistance, such as the existence of national poverty reduction and sustainable economic development programs, and anticorruption programs.[81] This requirement does not apply to allocation of emergency aid. The Ministry of Foreign Affairs, the Ministry of Economic Development and Trade, and the Ministry of Finance are charged with compiling factual and analytical data on the implementation of anticorruption activities and efforts to ensure transparency in the use of IDA.[82] The Ministry of Foreign Affairs and the Ministry of Finance are also responsible for assessing the cost-effectiveness of federal spending on IDA.[83]

B. Regulation of Private Contributions

As noted above, the amount of private Russian contributions to international development is insignificant. Amendments to the Tax Code enacted in July 2011 and entering into force from January 2012 provide for reducing the taxable income of private individuals to the extent of contributions made to charitable funds and socially oriented nongovernmental organizations.[84]

III. Foreign Aid Appropriations Process

According to the IDA Concept, Russia provides assistance on a multilateral basis, a trilateral basis, and a bilateral basis.[85] The majority of Russian ODA (more than 60% in 2010[86]) is provided through multilateral channels, including through UN organizations and the World Bank (i.e., in the form of untied voluntary contributions), since aid delivery channels and a legislative framework to deliver the aid have yet to be developed.[87]

---

[79] EHF & UNDP, *supra* note 19, at 9.

[80] IDA Concept, *supra* note 3, at 13.

[81] *Id.* at 6–7.

[82] *Id.* at 12.

[83] *Id.*

[84] Sotsial'nye uslugi osvobodili ot NDS, a blagotvoritel'nost' – ot NDFL [Social Services Are Exempted From VAT, and Charity From the Personal Income Tax], KADIS (July 25, 2011), http://www.kadis.ru/news/98058 (in Russian).

[85] RCICD, *supra* note 74.

[86] Claire Provost, *The Rebirth of Russian Foreign Aid*, GUARDIAN.CO.UK (May 25, 2011), http://www.guardian.co.uk/global-development/2011/may/25/russia-foreign-aid-report-influence-image.

[87] PARIS 21, *supra* note 72.

Bilateral assistance projects focus on a relatively limited number of recipient countries, such as Central Asian countries that share with Russia a common language and legacy of the Soviet health system, and countries where it is possible to make tangible, evaluable contributions.[88]   Assistance provided on a trilateral basis implies application of financial and technical capacity of traditional donor countries and international organizations and delivery of aid through trust funds of the World Bank, the UN institutions, and other organizations. At the same time, Russia retains the right to select recipient countries and areas of assistance, and to use Russian technical assistance specialists.[89]

Federal budget funds for development assistance activities are allocated according to procedures established by the Budget Code of the Russian Federation.[90]   The Ministry of Economic Development prepares annual plans for ODA in collaboration with international organizations, while the Ministry of Finance ensures that the agreed-upon ODA spending is included in the draft federal budget, informs budget funding administrators and beneficiaries of the overall budget schedule and of limits on ODA spending, and cooperates with the Federal Treasury to ensure timely financing of relevant spending items.[91]   However, proper spending of the funds is the responsibility of the federal executive bodies, which submit proposals each year to the Ministry of Finance on ODA volumes agreed-upon with the Ministry of Foreign Affairs together with justification for inclusion of their proposals in long-term financial plans and the federal budget.[92]

IV. Implementing Agencies

The following agencies are responsible for ODA according to the IDA Concept: the President; the Parliament; the Ministry of Foreign Affairs; the Ministry of Finance; the Ministry of Economic Development; the Ministry of Civil Defense, Emergencies and Disaster Relief; the Ministry of Industry and Trade; and the Ministry of Energy.[93]   The actual list of government agencies involved in implementing ODA policy also includes the Ministry of Natural Resources and Environment; the Ministry of Regional Development; the Ministry of Education and Science; the Federal Agency for the CIS, Compatriots Living Abroad and International Humanitarian Cooperation (*Rossotrudnichestvo*); and other agencies.[94]

The Ministries of Foreign Affairs and Finance are the main decision-making authorities with respect to ODA, including the prioritization of countries and regions, the political expediency of aid, the amount of aid, delivery channels, types, and terms.[95]   They provide

---

[88] Center for Strategic and International Studies, Russia's Global Health Leadership (May 29, 2011), http://csis.org/files/attachments/110519Summary.pdf.

[89] IDA Concept, *supra* note 3, at 9.

[90] *Id.* at 10.

[91] EHF & UNDP, *supra* note 19, at 10.

[92] *Id.*

[93] Rakhmangulov, *supra* note 1, at 53.

[94] EHF & UNDP, *supra* note 19, at 9.

[95] *Id.* at 9.

information support for ODA operations, submit official information to foreign governments and international organizations, and jointly prepare annual reports on outcomes of Russia's participation in ODA.[96] The Ministry of Finance is also responsible for analytical accounting of funds allocated by the Russian Federation to ODA.[97] Russia's humanitarian aid is controlled by the Ministry for Civil Defense, Emergencies and Elimination of Consequences of Natural Disasters.[98]

Rossotrudnichestvo was established under the jurisdiction of the Ministry of Foreign Affairs and is engaged in facilitation and development of international relations between Russia and the CIS member states and other states, as well as in the sphere of international humanitarian cooperation.[99] It is not the Russian agency for international development, creation of which is expected in the next year or two, because it is involved in aid programs only for the CIS member states.[100] Experts do not consider *Rossotrudnichestvo* as a serious IDA actor given its and its predecessors' specialization in promoting Russian language, culture, science, and educational relations.[101]

V. Other Types of 'Aid'

A. Emergency Aid

Even during extreme economic hardship in the early 1990s, Russia actively participated in humanitarian operations. Russian aid provided during the humanitarian operations after the earthquake in Haiti amounted to about US$5 million, and Russia donated an additional US$8 million following the Haiti Donors' Conference in March 2010.[102] Russia's largest single contribution, US$20 million, was made in 2008 in response to the earthquake in the Sichuan Province of China.[103]

B. College Scholarships to Foreign Students

The Concept for the Long-Term Social and Economic Development of the Russian Federation provides for creation of a system of incentives, including financial incentives, for foreign citizens to study in Russian institutions of higher education and for promotion of exchange programs for the development of economic ties with the countries participating in the joint educational programs.[104]

---

[96] *Id.*

[97] *Id.*

[98] *Country Profile: Russia*, GLOBAL HUMANITARIAN ASSISTANCE, http://www.globalhumanitarian assistance.org/countryprofile/russia (last visited Nov. 16, 2011).

[99] Rakhmangulov, *supra* note 1, at 53.

[100] *Id.*

[101] EHF & UNDP, *supra* note 19, at 13.

[102] IORI, *supra* note 5.

[103] GLOBAL HUMANITARIAN ASSISTANCE, *supra* note 98.

[104] Rakhmangulov, *supra* note 1, at 59.

According to various sources, students from 161 states were granted approximately 9,000 scholarships funded by the Russian federal budget in 2009.[105] Pursuant to a government decision, the number of foreign citizens and compatriots whose studies in government educational institutions of higher and professional education is supported by federal funds cannot exceed 10,000.[106]

C. Foreign Remittances

Russia is second only to the United States with respect to the number of migrants in its territory (12.3 million), and it is the fourth largest source of remittances in the world with US$18.6 billion (2% of GDP) transferred in 2010.[107] The IDA Concept emphasizes the importance of facilitating the simplification and cost-reduction, and enhancing the security and efficiency, of money remittance systems.[108]

Prepared by Peter Roudik
Director of Legal Research
and Nerses Isajanyan
Foreign Law Consultant
December 2011

---

[105] *Id.* at 60.

[106] Ministry of Education Resolution No. 179, May 26, 2009, ROSSIISKAIA GAZETA, June 24, 2009, *at* http://www.rg.ru/2009/06/24/inostrancy-vuzy-dok.html (official publication).

[107] THE WORLD BANK, MIGRATION AND REMITTANCES FACTBOOK 2011 at 1, 15 & 16 (2d ed.), *available at* http://siteresources.worldbank.org/INTLAC/Resources/Factbook2011-Ebook.pdf.

[108] IDA Concept, *supra* note 3, at 9.

LAW LIBRARY OF CONGRESS

SAUDI ARABIA

REGULATION OF FOREIGN AID

Executive Summary

Saudi Arabia is a leading provider of official development assistance to developing countries, averaging 1.5% of its gross national income (GNI) for the period between 1973 and 2008, according to a study conducted by the World Bank. Saudi Arabia channels its assistance through the Saudi Fund for Development established specifically for this purpose and is also a generous donor of humanitarian aid, totaling $2.1 billion for the period between 2000 and 2010.

I. Introduction

A. Official Development Assistance Figures

According to a study conducted by the World Bank, the Kingdom of Saudi Arabia, Kuwait, and the United Arab Emirates have been among the most generous in the world in providing official development assistance (ODA) to developing countries, averaging 1.5% of their gross national income (GNI) during the period from 1973 to 2008. This rate is about twice as much as the 0.7% target set by the United Nations and about five times the average assistance provided by Organisation for Economic Co-operation and Development (OECD) member states, with Saudi Arabia leading the other two countries, Kuwait and the United Arab Emirates.

Saudi Arabia's high ODA average of the 1970s and 1980s declined through 2001, but started rising again in 2002 both in terms of the amounts provided and the GNI percentage.[1]

B. Private Contribution Figures

According to the Saudi Arabia Market Information Resource and Directory (SAMIRAD), the Saudi Government formed official and national committees in each of the cities in the kingdom, under the auspices of a high ministerial committee tasked with coordinating private contributions, to help alleviate the ill effects of the persistent drought in Africa. The government provided aid in money and in kind payments and called on its citizens to give generously.

---

[1] Mustapha Rouis, *Arab Development Assistance: Four Decades of Cooperation*, MENA KNOWLEDGE AND LEARNING: QUICK NOTES SERIES No. 28 (World Bank, Aug. 2010), http://siteresources.worldbank.org/INTMENA/Resources/QuickNote28-ArabODA.pdf.

Through 1988, the total value of aid provided amounted to 325 million Saudi Riyals.[2] No relevant information about the status of such private aid has been found for the period after 1988.

C. Snapshot of Foreign Aid Activity

Between 1975 and the end of 2010, Saudi Arabia financed 472 development projects in 77 countries, in an amount totaling 33,258.99 million Saudi Riyals. The geographical distribution of these projects is as follows: 43 in Africa, 27 in Asia, and 7 in other parts of the world.[3]

II. Legal Framework

A. Regulation of ODAs

1. Overview

Saudi Arabia authorized official development assistance participation by issuing Royal Decree No. M/48 dated August 14, 1394 Hijri (corresponding to September 1, 1974), pursuant to which the Saudi Fund for Development (the Fund) was established.

The Fund's objective is to participate in financing developmental projects in developing countries through granting loans.[4]

2. Restrictions

The assistance provided by the Fund is not subject to any specific restrictions except for the following:

- The project being financed must benefit the country that receives the loan economically or socially;

- The loan should be disbursed and paid back in Saudi Riyals;

- The loan amount granted must not exceed 5% of the Fund's capital or 50% of the total cost of the project; and

- The aggregate amount of loans granted at the same time to any country must not exceed 10% of the Fund's capital.[5]

---

[2] *Saudi Aid at the National Level*, SAMIRAD, http://www.saudinf.com/MAIN/l109.htm (last visited Oct. 21, 2011). At the current exchange rate, one Saudi Riyal equals approximately US$0.266647.

[3] SAUDI FUND FOR DEVELOPMENT, ANNUAL REPORT 2010, http://www.sfd.gov.sa/cs/groups/public/ documents/document/mdaw/mtqx/~edisp/121-document-141993.pdf (in English; last visited Oct. 21, 2011).

[4] Saudi Royal Decree No. M/48 of 1974 (Royal Decree), art. 1, Bureau of Experts at the Council of Ministers, http://boe.gov.sa/ViewSystemDetails.aspx?lang=ar&SystemID=237 (in Arabic).

[5] *Id.* art. 7(a–d).

3. Policy Considerations

The Board of Directors of the Fund is vested with the authority to adopt rules and regulations under which loans are granted and recalled in a manner consistent with Royal Decree No. M/48 of 1974.[6] However, the Council of Ministers may dispense with any of the conditions prescribed in the Decree provided its decision is based on a recommendation made by the Board of Directors of the Fund and a proposal offered by the Minister of Finance and National Economy as to whether such dispensation is justified.[7]

4. Discretionary Aid

There are no provisions in the charter of the Fund as established by Royal Decree No. M/48 of 1974 to allow it to give discretionary aid outside the norms described therein. However, Saudi Arabia is known to have given and continues to give large contributions for humanitarian aid purposes, whether directly or through international or regional organizations. For example, according to a report citing as a source Development Initiatives, based on data from the Financial Tracking Service of the United Nation's Office for Coordination of Humanitarian Affairs, Saudi Arabia has given a total of US$2.1 billion in humanitarian aid between 2000 and 2010.[8]

5. Oversight

Notwithstanding the role and authority of the general financial inspection department within the Saudi government, the Board of Directors of the Fund may appoint one or more inspectors and financial auditors.[9]

B. Regulation of Private Contributions

Following the terrorist attacks of September 11, 2001, in the United States, Saudi Arabia is believed to have adopted measures to ensure that contributions by individuals and private organizations are not channeled to terrorist organizations. However, we were unable to find research sources to identify such measures or the status of the various committees referred to in section I.B, above.

III. Foreign Aid Appropriation Process

In addition to the disbursement processes for official development assistance adopted by the Board of Directors of the Fund, Saudi Arabia participates in the following regional and international development institutions, each of which disburses the funds appropriated to it according to its own rules and regulations: Arab Monetary Fund, Arab Fund for Economic and

---

[6] *Id.* art. 4.

[7] *Id.* art. 7, last para.

[8] Kerry Smith, *Non-DAC Donors: Arab Donors' Humanitarian Aid Contributions*, GLOBAL HUMANITARIAN ASSISTANCE, http://www.globalhumanitarianassistance.org/wp-content/uploads/2011/07/Arab-donors-humanitarian-aid.pdf (cut and paste URL into browser; last visited Oct. 21, 2011).

[9] Royal Decree art. 12.

Social Development, Arab Bank for Economic Development in Africa, Arab Investment Guarantee Corporation, Islamic Development Bank, OPEC Fund for International Development, International Bank for Reconstruction and Development, International Monetary Fund, International Development Agency, International Finance Corporation, International Fund for Agricultural Development, Multilateral Investment Guarantee Agency, African Development Bank, African Development Fund, Arab Authority for Agricultural Investment and Development, Islamic Corporation for Investment Insurance and Export Credit, Islamic Corporation for Private Sector Development, International Islamic Trade Financing Corporation, Islamic Solidarity Fund for Development, and the Special Account for financing small and medium size projects in Arab countries.[10]

IV. Implementing Agencies

As explained above, the only agency that implements Saudi policy on providing official development assistance to developing countries is the Saudi Fund for Development.

V. Other Types of 'Aid'

We were unable to determine whether other types of aid have been regulated in Saudi Arabia.

Prepared by Issam M. Saliba
Senior Foreign Law Specialist
October 2011

---

[10] For Saudi contribution amounts and percentages of the total capital of each institution, *see* SAUDI FUND FOR DEVELOPMENT, ANNUAL REPORT 2010, App. 2, *supra* note 3.

LAW LIBRARY OF CONGRESS

SOUTH AFRICA

REGULATION OF FOREIGN AID

Executive Summary

South Africa has robust and fast-growing foreign aid programs. However, the funding and implementation of these programs are fragmented across different government institutions and regional and international organizations. The lack of a central implementing institution or a reporting mechanism makes obtaining the complete picture of South Africa's aid programs difficult.

One of the most visible aid programs is the African Renaissance and International Cooperation Fund (ARF). It is administered by the Department of International Relations and Cooperation and supports numerous projects in Africa in accordance with its stated objectives.

The African Renaissance and International Cooperation Fund Act, the law which governs the ARF, gives the executive body wide discretion to negotiate most assistance agreements and impose restrictions.

Funds for the ARF come from different sources including parliamentary appropriations, which is the primary source. Transparency and accountability in the way that the ARF is administered are insured through mandatory annual reports issued by the ARF and annual auditing by the Auditor General, an independent constitutional body.

I. Introduction

A. Official Development Assistance Figures

The complete picture of development assistance figures in South Africa is difficult to obtain. This is mainly because development assistance in South Africa is highly fragmented and the country has yet to establish a system for collecting accurate and complete data.[1]

Although data on assistance provided through the African Renaissance and International Cooperation Fund (ARF), one of South Africa's foreign aid programs, is available, it does not give an accurate picture of all foreign aid programs in South Africa. ARF accounts for only a

---

[1] WOLFE BRAUDE ET AL., EMERGING DONORS IN INTERNATIONAL DEVELOPMENT ASSISTANCE: THE SOUTH AFRICA CASE 13 (South African Inst. of Int'l Affairs, Jan. 2008), *available at* http://web.idrc.ca/uploads/user-S/12441475471Case_of_South_Africa.pdf.

small percentage of the overall assistance that South Africa provides, with most of it coming from other government institutions that do not produce accurate and complete reports.[2]

Assistance through the ARF has increased dramatically through the years since its inception in 2001. In 2003/04 ARF spending was limited to ZAR50 million (about US$7million).[3] By 2007/08, the expenditure rose dramatically to US$36.4 million.[4]

Only select figures on overall foreign aid expenditures by South Africa are available. Information extracted from the South African Treasury shows that in 2008/09, South Africa's expenditure through regional and international organizations (the United Nations, the African Union, the Southern African Development Community (SADC), and others) amounted to US$19.6 million.[5] Expenditure on humanitarian assistance on the same year was US$2.9 million.[6] South Africa has also contributed US$7 million to the India-Brazil-South Africa (IBSA) Poverty Alleviation Fund since its establishment in 2004.[7]

Information on foreign aid expenditure patterns shows that foreign aid assistance that South Africa provides emphasizes education and peacekeeping programs. Expenditures made by the South African Department of Education in 2004 accounted for 36% of the overall aid that South Africa provided that year.[8] Expenditure on peacekeeping in the same year, which was over ZAR500 million (about US$70.5 million), was the second largest.[9]

B. Private Contribution Figures

It has not been possible to locate private contribution figures. A search of the Law Library's holdings on South Africa as well as online searches yielded no results.

C. Snapshot of Foreign Aid Activity

South Africa's strong and growing commitment to foreign aid and development assistance puts it on par with prominent emerging donor nations like China, Brazil, and India. Its foreign aid programs are currently scattered across numerous institutions, including

- the African Renaissance and International Cooperation Fund (ARF);

---

[2] *Id.* at 5.

[3] *Id.* at 13.

[4] Kimberly Smith et al., Beyond the DAC: The Welcome Role of Other Providers of Development Co-operation 5 (OECD Development Cooperation Directorate Issues Brief, May 2010), http://www.oecd.org/dataoecd/58/24/45361474.pdf.

[5] *Id.*

[6] *Id.*

[7] *See IBSA Fund*, IBSA (Jan. 13, 2010), http://www.ibsa-trilateral.org/index.php?option=com_content&view=article&id=29&Itemid=79.

[8] BRAUDE ET AL., *supra* note 1, at 15.

[9] *Id.*

- programs at the national, provincial, and local government levels;

- the India-Brazil-South Africa (IBSA) Poverty Alleviation Fund;

- multilateral programs through concessional lending institutions such as the African Development Bank (AFDB) and the World Bank; and

- Southern African Customs Union (SACU) Agreements on Revenue Sharing.[10]

The ARF was established in 2001, although aid programs were channeled through a similar fund long before that.[11] The ARF accounts for a small percentage of the overall foreign aid that South Africa provides. However, it remains the most visible and transparent of all aid programs in South Africa.

The majority of foreign aid programs in South Africa are carried out by government institutions at the national, provincial, and local levels. These programs take many forms. Some examples include the capacity-building training programs offered by the Department of Agriculture and the Reserve Bank to members of counterpart institutions in different African countries, subsidies provided to foreign students to study in South Africa, the South African military's peacekeeping missions, and South African Police Services members' participation in various nations as observers in conflict areas or in monitoring elections.[12]

The IBSA Poverty Alleviation Fund is yet another program through which South Africa provides foreign assistance. Established in 2004 by India, Brazil, and South Africa, its function is to "identify replicable and scalable projects that can be disseminated to interested developing countries as examples of best practices in the fight against poverty and hunger."[13] Each member contributes US$1 million annually.[14]

South Africa also provides assistance through the SACU. The SACU is a customs union between South Africa, Botswana, Namibia, Lesotho, and Swaziland. Customs, excise, and other trade-related duties levied are credited into a common revenue pool and the funds from this pool are then paid to a development fund, with the remainder distributed among members according to a revenue-sharing formula adopted under the 2002 SACU Agreement.[15] This is one of the ways in which South Africa provides assistance to members of the SACU.

---

[10] Department of International Relations & Co-operation, Establishment of South Africa Development Partnership Agency (SADPA) 11 (Presentation to the NCOP Select Committee on Trade and International Relations, Aug. 3, 2011), *available at* http://www.pmg.org.za/files/docs/110803sadpa-edit.pdf.

[11] African Renaissance and International Co-operation Fund Act No. 51 of 2000, 425 REPUBLIC OF SOUTH AFRICA GOVERNMENT GAZETTE No. 21798 (Nov. 24, 2000), http://www.info.gov.za/view/DownloadFile Action?id=68220 (official source).

[12] BRAUDE ET AL., *supra* note 1, at 17, 18.

[13] IBSA, *supra* note 7.

[14] *Id.*

[15] BRAUDE ET AL., *supra* note 1, at 14, 15; *see also About SACU: SACU Agreements*, SACU, http://www.sacu.int/about.php?id=400 (last visited Aug. 17, 2011).

The fragmented nature of the South African aid programs is likely to change soon when the ARF is phased out. A plan to replace the ARF with another fund, the South African Development Partnership Fund, is being developed. This fund will be administered by an independent agency, the South African Development Partnership Agency (SADPA).[16] One of the key changes that the establishment of the new fund is expected to bring about is the coordination of all foreign aid programs in South Africa.[17]

II. Legal Framework

A. Regulation of ODAs

1. Overview

The discussion that follows focuses on the ARF regulatory framework, mainly because it is the most visible program for foreign assistance. As mentioned above, the ARF was established in 2001 through the African Renaissance and International Cooperation Fund Act to replace a similar program that had existed since 1968.[18] Although an effort to replace the ARF is in the works, it remains in operation today.

One key change brought about with the establishment of the ARF was an emphasis on a multilaterally oriented approach to foreign aid, a stark difference from its predecessor, the Economic Cooperation and Promotion Loan Fund. Although the law controlling the preceding fund did not expressly so state, its legislative history shows that its implementation was geared towards providing foreign assistance on a bilateral basis.[19] This was in part because South Africa, due to its apartheid policies, was denied membership to most intergovernmental organizations through which it could advance multilateral assistance programs.[20] With the

---

[16] *South African Development Partnership Agency (SADPA) Establishment Meeting: Summary*, PARLIAMENTARY MONITORING GROUP (Aug. 3, 2011), http://www.pmg.org.za/report/20110803-department-international-relations-co-operation-legislation-establish.

[17] *Id.*

[18] The 1968 Fund was established through the Economic Cooperation and Promotion Loan Fund Act No. 68 of 1968, STATUTES OF THE REPUBLIC OF SOUTH AFRICA 603–05 (1968) (official source), and was amended twice through the Economic Cooperation and Promotion Loan Fund Amendment Act No. 29 of 1986 & Economic Co-operation Promotion Loan Fund Amendment Act No. 16 of 1998. 395 REPUBLIC OF SOUTH AFRICA GOVERNMENT GAZETTE No. 18928 (May 27, 1998), http://www.info.gov.za/view/DownloadFileAction?id=91577 (official source). The 1968 Fund was initially started by the apartheid regime in South Africa for two purposes: (1) With the program, the government hoped to win friends in the international arena and their votes in the intergovernmental organizations, particularly the friendship and votes of African countries including Lesotho, Gabon, and Ivory Coast with which South Africa enjoyed close ties, BRAUDE ET AL., *supra* note 1, at 5; and (2) The program was also intended to provide assistance to the segregated black areas that South Africa carved out as autonomous regions during their brief stint as independent states, including the former Republics of Transkei, Bophuthatswana, Venda, and Ciskei, the assistance to which ended in 1994 after these regions rejoined South Africa. *Id.*; *see also* Economic Co-operation Promotion Loan Fund Amendment Act No. 16 of 1998.

[19] *See* University of the Witwatersrand, The School of Law, Annual Survey of South African Law 1968 at 58 (1969).

[20] *Id.*

establishment of the ARF the multilateral approach to foreign aid and development assistance became central.[21]

Another notable change to the South African foreign aid programs as the result of the establishment of the ARF in 2001 came in the form of streamlining the objectives of the fund. The stated objectives of the ARF are relatively well defined to enable the efficient disbursement of resources earmarked for assistance and allow for greater South African participation in problem solving. The objectives of the previous program were general in that they were limited to the "promotion of economic cooperation between the Republic and other countries by granting loans and other financial assistance in respect of development projects in such countries."[22] The stated objectives of the ARF are much more targeted both geographically and in terms of issues addressed, and include

- cooperation between South Africa and other countries, particularly African countries;
- the promotion of democracy and good governance;
- the prevention and resolution of conflict;
- socioeconomic development and integration;
- humanitarian assistance; and
- human resources development.[23]

This allows the South African government to get involved in identifying and funding specific programs proactively. As shown in ARF's 2009–2010 Annual Report, South Africa has utilized the ARF to fund a wide range of programs in different African countries in line with the above objectives, including its participation in the 2010 general elections in Sudan, economic revitalization projects in Zimbabwe, implementation of a medical project in Sierra Leone,[24] and a museum project in Guinea.[25]

2. Implementing Agencies

---

[21] *Establishment of the African Renaissance and International Co-Operation Fund*, DEPARTMENT OF INTERNATIONAL RELATIONS AND COOPERATION, http://www.dfa.gov.za/foreign/Multilateral/profiles/arfund.htm (last visited Aug. 16, 2011).

[22] Economic Cooperation and Promotion Loan Fund Act § 3, *as amended*, http://www.info.gov.za/view/DownloadFileAction?id=91577.

[23] African Renaissance and International Cooperation Fund Act § 4, http://www.info.gov.za/view/DownloadFileAction?id=68220.

[24] Department of International Relations and Cooperation, African Renaissance and International Co-operation Annual Report 2009–2010 at 5, http://www.dfa.gov.za/department/report_2009-2010/annualreportarf2009-2010.pdf.

[25] Department of International Relations and Cooperation, African Renaissance and International Co-operation Annual Report 2006–2007 at 6, http://www.dfa.gov.za/department/report_2006-2007/arf%20report.pdf.

The ARF is under the Department of International Relations and Cooperation (the Department), which until May 2009 was known as the Department of Foreign Affairs.[26] Specifically, the fund is under the direct control of the Director-General of the Department, subject to the direction of the Minister.[27]

The disbursement of money from the ARF appears to be a role shared between the Department of International Relations and Cooperation and the Department of Finance. This is evident both in the decision making procedure carved out for the Minister of the Department as well as through the staffing of an Advisory Committee, a body that plays a large role in the process of the disbursement of funds. Most disbursements from the fund are made by agreements between the fund and the relevant recipient party on the recommendations of an Advisory Committee to the Minister who acts in consultation with the Minister of Finance.[28] The Advisory Committee consists of the Director-General or his/her representative and three additional representatives of the Department appointed by the Minister, as well as two representatives of the Department of Finance.[29]

There does not appear to be a centralized implementation organization comparable to the United States Agency for International Development or the French Development Agency in South Africa. Implementation, much like the aid programs themselves, appears to be fragmented. This is evident in recent projects that were funded through the ARF. For instance, the implementation of a capacity-building training project in the Democratic Republic of the Congo (DRC) in 2008/09 was made through the Public Administration, Leadership and Management Academy (PALAMA), while the South African Departments of Public Works, International Relations and Cooperation and Defense as well as the Freedom Parks Trust participated in a project to upgrade a leadership school in Uganda the same year.[30]

Aid provided by other South African institutions is implemented by those institutions. For instance the South African Police Services (SAPS) has provided assistance to African countries in different roles including observers in Darfur and election monitoring in the Democratic Republic of the Congo.[31] For these projects/missions, SAPS would also act as the implementing body.[32]

---

[26] BuaNews (Tshwane), *Department Of Foreign Affairs Renamed, Restructured* (May 10, 2009), *available at* http://allafrica.com/stories/200905100043.html.

[27] African Renaissance and International Cooperation Fund Act § 2, http://www.info.gov.za/view/DownloadFileAction?id=68220.

[28] *Id.* § 5.

[29] *Id.*

[30] DEPARTMENT OF INTERNATIONAL RELATIONS AND COOPERATION, AFRICAN RENAISSANCE FUND ANNUAL REPORT 2008–2009 at 2–3, http://www.dfa.gov.za/department/report_2008-2009/annualreportarffinal08-09.pdf.

[31] BRAUDE ET AL., *supra* note 1, at 17.

[32] *Id.*

Foreign aid funds from South Africa are also channeled through international multinational organizations[33] or managed by institutions of the recipient countries.[34]

3. Restrictions

The African Renaissance and International Cooperation Fund Act does not expressly impose any restrictions on eligibility to receive assistance from the ARF. However, this does not preclude the executive body (i.e., the Minister of International Relations and Cooperation) from imposing restrictions, as he/she enjoys unfettered powers to negotiate the terms of assistance agreements so long as they are within the stated objectives of the ARF.[35] Yet, South Africa in practice appears reluctant to attach strings to the assistance that it provides. A recent financial assistance agreement negotiated with Swaziland in which South Africa agreed to provide a conditional guarantee for loans to the Central Bank of Swaziland in the amount of ZAR2.4 billion (US$350 million) from the South African Reserve Bank is a good example of this reluctance. In the negotiation process South Africa was able to convince Swaziland to agree to implement some reform measures, including

- confidence building measures to be undertaken by the Government of the Kingdom of Swaziland,

- fiscal and related technical reforms required by the IMF to be implemented by the Government of the Kingdom of Swaziland,

- capacity building support to be provided by South Africa, and

- cooperation in multilateral engagements.[36]

However, there do not appear to be strict enforcement mechanisms to ensure that Swaziland adheres to the agreed terms and follows through on its promise to introduce reforms. This is illustrated by a statement issued by the South African government on the loan agreement, which calls for a host of reforms to be introduced but at the same time is soft on ensuring strict implementation through, among other things, continued monitoring and assessment schedules.[37] The South African government's unwillingness to impose strict restrictions also appears evident from the schedule it established for releasing the loan funds in three installments in August 2011,

---

[33] Smith et al., *supra* note 4, at 5.

[34] *See* Department of International Relations and Cooperation, Media Statement on an Agreement to Provide Financial Assistance to the Government of the Kingdom of Swaziland (Aug. 3, 2011), http://www.dfa.gov.za/ docs/2011/swaz0803.html.

[35] African Renaissance and International Cooperation Fund Act § 5, http://www.info.gov.za/ view/DownloadFileAction?id=68220. Under this law, all loans or other financial assistance, except those involving the promotion of democracy and good governance or the prevention or resolution of conflict, are required by law to be based on an agreement between South Africa and the recipient party. *Id.*

[36] Department of International Relations and Cooperation, Media Statement on an Agreement to Provide Financial Assistance to the Government of the Kingdom of Swaziland (Aug. 3, 2011), http://www.dfa.gov.za/ docs/2011/swaz0803.html.

[37] *Id.*

October 2011, and February 2012—a time frame too short for implementing any reform and a sign that South Africa does not intend to strictly implement the terms of the agreement.[38]

This has incensed rights groups in both Swaziland as well as South Africa, who maintain that the loan should have been made contingent on tangible political and economic reforms.[39]

4. Discretionary Aid

It appears that all of the aid provided by South Africa can be characterized as discretionary and that aid provided through the ARF can be geared towards any project. The only requirement is that the assistance should fit the broadly stated objectives of the ARF. Other institutions, which account for the majority of the overall aid that South Africa provides, appear to enjoy even more flexibility in identifying and funding projects.

5. Oversight

The African Renaissance and International Co-operation Fund Act includes several oversight mechanisms put in place to ensure the fund's transparency and accountability. The Director General of the Department of International Relations and Cooperation, who runs the ARF and is also a member of the Advisory Committee that makes recommendations to the Minister of International Relations and Cooperation on disbursement, is the accounting officer of the fund and is required to keep records of the fund's finances and issue annual reports.[40] The ARF is also subject to accountability and transparency requirements set forth under the Public Finance Management Act.[41] In addition, it is subject to annual auditing by the Auditor-General, an independent constitutional body directly accountable to the National Assembly.[42]

6. Policy Considerations

South Africa's policy considerations have evolved over the years. The Economic Cooperation and Promotion Loan Fund, which was phased out in 2001, was geared towards winning allies in the international arena at the time that the country was facing increasing isolation mainly due to its apartheid policy.[43] At the time, South Africa also had a policy of not

---

[38] South African Press Association, *Conditions Attached to Loan* (Aug. 3, 2011), *available at* http://allafrica.com/stories/201108031278.html.

[39] Delia Robertson, *Activists Condemn South Africa Loan to Swaziland*, VOICE OF AMERICA (Aug. 4, 2011), http://www.voanews.com/english/news/africa/southern/Swaziland-Activists-Criticize-South-African-Bailout-126771148.html.

[40] African Renaissance and International Cooperation Fund Act § 6, http://www.info.gov.za/view/DownloadFileAction?id=68220.

[41] Public Finance Management Act No. 1 of 1999, §§ 46–57, *as amended through* 2009, 405 REPUBLIC OF SOUTH AFRICA GOVERNMENT GAZETTE No. 19814, http://www.treasury.gov.za/legislation/PFMA/act.pdf (official source).

[42] *Id*; CONSTITUTION OF THE REPUBLIC OF SOUTH AFRICA [S. AFR. CONST.] §§ 181, 188, http://www.info.gov.za/documents/constitution/1996/96cons9.htm (last visited Aug. 17, 2011).

[43] BRAUDE ET AL., *supra* note 1, at 5.

providing assistance through international organizations in which it was denied membership.[44] With the democratization of South Africa in the 1990s it no longer had the need to continue these policies.

Certain policy considerations appear evident in South Africa's current assistance programs. For instance, a look at the preamble to the African Renaissance and International Cooperation Fund Act reveals geography and issue-based policy considerations; the Act places emphasis on cooperation with African countries including through promotion of democracy and conflict resolution, as well as economic development and integration.[45] South Africa's assistance disbursement patterns show a preference towards neighboring countries, particularly member states of the South African Development Community (SADC).[46] Disbursement patterns also show that South Africa's aid policy favors education and peacekeeping assistance.[47]

B. Regulation of Private Contributions

Income tax law incentivizes charitable donations by allowing deductions. A person who makes a "bona fide" donation to any approved public benefit organization[48] during the year of assessment is eligible for up to a 10% deduction from his/her taxable income.[49]

III. Foreign Aid Appropriations Process

The resources allocated to the ARF have more than one source. The primary source of funding is parliamentary appropriations.[50] For instance, in 2009/10, ZAR631.4 (about US$87.4

---

[44] University of the Witwatersrand, *supra* note 19.

[45] African Renaissance and International Co-operation Fund Act, Preamble.

[46] BRAUDE ET AL., *supra* note 1, at 3.

[47] *Id.* at 15.

[48] The Income Tax Act 58 of 1962 § 30, 15 & 16 STATUTES OF THE REPUBLIC OF SOUTH AFRICA (last updated 2007), http://www.sars.gov.za/lnb/mylnb.asp?/jilc/kilc/alrg/ulrg/vlrg/72k0a#4ae. A Public Benefit Organization is defined as

> any organization
>
> (*a*) which is— (i) a non-profit company as defined in §1 of the Companies Act, 2008 (Act No. 71 of 2008), or a trust or an association of persons that has been incorporated, formed or established in the Republic; or (ii) any branch within the Republic of any company, association or trust incorporated, formed or established in any country other than the Republic that is exempt from tax on income in that other country;
>
> (*b*) of which the sole or principal object is carrying on one or more public benefit activities, where—(i) all such activities are carried on in a non-profit manner and with an altruistic or philanthropic intent; (ii) no such activity is intended to directly or indirectly promote the economic self-interest of any fiduciary or employee of the organization, otherwise than by way of reasonable remuneration payable to that fiduciary or employee; and
>
> (*c*) where each such activity carried on by that organization is for the benefit of, or is widely accessible to, the general public at large, including any sector thereof (other than small and exclusive groups). (*Id.*)

[49] *Id.* § 18A, http://www.sars.gov.za/lnb/mylnb.asp?/jilc/kilc/alrg/ulrg/vlrg/u1k0a.

million) was appropriated from Parliament, while only ZAR34 million (about US$4.7 million) came from other sources.[51]

The national appropriations process requires the passage of an appropriations law ("money bill") by Parliament. Before the start of every financial year, the Minister of Finance is required to submit an annual budget to the National Assembly.[52] Once the annual budget proposal is introduced before the National Assembly, each Department submits to Parliament "measureable objectives for each main division within the Department's vote."[53] Enacting an appropriations bill into law requires the adoption of the bill by both houses of Parliament, the National Assembly and the National Council of Provinces, and presidential assent.[54]

Other sources of funding for the ARF include

- money that was part of the Economic Cooperation and Promotion Loan Fund that had not been spent at the time the ARF was established in 2001,[55]

- any amount received as payment for loans made from the ARF,

- interest on loans or investments made from the ARF, and

- any other source.[56]

Private donations fall under the "any other source" category of sources of funds that replenish the ARF's coffers.

V. Other Types of 'Aid'

No information on other types of aid, such as aid through religious ministries or remittances, was located.

Prepared by Hanibal Goitom
Foreign Law Specialist
September 2011

---

[50] African Renaissance and International Cooperation Fund Act § 2, http://www.info.gov.za/ view/DownloadFileAction?id=68220.

[51] African Renaissance and International Co-operation Annual Report 2009–2010, *supra* note 24, at 5.

[52] Public Finance Management Act § 26.

[53] *Id.* Votes are the main segments into which the appropriations act is divided. *Id.* § 1.

[54] S. AFR. CONST. § 77, http://www.info.gov.za/ documents/constitution/1996/96cons9.htm (last visited Aug. 17, 2011).

[55] African Renaissance and International Cooperation Fund Act § 2, http://www.info.gov.za/ view/DownloadFileAction?id=68220.

[56] *Id.*

LAW LIBRARY OF CONGRESS

SOUTH KOREA

REGULATION OF FOREIGN AID

Executive Summary

South Korea became the twenty-fourth member of the Development Assistance Committee (DAC) of the Organisation for Economic Co-operation and Development (OECD) in 2010. It is the first former aid recipient to join OECD/DAC, and it is making efforts to increase its official development assistance (ODA) amount and untie its ODA to catch up with other DAC members.

South Korea endeavors to share its development experience with other developing countries. The country has concentrated its international aid efforts on human resources development through technical cooperation and transfer of economic development experience. The geographic area of focus of South Korean ODA has been Asia, but South Korea is increasing its bilateral aid to Africa.

South Korea enacted the Framework Act on International Development Cooperation in 2010 for the effective and systematic performance of ODA. The basic principle of South Korea's ODA is "contribution to poverty eradication and sustainable development in developing countries aiming at peace and prosperity of the world as well as humanitarian causes."[1] Under the Act, the Committee for International Development Cooperation (CIDC) was established to make a comprehensive national ODA plan. ODA has primarily been managed by two agencies and coordination was needed. The Ministry of Foreign Affairs and Trade (MOFAT) controls grants and technical cooperation and the Ministry of Strategy and Finance (MOSF) is responsible for loans to developing countries.

I. Introduction

A. Official Development Assistance Figures

In 2009, South Korea reported to the Development Assistance Committee (DAC) of the Organisation for Economic Co-operation and Development (OECD) net Official Development Assistance (ODA) of US$850.7 million, which comprised US$615.81 million in bilateral ODA

---

[1] *See infra* note 20 and related text.

and US$234.94 million in multilateral ODA.[2] Preliminary data suggest that Korea's ODA amounted to US$1,202.51 million in 2010.[3] South Korea's net ODA was 0.1% of its Gross National Income (GNI).[4] Although Korea's ODA volume is still modest, the Korean government plans to increase the nation's ODA/GNI ratio to 0.15% by 2012 and to 0.25% by 2015.[5]

In addition to aid to other countries, South Korea provides aid to the northern part of the Korean peninsula. Under the South Korean Constitution, that area is a part of South Korea although the government of North Korea, the Democratic People's Republic of Korea, controls it.[6] South Korea estimated this assistance at US$558 million in 2007, its highest year, but since assistance to North Korea is not formally reported to the DAC, it is not officially verified or recorded as ODA. South Korea's aid to North Korea declined dramatically since the administration changed in early 2008.[7] For example, food aid from South to North Korea was 430,550 tons in 2007, but 8,605 tons in 2008 and 7,568 tons in 2010.[8]

B. Private Contribution Figures

It has not been possible to locate private contribution figures.

C. Snapshot of Foreign Aid Activity

South Korea became the first former aid recipient to join the OECD/DAC in January 2010.[9] It is very proud of this successful development history and views it as a model for poverty reduction. "Understanding that sharing its successful development experience with

---

[2] *ODA by Donor*, OECD.STATEXTRACTS, http://stats.oecd.org/Index.aspx?DatasetCode=ODA_DONOR (select Korea in "Donor" field, then select Net Disbursements in "Flow type" field) (last visited Nov. 10, 2011).

[3] *Id.*

[4] GNI is "the Gross Domestic Product (GDP) less net taxes on production and imports, less compensation of employees and property income payable to the rest of the world plus the corresponding items receivable from the rest of the world." *Glossary of Statistical Terms: Gross National Income (GNI)*, OECD, http://stats.oecd.org/glossary/detail.asp?ID=1176 (last updated Mar. 5, 2003).

[5] *What is the Role of Korea in Development Cooperation?*, ECONOMIC DEVELOPMENT COOPERATION FUND (EDCF) (Sept. 24, 2010), http://www.edcfkorea.go.kr/edcfeng/bbs/faq/view.jsp?no=9848&bbs_code_id=1317863854370&bbs_code_tp=BBS_8&code_tp=F01_22&code_tp_up=F01.

[6] Article 3 of the Constitution states, "[t]he territory of the Republic of Korea shall consist of the Korean peninsula and its adjacent islands." CONSTITUTION OF THE REPUBLIC OF KOREA, Oct. 29, 1987, English translation available on the National Assembly's website, *at* http://korea.assembly.go.kr/res/low_01_read.jsp?board id=1000000035 (last visited Nov. 10, 2011).

[7] Cho Jong Ik, *NK Economy Stays in the Mire*, DAILYNK (July 7, 2011), http://www.dailynk.com/english/read.php?cataId=nk00100&num=7923.

[8] Numbers are available through the World Food Program's database at http://www.wfp.org/fais/reports/quantities-delivered-report (select "Donor," "Recipient," and "year" in Y1, Y2, and X dimension boxes of the top section, then, select "Republic of Korea," "Democratic People's Republic of Korea," and "select all" in Donor, Recipient and Year in the second top section) (last visited Nov. 10, 2011).

[9] *S. Korea Becomes First Former Aid Recipient to Join OECD Development Assistance Committee*, HANKYOREH (Nov. 26, 2009), http://english.hani.co.kr/arti/english_edition/e_international/389918.html.

developing countries is the most effective means of assistance, to date Korea has concentrated its international aid efforts on human resources development through technical cooperation and transfer of economic development experience."[10] By "capacity building of partner countries," Korea can "help them achieve self-reliance."[11] This policy was also chosen because it is practical for South Korea in the context of its limited ODA budget. South Korea also focuses on economic infrastructure assistance. In this area, South Korea has assisted partner countries in reducing the "digital divide" by aiding development of their information technology industry.[12]

The geographic area of focus of South Korean ODA is Asia. "In 2008, Korea spent 56 percent of its gross bilateral aid . . . in Asia, and nearly 70 percent of this funding was focused on East Asia. . . . But Korea has recently increased its ODA to Africa, doubling its support to the region."[13] In particular, the Korean International Cooperation Agency (KOICA) greatly expanded its grants to Africa because most of the least developed countries are located there.[14] South Korea also assists Iraq, Afghanistan, and the Palestinian Territories under the theme of "Assistance for the Reconstruction of Fragile States and Peace-Building."[15]

The South Korean government joined an international drug purchasing entity, UNITAID. UNITAID chose a tax on airline tickets as the most appropriate means of providing sustainable funding.[16] The South Korean government introduced an "air-ticket solidarity levy" in 2007.[17] International flight passengers departing from South Korea must pay KRW1,000 (about US$0.9).[18] A large proportion of the collected levy contributed to UNITAID supports the treatment of HIV/AIDS, tuberculosis, and malaria in developing countries. The remainder goes toward disease eradication projects in Africa that are run by South Korean nongovernmental organizations or African governments.[19]

---

[10] Kang-ho Park, Korea's Role in Global Development, Brookings Northeast Asia Commentary, No. 36 (Feb. 2010), http://www.brookings.edu/opinions/2010/0209_korea_global_development.aspx.

[11] *Policy & Directions*, EDCF, http://www.edcfkorea.go.kr/edcfeng/about/overview/policy.jsp (last visited Jan. 24, 2012).

[12] *Id.*

[13] Park, *supra* note 10.

[14] Ministry of Foreign Affairs and Trade (MOFAT), 2011 Diplomatic White Paper, pt. 5, at 237, http://www.mofat.go.kr/english/political/_whitepaper/index.jsp (click "White Paper," then "2011 Diplomatic White Paper (Part 4-7)," then "Part 5") (last visited Nov. 9, 2011).

[15] *Id.* at 238.

[16] *How UNITAID Came About*, UNITAID, http://www.unitaid.eu/en/component/content/article/159.html (last visited Nov. 10, 2011).

[17] *Air-ticket Solidarity Levy*, ODA Korea, http://www.odakorea.go.kr/eng/operations/innovative.php (last visited Nov. 10, 2011).

[18] Korea International Cooperation Agency Act, Act No. 4313, Jan. 14, 1991, *last amended by* Act No. 10095, Mar. 17, 2010, art. 18-2, para. 1. An English translation is available through the website of the Korea Legislative Research Institute (KLRI), *at* http://elaw.klri.re.kr/eng/main.do (last visited Nov. 14, 2011). A membership registration at no cost is required to obtain the translation (click "sign up" in upper left-hand corner). KLRI is a government-funded research institute.

[19] *Air-ticket Solidarity Levy*, *supra* note 17.

II. Legal Framework

A. Regulation of ODAs

1. Overview

The basic principle of South Korea's ODA is "contribution to poverty eradication and sustainable development in developing countries aiming at peace and prosperity of the world as well as humanitarian causes."[20]   South Korea enacted the Framework Act on International Development Cooperation in 2010 for the effective and systematic performance of ODA.[21]

There are two main agencies involved in managing ODA: the Ministry of Foreign Affairs and Trade (MOFAT) controls grants and technical cooperation and the Ministry of Strategy and Finance (MOSF) is responsible for loans to developing countries.[22]   MOFAT and MOSF, respectively, must develop Five-Year Basic Plans and submit them to the Committee for International Development Cooperation (CIDC), which is under the Prime Minister's jurisdiction.[23]   Based on these Basic Plans, the CIDC makes a comprehensive plan for Korea's international development assistance.[24]

In addition, various national government agencies, local governments, and public organizations implement ODA. They submit annual international development assistance plans to MOFAT and MOSF.[25]   MOFAT and MOSF examine whether their plans fall under the Basic Plans and coordinate them.[26]   CIDC may discuss related issues with MOFAT, MOSF, and select countries on which South Korean ODA is focused.[27]   In October 2010, CIDC adopted the "Strategic Plan for International Development Cooperation," which outlined key strategies and plans to strengthen Korea's international cooperation capacity.[28]

---

[20] MOFAT, 2010 Diplomatic White Paper, pt. 5, at 190, http://www.mofat.go.kr/english/political/ whitepaper/index.jsp (click "White Paper," then "2010 Diplomatic White Paper (Part 4-7)," then "Part 5") (last visited Nov. 7, 2011).

[21] Framework Act on International Development Cooperation, Act No. 9938, Jan. 25, 2010, art. 1. An English translation of this act is not available on the KLRI website.

[22] *Id.* art. 9, para. 1.

[23] *Id.* art. 8, para. 1.

[24] *Id.* art. 8, para. 2.

[25] *Id.* art. 11, para. 1.

[26] *Id.* art. 11, paras. 2, 3.

[27] *Id.* art. 12.

[28] *ODA/Development Cooperation*, MINISTRY OF FOREIGN AFFAIRS AND TRADE (MOFAT), http://www.mofat.go.kr/ENG/policy/oda/index.jsp?menu=m_20_110 (last visited Nov. 2, 2011) (click on "Policy Issues").

2. Implementing Agencies

As stated in the previous section, South Korea has a dual system of ODA. For bilateral aid, KOICA, under the guidance of MOFAT, controls grants and technical cooperation for South Korea's ODA, while the Economic Development Cooperation Fund (EDCF) of Korea's Export-Import Bank, under the guidance of MOSF, is responsible for loans.[29] Multilateral aid is also split, with MOFAT responsible for the UN agencies and MOSF responsible for the international development banks.[30] In addition, approximately thirty institutions, including national government agencies and municipal governments, participate in the execution of ODA programs.[31] In its 2008 Special Review of Korea, the DAC recommended that the South Korean government establish "a single entity with sole authority over development cooperation objectives, policy, and strategy."[32] Although CIDC was established as a coordinating body in 2008,[33] "intra-governmental coordination is a challenge, and the Korean development community remains fragmented."[34]

3. Restrictions

Historically, South Korea's ODA has been heavily tied. In 2007, only a quarter of South Korean aid was untied. South Korea established a road map to reduce its tied aid. The country plans to untie 75% of its ODA by 2015.[35]

The DAC High Level Meeting adopted a recommendation on untying aid to the least developed countries in April 2001.[36] South Korea must fully comply with the DAC recommendation on untying aid within a reasonable time frame after it joins the DAC.[37]

4. Discretionary Aid

Information on discretionary aid was not available.

---

[29] Ahn Eungho, Korea's Development Cooperation Experience, Korea EXIM-Bank (paper presented at the Jeju Peace Institute-Friedrich Nauman Foundation for Liberty Joint Workshop, Oct. 18-20, 2010), *available at* http://www.jpi.or.kr/board/run/download.php?board_id=jpiworld&page=4&row_per_page=15&page_per_block=10&pds_uid=3899.

[30] OECD/DAC, DEVELOPMENT COOPERATION, DEVELOPMENT CO-OPERATION OF THE REPUBLIC OF KOREA: DAC SPECIAL REVIEW 10 (Aug. 8, 2008), http://www.oecd.org/dataoecd/53/50/42347329.pdf.

[31] 2010 Diplomatic White Paper, *supra* note 20, at 191; Jin-myong Kim, *ODA wa tojōkoku hōmon ji no temiyage?* [*Is ODA Like a Souvenir When an Official Visits a Developing Country?*], CHOSUNILBO, July 14, 2011 (in Japanese; on file with author).

[32] DAC SPECIAL REVIEW, *supra* note 30.

[33] 2010 Diplomatic White Paper, *supra* note 20, at 191.

[34] Park, *supra* note 10; Kim, *supra* note 31.

[35] Park, *supra* note 10.

[36] Untying Aid to the Least Developed Countries, OECD Policy Brief, at 1 (July 2001), http://www.oecd.org/dataoecd/16/24/2002959.pdf.

[37] DAC SPECIAL REVIEW, *supra* note 30, at 24.

5. Oversight

CIDC developed guidelines in December 2009 for an integrated ODA evaluation system, to evaluate ODA policies and results.[38] The evaluations examine appropriateness, efficiency, effectiveness, influence, and sustainability. Evaluations may be performed by the implementing agency or outside experts, or joint evaluations may be conducted with aid-receiving countries or other donor agencies. In the process of evaluating, CIDC considers the opinions of aid-receiving countries and MOFAT overseas offices.[39] CIDC submits ODA evaluation results to the National Assembly annually.[40]

6. Policy Considerations

Information on policy considerations was not available.

B. Regulation of Private Contributions

Information on the regulation of private contributions was not available.

III. Foreign Aid Appropriations Process

"MOSF establishes the annual budget and national fiscal management plan to support public expenditure for national development activities."[41] The general budget process is discussed below.

The Constitution states that the Executive formulates the budget bill for each fiscal year and submits it to the National Assembly within ninety days before the beginning of a fiscal year. The National Assembly must decide on it within thirty days before the beginning of the fiscal year.[42] Within the executive branch, the Ministry of Planning and Budget (MPB) prepares the budget proposal.[43]

> At the beginning of a new budget cycle, the guidelines for the budget requests and the principle of the budget formulation are decided by MPB. Certain national priorities decided by the President are reflected in the guidelines for budget requests. The head of each administrative agency prepares a budget request in accordance with the guidelines

---

[38] Framework Act on International Development Cooperation, Act No. 9938, Jan. 25, 2010, art. 13, para. 1. 2011 Diplomatic White Paper, *supra* note 14, pt. 5, at 234.

[39] Framework Act on International Development Cooperation Enforcement Order, Presidential Decree No. 22296, July 21, 2010, *last amended by* Presidential Decree No. 23229, Oct. 17, 2011, art. 11.

[40] Framework Act on International Development Cooperation, art. 13, para. 2.

[41] DAC SPECIAL REVIEW, *supra* note 30, at 19.

[42] Constitution of the Republic of Korea, Oct. 29, 1987, art. 54, para. 2.

[43] Joonook Choi, International Cooperation Behind National Borders: Country Case Study on the Republic of Korea 6 (2005) (UNDP/ODS Background Paper), http://www.undp.org/thenewpublicfinance/casestudies/ccs_korea.pdf.

of the Budget Office. Each agency makes its budget appropriation request by categorizing the objectives and the logistical features of each project.[44]

The Budget Office in the MPB reviews the budget proposal of each ministry and agency, negotiates changes of proposals, and prepares a comprehensive government budget proposal. The proposal is sent to the State Council presided over by the President. After the State Council confirms the budget proposal, the proposal is sent to the National Assembly.[45] The National Assembly has authority to change the proposal, but it has not played a significant role in budget-making in the past.[46]

The main funding sources for the EDCF have been contributions from the government's general budget account and borrowings from the government's special budget account.[47] In addition, the Foreign Economic Cooperation Fund Act allows the EDCF to obtain funds from other financial sources, such as contributions from governmental funds, deposits from the National Bond Management Fund, and profit earned from the operation of the EDCF.[48]

As of the end of 2009, the accumulated total of the EDCF had reached KRW2,470 billion. Total contributions from the government amounted to KRW1,380 billion, accounting for about 55.9% of the total fund. The net borrowings from the government reached KRW96.0 billion, about 4% of the total fund, while total reserves were KRW994.0 billion (about 40.2%).[49]

IV. Other Types of 'Aid'

A. Humanitarian Assistance

South Korea "supports and participates in the collective efforts of the international society in promoting humanity and protecting human rights of those in crises caused by hunger, diseases and natural and man-made disasters."[50] South Korea provided US$24.6 million in humanitarian assistance in 2006, which accounted for 3.6% of the country's total bilateral ODA.[51] South Korea plans to increase the budget for overseas emergency relief to 6% of the overall ODA budget by 2015.[52]

---

[44] *Id.*

[45] *Id.*

[46] *Id.*

[47] *Funding Resources*, EDCF, http://www.edcfkorea.go.kr/edcfeng/data/fund.jsp (last visited Jan. 24, 2012).

[48] Foreign Economic Cooperation Fund Act, Act No. 3863, Dec. 26, 1986, *last amended by* Act No. 8852, Feb. 29, 2008, art. 4, English translation available through the website of the KLRI, *at* http://elaw.klri.re.kr/eng/main.do.

[49] EDCF, *supra* note 47.

[50] *Humanitarian Assistance*, ODA KOREA, http://www.odakorea.go.kr/eng/operations/humanitarian.php (last visited Nov. 9, 2011).

[51] *Id.*

[52] 2011 Diplomatic White Paper, *supra* note 14, at 243.

Regarding emergency aid, the Overseas Emergency Relief Act was enacted in 2007 to provide a systematic response in the event of large-scale overseas disasters.[53] MOFAT is a coordination agency for governmental emergency relief activities.[54] It has a budget for a natural disaster emergency relief fund for foreign countries. The amount has been recently criticized as too small. For developing countries, a portion of the ODA budget can be used. During 2011, the emergency relief budget for developing countries was US$16.8 million, which is 1.1% of the ODA budget. For developed countries, however, it is only US$200,000.[55]

B. Foreign Remittances

The Bank of Korea stated that foreign remittances in 2010 amounted to nearly US$10 billion: US$1.8 billion from short-stay (less than one year) foreign workers and US$8.89 billion combined from long-stay foreign workers and South Koreans who sent money to overseas South Koreans. The Bank of Korea estimated that most of the US$8.89 billion was from foreigners, not from South Koreans.[56]

Prepared by Sayuri Umeda
Senior Foreign Law Specialist
November 2011

---

[53] *Overseas Emergency Relief,* ODA KOREA, http://www.odakorea.go.kr/eng/operations/emergency.php (last visited Nov. 9, 2011).

[54] Overseas Emergency Relief Act, Act No. 8317, Mar. 29, 2007, arts. 7–14.

[55] Kuni no hinkaku ni miau kaigai kyuen yosan o wariate yo [Allocate Emergency Foreign Aid Budget that Matches National Power and Pride], CHOSUNILBO (Mar. 16, 2011), (in Japanese, on file with author).

[56] Yonhap news, *Gaikokujin rodosha no kaigai sokin sakunen 100 oku doru ni semaru* [Foreign Remittance by Foreign Workers Amounted to Almost 10 billion Dollar], WOW KOREA (Jan. 28, 2011), http://www.wowkorea.jp/news/Korea/2011/0128/10079658.html (in Japanese).

LAW LIBRARY OF CONGRESS

SWEDEN

REGULATION OF FOREIGN AID

Executive Summary

Sweden is one of the few countries in the world that meets the UN target of giving more than 0.7% of GNI in foreign aid. In fact, Sweden gives some 0.98% of its GNI as foreign aid annually. While the government provides for most of the aid, new legislative efforts are underway to promote private donations through tax deductions in an effort to keep pace with the rest of the Scandinavian nations. Swedish development cooperation (aid) primarily targets fewer areas, with the Swedish government wanting to be a bigger player in fewer recipient states. The three largest recipient nations of Swedish aid are Tanzania, Afghanistan, and Mozambique. In addition to its focus on the poorest countries of the world, Sweden also maintains a strong presence and commitment to the democratization process in Eastern Europe and the Baltic Area.

I. Introduction

A. Official Development Assistance Figures

According to official Organisation for Economic Co-operation and Development (OECD) figures, Sweden's preliminary Net Development Assistance for 2010 is US $4,527 million compared to the 2008 high of US $4,732 million.[1] Stated as a percentage, the estimated aid for 2010 is 0.98% of total gross national income (GNI).[2] When the Swedish budget for 2011 was set, the goal was 1%.[3] The administrative costs associated with refugees are deducted from this initial figure.[4] The budget for development cooperation also includes Swedish Krona (SEK) 20.3 million (approximately US$3.03 million) in administrative costs associated with Sweden's commitments in the Baltic Area "[which] is not classified as development cooperation."[5]

---

[1] Development Aid: Net Development Assistance (ODA), DOI 10.1787/20743866-table 1 (measured in US dollars), OECDiLIBRARY (Apr. 13, 2011), *available at* http://www.oecd-ilibrary.org/development/development-aid-net-official-development-assistance-oda_20743866-table1.

[2] *Id.*

[3] *See* REGERINGSKANSLIET (Swedish government website), http://www.sweden.gov.se/sb/d/3102/a/114382 (last visited Sept. 6, 2011).

[4] *Frågor och svar om bistånd* [Questions and Answers on Development Assistance], REGERINGSKANSLIET (Mar. 18, 2008; updated Sept. 15, 2011), http://www.sweden.gov.se/sb/d/4759.

[5] *Id.*

Swedish aid is mainly distributed through multilateral, governmental, and public agencies.[6] Less than 3% of Swedish aid is distributed through private channels.[7]

The distribution of official development assistance (ODA) between different sectors in 2010 was divided as follows: agriculture and forestry, 2%; peace and security, 2%; research, 3%; budget support to fight poverty, 3%; education, 3%; market development, 3%; sustainable development, 4%; environment, 5%; health, 7%; conflict, democracy, human rights, and equality, 9%; humanitarian aid, 15%; and miscellaneous, 42%.[8]

In 2010, Swedish bilateral aid was distributed among twenty countries and totaled SEK 15,413 million (approx. US$2,289 million), including non-ODA countries.[9] The bilateral aid is about 50% of the total aid, which is SEK 31,430 million (approx. US$4,778 million).[10] OECD figures for Swedish total development cooperation were US$3,954.96 million in 2006, US$4,338.94 million in 2007, US$4,734.56 million in 2008, US$4,552.37 million in 2009, and US$4,526.62 million in 2010.[11]

On Sweden's current and past commitments to development cooperation, the OECD Peer Review states: "Sweden is providing crucial leadership within the international donor community. It remains a leading advocate of increased aid flows to developing countries, and has led by example with aid allocations exceeding the UN target of 0.7% of GNI every year since 1975 and reaching 0.98% in 2008."[12]

B. Private Contribution Figures

In 2009, according to official OECD figures, the Swedish Net Private Aid was US$2,473 million.[13] Swedish private contributions were especially high following the tsunami catastrophe of 2004.[14] The Swedish Red Cross has published donation figures totaling SEK 299 million

---

[6] Multilateral organizations-53%, public sector-24%, international organizations-8%, Swedish organizations-8%, organizations in the recipient country-3%, private and miscellaneous-3%, and unspecified-1%. *Vem genomför biståndet?* [Who Implements Assistance?], OPEN AID (government website), http://www.openaid.se/organizations (last visited .

[7] *Id.*

[8] *Vad används biståndet till?* [What Is the Assistance Used For?], OPEN AID, http://www.openaid.se/sectors/ (last visited Sept. 6, 2011).

[9] Sveriges utvecklingssamarbete i siffror [Sweden's Development Cooperation in Numbers]: Multilateralt utvecklingssamarbete [Multilateral Development Cooperation], SIDA (June 1, 2011), http://sidapublications.citat. se/interface/stream/mabstream.asp?filetype=1&orderlistmainid=3159&printfileid=3159&filex=4352431991895.

[10] *Id.*

[11] *ODA by Donor* (Sweden), OECD.STATEXTRACTS, http://stats.oecd.org/Index.aspx?DatasetCode= ODA_DONOR (also provides detailed statistics on bilateral and multilateral aid) (data extracted on Sept. 20, 2011).

[12] *Sweden (2009) DAC Peer Review – Main Findings and Recommendations*, OECD, http://www.oecd.org/document/1/0,3343,en_2649_34603_43278401_1_1_1_1,00.html (last visited Sept. 7, 2011).

[13] *Table 5. Total Net Private Flows by DAC Country*, OECD, http://www.oecd.org/dataoecd/31/38/ 47452671.xls (last visited Sept. 20, 2011).

[14] *See* RÖDA KORSET, http://www.rodakorset.se (last visited Sept. 14, 2011).

(approximately US$45 million) for 2010.[15]   Together with contributions from the European Union (EU) and Swedish government, the Swedish Red Cross budget totaled SEK 851 million (approximately US$87 million), of which approximately half (SEK 433 million) is used for their international efforts.[16]

C. Snapshot of Foreign Aid Activity

General

Sweden sends aid to twenty countries, primarily focusing on Tanzania, Afghanistan, and Mozambique, which each received more than SEK 600 million (approx. US$90 million) in aid during 2010.[17]   Sweden has recently refocused its bilateral resources from certain areas (such as Botswana, Namibia, South Africa, India, Indonesia, China, and Vietnam) to others (including Afghanistan, Somalia, Democratic Republic of Congo, Liberia, Sierra Leone, West Bank–Gaza, Colombia, and Guatemala).[18]

Current projects include a Pungwe River project led by the Swedish International Development Cooperation Agency (SIDA).[19]   Anticipated projects include a water project ("Water Aid Innovation Challenge") in ODA countries.[20]   Through the EU, Sweden also contributes to the payment of Palestinian teachers and doctors.[21]   In addition, Sweden participates in multilateral efforts with organizations such as the International Development Association, the World Bank, the Multilateral Investment Guarantee Agency, the UN Development Programme, UNICEF, UN Women, UN-HABITAT, and the Global Water Partnership Organization.[22]

---

[15] *See Svenska Röda Korset 2010* [*Swedish Red Cross (Annual Report) 2010*] RÖDA KORSET at 24, http://www.redcross.se/PageFiles/1046/Arsredovisning_2010.pdf.

[16] Id.

[17] SIDA, *supra* note 9.

[18] Ministry of Foreign Affairs, Focused Bilateral Development Cooperation (Aug. 27, 2007) at 8, http://www.regeringen.se/content/1/c6/08/66/21/496f32e6.pdf. For additional information regarding Sweden's policy shift, *see infra*, section II.A.6.

[19] *Pungwefloden–en gemensam vattenresurs för miljontals människor* [Pungwe River–A Common Water Resource for Millions of People], SIDA (Aug. 17, 2011; updated Sept. 20, 2011), http://www.sida.se/Svenska/Lander--regioner/Afrika/Mocambique/Program-och-projekt1/Pungwefloden-en-gemensam-vattenresurs/.

[20] Press Release, Ministry of Foreign Affairs, *Regeringens satsningar inom biståndspolitiken* [Government Initiatives in Development Policies] (Sept. 20, 2011), *available at* http://www.regeringen.se/sb/a/175917.

[21] *Svenska biståndspengar går till läkare och lärare i Palestina* [Swedish Aid Money Goes to the Doctors and Teachers in Palestine], SIDA (Sept. 1, 2011; updated Sept. 2, 2011), http://www.sida.se/Svenska/Nyhetsarkiv/2011/September-2011/Svenska-bistandspengar-till-Palestina/.

[22] Ministry of Foreign Affairs, Regleringsbrev för budgetåret 2011 avseende Styrelsen för internationellt utvecklingssamarbete [Appropriation for the Year 2011 Regarding the Board for International Development Cooperation] (July 28, 2011) (III:2) UF2011/45027/UD/USTYR at 12–15, *available at* http://www.esv.se/Verktyg--stod/Statsliggaren/Regleringsbrev/?RBID=13684.

Aid is being used as a tool to promote the Swedish policy of gender equality and to decrease the level of corruption in developing countries. Allocation of foreign aid is divided in types of aid; thus the budget allocates more aid to certain forms than others.[23] Favored projects include water safety, gender equality, HIV prevention and treatment, and democratization efforts, among others.

Trade and Aid

Sweden has changed its policies to focus more on increasing trade and less on aid. Still, trade with African countries constitutes only 3% of total Swedish exports and even less in total imports in 2010.[24] Examples of current free trade efforts include the Trade Mark East Africa project, to which Sweden has pledged SEK 30 million to be distributed over a three-year period.[25]

The Swedish development cooperation effort has been ranked the best in the world by the US-based Center for Global Development as recently as 2010.[26]

II. Legal Framework

A. Regulation of ODAs

1. Overview

ODA is accounted for and regulated by the Swedish annual budget (for 2011 in Prop. 2010/11:1 Utgiftsområde 7)[27] and is then distributed by the implementing agencies through a "letter of appropriation" from the government, which specifies the allocation of the budget and the division of resources among different areas and sections of ODA. Most resources are distributed through multilateral organizations or the public sector.[28] In 2010, only 3% of all Swedish ODA was distributed through the private sector.[29]

---

[23] See id.

[24] *See* Exportrådet [Swedish Trade Council], *Svensk Export 2010* [Swedish Export 2010], http://www.swedishtrade.se/PageFiles/134234/Exportstatistik_2010_110307.pdf (last visited Sept. 20, 2011).

[25] *See Konkurrenskraftig handel i Östafrika* [*Competitive Trade in Eastern Africa*], SIDA (Jan. 26, 2011), http://www.sida.se/Svenska/Kontakta-oss/For-medier/Aktuella-Beslut/Aktuella-beslut-2010/Aktuella-beslut-december/Konkurrenskraftig-handel-i-Ostafrika/.

[26] *See Country Report Sweden*, CENTER FOR GLOBAL DEVELOPMENT, http://www.cgdev.org/section/ initiatives/_active/cdi/_country/sweden (last visited Sept. 7, 2011). For a summary, visit the Swedish news site, TheLocal.se, which provides Swedish news in English at http://www.thelocal.se/16158/20081205/ (last visited Sept. 7, 2011).

[27] Proposition [Prop.] 2010/11:1 Budgetpropositionen för 2011 Utgiftsområde 7 Bilaga 1 [government bill], *available at* http://www.regeringen.se/content/1/c6/15/33/07/53ddf3aa.pdf.

[28] *Vem genomför biståndet?*[Who Implements the Aid], OPEN AID, http://www.openaid.se/organizations (last visited Sept. 6, 2011).

[29] *Id.*

2. Implementing Agencies

Ministry of Foreign Affairs

The Swedish Ministry of Foreign Affairs allocates the majority of the Swedish ODA budget through implementation agencies (mainly SIDA) or multilateral organizations.[30]

SIDA – The Swedish International Development Cooperation Agency

The main Swedish implementing agency for foreign aid and development is SIDA, the Swedish International Development Cooperation Agency,[31] which is responsible for approximately 50% of the Swedish ODA budget.[32] SIDA's mandate is regulated in *Myndighetsförordningen* (Agency Regulation)[33] and *Regeringens förordning med instruktion för Styrelsen för internationellt utvecklingssamarbete* (Government Regulation with Instruction for the Swedish International Development Cooperation Agency),[34] as well as yearly appropriation letters and "individual governmental decisions."

In the Letter of Appropriation for 2011, the Swedish government especially focuses on SIDA's finances and how SIDA needs to balance its budget and revise its risks.[35] The Swedish government also specifies "three thematic areas" on which SIDA should focus: "democracy and human rights, environment and climate as well as the promotion of equality and human rights as part of development."[36] The Government also calls for more substantial oversight of these specific areas.[37]

The *Swedish Förordning (2010:1080) med instruktion för Styrelsen för internationellt utvecklingssamarbete (Sida)* (Swedish authority regulation with instruction for SIDA)[38] includes

---

[30] *See* BUDGETLAG (Svensk Författningssamling [SFS] 2011:203).

[31] SIDA, http://www.sida.se/English/About-us/Organization/ (last visited Sept. 6, 2011).

[32] *Sida förfogar över hälften av Sveriges biståndsbudget* [SIDA Has More Than Half of Sweden's Aid Budget], SIDA (June 24, 2009; updated Jan. 26, 2011), http://www.sida.se/Svenska/Om-oss/Budget/.

[33] MYNDIGHETSFÖRORDNING (Svensk författningssamling [SFS] 2007:515), *available at* http://www.riksdagen.se/webbnav/index.aspx?nid=3911&bet=2007:515.

[34] REGERINGENS FÖRORDNING MED INSTRUKTION FÖR STYRELSEN FÖR INTERNATIONELLT UTVECKLINGSSAMARBETE (Svensk Författningssamling [SFS] 2010:1080), http://www.riksdagen.se/webbnav/index.aspx?nid=3911&bet=2010:1080.

[35] Ministry of Foreign Affairs, Regleringsbrev för budgetåret 2011 avseende Styrelsen för internationellt utvecklingssamarbete [Swedish Government Letter of Appropriation for 2011 regarding the Swedish International Development Cooperation Agency] (Dec. 22, 2010), *available at* http://www.sida.se/Global/About%20 Sida/Regleringsbrev/Regleringsbrev%202011.pdf (translation by author).

[36] *Id.* (translation by author).

[37] *Id.*

[38] REGERINGENS FÖRORDNING MED INSTRUKTION FÖR STYRELSEN FÖR INTERNATIONELLT UTVECKLINGSSAMARBETE [Government Regulation with Instruction for International Development Cooperation] (Svensk Författningssamling [SFS] 2010:1080*),* http://www.riksdagen.se/webbnav/?nid=3911&bet=2010:1080 (translation by author).

provisions for cooperation with other national and international agencies (5§) as well as special allocation of resources for research and development (9§). A comprehensive list of the agency's authority is found in section 4, which, among other things, provides that SIDA "may decide on and distribute aid or other type of financing in support of efforts taken [bilaterally]."[39] SIDA may also cancel procedural agreements (4§ p. 2), and "after agreement with the other party to redistribute resources between bilateral agreements" (4§ p. 3) "demand that a ministry of another country with which Sweden has a bilateral development cooperation agreement, or where Sweden contributes humanitarian aid, provide SIDA with such information which is necessary for its operations."[40] Generally SIDA has broad discretion to act in day-to-day operations as well as plan future strategies regarding development aid.[41] However, if the development cooperation "is of special importance for Swedish [diplomatic relations] with a country or [relations] with an international organization [and] is canceled, SIDA must immediately contact the Government Offices (Ministry of Foreign Affairs)."[42] In addition to its implementation functions, SIDA also has an advisory function by advising the government on how the budget should be allocated with regard to international development cooperation.[43]

Folke Bernadotte Academy

Although the main purpose of the Folke Bernadotte Academy[44] is to promote peace and security in the world,[45] the Academy is involved in development cooperation efforts, especially through the "security sector reform program" (SSR program).[46] Through this program, the Folke Bernadotte Academy mainly provides "grants for capacity development and operational efforts."[47]

Swedfund International AB

Swedfund is a state-owned corporation with the primary purpose of investing in Swedish projects abroad. However, it also strives to increase the level of development of the host

---

[39] *Id.* 4 § no. 1 (translation by author).

[40] *Id.* 4 § no. 11 (translation by author).

[41] *See id.* 4 § nos. 1–11, which includes assigning powers to another agency, conferring powers, and "cooperating with other nations, EU, international and multilateral organizations" (no. 6) (translation by author), etc.

[42] *Id.* 4 § para. 2. (translation by author).

[43] SIDA, *supra* note 9.

[44] FOLKE BERNADOTTE ACADEMY, http://www.folkebernadotteacademy.se/en/About-FBA/ (last visited Sept. 20, 2011).

[45] *Id.*

[46] *SSR-programmet* [SSR Program], FOLKE BERNADOTTE ACADEMY, http://folkebernadotteacademy. se/Kunskapsomraden/Sakerhetssektorreform/SSR-programmet/ (last visited Sept. 9, 2009) (translation by author).

[47] *See id.* (translation by author).

country.[48]   According to its own records and statements, "Swedfund does not invest in corporations that manufacture or sell weapons, tobacco or alcohol."[49]

Coordination Between Implementing Agencies

Because Sweden has several agencies that participate in activities that may overlap (e.g., peace and security, development cooperation), the government has assigned each agency one area for which they are primarily responsible for coordination and reporting. For instance, SIDA is responsible for coordinating international development cooperation.[50]   Folke Bernadotte Academy is responsible for providing the Ministry of Foreign Affairs with a coordination report each month for "security policy efforts."[51]

In addition, the Swedish government has adopted a Politics for Global Development (PGU) policy aimed at coordinating not only efforts among development cooperation agencies but across government agencies as a whole to make all government efforts, including civil and military, as efficient in fostering development as possible.[52]

3. Restrictions

General restrictions on exports (and thus also indirectly on foreign aid) are covered by law. For example, Sweden prohibits trade with weapons[53] and requires licenses for the export of nuclear technology,[54] which, depending on the use of the nuclear technology, may be banned altogether.[55] However, most restrictions on aid and development are made in the annual letter of appropriation from the government.[56] For example, SIDA's development cooperation efforts

---

[48] *See* Ägaranvisningar för Swedfund International AB (556436-2084) (Apr. 27, 2011), http://www.swedfund.se/wp-content/uploads/2011/04/Agaranvisningar-201104271.pdf.

[49] *See* Swedfund International AB website, http://www.swedfund.se/om-swedfund/ (translation by author).

[50] *See* SIDA's most recent report on joint efforts and coordinated projects, *Sveriges utvecklingssamarbete i siffror 2011*, *supra* note 9.

[51] *Samordning av svenska insatser* [Coordination of Swedish Efforts] (Jan. 13, 2010), FOLKE BERNADOTTE ACADEMY http://folkebernadotteacademy.se/Utlandsuppdrag/Vara-insatser/Samordning-av-svenska-insatser/.

[52] *Politik för Global Utveckling* [Policies for Global Development] (June 9, 2009, updated Mar. 31, 2011), SIDA, http://www.sida.se/Svenska/Bistand--utveckling/Internationellt-samarbete-/Politik-for-global-utveckling-PGU/.

[53] 4 § LAG OM KRIGSMATERIEL (Svensk författningssamling [SFS] 1192:1300), *available at* http://www.riksdagen.se/webbnav/index.aspx?nid=3911&bet=1992:1300. Note that the new 6§ para. 2 no. 5 LAG OM KRIGSMATERIEL, which will come into force on June 30, 2012, specifies that "humanitarian aid [in response to a] catastrophe" is exempt. *Id.*

[54] 7c § LAG OM KÄRNTEKNISK VERKSAMHET (Svensk författningssamling [SFS] 1984:3), *available at* http://www.riksdagen.se/webbnav/index.aspx?nid=3911&bet=1984:3.

[55] 9 § LAG OM KONTROLL AV PRODUKTER MED DUBBLA ANVÄNDNINGSOMRÅDEN OCH AV TEKNISKT BISTÅND (Svensk författningssamling [SFS] 2000:1064), *available at* http://www.riksdagen.se/webbnav/index.aspx?nid=3911&bet=2000:1064.

[56] *See* Ministry of Foreign Affairs, *Regleringsbrev för budgetåret 2011 avseende Styrelsen för internationellt utvecklingssamarbete* [Swedish Government Letter of Appropriation for 2011 regarding the Swedish

must comply with the OECD's "DAC [Development Co-operation Directorate] guidelines covering what can be classified as development cooperation."[57] Moreover, "aid may only be given to countries that DAC defines as development countries."[58] However, the government has provided an explicit exception from this requirement for the support that goes to "Eastern and Central Europe."[59] Restrictions also include the requirement that the use of the appropriation funds be "in accordance with [the applicable] Swedish policy."[60] (For further discussion on this topic, see section II.A.4 on Discretionary Aid, below.)

Criminalization of Certain Types of Aid Measures

Proposed restrictions on development aid include a "permit requirement" for any technical assistance that is given to a third country (i.e., non EU/European Economic Area country) and can be found in Swedish Proposition 2010/11:112 *Genomförande av direktiv om överföring av krigsmateriel* [Implementation of Directive on Defense Transfers], which is a step in the Swedish implementation of the EU Defense Transfers Directive.[61] These proposed changes would become effective on June 30, 2012.[62] The proposed legislation would make it a crime to send technical equipment as aid without first being certified by the Swedish government.[63]

Conditional Aid

Sweden does not use "tied aid," but it does impose conditions on the recipients of foreign aid. The distribution of development cooperation aid must comply with special strategies and policy decisions but generally is not regulated by law.[64] This means that the regulation of Swedish foreign aid is very flexible, but the flexibility of the government to adopt new policies also risks creating a framework that is neither consistent nor predictable.

International Development Cooperation Agency] (Dec. 22, 2010), *available at* http://www.sida.se/Global/About%20 Sida/Regleringsbrev/Regleringsbrev%202011.pdf.

[57] *Id.* at 8.

[58] *Id.*

[59] *Id.* at 8 (translation by author). Note, however, that in 2011 no appropriation was provided for. *Id.*

[60] *See, e.g.*, the requirement that appropriation funds for HIV/AIDS "must be used in accordance with the policy for Sweden's international HIV and AIDS work." Regleringsbrev, *infra* note 69, at 17 (translation by author).

[61] Proposition [Prop.] 2010/11:112 Genomförande av direktiv om överföring av krigsmateriel [government bill], *available at* http://www.regeringen.se/content/1/c6/16/67/70/94dc42de.pdf.

[62] *Id.*

[63] *Id.* The proposed legislation thus would expand the certification requirements from nuclear technologies to all technical assistance.

[64] For a comprehensive list of Sweden's policies and strategies on development cooperation, see SIDA's website, http://www.sida.se/Svenska/Om-oss/Sa-styrs-vi/Policyer-och-strategier/.

Aid in Violation of Swedish Policy

Sweden has been criticized for its policies surrounding the sale of JAS 39 Gripen fighter airplanes to South Africa because of suspicion of bribes and corrupt behavior, which were also connected with development aid policies.[65]

4. Discretionary Aid

The discretion given to the implementing agencies, although broad in terms of the scope and nature of activities within each sector of the budget, is rather limited between sectors or countries on redistribution of appropriated sums.[66]   The annual budget and the letter of appropriation specify the allocation of the resources to be used in different countries as well as the funding for different multilateral efforts.[67]   To increase the flexibility of its operations, the Swedish government has granted SIDA the authority to "exceed [or] alternatively [use less than] the annual strategy amount [appropriated] for a [specific] country or region with 10%" in the "humanitarian efforts and conflict resolution" part of the budget.[68]   However, no corresponding authority has been given for the EU or UN amounts (i.e., SIDA's multilateral budget).[69]   The power to contract has also been reduced by the letter of appropriation for 2011, which provides that at least 50% of the annual volume should be "unallocated 2 ... years after the strategy expires."[70]

Moreover, because there are currently investigations into the effectiveness of foreign aid distributed through international funds, SIDA "shall until further notice refrain from making decisions on *new* economic commitments to foreign funds, corporations and non-governmental or multilateral institutions that are used to channel aid."[71]

Restrictions on the implementing agencies' discretion include government-imposed ceilings for "global subject strategic development efforts" covering each international organization (such as the International Center for Transitional Justice and the International Legal Assistance Consortium (ILAC)), as specified in the letter of appropriation.[72]   Also, the

---

[65] *See* Nils Resare, *Mutor, makt och bistånd : JAS och Sydafrikaaffären; see also* Holmström, Mikael, *Saab anklagar BAE for mutbrott* [Saab Accuses BAE of Bribe Crimes], SVD (June 16, 2011), *available at* http://www.svd.se/naringsliv/saab-anklagar-bae-for-mutbrott_6249666.svd.

[66] *See* Ministry of Foreign Affairs, Regleringsbrev för budgetåret 2011 avseende Styrelsen för internationellt utvecklingssamarbete, (July 28, 2011) (III:2) UF2011/45027/UD/USTYR, *available at* http://www.esv.se/Verktyg--stod/Statsliggaren/Regleringsbrev/?RBID=13684.

[67] For a detailed overview of the spending allocated to the World Bank Group, including regional development banks, *see id.* at 12.

[68] *Id.* at 7 ("General conditions covering appropriation items ap.1, ap.2, ap.5, ap.6, ap.7, ap.9, ap.17, ap.21, ap.22, ap.23, ap.24, ap.25, ap.26, ap.26.1, ap.26.2, ap.32 and ap.33") (translation by author).

[69] *See id.* at 6–7 (appropriation posts 34-38 are not included in the +/- 10% exception).

[70] *Id.* at 7.

[71] *Id.* at 8 (translation by author) (emphasis added by author).

[72] *Id.* at 10 (translation by author).

appropriation decision covering the allocation heading "Research" specifies sub-requirements; for example, at least SEK 75 million (approx. US$11.3 million) should go toward "diseases that primarily affect poor children and at least SEK 25 million [approximately US$3.7 million] should cover research on securing future food supplies."[73]

5. Oversight

Foreign Ministry

The Foreign Ministry has its own oversight agency, UD-USTYR, which is responsible for the "direction and methods of development cooperation."[74] UD-USTYR has oversight over the complete development cooperation budget and investigates the efficiency of the aid and cases pertaining to SIDA's activities, among other things.[75]

Riksrevisionen

The main oversight agency in Sweden is the *Riksrevisionen* (Swedish National Audit Office). *Riksrevisionen* conducts yearly investigations of Swedish government actions. These investigations are made pursuant to Swedish legislation that requires audits of governmental activity.[76] An investigation into Swedish contributions to international operations (*Svenska bidrag till internationella insatser*) was conducted in 2011.[77] The most recent report by the agency criticized the lack of concrete examples and statistics on development cooperation provided by the government to the *Riksdag* (parliament).[78]

SADEV

SADEV, the Swedish Agency for Development Evaluation (*Institutet for utvärdering av internationellt utvecklingssamarbete*),[79] is governed by *Myndighetsförordningen* (Agency Regulation) and a special governmental instruction.[80] Thus, unlike SIDA, SADEV's mission is

---

[73] *Id.* at 12 (translation by author).

[74] Swedfund International AB, http://www.swedfund.se/om-swedfund/ (last visited Sept. 14, 2011) (translation by author).

[75] Regeringskansliet, *Enheten för styrning och metoder i utvecklingssamarbetet* [The Section for Governance and Methods in Development Cooperation] (Feb. 2, 2006, updated Sept. 21, 2010), http://www.sweden.gov.se/sb/d/2868/a/57420.

[76] *See* 2 § para. 1 and 9 § LAGEN OM REVISION AV STATLIG VERKSAMHET M.M. (Svensk Författningssamling [SFS] 2002:1022).

[77] Riksrevisionen, RiR 2011:14 *Svenska bidrag till internationella insatser* (Swedish National Audit Report) (Mar. 29, 2011), *available at* http://www.riksrevisionen.se/PageFiles/10853/Anpassad_11_14%20 Svenska%20bidrag%20till%20internationella%20insatser.pdf.

[78] *Id.* at 29.

[79] SADEV, http://www.sadev.se/en/About-SADEV/.

[80] MYNDIGHETSFÖRORDNINGEN (Svensk författningssamling [SFS] 2007:515) and Instruktion för Institutet för utvärdering av internationellt utvecklingssamarbete [Instruction for Swedish Agency for Development

not reviewed annually through a letter of appropriation but through a more lengthy process of revising the instruction. The main purpose of SADEV is to evaluate the entire Swedish international development cooperation effort.[81]

OECD

Internationally, Swedish development efforts are also scrutinized by the OECD. The OECD, although very positive about Swedish ODA efforts overall, still recognizes problem areas in the Swedish ODA approach, mainly with respect to the fact that "Sweden has not yet been able to address previous recommendations, notably in reducing the complexity of the policy framework and providing independent monitoring and evaluation of policy coherence for development."[82] This continued to be the Swedish "Achilles' heel" during 2011.[83]

SIDA

Oversight is also maintained by the implementing agencies themselves. SIDA has an internal audit system, *Sekretariatet för utvärdering (UTV)* (Secretariat for Evaluation), that contributes to both international and domestic evaluations.[84]

Moreover, SIDA must submit an annual financial report to the government each year analyzing the successes and effectiveness of its efforts.[85] The report is divided into subparts corresponding to each of the government's delegated activities and includes statistics on the number of efforts, the cooperation partners, other agency involvement, and the costs associated with each effort.[86] In addition, in 2010 SIDA commissioned an evaluation of its humanitarian assistance, which was published in November 2010.

To safeguard against fraud and corruption, SIDA has adopted an anticorruption code of conduct.[87] The SIDA definition of corruption is "abuse of trust, power or position that results in improper benefit." According to SIDA's anticorruption code, corruption includes "[the giving

---

Evaluation] (Svensk Författningssamling [SFS] 2007:130), *available at* http://www.riksdagen.se/webbnav/index. aspx?nid=3911&bet=2007:1300.

[81] SADEV website, *supra* note 79.

[82] OECD Sweden (2009) DAC Peer Review – Main Findings and Recommendations, *available at* http://www.oecd.org/document/1/0,3343,en_2649_34603_43278401_1_1_1_1,00.html (last visited Sept. 7, 2011).

[83] *See* Betänkande 2010/11:UU2 Utgiftsområde 7 – Internationellt Bistånd [Parliamentary Committee Report], *available at* http://www.riksdagen.se/webbnav/index.aspx?nid=3322&rm=2010/11&bet=UU2.

[84] SIDA website (June 15, 2009, updated June 16, 2011), *Så arbetar vi med utvärdering*, http://www.sida.se/Svenska/Om-oss/Sa-arbetar-vi/Utvardering/Ansvar-utvardering/.

[85] *See* SIDA, Annual Financial Report 2009, *available at* http://www.sida.se/Global/About%20Sida/ Budget/Sidas%20%c3%a5rsredovisning%202009%20slutversion.pdf.

[86] *See id.*

[87] SIDA, Antikorruptionsregel [Anti-Corruption Rule], http://www.sida.se/Global/About%20Sida/ Sidas%20antikorruptionsregel.pdf (last visited Sept. 9, 2011).

and taking of bribes,] blackmail, nepotism, but also embezzlement, scams and conflicts of interest."[88]

Ekonomistyrningsverket

The *Ekononomistyrningsverket* (ESV) (Swedish National Financial Management Authority)[89] coordinates all accounting of Swedish finances, including spending for development cooperation.[90] ESV does not itself conduct any accounting but coordinates the accounting by various governmental agencies.[91] In addition, it analyzes relevant spending policies and assess risks associated with the budget.[92]

6. Policy Considerations

The Swedish government applies what it refers to as a "country focus process" (focused bilateral development cooperation), which is outlined in a memorandum by the Ministry of Foreign Affairs.[93] The memo highlights five issues to address when choosing a bilateral development partner: (1) the needs of the recipient country, (2) the prospective efficiency of the results, (3) the potential influence Sweden might have on the democratization process, (4) whether Sweden has a comparative advantage in the recipient country compared to other donor nations, and (5) "Sweden's overall links with each country."[94]

However, certain types of aid remain unaffected by the "country focus approach."[95] Examples include "humanitarian aid, multilateral aid, support to Swedish nongovernmental organisations via the frame organisations, [and] independent research cooperation."[96] Sweden has expressed a devotion to the promotion of human rights and in 2008 reduced the amount of aid distributed through the United Nations Development Programme (UNDP) as a direct result of Sweden's belief that UNDP was not adequately committed to "pushing for" human

---

[88] *See Vårt arbete mot korruption – Korruption hindrar utveckling* [Our Efforts Against Corruption – Corruption is an Obstacle for Development] (June 24, 2009, updated Mar. 25, 2011). SIDA, http://www.sida.se/Svenska/Om-oss/Sa-arbetar-vi/Vart-arbete-mot-korruption/ (translation by author).

[89] Ekonomistyrningsverket's website, http://esv.se/Snabblankar-i-toppen/English1/ (last visited Sept. 14 2011).

[90] 3 § no. 4 Förordning med instruktion för Ekonomistyrningsverket (Svensk författningssamling [SFS] 2010:1764), *available at* http://www.riksdagen.se/webbnav/index.aspx?nid=3911&bet=2010:1764.

[91] Ekonomistyrningsverket, http://www.esv.se (last visited Sept. 14, 2011).

[92] *Id.*

[93] Ministry of Foreign Affairs, *Focused bilateral development cooperation* (Aug. 27, 2011), *available at* http://www.sweden.gov.se/content/1/c6/08/66/21/496f32e6.pdf.

[94] *See id.* at 4–5.

[95] *Id.* at 9.

[96] *Id.*

rights protections.[97] Swedish efforts also include a focus on gender equality in the distribution of aid.[98]

Reevaluation of Aid Policy

The Swedish government is currently overhauling the Swedish International Development Cooperation Agency.[99] The overhaul includes analyses of which countries should receive development cooperation and how aid measures are monitored and reported.

The Swedish government is attempting to make aid more efficient and focused, leaving certain areas in favor of others, and mainly focusing on Africa and the Baltic Region. No change in the amount allocated is intended, but rather a shift in purpose.[100]

The Minister for International Development Cooperation, Gunilla Carlsson, has made it her priority to open up access to foreign aid data and has launched a website devoted solely to making foreign aid data, and especially the fight against corruption, transparent and accessible.[101] The project is outlined in the Swedish report *Öppna biståndet* (*Make the Aid More Transparent*)[102] and summarized in English on the English website version.[103] Sweden has also launched a website covering the Swedish ODA and military operations in Afghanistan, as a part of its policy to make its international involvements more transparent.[104]

B. Regulation of Private Contributions

Sweden is the only Scandinavian country that does not provide a tax deduction for private aid donations to nonprofit organizations, such as the Red Cross.[105] However, *Aktiebolag*

---

[97] *See* Gunilla Carlsson, *Mindre bidrag till FN* [Less Assistance to United Nations],January 4, 2008, Regeringskansliet, http://www.regeringen.se/sb/d/10080/a/95478 (translation by author).

[98] *See* Swedish Government Report, On Equal Footing: Policy for Gender Equality and the Rights and Role of Women in Sweden's International Development Cooperation 2010-2015 (Article no: UD 10.062 ISBN: 78-91-7496-428-8) (Aug. 2010), *available at* http://www.sweden.gov.se/content/1/c6/15/22/97/a962c4c8.pdf.

[99] *See* Ministry of Foreign Affairs, *Bistånd och utveckling*, http://www.sweden.gov.se/sb/d/2355 (last visited Sept. 9, 2011).

[100] *Id.*

[101] *See* Open Aid, http://www.openaid.se (last visited Sept. 20, 2011).

[102] Öppna Biståndet – Genomförandeplanen, http://www.regeringen.se/content/1/c6/13/53/41/f90270ba.pdf (last visited Sept. 6, 2011), and http://www.oppnabistandet.nu.

[103] Government Offices of Sweden, *Swedish Development Cooperation*, http://www.sweden.gov. se/sb/d/3102/a/86621 (last visited Sept. 6, 2011).

[104] *See* Swedish Government website on Sweden's efforts in Afghanistan, http://www.swedeninafghanistan.se/ (last visited Sept. 7, 2011).

[105] *See* Statens Offentliga Utredningar [SOU] 2009:59 Skatteincitament för gåvor till forskning och ideell verksamhet [Tax Incentives for Gifts to Research and Non-Profits] [government report series] at 60-63, *available at* http://www.regeringen.se/content/1/c6/12/85/17/e37b11c9.pdf. For an overview of the Danish and Norwegian systems, *see* http://um.dk/da/danida/det-goer-vi (Denmark), http://www.skatteetaten.no/en/Artikler/Donations-to-certain-voluntary-organisations-and-religious-and-beliefs-based-communities-/ (Norway).

(Incorporated Shareholder Corporations) do have a right to deduct Christmas gifts, which may include planting a tree in the name of an employee. A more controversial example is that *Rädda Barnen* (Save the Children, Sweden) sold Christmas trees for SEK 150,000 (approx. US$22,387), for the benefit of their local and international efforts, which could be given as Christmas presents to their corporate employees and thereby become deductible.[106] Less expensive alternatives included a box of chocolates for SEK 5,500[107] (approx. US$821) and a Christmas flower for SEK 8,000 (approx. US$1,194).[108] The right to deduct the difference between the market value for a chocolate box and the paid price depends on the quantity of sponsoring services the donor receives.[109]

The Christian Democrat Party (currently part of the governing coalition) has suggested that a tax deduction be introduced for both corporations and individuals and that such action could double the current total Swedish ODA.[110] A state investigation as part of a legislative effort has also been conducted.[111] The proposed fall budget (*höstbudget*),[112] which was delivered to the *Riksdag* on September 20, 2011, proposed to make "gifts to organizations, nonprofit organizations, religious and belief-based communities" deductible, provided that the recipient is involved in activities that benefit people in need "or promote research and development."[113] However, this newly proposed deduction is intended *only for private individuals* and not legal persons such as corporations or state actors.[114] The proposal would cover gifts ranging between SEK 200 (approx. US$30) and SEK 6, 000 (approx. US$895) and donors would receive a 25% tax deduction.[115]

According to the government proposal, the recipients of deductible gifts under this new law should be limited to organizations with "an objective of conducting support activity to the

---

[106] E24, *En julgran för 150 000* (Oct. 11, 2010, 15:59, updated 17:37) http://www.e24.se/entreprenor/en-julgran-for-150-000_2357233.e24.

[107] E24, *Rädda barnens julkampanj*, Bildspel (picture 2), http://www.e24.se/entreprenor/radda-barnens-julkampanj_2352621.e24#?imgID=1.

[108] E24, *Rädda Barnens julkampanj*, Bildspel (picture 3), http://www.e24.se/entreprenor/radda-barnens-julkampanj_2352621.e24#?imgID=2.

[109] *See* Statens Offentliga Utredningar [SOU] 2009:59 Skatteincitament för gåvor till forskning och ideell verksamhet [Tax Incitements for Gifts to Research and Non Profit Activity][government report series], at 71, *available at* http://www.regeringen.se/content/1/c6/12/85/17/e37b11c9.pdf.

[110] Hasse Boström, *Avdragsrätt ska öka det frivilliga biståndet*, DAGEN, (Mar. 5, 2008, 06:00) http://www.dagen.se/dagen/article.aspx?id=150696 (translation by author).

[111] Statens Offentlia Utredningar [SOU] 2009:59 Skatteincitament för gåvor till forskning och ideell verksamhet, *supra* note 111.

[112] *See* discussion on Swedish fall budget above.

[113] Lars Larsson, *Gåvor föreslås bli avdragsgilla*[Gifts Suggested to Become Deductible], DN.SE (Sept. 1, 2011, 6:17 PM), http://www.dn.se/ekonomi/gavor-foreslas-bli-avdragsgilla (translation by author).

[114] *Id.* (emphasis added by author).

[115] Annika Creutzer, *Skatteavdrag för gåva ett dumt förslag*[Tax Deduction for Gift a Stupid Suggestion], DAGENS INDUSTRI, (Sept. 2, 2011, at 12:59 PM, updated Sept. 5, 2011, at 10:25 AM), http://www.e24.se/pengar/din-ekonomi/skatter-och-deklarationer/sankt-skatt-for-gava-i-budgetpropositionen_3029722.e24.

benefit of people in need or to promote scientific research or completely or in part conduct such activity."[116]

III. Foreign Aid Appropriations Process

A. General

Budget and Appropriation Procedure Law

The appropriation process for the Swedish budget is governed by the Swedish Constitution[117] and budget law.[118] The *Riksdag* decides on the budget after receiving a budget proposal from the government.[119] The governmental proposal is supposed to include guidelines for expenditures beyond the current budget year (RF 9:6) as well as a budget ceiling for the upcoming three years.[120] The governmental expenditure appropriation must be made as general appropriations (3 ch. 2§), but the government may make limitations and conditions for "the use of the [appropriated funds]" (3 ch. 11§).[121] Before submitting a budget, the government hears suggestions from the relevant implementing agencies.

General Procedure

The government generally sends a *vårbudget* (Spring Fiscal Policy Bill) to the *Riksdag* in April (April 15 at the latest) and the *Riksdag* decides on the budget in June.[122] The Spring Fiscal Policy Bill covers the general policy with a long-term perspective.[123] There is also a budget proposition during the fall, *höstbudget* (Budget Bill), which outlines the actual budget for the upcoming year.[124] The *Riksdag* decides on this Budget Bill in December after discussions between the government and Riksdag.[125]

---

[116] Statens Offentlia Utredningar [SOU] 2009:59 Skatteincitament for gåvor till forskning och ideell verksamhet, Stockholm June 17, 2009 [government report series] at 91, *available at* http://www.regeringen.se/content/1/c6/12/85/17/e37b11c9.pdf (translation by author).

[117] REGERINGSFORMEN [RF] [Constitution].

[118] BUDGETLAG (Svensk Författningssamling [SFS] 2011:203).

[119] REGERINGSFORMEN [RF] 9:1-2 [Constitution].

[120] 2 ch. 2 § para. 2 BUDGETLAG (SFS 2011:203).

[121] BUDGETLAG (Svensk Författningssamling [SFS] 2011:203).

[122] Government Offices of Sweden, *State Budget Procedure* (Apr. 23, 2004, updated Apr. 8, 2011), http://www.sweden.gov.se/sb/d/2855/a/18833.

[123] *Id.*

[124] *Id.*

[125] *Id.*

B. Bilateral and Multilateral Agreements

The government enters into all agreements with foreign states as well as multilateral organizations (RF 10:1). However, the *Riksdag* must accept certain agreements (RF 10:3). As part of its power to enter into agreements with states and multilateral organizations, the Swedish government may also assign contracting powers to relevant governmental agencies to enter into such agreements, provided that those agreements do not require the *Riksdag*'s or *Utrikesnämnd*'s[126] participation (RF 10:2). Thus, in regard to foreign aid, the Swedish government may delegate its mandate by asking SIDA (or another government agency) to enter into bilateral agreements.

C. Allocation – Bilateral/Multilateral Aid

When presenting the budget to the Riksdag, the government includes a special budget for development assistance, which also includes a minor allocation for certain administrative costs associated with the Swedish asylum process.[127] In addition, the government sends the implementing agencies "letters of appropriation" that specify in greater detail the allocation of both bilateral and multilateral aid.[128] The letters of appropriation include separate posts for bilateral aid (divided into regions), multilateral aid, and administrative costs.[129]

IV. Other Types of 'Aid'

A. Aid to College and University Students from ODA Countries

Until recently, university education in Sweden was free for all foreign students. As of July 31, 2011, college and university education is now *avgiftsbelagd* (tuition based) for all students who are not citizens of an EEA (European Economic Area) country (commonly known as third-country citizens), or are not permanent residents of Sweden or the family members of EES citizens who have permanent residence in Sweden. These students must also pay an application fee unless they are participating in an exchange program or have studied at a Swedish University during the preceding semester.[130] Non-EES citizens who are legally present in Sweden for reasons other than pursuing a university education are also exempted.[131]

---

[126] The Utrikesnämnd is a *samrådsorgan*, which discusses relevant issues following a request by four of its members. The Utrikesnämnd provides the Government with relevant information on issues that are of importance to Sweden's foreign affairs (REGERINGSFORMEN (RF) [CONSTITUTION] 10:6). The Utrikesnämnd does not have a decision mandate.

[127] *See* Proposition [Prop.] 2010/11:1 Budgetpropositionen för 2011 Utgiftsområde 7 Bilaga 1[Budget Bill for 2011 Expense Post 7 Attachment 1], *available at* http://www.regeringen.se/content/1/c6/15/33/07/53ddf3aa.pdf.

[128] *See* Regleringsbrev SIDA, Swedfund.

[129] For a detailed example, *see* 2011 Letter of Appropriation for SIDA, *supra* note 35.

[130] *See* Regeringsbeslut U2009/7345/UH *Uppdrag om förberedande åtgärder inom högskoleområdet* (Dec. 17, 2009) at 1–2, *available at* http://www.vhs.se/Global/Anm%c3%a4lningsavgifter/Regeringsuppdrag%20om%20 anm%c3%a4lningsavgifter.pdf?epslanguage=sv.

[131] *Id.*

The change in policy has mainly been a result of the rapid increase in foreign students at Swedish universities. Since 1999 the number has tripled and now "constitute[s] more than eight percent of all students in Sweden."[132] To accommodate talented students with limited means, the Swedish government has made two different scholarship programs available, one covering both the education fee and living expenses and one covering only the education fee.[133] In total, 90 million SEK (approximately US$13.5 million) will be spent on these scholarships in the 2011–2012 academic year.[134]

Because the education fee must be paid to the educational institution even before a visa is granted by the *Immigrationsmyndigheten* (Immigration Authority), it is probable that the number of students from developing countries will decrease significantly.

Government student loans and grants are given to students who are Swedish citizens or EU-members or *"likställda EU medborgare"* (persons who by law are to be treated equally to EU citizens).[135] These policies tend to disadvantage citizens of ODA recipient countries because most Swedish ODA recipient countries are not part of the EES.

B. Aid Through Asylum or Emigration

With a large number of asylum seekers each year (31,819 in 2010),[136] of whom more than half come from Serbia, Somalia, and Afghanistan, Sweden has taken steps to provide more humane living conditions for noncitizens and undocumented immigrants.

1. Free Health and Dental Care for Undocumented Immigrants

Sweden is considering a proposal to give all undocumented immigrants health care and to provide free schooling for undocumented children between the ages of six to sixteen, or up to age eighteen if the student wishes to pursue a secondary education.[137] Undocumented children are already receiving free health care in Sweden. Adult undocumented immigrants, however, only receive emergency treatment.

---

[132] Proposition [Prop.] 2009/10:65 Konkurrera med kvalitet – studieavgifter för utländska studenter [government bill][Compete With Quality – Student Fees for Foreign Students], *available at* http://www.sweden. gov.se/sb/d/12489/a/140001 (translation by author).

[133] *Id.*

[134] *See id.* at 31.

[135] *See* STUDIESTÖDSLAG (Svensk författningssamling [SFS] 1999: 1395).

[136] *See* Migrationsverket, *Applications for asylum received, 2010,* http://www.migrationsverket. se/download/18.46b604a812cbcdd7dba80008290/Inkomna+ans%C3%B6kningar+om+asyl+2010.pdf.

[137] Statens Offentliga Utredningar [SOU] 2011:48 Vård efter behov och på lika villkor – en mänsklig rättighet[Health Care According to Need and on Equal Terms – a Human Right] [government report series], Stockholm 2011.

2. Foreign Remittance

Foreign remittances were officially calculated to be about SEK 4 billion in 2006.[138] An article published in the Nordic Africa Institute's periodical, *Policy Notes Report*, argues that actual foreign remittances in 2007 were 30% higher than official figures, however.[139] This would mean that foreign remittances corresponded to approximately 0.175% of Sweden's GNI.[140] The Swedish government has worked to promote the transfer of foreign remittances by reducing the costs associated with international transfers without facilitating money laundering and the financing of terrorist activity.[141]

3. The Kosmopolit Project

The Swedish Minister for Trade, Ewa Bjoerling, started the project *Kosmopolit* in an effort to increase trade and integration.[142] The project allocates funds to stimulate and increase foreign trade with the immigrant's native country.[143]

Prepared by Edith Palmer, Chief
Foreign, Comparative and International Law Division II
Global Legal Research Center
and Elin Hofverberg
Law Library Intern
November 2011

---

[138] Mattias Engdahl, *Migrant Remittances: An Overview of Global and Swedish Flows*, POLICY NOTES 2009/5 at 3, *published by* The Nordic Africa Institute, Globalization, Trade and Regional Integration, http://nai.diva-portal.org/smash/record.jsf?pid=diva2:233024 (last visited Sept. 8, 2011).

[139] *Id.*

[140] *See id.*

[141] Skrivelse [Skr.] 200/08:89 Sveriges politik för global utveckling [government communications series] at 28, *available at* http://www.regeringen.se/content/1/c6/10/10/82/03480187.pdf.

[142] *See* Swedish government webpage on the Kosmopolit project *at* http://www.sweden.gov.se/sb/d/14317 (in English; last visited Oct. 21, 2011).

[143] *Id.*

LAW LIBRARY OF CONGRESS

UNITED KINGDOM

REGULATION OF FOREIGN AID

Executive Summary

  The United Kingdom has emerged as a major player in providing development assistance. It was one of the first countries to completely "untie" aid, meaning that aid is provided without being tied to any policy considerations, and has created a strong government department responsible for administering the UK's development assistance budget and policy, which, by law, must have the principal purpose of reducing poverty. The government has taken an evidence-based approach intended to provide relief not just from the effects of poverty but also from its causes. This has required close interdepartmental relations and a sharing of resources to achieve the best results. A public information campaign has also highlighted the work of development assistance provided by the UK.

I. Introduction

A. Official Development Assistance Figures

  In 2010 the United Kingdom (UK) provided official development assistance (ODA) that amounted to an estimated 0.56% of its gross national income (GNI). This is the highest amount of ODA to GNI that the UK has provided since the United Nations (UN) set a target rate of its prosperous members providing 0.7% GNI for ODA.[1] The 2010 UK percentage amounts to an estimated £8.3 billion (approximately US$13 billion), up from £7.2 billion (approximately US$11.5 billion) in 2009.[2] Of the 2010 amount, £5.3 billion (approximately US$8.5 billion) went to bilateral aid (£5.2 billion, or approximately US$8.3 billion, when excluding debt relief), and £2.9 billion (approximately US$4.6 billion) went to multilateral organizations, which include, *inter alia*, the UN, the World Bank, and the European Commission.[3]

  The Department for International Development (DFID) has stated that its budget will increase to £7.8 billion (approximately US$12.5 billion) by 2010–11, and by 2013 the UK aims to provide 0.7% of its GNI for development assistance, a dramatic rise from the 0.36% that was

---

[1] *Keeping the Promise: United to Achieve the Millennium Development Goals*, U.N. GAOR, 65th Sess., 9th plen. mtg. at 12–19, U.N. Doc. A/RES/65/1, http://www.un.org/en/mdg/summit2010/pdf/outcome_document N1051260.pdf.

[2] Department for International Development, *Statistical Release: Provisional UK Official Development Assistance as a Proportion of Gross National Income*, 2010, http://www.dfid.gov.uk/Documents/publications1/Statistical-Release-Provisonal-UK-ODA-Table.xls.

[3] *Id.*

provided for in 2007–8.[4] In 2009, a private member's bill was introduced to galvanize this commitment due to concern that the "target is otherwise vulnerable."[5] As with the majority of private members' bills, it was never enacted.[6] The full coalition government has maintained the position that the 0.7% target will be met by 2013 and stated that it will "enshrine this commitment in law";[7] however, no legislation has since been put forward.

The increase in funding toward the ODA/GNI target has been criticized by some Members of Parliament and the public because the steep increase occurred while budgets were being drastically cut for other departments within the UK.[8] However, despite this criticism, the government remains committed to meeting its targets and maintains that it has both a moral imperative and a national interest at stake to help lift developing countries out of poverty,[9] specifically stating as follows:

> On aid spending our commitment is clear – we won't balance the budget on the back of the world's poorest people. Confirming our commitment on aid is both morally right and in our national interest.[10]

B. Private Contribution Figures

In 2011, a nonprofit organization reported on the figures of private donations in the UK. It found that during 2009–2010, donations from private individuals amounted to an estimated £10.6 billion (approximately US$17 billion) across the entire UK.[11] In this period, 24% of these

---

[4] *Who we are and what we do*, DEPARTMENT FOR INTERNATIONAL DEVELOPMENT, http://www.dfid.gov.uk/About-DFID/Quick-guide-to-DFID/Who-we-are-and-what-we-do/ (last visited July 5, 2011).

[5] HOUSE OF COMMONS, DRAFT INTERNATIONAL DEVELOPMENT (OFFICIAL DEVELOPMENT ASSISTANCE TARGET) BILL, 2009–10, H.C. 404, at 3, http://www.publications.parliament.uk/pa/cm200910/cmselect/cmintdev/404/404.pdf. *See also* SECRETARY OF STATE FOR INTERNATIONAL DEVELOPMENT, THE INTERNATIONAL DEVELOPMENT (OFFICIAL DEVELOPMENT ASSISTANCE TARGET) BILL, 2009–10, Cm. 7792, http://www.official-documents.gov.uk/document/cm77/ 7792/7792.pdf.

[6] It has been noted that "[s]ome were critical of the decision to introduced draft legislation, as a crowded legislative programme suggested it would stand little chance of reaching the statute book before the 2010 General Election." House of Commons Library, *Aid: Meeting the 0.7% of UK national income target by 2013 & proposed legislation*, House of Commons Library Standard Note, 2010, SN03714, at 12, http://www.parliament.uk/briefing-papers/SN03714.pdf.

[7] *Id.* at 15.

[8] David Williamson, *Police applaud MP for criticising foreign aid*, WALESONLINE (Aug. 2, 2011), http://www.wales online.co.uk/news/wales-news/2011/08/02/police-applaud-mp-for-criticising-foreign-aid-91466-29159495/. *See also* DEPARTMENT FOR INTERNATIONAL DEVELOPMENT, AID UNDER PRESSURE: SUPPORT FOR DEVELOPMENT ASSISTANCE IN A GLOBAL ECONOMIC DOWNTURN, FOURTH REPORT OF SESSION 2008–09, 2008–09, H.C. 179-I, http://www.publications.parliament.uk/pa/cm200809/cmselect/cmintdev/179/179i.pdf.

[9] SECRETARY OF STATE FOR INTERNATIONAL DEVELOPMENT, *supra* note 5, at 4.

[10] House of Commons Library, *supra* note 6, at 15, *citing* Queen's Speech, *International development spending from 2013*, Number 10 website (May 2010).

[11] CHARITIES AID FOUNDATION, UK GIVING 2010 at 21 (Dec. 2010), http://www.cafonline.org/pdf /UK%20Giving%202010_101210.pdf.

donations went to overseas causes, totaling around £2.2 billion (approximately US$3.5 billion).[12] This increase from the average of 15% of donations that typically go to overseas causes was attributed to the earthquake disaster in Haiti and the successful appeal for funds in its aftermath.[13]

C. Snapshot of Foreign Aid Activity

The UK is providing foreign aid to over one hundred counties. The DFID's overall aim is to reduce poverty in poorer countries and to meet eight criteria, known as the Millennium Development Goals (MDGs) and set by the UN (these goals are listed in section II(A), below, under the heading "Regulation of ODA's").[14]

Foreign aid used toward achieving these goals has included funding for activities such as providing clean water and sanitation, giving developmental food aid and food security assistance; forgiving debt, and providing basic education. In 2010, key achievements were made in the following areas:

- Education: Trained over 95,000 teachers and building or reconstructing over 10,000 classrooms

- Health: Trained over 65,000 health professionals, vaccinated almost five million children against measles, delivered nearly nine million anti-malarial bed nets, administered anti-retroviral drugs to 150,000 people with HIV, and distributed nearly 500 million condoms

- Infrastructure: Provided 1.5 million people with clean water and 800,000 people with better sanitation, built or upgraded 1,500 kilometers of roads and maintained 3,000 kilometers

- Food and Social Assistance: Provided food to 1.5 million people and provided social assistance to 3.5 million[15]

II. Legal Framework

The DFID operates under the legal framework provided for by the International Development Act 2002.[16] This Act was necessary because the DFID operates using public money, which cannot be spent without parliamentary authorization regarding the manner and

---

[12] *Id.*

[13] *Id.*

[14] DEPARTMENT FOR INTERNATIONAL DEVELOPMENT, ANNUAL REPORT AND ACCOUNTS 2010–11, vol. 1, HC 989-I, 2010–11, at 4, http://www.dfid.gov.uk/Documents/publications1/departmental-report/2011/Annual-report-2011-vol1.pdf.

[15] Id.

[16] International Development Act 2002, c. 1. This Act repealed and replaced the Overseas Development and Co-operation Act 1980, c. 63.

purposes of its use.[17] The Act allows the Secretary of State for International Development to provide development assistance to countries or territories outside the UK if it is likely to contribute to a reduction in poverty or improve the welfare of the population.[18] Reducing poverty is the "core power" of the Act and, by law, must be the overall purpose for which any development assistance is provided.[19] The aim of this purpose is, in part, to "protect aid resources from pressures within government to spend money on aims other than poverty reduction."[20] This, combined with the strong political figure of a cabinet minister as the head of the organization, has helped to move development assistance higher on the national agenda.[21]

There are certain exceptions to the requirement that the core aim of poverty reduction must be met for assistance to be provided. These exceptions include assistance provided for humanitarian relief,[22] to the overseas territories[23] of the UK, and to multilateral development banks.[24] The UK's overseas territories were excepted "in recognition of the continuing special relationship between the UK and Overseas Territories."[25]

The term "development assistance" is defined in the Act as "furthering sustainable development [which is not just limited to environmental or economic aims][26] . . . or improving

---

[17] *International Development Act 2002*, DEPARTMENT FOR INTERNATIONAL DEVELOPMENT, http://www.dfid.gov.uk/About-DFID/History1/International-Development-Act-2002/ (July 13, 2011).

[18] International Development Act 2002, c. 1, § 1.

[19] DEPARTMENT FOR INTERNATIONAL DEVELOPMENT, *supra* note 17.

[20] Danielle Goldfarb & Stephen Tapp, *How Canada Can Improve Its Development Aid: Lessons from Other Aid Agencies*, BNET (Apr. 15, 2006), http://findarticles.com/p/articles/mi_hb1414/is_232/ai_n29264581/pg_7/.

[21] *History*, DEPARTMENT FOR INTERNATIONAL DEVELOPMENT http://www.dfid.gov.uk/About-DFID/History1 (last visited Aug. 16, 2011).

[22] DFID has stated that its humanitarian assistance "is guided by the core principles of humanitarianism set out in the Principles for Good Humanitarian Donorship, namely *humanity* (the centrality of saving human lives and relieving suffering wherever it is found); *neutrality* (humanitarian assistance should not favour any side in an ongoing conflict); and *independence* (humanitarian objectives should be independent of any political or military objectives). Humanitarian assistance should be designed as far as possible to complement and pave the way for other forms of engagement." Department for International Development, *Working Effectively in Conflict-affected and Fragile Situations*, Mar. 2010, Briefing Paper G, http://www.dfid.gov.uk/Documents/publications1/governance/Building-peaceful-states-G.pdf.

[23] The British overseas territories are Anguilla, Bermuda, British Antarctic Territory, British Indian Ocean Territory, British Virgin Islands, Cayman Islands, Falkland Islands, Gibraltar, Montserrat, Pitcairn Islands, St. Helena and Dependencies, South Georgia and the South Sandwich Islands, the Sovereign Base Areas of Akrotiri and Dhekelia in Cyprus, and the Turks and Caicos Islands. *List of Crown Dependencies & Overseas Territories*, FOREIGN AND COMMONWEALTH OFFICE, http://www.fco.gov.uk/en/publications-and-documents/treaties/uk-overseas-territories/list-crown-dependencies-overseas (last visited Aug. 30, 2011).

[24] International Development Act 2002, c. 1, §§ 2-3.

[25] DEPARTMENT FOR INTERNATIONAL DEVELOPMENT, *supra* note 17.

[26] *Id.*

the welfare of the population."[27]   The Act does not further define the terms "poverty," "sustainable development,"[28] or "welfare," because

> to do so might reduce the United Kingdom's ability to offer assistance . . . . Poverty is a complex phenomenon and the actions required to reduce it will necessarily be varied. The power in section 1 is designed to ensure that the Secretary of State will be able to support a wide range of activities and organisations.[29]

Despite there being no specific statutory definition, there has been much discussion on what the term "poverty" includes. The UK does not interpret it as encompassing the condition of poverty alone, but also as including the underlying causes of poverty, such as conflict, economic difficulties, and corruption.[30] Thus, under the Act, the Secretary of State may provide assistance that is "preparatory to, or will facilitate the provision of, assistance" permitted under the Act, such as commissioning research intended to provide insight into ways to reduce poverty.[31]

As noted above, the 2002 Act is necessarily broad to allow assistance to be provided in many ways. The most common form of assistance, financial assistance, is specifically defined in the 2002 Act.[32] This definition allows the Secretary of State to provide financial assistance not only through the traditional means of grants and loans, but also through guarantees and the purchase of equities or other company securities, or any combination of the above methods.[33]

A. Regulation of ODAs

1. Overview

A 1997 government paper marked a shift in policy and a move away from providing purely economic assistance to developing countries. Instead, the reduction of poverty was made the overarching aim of the UK's provision of development assistance.[34] To achieve this aim, the DFID is working to reach the MDGs, which aim to halve world poverty by 2015. These goals offer a "quantifiable and measurable"[35] way in which this can be achieved[36] and are to

---

[27] International Development Act 2002, c. 1, § 1(2).

[28] The term sustainable development is, however, clarified in the Act to ensure that it is not interpreted too narrowly. It "includes any development that is, in the opinion of the Secretary of State, prudent having regard to the likelihood of its generating lasting benefits for the population of the country . . . in relation to which it is provided." International Development Act 2002, c. 1, § 1(3).

[29] International Development Act 2002, c. 1, Explanatory Notes, ¶ 18.

[30] Owen Barder, *Reforming Development Assistance: Lessons from the U.K. Experienc*e, Center for Global Development: Working Paper 70, Oct. 2005, http://www.cgdev.org/files/4371_file_WP_70.pdf.

[31] International Development Act 2002, c. 1, Explanatory Notes, ¶ 23.

[32] International Development Act 2002, c. 1, § 5.

[33] *Id.* § 6.

[34] *Id.* § 1. *See also* DEPARTMENT FOR INTERNATIONAL DEVELOPMENT, *supra* note 14, ¶ 1.6.

[35] Barder, *supra* note 30.

- Eradicate extreme poverty and hunger

- Achieve universal primary education

- Promote gender equality and empower women

- Reduce child mortality

- Improve maternal health

- Combat HIV/AIDs, malaria, and other diseases

- Ensure environmental sustainability

- Develop a global partnership for development[37]

The DFID has set out its priorities for 2011–2015 in meeting these goals, which include honoring its international commitments; increasing transparency in aid provided; boosting wealth creation; strengthening governance and security in unstable areas; improving the lives of girls and women; and combating climate change.[38]

As noted above, the work of the DFID in meeting these objectives must be within the legal framework of the 2002 Act. Specifically, two conditions must be met before development assistance will be given. The assistance must: (1) further sustainable development or improve the welfare of the population; and (2) be likely to contribute to a reduction in poverty.[39]

2. Implementing Agencies

The body responsible for administering the UK's development assistance budget is the DFID. This body replaced the Overseas Development Administration (ODA), which formed part of the Foreign and Commonwealth Office.[40] The DFID was established in 1997 as a government department headed by a minister, with the overarching aim of reducing poverty.[41] To achieve this, financially the UK is striving to provide 0.7% of its GNI as ODA and it is working toward meeting the MDGs set by the UN. The DFID has two headquarters in the UK: one in London, England, and one in East Kilbride, Scotland, in addition to offices in over 40 developing countries worldwide.[42]

---

[36] DEPARTMENT FOR INTERNATIONAL DEVELOPMENT, *supra* note 4.

[37] Department for International Development, *DFID in 2009–10: Response to the International Development (Reporting and Transparency) Act 2006* (2010), http://www.dfid.gov.uk/Documents/ publications1/departmental-report/2010/dfid-in-2009-10-revised-6-sept-2010.pdf.

[38] International Development Act 2002, c. 1, § 1. *See also* DEPARTMENT FOR INTERNATIONAL DEVELOPMENT, *supra* note 14, ¶ 1.7.

[39] DEPARTMENT FOR INTERNATIONAL DEVELOPMENT, *supra* note 17.

[40] DEPARTMENT FOR INTERNATIONAL DEVELOPMENT, *supra* note 21.

[41] *Id. See also* Barder, *supra* note 30.

[42] DEPARTMENT FOR INTERNATIONAL DEVELOPMENT, *supra* note 4.

The DFID also bears responsibility for the UK's policies relating to development assistance, which includes aspects of environmental policy, trade, conflict prevention, political relationships, international economy, and migration. The reason for including these within the remit of the DFID was "recognition that there were important limits on what aid alone could achieve. A great many other policies pursued by rich nations have as much, or more, impact on the reduction of poverty."[43] By creating a governmental department whose sole responsibility was the reduction of poverty, the government hoped to give greater weight to this long-term interest of the UK, which had frequently been sidelined by short-term political and commercial concerns. A report on the work of DFID noted that

> [a]n important motivation for the establishment of a separate department was to increase the attention paid within Government to the UK's long-term strategic interests, so that these might be properly balanced against short-term pressures. For example, it was recognized that it was in the UK's long-term commercial interests that Africa should emerge as an economically strong trading partner; and in the UK's security interests that there should be reductions in poverty and inequality and improvements in governance in developing countries. But these long-term interests had not always been given weight alongside short-term commercial and strategic concerns. By creating a department with a long-term agenda for global poverty reduction, the intention was to create institutional pressures within government to ensure that the UK's long-term interests were taken into account alongside short-term pressures.[44]

As a governmental department, the DFID has achieved considerable success.[45] A report by the Canadian government has noted that the DFID is "generally considered to be the best [development agency] in the world."[46] It has received praise from *The Economist*, which describes it as "a model for other rich countries."[47]

Coordination with Other Agencies

The 2002 Act provides for other specified bodies[48] to enter into and carry out agreements to further sustainable development; improve the welfare of the population; or alleviate the effects of a disaster or emergency, outside the UK. These bodies may not provide any financial

---

[43] Barder, *supra* note 30, at 21.

[44] *Id.* at 14.

[45] *Id.*

[46] *Id.* (citing ROBERT GREENHILL, MAKING A DIFFERENCE: EXTERNAL VIEWS ON CANADA'S INTERNATIONAL IMPACT (Global Voices Project: Interim Report, Jan. 2005), http://idl-bnc.idrc.ca/dspace/bitstream/10625/33024/1/120694.pdf.

[47] *Id.* (citing *Aid Policy*, THE ECONOMIST, Oct. 31, 2002).

[48] These bodies are the British Tourist Authority; a Health Authority, a Health Board, a National Health Service Trust, a Primary Care Trust, the Public Health Laboratory Service Board, a Special Health Authority, a Special Health Board, and the Wales Tourist Board. International Development Act 2002, c. 1, § 9.

assistance, and the Secretary of State[49] must consent to any agreements before they are entered into.[50]

As noted above, the UK established the DFID as a government department with its own minister. As a result of this, development assistance has a higher profile on the political agenda and policy coherence across the entire government is strived for; the aims of DFID are frequently considered in the policy decisions of other government departments.

The government has specifically noted that the role of DFID in reducing poverty

is not an exclusive role, and DFID works jointly with a number of other UK Government departments, including those with responsibility for:

- the economy—Her Majesty's Treasury (HMT);

- foreign affairs and diplomacy—the Foreign and Commonwealth Office (FCO);

- defence, conflict prevention and post-conflict reconstruction—the Ministry of Defence (MOD);

- the promotion of international trade, enterprise and innovation—Department of Trade and Industry (DTI) [now the Department for Business, Innovation and Skills (BIS)];

- the pursuit of sustainable development—the Department for Environment, Food and Rural Affairs (DEFRA).[51]

The government has actively pursued interdepartmental arrangements to ensure a "joined up" approach to providing development assistance. While this approach may at first look similar to tied aid, the government has emphasized that "the aim is for policy coherence and joined-up strategies where possible, while preserving the independence, neutrality and impartiality of [development assistance and] humanitarian aid."[52]

There was initially friction between some government departments and the DFID; however, there was soon a realization of "the need to build support among developing countries and civil society organizations for their own policies with an international dimension," and the DFID was regarded "as a potentially useful ally in building international support."[53]

---

[49] If the agreement involves Scotland or Wales, the appropriate devolved body must also provide their consent.

[50] International Development Act 2002, c. 1, § 9.

[51] DEPARTMENT FOR INTERNATIONAL DEVELOPMENT, DEPARTMENTAL REPORT 2005, 2006, Cm. 6354, ¶ 6, http://www.dfid.gov.uk/Documents/publications1/departmental-report/2005/CHAP-01.pdf?epslanguage=en.

[52] Department for International Development, Working Effectively in Conflict-affected and Fragile Situations Briefing Paper C: Links between Politics, Security and Development, 2010, http://www.dfid.gov.uk/Documents/publications1/governance/building-peaceful-states-C.pdf.

[53] Barder, *supra* note 30, at 19.

An example of these kinds of arrangements is the Conflict Pool, which has brought together the resources of the Ministry of Defence, the Foreign and Commonwealth Office, and the DFID, with the aim of providing a "more strategic approach to conflict resolution."[54] The government notes that "it is valued as a means of coordinating the discretionary conflict work of the three departments by joining up UK expertise in development, diplomacy and defence."[55] The Pool's budget for 2009–10 was £100 million (approximately US$160 million), and an additional £71 million (approximately US$113 million) was added from the budgets of the three departments that form part of the Pool.[56] This budget is allocated to each of the agencies once the Pool approves the strategy to be followed.[57]

Another example is the "joined up" inter-agency approach, enshrined in the recently established £269 million Stabilisation Aid Fund and Stabilisation Unit. This unit is jointly operated by the DFID, the Foreign and Commonwealth Office, and the Ministry of Defence.[58] The Stabilisation Unit works with countries that have been affected by conflict and instability to establish peace and security.

The DFID also works with a number of international bodies, nongovernmental organizations, and charities—most prominently the World Bank, the UN, and the European Union. It considers that these bodies "have the skills and access to further our aims of poverty reduction and sustainable development."[59] Around 40% of the DFID's budget goes toward working with these multilateral partners,[60] due to the recognition that

> Britain could make only a modest difference on its own; but that there was much that the international community could do by working together. This led to a much more positive view of the need to work closely with other donors. Together with a raft of policy papers on particular topics, embracing collaboration with others helped DFID to become extremely influential throughout the development community after 1997.[61]

---

[54] *Conflict Pool*, FOREIGN AND COMMONWEALTH OFFICE, http://www.fco.gov.uk/en/about-us/what-we-do/spend-our-budget/funding-programmes1/conflict-funding/conflict-pool/ (last visited Aug. 24, 2011).

[55] Department for International Development, Foreign and Commonwealth Office, Ministry of Defence, *Conflict Pool Annual Report 2009/2010*, 2010, at 1, http://www.fco.gov.uk/resources/en/pdf/publications/annual-reports/conflict-pool-report-09-10.

[56] *Id.* at 47.

[57] DEPARTMENT FOR INTERNATIONAL DEVELOPMENT, DEPARTMENTAL REPORT 2006, Cm. 6824, 2006, ¶ 7.13, http://www.dfid.gov.uk/Documents/publications1/departmental-report/2006/CHAP%2007.pdf.

[58] *What is Stabilisation*, STABILISATION UNIT (Foreign and Commonwealth Office, Ministry of Defence and UKAid), http://www.stabilisationunit.gov.uk/about-us/what-is-stabilisation.html (last visited Aug. 22, 2011); CABINET OFFICE, THE NATIONAL SECURITY STRATEGY OF THE UNITED KINGDOM, 2007–8, Cm.7291, http://interactive.cabinetoffice.gov.uk/documents/security/national_security_strategy.pdf.

[59] *Who DFID works with*, DEPARTMENT FOR INTERNATIONAL DEVELOPMENT, http://www.dfid.gov.uk/About-DFID/Quick-guide-to-DFID/Who-DFID-works-with (last visited Aug. 16, 2011).

[60] *Id.*

[61] Barder, *supra* note 30, at 16.

Limits on Recipients

The UK incorporates UN sanctions into its national law through the use of statutory instruments, which are secondary legislation.[62] These sanctions tend to be focused on trade and on specific individuals, rather than prohibiting humanitarian and/or development assistance to hostile states overall.

The UK has provided development assistance to people in need in hostile states. In these cases, the assistance is typically not provided to the government, but to humanitarian organizations and nongovernmental organizations that work in that country. One reason for this is that a technical analysis issued by the DFID determined "that poverty and fragile states created fertile conditions for conflict and the emergence of new security threats including international crime and terrorism" and "committed itself to pay greater attention to regional conflict and insecurity."[63] The DFID recently stated that 30% of its aid will go to war-torn and unstable countries by 2014.[64] The aim of the government in pushing such a large percentage of aid in this area is to "help address the causes of conflict, strengthen security and justice, lay the foundations for growth and improve access to basic services."[65]

An example of providing aid in a hostile state can be found in the immediate period after September 11, 2001, when the UK increased the amount of development assistance to the people of Afghanistan. It accepted "that a certain amount of assistance might not reach its intended targets" and reasoned that this was "a small price to pay for saving lives."[66] To minimize the amount of assistance being taken by the Taliban, the DFID used international humanitarian organizations and nongovernmental organizations that had "experience in the region and a track record of deliver[y]."[67] In this case, to avoid breaching any UN-imposed sanctions, the government announced that it was working diligently "to secure humanitarian exemptions in line with our 'smart sanctions' policy."[68]

3. Restrictions

As noted above, other than for certain exceptions, poverty reduction is the sole purpose for the provision of development assistance. It should be noted that the government has used the

---

[62] *See, e.g.*, the following statutory instruments implementing a number of UN sanctions that served to restrict transactions with Iraq: The Iraq (United Nations Sanctions) Order 2000, SI 2000/3241, and the Export of Goods (Control) (Iraq and Kuwait Sanctions) Order 1990, SI 1990/1640.

[63] Statement by the Secretary of State for International Development, the Bilateral and Multilateral Aid Reviews (Mar. 1, 2011), http://www.dfid.gov.uk/Media-Room/Speeches-and-articles/2011/BAR-MAR-oral-statement/.

[64] Id.

[65] Id.

[66] *The Afghanistan Crisis*, DEPARTMENT FOR INTERNATIONAL DEVELOPMENT (Oct. 2001), *available at* http://webarchive.nationalarchives.gov.uk/+/http://www.dfid.gov.uk/faqs/files/faq_afghanistan.htm.

[67] *Id.*

[68] *Id.*

term "poverty reduction," which is significantly broader, rather than "poverty relief." The government commissioned research to better understand the causes of poverty, which led to the expansion of its program and the inclusion of additional areas, including institution building; governance reform; security; and access to justice programs with the aim of reducing poverty.[69] While issues in these different areas contributes in some way to causing poverty, care has to be exercised that assistance given keeps the purpose of poverty reduction as its main aim. The government has noted the difficulty posed by the policy overlap in these different areas:

> The distinction between humanitarian, development and stabilisation activities is sometimes not clear cut. Stabilisation can be seen as filling the gap between emergency humanitarian assistance and longer term development assistance, though, as the definition above shows, it is more than that. The most fundamental distinctions are between the explicitly political aims of stabilisation (aiming to promote peaceful political processes); the strictly neutral role of humanitarian assistance; and the apolitical poverty-focused rationale for development activity.[70]

Tied Aid

The British government expressed its opposition to tying aid in a White Paper published in 2000, stating that it is

> totally committed to the multilateral untying of aid. Tied aid is one of the most damaging carry-overs from the past. It is damaging for three reasons. The first is value for money. It is estimated that tying aid to the purchase of goods and services from the donor country reduces the value of that aid by around 25% . . . it is grossly inefficient. It leads to developing countries being supplied with incompatible pieces of equipment provided by different development agencies, each with separate requirements . . . [and] it encourages a donor driven approach to development. It signals that development agencies' major concern is not development, but their national contracts.[71]

The government announced that it would completely untie all UK development assistance beginning April 1, 2001.[72] This was enshrined in the 2002 Act,[73] which was drafted to ensure that any assistance provided to promote UK trade, or for commercial or political reasons, is challengeable in the courts.[74] It noted that untying development assistance served to create a single, clear mission of reducing and eliminating poverty. This single mission became a

---

[69] Barder, *supra* note 30, at 24.

[70] STABILISATION UNIT, *supra* note 58.

[71] Department for International Development, Eliminating World Poverty: Making Globalisation Work for the Poor, White Paper on International Development, 2000, Cm. 5006, ¶¶ 320–322, http://webarchive.nationalarchives.gov.uk/+/http:/www.dfid.gov.uk/Documents/publications/whitepaper 2000.pdf.

[72] *Id.* ¶ 323.

[73] DEPARTMENT FOR INTERNATIONAL DEVELOPMENT, *supra* note 17.

[74] *Id.*

"powerful motivating, unifying and guiding force"[75] for staff because they no longer had to consider commercial, political, or strategic objectives as factors when distributing assistance.

In the early days after the prohibition on tied aid was introduced, there were some struggles regarding the use of development assistance to achieve political aims. For example, in an attempt to reduce the number of asylum seekers, the Home Office proposed that aid in developing countries be conditional upon their acceptance of the return of failed asylum seekers.[76] The head of the DFID at the time strongly opposed the use of development aid in this manner and successfully argued that it was illegal because it was not for poverty reduction.[77] Before this policy announcement and subsequent Act, the UK did tie aid, at 8.5% in 1999, down from 28% in 1997.[78]

Conditionality

While tied aid is prohibited and poverty reduction is the central aim, the UK does require countries that receive its development assistance to adhere to certain conditions, which if not met have a direct effect on the terms under which aid is supplied. The DFID has specifically stated that it does not use these conditions to "impose specific policy choices on countries."[79] Rather,

> [t]he UK policy on conditionality is that DFID's aid is based on three shared commitments with partner governments: poverty reduction and meeting the MDGs; respecting human rights and other international obligations; and strengthening financial management and accountability and reducing the risk of funds being misused thorough weak administration or corruption. If partner governments move away from these conditions, DFID can suspend, interrupt, delay or change how it delivers its aid. DFID does not use conditions to impose specific policy choices on countries.[80]

The UK details in its annual report country-by-country instances where its aid has been interrupted as a result of a breach of conditions by the recipient. An example of this is in Uganda, where a lack of action taken against corruption resulted in £5 million (approximately US$8 million) of development assistance being withheld.[81]

---

[75] Sir John Vereker, Blazing the Trail: Eight Years of Change in Handling International Development, 20 DEV. POL'Y REV. 133 (2002).

[76] Barder, *supra* note 30.

[77] *Id.* at 21.

[78] Press Release, Department for International Development, Untie all development assistance to make it more effective, says Short (Dec. 11, 2000), *available at* http://webarchive.nationalarchives.gov.uk/+/http://www.dfid.gov.uk/news/PressReleases/files/pr11_1dec00.html.

[79] DEPARTMENT FOR INTERNATIONAL DEVELOPMENT, *supra* note 14, at 166.

[80] *Id.*

[81] DEPARTMENT FOR INTERNATIONAL DEVELOPMENT, *supra* note 14, at 96.

4. Discretionary Aid

The DFID's budget includes a contingency reserve of £100m (approximately US$160 million) per year that can be used for emergency crises. This funding is discretionary as the government does not "pre-allocate resources for specific humanitarian crises."[82] This discretionary fund has also been used to accommodate changes in the exchange rate.[83]

The Conflict Pool, discussed briefly above, also provides discretionary funding for "conflict prevention, stabilisation and peacekeeping activities."[84]

5. Oversight

The work of the DFID is subject to many oversight mechanisms, some of which are set out by law. Specifically, the DFID operates under the Development Act (Reporting and Transparency) 2006 Act (hereinafter the 2006 Act).[85] This Act requires the Secretary of State to report annually on the total expenditure of international aid, the effectiveness of the aid in achieving the MDGs, and the transparency of the aid. These reporting requirements are reflective of the government's intention that the success of development assistance not be measured by spending targets alone (i.e., spending a percentage of the GNI on ODA) but also by how effective it is in reducing poverty.[86]

In addition to the requirements of the 2006 Act, the government has also attempted to increase oversight of how development assistance is used. In its 2010–11 Annual Report, the DFID announced that transparency and accountability are "watchwords" and on June 3, 2010, the Secretary of State announced a new Aid Transparency Guarantee. This guarantee is that aid will be completely transparent not only to UK citizens, but to those in the countries in which aid is provided. The government considers this guarantee essential for aid to be effective and to give value for money.[87] The guarantee requires the DFID to publish on its website detailed information about all new projects into which it enters and to publish a summary of information on the projects in both English and the major local language(s) of the country in which the

---

[82] *Enquiry into Preparing for the Humanitarian Consequences of Possible Military Action Against Iraq*, INTERNATIONAL DEVELOPMENTAL COMMITTEE (Feb. 2003), *available at* http://webarchive.national archives.gov.uk/+/http://www.dfid.gov.uk/News/News/files/idc_enquiry_memo_12feb03.htm.

[83] INTERNATIONAL DEVELOPMENT COMMITTEE, DFID'S PERFORMANCE IN 2008–09 AND THE 2009 WHITE PAPER, 2009–10, H.C. 48-II, at Ev 12, Q52, http://www.publications.parliament.uk/pa/cm200910/cmselect/cmintdev/48/48ii.pdf.

[84] FOREIGN AND COMMONWEALTH OFFICE, *supra* note 54.

[85] Development Act (Reporting and Transparency) 2006, c. 31.

[86] Barder, *supra* note 30, at 14. *See also* Development (Reporting and Transparency) Act 2006, c. 31.

[87] *The UKAid Transparency Guarantee*, DEPARTMENT FOR INTERNATIONAL DEVELOPMENT (June 3, 2010), http://www.dfid.gov.uk/Media-Room/News-Stories/2010/The-UKAid-Transparency-Guarantee/.

assistance is being provided.[88]   Additionally, as of April 1, 2011, the DFID must publish every financial transaction over the amount of $500 as part of the government's Transparency Drive.[89]

To ensure that the internal functions of the DFID are conducted appropriately, the DFID has its own internal audit department, which provides an "independent and objective opinion on the adequacy of systems of risk management, control and governance, by measuring and evaluating their effectiveness in achieving DFID's objectives."[90]

Within the internal audit department, there is a specialist Counter Fraud Unit that is split into two sections, the intelligence section and the investigation section. The intelligence section looks at "the wider aspects of fraud and corruption,"[91] while the investigation section delves into these matters.

Additional oversight is provided by the National Audit Office[92] which observes public spending by Parliament. This office conducts audits of the DFID's accounts and reports to Parliament and the Public Accounts Committee, which analyses DFID's spending with respect to value for money.[93] Within Parliament, the International Development Committee scrutinizes the DFID's annual report and has the authority to hold inquiries into particular areas of the DFID's work.[94]

Despite the oversight provided by the bodies discussed above, the government considered that the commitment to spend 0.7% of its GNI on ODA by 2013, particularly at a time when funding was being decreased for other government departments, required greater independent scrutiny.[95] As a result, it established the Independent Commission for Aid Impact on May 12, 2011.[96] This Commission scrutinizes the use of all UK ODA to "maximise value for money and

---

[88] *UK Aid Transparency Guarantee*, DEPARTMENT FOR INTERNATIONAL DEVELOPMENT, http://www.dfid.gov.uk/Global-Issues/What-transparency-means-for-DFID/UK-Aid-Transparency-Guarantee/ (last updated Nov. 17, 2010).

[89] DEPARTMENT FOR INTERNATIONAL DEVELOPMENT, ANNUAL REPORTS AND ACCOUNTS, H.C. 989-II, 2010–11, ¶ 5.5.1, http://www.dfid.gov.uk/Documents/publications1/departmental-report/2011/Annual-report-2011-volII.pdf.

[90] *Id.* at 32.

[91] *Id.* at 33.

[92] NATIONAL AUDIT OFFICE, http://www.nao.org.uk/ (last visited Aug. 25, 2011).

[93] Barder, *supra* note 30, at 29.

[94] International Development Act 2002, c. 1, § 6. *See also International Development Committee*, WWW.PARLIAMENT.UK, http://www.parliament.uk/business/committees/committees-archive/international-development/indcom (last visited Aug. 24, 2011).

[95] *Role and core values*, INDEPENDENT COMMISSION FOR AID IMPACT, http://icai.independent.gov.uk/about/background/how-we-work/ (last visited Aug. 24, 2011).

[96] *Founding Documents*, INDEPENDENT COMMISSION FOR AID IMPACT, http://icai.independent.gov.uk/about/background/founding-documents/ (last visited Aug. 25, 2011).

impact."[97] It reports its findings to the Parliamentary International Development Select Committee and publishes its reports on its website.[98]

The UK is also a party to the Paris Declaration on Aid Effectiveness. This Declaration outlines five commitments to improve aid and includes quantifiable targets[99] that are monitored biannually by the Organisation for Economic Co-operation and Development (OECD) to assess progress of the signatories toward the commitments, with a target date of 2010.[100] The last review was in 2008, and a review of whether the targets were met in 2010 is to be completed at the end of 2011.[101]

6. Policy Considerations

The DFID is responsible ensuring "a joined-up development policy across the Government as a whole"[102] with regard to the policy and provision of development assistance. This approach underpins the government's belief that development assistance should not be provided in a vacuum and that its success depends on the interaction of a number of policies, including trade and foreign relations, as discussed above.[103] The DFID formulates its policy "on evidence, focusing on outcomes rather than inputs, and increasing the transparency of policy making and use of resources."[104]

The DFID has elaborated on the provision of development assistance in a number of policy papers (White Papers) and briefing papers.[105] These papers provide a more detailed look and discuss the UK's approach in providing assistance in a variety of scenarios.[106]

The DFID's current policy is to reduce poverty by following the UN's MDG goals. In 2010 the UK undertook an extensive review of both its bilateral and multilateral aid.[107] The end

---

[97] Id.

[98] Id.

[99] *Assessing progress on implementing the Paris Declaration and the Accra Agenda for Action*, OECD, http://www.oecd.org/document/44/0,3746,en_2649_201185_43385196_1_1_1_1,00.html (last visited Aug. 24, 2011).

[100] DEPARTMENT FOR INTERNATIONAL DEVELOPMENT, *supra* note 89, ¶ 5.5.1.

[101] OECD, *supra* note 99. Information on the UK and its progress toward the targets set by the Paris Declaration is available at: DEPARTMENT FOR INTERNATIONAL DEVELOPMENT, ANNUAL REPORTS AND RESOURCE ACCOUNTS, H.C. 867-II, 2008–09, annex F, http://www.dfid.gov.uk/Documents/publications1/departmental-report/2009/volume2.pdf?epslanguage=en.

[102] Barder, *supra* note 30, at 15.

[103] *Id.*

[104] *Id.* at 26.

[105] *See, e.g.*, DEPARTMENT FOR INTERNATIONAL DEVELOPMENT, *supra* note 21.

[106] *Id.*

[107] House of Commons Library, *The bilateral and multilateral aid reviews*, Standard Note, SN/EP/5906, 2011, http://www.parliament.uk/briefing-papers/SN05906.pdf.

result of this was controversial because the government sought to increase the value for money by increasing the amount of development assistance to extremely poor countries and removing aid from other countries where the situation was no longer as dire.[108] The DFID set, in conjunction with the Treasury, a public target to change the proportion of development assistance for bilateral programs and increase it to low-income countries from 78 to 90%, thus shifting resources to focus on the poorest countries. This later became known as the 90-10 rule, where 90% of aid goes to the poorest countries and the remaining 10% to others.[109]

Within these countries, the areas upon which the DFID is currently focusing include tackling health needs and disease, malnutrition, and climate change; encouraging wealth creation by emphasizing property rights; encouraging investment and trade in poor countries; and addressing the root causes of conflict in an attempt to provide stability in some countries.[110]

The UK has attempted to move toward working in partnership with developing countries in need of assistance. Specifically, where developing countries have demonstrated a commitment to the elimination of poverty and cohesive policies in this area, the UK has announced that it will provide a longer term commitment and greater resources, and will allow more flexibility in how the developing country may use the resources provided:[111]

> where we have confidence in the policies and budgetary allocation process and in the capacity for effective implementation in the partner government, we will consider moving away from supporting specific projects to providing resources more strategically in support of sector-wide programmes or the economy as a whole.[112]

As noted above, the DFID has a large number of field offices in developing countries, allowing them to work closely in the provision of development assistance. This decentralization of management is intended to "promote dialogue with recipient countries."[113]

B. Regulation of Private Contributions

No tax relief is provided for individuals who donate to charities in the UK. Instead, tax relief is provided for charities that are properly registered in the UK. This tax relief applies to trading profits; income from land and property; and general income. Charities can also reclaim tax paid by UK residents who donate to them through a scheme known as "gift aid." Under this scheme, registered charities can reclaim tax at the basic rate of 22%, provided the donor has filled in the correct information on the Gift Aid Declaration. Individuals in tax brackets higher

---

[108] *Id. See also* Barder, *supra* note 30, at 17.

[109] Barder, *supra* note 30, at 17.

[110] Department for International Development, *UKAid: Changing lives, delivering results*, 2011, http://www.dfid.gov.uk/Documents/publications1/mar/BAR-MAR-summary-document-web.pdf.

[111] SECRETARY OF STATE FOR INTERNATIONAL DEVELOPMENT, ELIMINATING WORLD POVERTY: A CHALLENGE FOR THE 21ST CENTURY, Cm. 3789, 1997, ¶ 2.21, http://webarchive.nationalarchives.gov.uk/+/http://www.dfid.gov.uk/policieandpriorities/files/whitepaper1997.pdf.

[112] *Id.* ¶ 2.22.

[113] Barder, *supra* note 30, at 16 (citing *Aid Policy*, THE ECONOMIST, Oct. 31, 2002, at 18).

than the basic rate of tax that charities can reclaim may claim the difference between the basic rate and the higher rate of tax. For example, an individual paying a higher rate of income tax of 40 or 50% who makes a donation to charity may reclaim the 18 or 28% difference in tax paid.[114] For example, a donation of £100 (approximately US$160), is worth £125 (approximately US$200) to the charity, and the higher-rate taxpayer would be able to claim back £25 (approximately US$40) if they are in the 40% tax bracket or £37.50 (approximately US$60) if they are in the 50% tax bracket.[115]

III. Foreign Aid Appropriations Process

The UK's budget is the major financial statement of the government, typically delivered in spring by the Chancellor of the Exchequer.[116] The budget is then debated by Parliament, which must then approve it.

The DFID is responsible for the vast majority of the UK's development assistance budget. It has two separate allocations in the budget controlled through setting Departmental Expenditure Limits (DEL), and a separate budget allocation within the public expenditure controlled as an Annually Managed Public Expenditure. Within the DEL the two allocations are for current spending (which includes an amount for administration costs) and for net capital expenditure. The total budget for DEL in 2010–2011 was £7.5 billion (approximately US$12 billion), from which £1.6 billion (approximately US$2.57 billion) went to bilateral aid in Africa; £7.9 million (approximately US$12.64 million) to bilateral aid in South Asia; and £4 million (approximately US$6.4 million) to bilateral aid in countries in other parts of the world.[117] The Annual Reports and Accounts note that UK payments made to the European Community for development purposes are taken from the consolidated fund.[118]

The DFID has not been unharmed by the budget cuts across the government, with the coalition promising to halve public sector borrowing over the next four years.[119] It was not included in the £6.2 billion (approximately US$10 billion) public spending cuts, but was requested to make "efficiency savings of [its] own, but [told] that these would be recycled back

---

[114] Finance Act 2000, c. 17, http://www.legislation.gov.uk/ukpga/2000/17/contents.

[115] *Giving to charity through Gift Aid*, HER MAJESTY'S REVENUE AND CUSTOMS, http://www.hmrc.gov.uk/individuals/giving/gift-aid.htm (last visited Aug. 31, 2011).

[116] *Budget*, HER MAJESTY'S TREASURY, http://www.hm-treasury.gov.uk/about_budget.htm (last visited Aug. 29, 2011). *See also* ERSKINE MAY, ERSKINE MAY'S TREATISE ON THE LAW, PRIVILEGES, PROCEEDINGS AND USAGE OF PARLIAMENT 910 (Sir. William McKay et al. eds., 23rd ed. 2004).

[117] DEPARTMENT FOR INTERNATIONAL DEVELOPMENT, *supra* note 89, at 54.

[118] *Id.* at 1.

[119] HER MAJESTY'S TREASURY, *supra* note 116, ¶ 6.20.

within [its] budget" in 2010–11.[120]   As a result of this, the DFID is to deliver an additional £155 million (approximately US$250 million) of new efficiency savings in 2010–11.[121]

IV. Other Types of 'Aid'

In addition to its ODA commitment, the UK provides aid in a number of other ways. The following subheading highlights the different ways in which the UK attempts to meet its goal of reducing poverty.

Emergency Aid

The DFID has a contingency reserve that is intended for use in unforeseen emergencies. At one point the reserve was £100 million (approximately US$160 million). This amount was cut by 60% to meet the £155 million (approximately US$250 million) in efficiency savings required as a result of budget cuts across the whole government.[122]

Religious Workers and Scholarships

Individuals may enter the UK to pursue religious work on a visa for up to two years, or enter as a Minister of Religion.[123]   This work includes "preaching, pastoral work and non-pastoral work."[124]   The UK also has a Commonwealth Scholarship Commission, funded by the DFID, which offers scholarships to students from developing Commonwealth countries.[125]   The criteria for selection for these scholarships include the "likely impact of the work on the development of the candidate's home country."[126]

---

[120] Her Majesty's Treasury, Press Release 06/10, Speech by the Chief Secretary to the Treasury, Rt Hon David Laws MP, announcing £6.2 billion savings (May 24, 2010).

[121] HER MAJESTY'S TREASURY, BUDGET 2009: BUILDING BRITAIN'S FUTURE, 2009, 2008-09, H.C. 407, at 131, http://downloads.bbc.co.uk/news/nol/shared/bsp/hi/pdfs/22_04_09bud09_completereport_2591.pdf. *See also* House of Commons Library, *supra* note 6.

[122] *Addendum to DFID's Value for Money (VfM) Delivery Agreement*, DEPARTMENT FOR INTERNATIONAL DEVELOPMENT, Apr. 22, 2009, *available at* http://webarchive.nationalarchives.gov.uk/+/http://www. dfid.gov.uk/Media-Room/News-Stories/2009/Budget-2009---keeping-our-promises-to-the-worlds-poorest-people/Addendum-to-DFIDs-Value-for-Money-VfM-Delivery-Agreement/. *See also* House of Commons Library, *supra* note 6, at 8.

[123] *Tier 2 (Minister of Religion)*, UK BORDER AGENCY, http://www.ukba.homeoffice.gov.uk/visas-immigration/working/tier2/ministerofreligion/ (last visited Aug. 29, 2011).

[124] *Id.*.

[125] *Commonwealth Scholarships – developing Commonwealth country citizens*, COMMONWEALTH SCHOLARSHIP COMMISSION IN THE UNITED KINGDOM, http://cscuk.dfid.gov.uk/apply/scholarships-developing-cw/ (last visited Aug. 29, 2011).

[126] *Id.*

Foreign Remittance

Migrant workers from developing countries who have secured work in developed countries have also played an important role in helping to lift their families in the home country out of poverty by sending them money. The World Bank previously estimated that foreign remittances were at one point twice the amount of global aid.[127] The amount of remittance as a percentage of income that workers in the UK send to their families in foreign countries has declined over recent years as a result of the economic crisis, to between 5 and 15%.[128] Remittance from the UK goes primarily to India, Pakistan, Nigeria, Jamaica, and Ghana.[129] The UK supports foreign remittances and has regulated them to ensure transparency and ease of use. For example, these transactions must be executed in a currency agreed upon between the parties and, when a currency conversion service is offered, the exchange rate must be disclosed.[130]

Debt Relief

The UK is committed to reducing developing countries' debt. In 2010–11 the UK provided over £124 million (approximately US$200 million) in debt relief, with £111 million (approximately US$178 million) of this given toward the Heavily Indebted Poor Countries (HIPC) initiative and the Multilateral Debt Relief Initiative. The UK also has its own Multilateral Debt Relief Initiative, through which it provides over £10 million (approximately US$16 million) in debt relief to eight countries.[131]

'Vulture Funds'

The end of 2009 saw renewed legislative efforts to tackle poverty in developing countries in the wake of a judgment from the High Court in London that ordered Liberia to repay a US$20 million debt, an amount equal to around 5% of the Liberian government's annual budget.[132] This debt dated from 1978, and had been acquired at a fraction of the real price from the secondary market by two private investment funds.[133] Funds that are acquired in such a way are frequently referred to as "vulture funds" because the investment funds that purchase these debts get them at significantly less than face value and then pursue legal action to obtain the full value from the country, plus accrued interest. Repayment of this type of debt is damaging to developing

---

[127] CABINET OFFICE, *supra* note 58, ¶ 3.52.

[128] DEPARTMENT FOR INTERNATIONAL DEVELOPMENT, *supra* note 8, ¶ 14.

[129] House of Commons Library, *Migration and Development; The role and impact of remittances*, House of Commons Library Standard Note, SN/EP/3925, 2008, at 6.

[130] The Payment Services Regulations 2009, SI 2009/201, ¶¶ 36, 49, http://www.opsi.gov.uk/si/ si2009/uksi_20090209_en_6#pt5-pb4-l1g49.

[131] DEPARTMENT FOR INTERNATIONAL DEVELOPMENT, *supra* note 14, at 34.

[132] *Liberia ordered to pay 'vulture funds' over 1978 debt*, BBC NEWS (Nov. 26, 2009), http://news.bbc.co. uk/2/hi/africa/8380117.stm.

[133] *UN expert on foreign debt regrets British court order that Liberia must pay 1978 debt to 'vulture funds,'* UNITED NATIONS HUMAN RIGHTS, Dec. 17, 2009, http://www.ohchr.org/en/NewsEvents/Pages/DisplayNews. aspx?NewsID=9689&LangID=e.

countries because it "diverts the resources provided through debt relief, which are intended to support development and poverty reduction in the country."[134]

To prevent this from happening to the forty countries[135] that qualify for the World Bank and International Monetary Fund's Highly Indebted Poor Countries Initiative (HIPC), a Member of Parliament introduced the Debt Relief (Developing Countries) Bill 2010 as a private member's bill.[136] The bill was pushed through Parliament and enacted.[137] It aims to stop private investment funds from obtaining the face value of debts purchased from countries subject to the HIPC by legal action in the UK.[138] Instead, it subjects the investment funds that have purchased these debts to the same reductions of 67–90% of the original value of the debt as apply to public creditors (multilateral institutions and sovereign lenders) if they enforce their claims in the UK.[139] The Act applies to any public debt that was created before June 8, 2010,[140] and "applies to any current or future court judgments or arbitral awards obtained with respect to the payment of HIPC countries' debt, if at any point the creditors attempt to enforce such judgments in UK courts."[141] To ensure that the Act does not deter commercial creditors from participating in restructuring debt from HIPC countries, it specifically excludes debts that would be eligible if the HIPC country did not "affirmatively offer to repay its commercial creditors under the HIPC formula."[142] It also provides that if enforcement action is taken as a result of default on a restructured debt, the "HIPC-formula write-downs will apply to the original amount of the debt, and not to the restructured lower amount."[143]

---

[134] Debt Relief (Developing Countries) Act 2010, c. 22, Explanatory Notes, ¶ 5, http://www.legislation.gov.uk/ukpga/2010/22/notes/division/2.

[135] A list of qualifying countries is available at: International Monetary Fund, *Debt Relief Under the Heavily Indebted Poor Countries (HIPC) Initiative*, IMF (Sept. 6, 2011), http://www.imf.org/external/np/exr/facts/hipc.htm.

[136] House of Commons Library, *Debt relief & 'vulture funds': the Debt Relief (Developing Countries) Act 2010*, Standard Note, SN/EP/5658, 2010, http://www.parliament.uk/briefing-papers/SN05658.pdf.

[137] Debt Relief (Developing Countries) Act 2010, c. 22, http://www.legislation.gov.uk/ukpga/2010/22/contents. For an overview on the passage of the bill through Parliament, *see id.*

[138] Debt Relief (Developing Countries) Act 2010, c. 22, § 1, http://www.legislation.gov.uk/ukpga/2010/22/contents.

[139] Gavin McLean & Francis Fitzherbert-Brockholes, *The UK Debt Relief (Developing Countries) 2010 Act: Causes and Effects*, INSIGHT: CAPITAL MARKETS (Aug. 2010), http://www.whitecase.com/files/Publication/19c117d7-95d1-4e93-ad26-48c5a2d9f9a2/Presentation/PublicationAttachment/de49d681-2136-444e-b9f1-4fd01d7bdb07/alert_Vulture_Funds_v1.pdf.

[140] The government reportedly chose not to apply the law to debts incurred after this date because, in the absence of similar legislation in other major financial jurisdictions (notably New York), a forward-looking application of the law covering future indebtedness would chill the degree to which sovereign lenders and creditors would choose English law to govern future debts. *Id.*

[141] *Id.*

[142] *Id.*

[143] Debt Relief (Developing Countries) Act 2010, c. 22, § 6, http://www.legislation.gov.uk/ukpga/2010/22/contents. *See also id.*

This Act was welcomed by the UN's independent expert on foreign debt and human rights, who stated that it was "the first occasion on which a country has banned profiteering by 'vulture funds.' "[144]

International Finance Facility for Immunization

The UK is providing resources to the International Finance Facility for Immunisation (IFFIm). This supports immunization through guaranteeing funds that enable the IFFIm to sell "vaccine bonds" on the private market. The sale of these bonds makes funds immediately available for vaccination programs in developing countries.[145] The UK has currently pledged £1.38 billion (approximately US$2.2 billion) until 2026, and holds 45.14% of the total amounts pledged as of March 31, 2011.[146]

The Advance Market Commitment

The UK also provides financing to the Advance Market Commitment (AMC), which aims to create a market for vaccines in developing countries by creating incentives for pharmaceutical companies "to invest in research, development and production capacity for new vaccines that serve the poor." The UK has currently pledged $485 million (approximately US$776 million) to this Commitment.[147]

Environmental Transformation Fund

As noted above, the UK has included environmental concerns and climate change as part of its strategy to reduce poverty. The DFID, in conjunction with the Department of Energy and Climate Change (DECC), has established an £800 million (approximately US$1.2 billion) International Window of the Environmental Transformation Fund designed "to reduce poverty through environmental protection."[148] The fund is jointly managed by the DFID and DECC and its use must meet two criteria: "it must be scored as Official Development Assistance (ODA) and capital investment."[149] The DFID has committed £400 million to this fund.[150]

Prepared by Clare Feikert-Ahalt
Senior Foreign Law Specialist
October 2011

---

[144] *'Vulture Funds' – UN Expert on Foreign Debt Welcomes Landmark Law to Address Profiteering*, UNITED NATIONS HUMAN RIGHTS (Apr. 20, 2010), http://www.ohchr.org/en/NewsEvents/Pages/DisplayNews.aspx?NewsID=9976&LangID=E.

[145] *Overview*, IFFIM, http://www.iffim.org/about/overview/ (last visited Aug. 29, 2011).

[146] DEPARTMENT FOR INTERNATIONAL DEVELOPMENT, *supra* note 89.

[147] *Id.*

[148] *Id.*

[149] *Id.*

[150] *Id.*

www.ingramcontent.com/pod-product-compliance
Lightning Source LLC
Chambersburg PA
CBHW080243290526
45790CB00005B/1682